MW01635874

to

from

date

Truth for Today

Daniel Rendelman

Truth for Today
First Edition, January 2012

Printed in the United States of America

ISBN 1466486406 and ISBN 978-1466486409

This publication is available at special quantity discounts for bulk purchases of ten or more copies for ministry, sales promotions, and educational needs. For details visit www.emetministries.com.

The author may be contacted at emetministries@gmail.com.

A Note to the Reader:

This book uses many Hebrew terms in an effort to return to the truest meaning of the Bible. If you have questions about any words or usage please email the author at emetministries@gmail.com or visit www.emetministries.com.

The following are Hebrew terms used in the place of their English translations:

- Elohim = God
- YHWH = The LORD
- Y'shua = Jesus
- Moshiach = Messiah
- Messiah = Christ
- Ruach Ha Kodesh = Holy Spirit
- Kavod = Glory
- Teshuvah = Repentance
- Mitzvoth = Commandments
- Kadosh = Holy / Set Apart
- Chesed = Grace
- Shamayim = Heaven
- Torah = Five Books of Moses or the entire Bible
- Ahava = Love
- Shabbat = Sabbath
- Emunah = Faith / Trusting Belief

These terms are not used to offend but to teach and use the most accurate representation of the Biblical text. For more on the importance of the Hebrew language and the Sacred Name of YHWH Y'shua please visit www.emetministries.com.

January

TRUTH FOR TODAY

January 1

With the New Year comes fireworks, champagne, and the purchase of an updated calendar. The calendar industry reports sales in the billions with designs featuring comedy, landscapes, and of course swimsuit models. You can choose a desktop or wall chart of days but you can't choose to use the most accurate telling of time. Historians agree that the calendar of today has been through so many changes that it is almost impossible to know exactly what year it is.

Most of the world uses the error-filled Gregorian calendar that was made popular by Pope Gregory XII. This calendar shows the year to change on January 1. Yet before this dateline, several countries celebrated the New Year at different times. The Romans recognized March 1 while the Byzantine Empire held September 1 as the start of the year. The Jewish people still change their calendar in mid-September.

The Gregorian calendar is a supposed improvement upon the model created by Julius Caesar. When Caesar created his monthly calendar, he named each period of days after a different Greek god. January was named for Janus, the Roman mighty one of portals. May was named for Maia, the female deity of fertility. July was given its title after Julius Caesar himself. This isn't the only pagan connection to the modern calendar.

The Romans and Greeks had their pantheon of gods to honor. So, they developed a system of unified worship based on the calendar. This pattern continues today. Each day of the week actually retains its original name, given by the Romans, to signify the time to worship a different god. Monday is the day to worship the moon. Thursday is Thor's Day. Sunday is honored as "solis dias"- the venerable day of the sun.

Is the use of the titles for the days and months in direct opposition to the Biblical principle to not pronounce the names of false gods? Exodus 23:13, "And in all things that I have said to you take heed: and make no mention of other gods, neither let it be heard out of your mouth." Is it really the New Year? Check your Bible before you answer that question!

January 2

Perhaps we should return to the Biblical reckoning of time? Throughout the Scriptures there is only one day that is given a specific name. The Bible calls the Seventh day the "Sabbath" or "Shabbat" in Hebrew. All other days were counted off from the Sabbath. The months were also counted from the spring time of Passover and the month of "Aviv" as seen in Exodus 12:1-3.

The dating of our modern calendar is also incorrect. We are told that there have been at least 2000 years since the birth of Messiah. The term "AD" is short for "Anno Domini" or "in the year of our Lord." The problem is that Y'shua couldn't have been born in the year 1AD. The gospels show that the Savior's birth occurred during the reign of Herod the Great. Well, Herod's died in the spring of 4BC. Therefore, Messiah's birth had to take place at least four years before the traditional date! (Herod's death is recorded by Jewish historian Flavius Josephus in the Antiquities of the Jews, Book 17, Chapter 8.)

These calendar errors make a startling point. If we are misled concerning the actual dating of the year or naming of the days, then what other parts of our life and culture also contain error? Much time has passed since the events of the Bible took place. Sadly, as the calendars have changed so has mankind. The Almighty is the same yesterday, today, and forever.

Read more throughout this book for information on the original faith of the disciples. Learn about your heritage and live out your faith.

TRUTH FOR TODAY

January 3

"Speak to the children of Israel, that they bring you a red heifer without blemish, in which there is no defect and on which a yoke has never come. You shall give it to Eleazar the priest, that he may take it outside the camp, and it shall be slaughtered before him....Then the heifer shall be burned in his sight....And the priest shall take cedar wood and hyssop and scarlet and cast them into the midst of the fire burning the heifer....Then a man who is clean shall gather up the ashes of the heifer, and store them outside the camp in a clean place; and they shall be kept for the congregation of the children of Israel for the water of purification; it is for purifying from sin." (Excerpts from Numbers 19:2-9)

One mystery in the Torah is the section about the "parah adumah" or "red heifer." This holy cow was commanded to be used as a special offering. The parah adumah had the power to purify the uncleanliness of death. "Speak unto the children of Israel, that they bring thee a red heifer without spot wherein is no blemish, and upon which never came yoke," Numbers 19:2. The Messiah Y'shua was a fulfillment of YHWH's parah adumah as He was without spot of sin.

The book of Hebrews explains how the parah adumah pictured the Moshiach. The red cow was slain outside the gate like Y'shua, Hebrews 13:12. The entire heifer was to be consumed just as Y'shua gave his entire life for the Father's Kingdom. The ashes of the red cow were to be collected and stored in a clean place. The body of Y'shua was placed in a perfectly new tomb. Those same ashes were to be stored outside the city, just as the body of Y'shua lay in a tomb outside the city.

When the heifer was sacrificed there was hyssop, cedar and scarlet added. Y'shua was clothed in a scarlet robe and vinegar was given to him as he was crucified. The heifer was red – the color of blood that Y'shua shed for all mankind. The third day and the seventh day were days of purification after the parah adumah water was used. Y'shua rose on the third day and will return at the completion of the seventh day.

The sacrificial cow's ashes cleansed and purified all that touched it. "Therefore, brethren, since we have confidence to enter the holy place by the blood of Y'shua, by a new and living way which He inaugurated for us through the veil, that is, His flesh, and since we have a great priest over the house of YHWH, let us draw near with a sincere heart in full assurance of faith, having our hearts sprinkled clean from an evil conscience and our bodies washed with pure water," Hebrews 19:22. In Hebrews 9:13-14 we see that the blood of Y'shua is better than the blood of the red heifer. Praise YHWH today for the blood of our Messiah!

Truth For Today

January 4

Sin has caused mankind to "lose" or "fall short" of the glory of YHWH. The fall of Adam affected the spiritual DNA of mankind as we who were meant to be eternal can now experience death. The original temptation was to question the Almighty's warning of death. "Ye shall not surely die?" questioned the serpent. But die they did. As sin and the curses of sin entered humanity Adam and his sons would no longer have eternal life. Their spirit would be inclined towards evil. Noah's generation experienced this so much that they had to be washed away from the face of the earth.

Adam's sin created a rift of death in the spirit of man. No longer would mankind enter the world as perfect. Instead, we are each born with an inclination to sin because our spirit is first dead to YHWH and alive to sin. At birth our heart is "evil" and inclined to sin. Judaism calls this desire to receive for self alone the "yetzer hara" or the "evil inclination." Judaism though only provides the Torah as a remedy for the evil sinful nature. Torah does many things but it can't transform a person's spirit. Changing behavior through obeying the Torah does NOT change the spiritual DNA makeup of a person. Even the Pharisee Nicodemus was told that he "must be born again." Nick's obedience to the Torah couldn't bring him eternal life because it didn't change his spirit. Nicodemus, like all other Old Testament saints, didn't have the Holy Spirit inside of them and therefore did not experience the regeneration of YHWH. The Scripture says that at salvation a person is "translated from the kingdom of darkness into the kingdom of light."

According to Romans 10:9 and 10, a person is delivered from darkness (or "saved") when they "believe in their heart that Y'shua is their Master and confesses with their mouth that YHWH raised Him from the dead." A person who earnestly repents of their sins and turns from their wicked ways by calling upon the name of YHWH Y'shua is instantly born again in their spirit (and not their mind or body).

What happens in the spiritual realm is that the evil inclination or sinful nature instantly and completely is crucified and resurrected with Y'shua. The "yetzer hara" is replaced with a "yetzer tov" or "good spirit" that is joined completely with YHWH's Holy Spirit. Judaism says the "yetzer hara" and the "yetzer tov" are present in every person but this isn't true. Every born again person has had their old nature crucified and now the Spirit of YHWH dwells in them. Salvation is when the glory of creation is restored because your spirit is joined to YHWH's Spirit. We are now sons and daughters of YHWH, joint heirs with Y'shua, and the temple of the Holy Spirit.

What does this message mean to you today?

January 5

Thousands of years ago, YHWH gave man specific and direct instructions on how to live a life that is both spiritually and physically fulfilling. This set of loving instructions and teachings, much like a blueprint for living, is what the Hebrew language calls "torah." The Torah is the teachings found in the first five books of the Scriptures, often mistranslated as the word "law." There are laws in the Torah but the Torah is not just law, it is teaching. It is the way YHWH desires His people to live.

As man obeys the Torah through heartfelt love and devotion the natural result is blessing, fulfillment, and closeness with the Creator. But, there are times when man disobeys the Torah. There are times when mankind chooses to pay no attention to the Torah and do what feels right at the moment. There are times when the doctrines of man have so confused people that the Torah is ignored. There are times when the torah is forgotten and disregarded as meaningless laws for a generation past. These times of rebellion are what the Torah calls "sin." 1 John 3:4, "Everyone who sins breaks the Torah; in fact, sin is torah-lessness."

Sin results in separation from things holy or set-apart, including YHWH Himself. Sin makes a person unclean and "dead" or void of life spiritually speaking. "The wages of sin is death," Romans 3:23. Because YHWH is holy and full of life, things that are dead or unclean cannot approach Him.

This issue of sin presents a perplexing problem without some type of way to bridge the gap between holy and sinless YHWH and unclean and sinful man. A bridge is needed to cross the chasm to connect man with YHWH.

Teshuvah is that bridge. Teshuvah is the bridge YHWH has graciously provided man for relationship and closeness. Teshuvah is the bridge, built by Y'shua Himself. Teshuvah is the Hebrew word for "repentance" but it means much more than just saying "sorry." Teshuvah is turning from the sin, doing right, and correcting the mistake.

"Turn thou us unto thee, O YHWH, and we shall be turned; renew our days as of old," Lamentations 5:21. Through teshuvah sinful and disobedient man is returned to the state of obedience and righteousness. It is teshuvah that stops man from being overcome by evil and wickedness and restores man to the life before the sin occurred.

TRUTH FOR TODAY

January 6

"The grass withereth, the flower fadeth: but the word of our Elohim shall stand forever," Isaiah 40:8.

Understand that when Isaiah said this, the only scriptures the believers had at that time was actually the Torah of Moses. So, if you believe that this verse is true then you must believe that all the teachings, commandments, and principles in the scriptures are for you. They haven't passed away. In fact, this verse says that they shall "stand forever."

Man has created the doctrine of the dispensationalism. Dispensationalists teach that part of the Bible was for yesterday while part of it is for today. This is totally opposite of what the scriptures themselves teach in 1 Peter 1:25, "but the word (torah) of the YHWH endureth forever," and in Psalm 119:142, "Thy righteousness is an everlasting righteousness, and thy law is the truth."

If the word is eternal (which it is) that means it was to be followed yesterday, is to be obeyed today, and should be kept tomorrow. According to Ezekiel 36:26 this obedience to the Torah is to flow from a heart of love and not obligation. Our Savior based His complete life and ministry on the Torah given by the Almighty Father. He did not negate it nor abolish it. "Do not think that I have come to abolish the Law or the Prophets; I have not come to abolish them but to fulfill them. I tell you the truth, until heaven and earth disappear, not the smallest letter, not the least stroke of a pen, will by any means disappear from the Law until everything is accomplished," Matthew 5:17 & 18. Heaven and earth have not disappeared so then the Torah should still be followed.

YHWH and His Word are eternal and do not change. Nothing in the Bible has "passed away." YHWH expects the same from us as He did from people 2,000 years ago. YHWH expects us to obey His Word, trust Him, and love Him with all our might. Psalm 119:83, "For I am become like a wineskin in the smoke; yet do I not forget your chukim / rulings."

YHWH does not lie and is incapable of falsehood. The Word of YHWH is infallible or without error. The Scriptures contain no contradictions. YHWH has given us the Tanakh / Older Testament and the Brit Chadasha / Newer Testament so that we can know His will and therefore obey Him. Luke 4:4, "And Y'shua answered him, saying, It is written, That man shall not live by lechem alone, but by every word of YHWH." Yes, the Scriptures are powerful. Y'shua is the Living Word. Y'shua gave ineffable proof of the Scriptures through His life, ministry, death and resurrection. Y'shua fulfilled prophecies written of Him hundreds and thousands of years before He came to earth. Acts 1:3, "To whom also He showed Himself alive after His passion by many infallible proofs, being seen by them forty days, and speaking of the things pertaining to the malchut / kingdom of YHWH." Have you taken time today to read and study the Scriptures?

TRUTH FOR TODAY

January 7

With a mirror we can look at the sight in the glass and see an exact reflection. A mirror is a one-dimensional image of our three dimensional world. Unless it's a fun house at the carnival, what is seen in the mirror is an accurate reflection of our world. Like a mirror, this world echoes the deeper, hidden world of the Spirit. What we see and experience in the natural is a reflection of the supernatural. And vica-versa.

We live in the physical world of what we perceive. Yet, this is only 1% of reality. There remains 99% of the unseen.

What we do in the one percent affects the whole ninety-nine percent. To aid our daily struggles, we have been given several mitzvoth / commandments that will bridge the gap between recognition and our memory shortfalls. As we recall and heed these reminders, we are connecting to the supernatural; we are operating in the shadow of the 99%. "Let no one therefore judge you in eating or in drinking, or in respect of a Festival or a new moon or Sabbaths – which are a shadow of what is (yet) to come – but the Body of Messiah," Colossians 2: 16-17. The true reality is in Ha Shamayim / the Heavens, while the earth is merely a shadow of how life is supposed to be.

Our actions are a reflection of our attitudes and motives. Our obedience of YHWH's mitzvoth / commandments reflects our love of Him.

YHWH's reminders can literally fill our day, repeatedly calling us back to our Spiritual senses...while we touch the mezuzah on our doorposts and repeat the Shema daily, we are actually making a divine connection to the Almighty. As we eat of the bread and wine on Shabbat, we are uniting with the Holy One.

These links are the mitzvoth / commandments. Spiritually speaking, when we keep the mitzvoth, as habitually as wearing Tzittzit, we are bridging the gap between the 1% and the 99%. From the moment we wake up in the morning to the time close our eyes as we lie in bed, these emblems turn our thoughts heavenward. These reminders help us to fulfill, "From the rising of the sun to the going down of the same, YHWH's Name is to be praised," Tehillim / Psalm 113:3.

Here's the point, in the spirit realm closeness is determined by similarity. So, the more we act like YHWH, the more we think upon YHWH, the closer we are to YHWH. As we follow His word, we are actually moving as His shadow and in His shadow.

January 8

In the book of Genesis we find the original first family and the plan for all descendants who would come forth. If you want to know how to raise a Biblical family then just read in Beresheet / Genesis. The very first words, perhaps the very first commandment given to mankind explains YHWH's will for the family. "And Elohim blessed them, and Elohim said unto them, be fruitful, and multiply, and replenish the earth, and subdue it: and have dominion over the fish of the sea, and over the fowl of the air, and over every living thing that moveth upon the earth," Beresheet / Genesis 1:28. This is the key!

YHWH didn't declare that the family must have a budget or fire escape plan. He originally told them to "be fruitful and multiply." This was the purpose of family in the Garden and this is the purpose of family today.

Note that YHWH told them to 'be fruitful' before He told them to 'multiply.' Growth for the sake of growth is not a good thing. Life is not all about numbers and material possessions. Biblically, fruit should abound before growth occurs. Think of a woman with a large growth in her stomach. This could be a child or this growth could be a huge tumor. Growth does not always equal health. Yet, healthy beings grow naturally. A tree that receives water and sunlight will grow on its own. This is the same with our families and our ministries. Growth occurs as fruit abounds.

When YHWH instructed Adam and Chava to be fruitful, He used the word "parah." This Hebrew term means to "grow, increase, bear fruit like a vine, bring forth, to open." This word parah is used many times throughout the Scriptures in reference to the fruit of a vine. The family is not the vine, but is to produce life and goodness from the vine. This can be better understood when you reference the words of Y'shua. "Remain in me, and I will remain in you. No branch can bear fruit by itself; it must remain in the vine. Neither can you bear fruit unless you remain in me. I am the vine; you are the branches. If a man remains in me and I in him, he will bear much fruit; apart from me you can do nothing," Yochannan / John 15:4-5.

How can you lead your family to grow in the true vine?

Truth For Today

January 9

Genesis 18 shows that while Abraham was in the middle of his prayer time, he lifted up his eyes and saw a group of sojourners coming towards his tent. Abraham immediately ran to meet the visitors. (Can you imagine running just a few days after being circumcised?) The Jewish Talmud asserts that hospitality should take priority even over "welcoming the Divine presence."

Abraham greeted his visitors with sincerity and care. He gave them food and washed their feet. Abraham had Sarah prepare her "world famous" flour cakes for them to taste. Abraham showed hospitality to these visitors before he even knew who they were. This is true kindness. This is true chesed / grace.

The Hebrew word "chesed" is most often translated as "grace" or "kindness" in English Bibles. This term implies an action of unmerited favor in a physical manner. Grace isn't something you believe. Grace / chesed is something you do. Abraham showed grace to his visitors. In a similar fashion, Lot showed chesed to the visitors of Sodom and Gomorrah. He insisted that they spend the night in his home and not on the street. Perhaps it was the chesed that Lot showed to the visitors that allowed him to be rescued from destruction. Perhaps it was the kindness that Abraham shared that led to the blessing of Isaac. Kindness has reciprocal effects that set in motion chains of good events. When you reach out to someone to meet a need, you are in essence putting your needs in YHWH's hands. Abraham left his own tent of meeting to welcome guests and was never the same.

Y'shua said the greatest commandment was to love YHWH and to love your neighbor as yourself. One way in which we express love to YHWH is through the kindness / chesed that we show others. This week, look for new ways to be hospitable. Ask the Ruach HaKodesh/ Holy Spirit to reveal to you a way to show kindness each day of this week. Spend time in prayer for others and spend extra time meeting the needs of others. As you replicate Abraham's actions you will experience the blessing of chesed yourself.

January 10

"The time is coming," declares YHWH, "when I will make a new covenant with the house of Israel and with the house of Judah. It will not be like the covenant I made with their forefathers when I took them by the hand to lead them out of Egypt, because they broke my covenant, though I was a husband to them," declares YHWH. "This is the covenant I will make with the house of Israel after that time," declares YHWH. "I will put my law in their minds and write it on their hearts. I will be their Elohim, and they will be my people. No longer will a man teach his neighbor, or a man his brother, saying, 'Know YHWH,' because they will all know me, from the least of them to the greatest," declares YHWH. "For I will forgive their wickedness and will remember their sins no more," Jeremiah 31:31-33. This was a covenant of mercy. "YHWH was merciful with Israel and looked upon them with compassion because of His covenant with Avraham / Abraham, Yitzchak / Isaac and Ya'acov / Jacob," 2 Kings 13:23. The Prophet Isaiah agrees. "Though the mountains leave their place and the hills be shaken, My love shall never leave you nor my covenant of peace be shaken, says YHWH, who has rachamim / mercy on you," Yesha'yahu / Isaiah 54:10. YHWH has not and cannot forsake or replace His people. He longs to show mercy.

And to fulfill this covenant, to show mercy, was one reason why Y'shua came. He said "I came to seek and save the whole house of Israel," Matthew 15:24. This corresponds directly with Romans 15:8-9, "Now I say that Y'shua ha Moshiach was an servant to Israel for the emet / truth of YHWH, to confirm the promises made to our fathers: And that the nations might all esteem YHWH for His rachamim; as it is written, For this cause I will confess You among the nations, and sing to Your Name."

We are living in a time of rachamim and not judgment. This is startling to those that are used to a doom's day message of YHWH showing forth His wrath upon America through natural disasters like Hurricane Katrina. We'd much rather hear bad news so that we can cheer on the judgment of the sinners. But, YHWH is showing mercy to the whole house of Israel. YHWH is an el of rachamim / mighty one of mercy. As you show mercy and kindness to others YHWH will use you to restore His rule and reign in this earth. What can you do today to show mercy to someone?

TRUTH FOR TODAY

January 11

Rabbi Sha'ul or "Paul" reminds us in Colossians, chapter 1 verse 16, "All things were created by him, and for Him."

The universe and all it holds exists to bring praise to YHWH. In the Bible, the word most often translated "glory" is the Hebrew phrase "kavod." Dictionaries agree that YHWH's kavod is His "weight, attributes, heaviness, significance, praise, power, moral beauty, perfect character, visible presence, and honor." At certain places in the Bible, the kavod is spoken of as praise to YHWH. Other times the kavod is a physical manifestation, usually seen as light or fire. Mostly though, kavod is seen in the Scriptures as the significance of a person. YHWH's kavod is the manifestation of who YHWH is. YHWH's kavod is how significant He is. Another term translated "glory" is the Hebrew term "tifereth." While kavod denotes the energy and significance of YHWH, "tifereth" symbolizes YHWH's splendor and radiant flow. The terms are interchangeable as expressions of YHWH's magnificent power and might.

The world, including mankind, was formed to be a vessel of His presence. Adam was originally crowned with glory and enjoyed an unhindered relationship with the Almighty. Psalm 8:5, "For You have made him a little lower than the Elohim, and have crowned him with kavod and honor." But, sin entered the world because Adam chose the path of the desire to receive for self alone. Adam disobeyed YHWH and fell from glory. With this sin came separation from the Creator of His creation. The crown of glory that was once upon man was now lost. "For all have sinned, and come short of the tifereth of YHWH," Romans 3:23. Sin drove Adam out of the garden and pushed the glory away.

Y'shua the Messiah came to restore the glory of YHWH that was lost by Adam's sin. This mission was proclaimed upon the birth of Messiah, "And, see, the heavenly malach / angel of the Master YHWH came upon them, and the tifereth of YHWH shone around them: and they were greatly afraid. Tifereth to YHWH in the highest, and on earth shalom, and tov among men, with whom He is pleased," Luke 2:9, 14.

Y'shua came to earth amidst the glory, in order to bring glory to YHWH, by establishing peace between YHWH and men. Amidst the glory, Y'shua's mission is made clear. He came as "A Light to unveil the nations, and the tifereth of Your people Israel," Luke 2:32.

What did you learn today from this teaching?

January 12

We all have some areas of obedience where we could be more devoted. Yet, most of the time, we ignore these sinful problems. We hide them in our pockets until the right time to sneak away and enjoy. Who likes to control their thoughts anyway? Who wants to show respect to those in spiritual authority? Who doesn't stretch the truth, just a little? We reason that a little sin, here and there, doesn't count against us, if we know the Hebrew Names or keep the Biblical Sabbath. Sadly, we have heart disease. Our arteries are clogged with some wicked actions and bad thoughts.

This is why, in Mishlei / Proverbs, chapter 4, the scriptures say to "Keep thy heart with all diligence." We need to be watchmen, who are on the lookout for false concepts concerning the mitzvoth / commandments. One such deception that easily slips into our heart is the idea that the Creator wants us to obey Him. We've allowed the mitzvoth mindset to harden our hearts into believing that YHWH wants us to just obey the mitzvoth. However doing the right actions is not the pathway to pleasing the Almighty Elohim. We don't earn our place into heaven, no matter how Torah-observant we are. Our spiritual standing is not based on us memorizing the worship service, so the "amen" is said at just the right time.

Somehow, we have come to believe that when YHWH looks down from heaven upon us, that He measures our Torah obedience on a scale. We reason that, if we are doing Torah then, YHWH honors us, and we are ok. We've come to believe, write in our emails, and even tell others that YHWH wants us to be Torah-observant. We'll go to heaven, we'll be happy on earth, and life will be just fine. However, this is just not true. When YHWH looks from heaven, He is not looking in judgment towards our Torah obedience ONLY. He does not desire us to be robots, who blindly obey to just obey; He did give to us free will! Plainly, YHWH doesn't want our obedience. He doesn't really want us to keep kosher or speak Hebrew. What YHWH wants is us, in totality. He wants our life. Totally. Fully. YHWH wants our heart, our soul, and our devotion. He doesn't need our service.

Likewise, He doesn't get a thrill from our obedience when He doesn't have our heart. Sure, we can learn the mitzvoth. We can memorize the 613 commandments, we can keep the Noachide laws, and we can quote the Ten Commandments. But if we don't totally give our life to Him then, all the good works we do are just that. Good works and nothing else! It isn't the actions that earn us points in heaven; it is our heart condition that is most important. What pleases Him is the fact that our souls and very life have been yielded to the Almighty. YHWH wants us to submit our life totally to Him. That is the essential difference between obeying and submitting.

January 13

Loving YHWH makes your life kadosh / holy. We have had this backwards. We think that the commandments are what set us apart. This is NOT true. A person can keep all the commandments of the Bible and not love YHWH. Yes, they might be set apart from the world BUT a Torah-keeper without love is NOT set apart unto YHWH. We are to love Him FIRST and our obedience to the mitzvoth should be a result of our love to Him. We are then to show that ahava / love to others!

"If you love Me, keep My mitzvoth," Yochannan / John 14:15. Notice the order here – love Him FIRST and then keep the mitzvoth!

"Therefore you shall love YHWH your Elohim and shomer / keep His charge, and His chukim / judgments, and His mishpatim / rulings, and His mitzvoth, always." Devarim / Deuteronomy 11:1

"He that has My mitzvoth, and keeps them, he it is that loves Me: and he, who loves Me, shall be loved by My Abba, and I will love him, and will reveal Myself to him." Yochannan / John 14:21. Our obedience is PROOF that we love YHWH. When we choose to sin then we choose the love of self over the love of YHWH.

Mitzvoth are for us to connect to Him. Obedience to the commandments does not make YHWH love us more. YHWH does not love Torah keepers more than Torah breakers. His ahava / love is unconditional. The purpose of the mitzvot is to help us to know His divine will and walk in His ahava. "The Torah of YHWH is perfect, converting the soul," Psalm 19:7. We prove to YHWH that we are his disciples / talmidim by keeping His commandments. We prove to the world that we are disciples of YHWH by loving one another.

Make a choice to love YHWH more by loving someone more

January 14

The book of 1 John speaks vividly on the subject of sin. The definition and the remedy for sin are both discussed in 1 John 3:4-7, "Everyone who sins breaks the law; in fact, sin is lawlessness. But you know that he appeared so that he might take away our sins. And in him is no sin. No one who lives in him keeps on sinning. No one who continues to sin has either seen him or known him. Dear children, do not let anyone lead you astray. He who does what is right is righteous, just as he is righteous."

And here it is in plain and simple English in verse 4 "sin is LAWLESSNESS!" To be "sin less" a person must be "law full." So, evidently if the law remains to define sin, then the law of YHWH remains.

Wait a minute! Christianity teaches that believers are not under law but under grace. Mainstream Christianity says that the law has passed away and the "age of grace" has come. Many religious teachers do say the law is a bad, hindering set of confusing rules and regulations. Well, according to the above scripture "sin is lawlessness." If a person violates YHWH's laws then a person is sinning. Sin is not keeping or obeying the laws or commands of the Bible. Sin is a life without the law; i.e. "lawlessness."

The word "law" is a Greek interpretation of the Hebrew word "Torah." The word "torah" is Hebrew for "teaching or instruction." The "Law" that Torah is commonly translated into brings to mind a restraining order but this is simply not the case. Torah was given for the benefit of mankind, not to hinder mankind. Torah is the loving instructions and guidelines for living as YHWH's chosen people. The Torah is traditionally considered the first five books of the Old Testament, including the Decalogue or the Ten Commandments. Yet, the Law is not Jewish, it is Biblical.

One author has written, "Christians usually call the Torah "the Law," because most English translations of scripture translate Torah as Law. The reason this came about is because pre-Y'shua rabbis translated the Hebrew Scriptures into Greek, called the Septuagint. The Septuagint translated Torah into the Greek word "nomia" or "nomos." The term nomos was used in the Greek culture to mean an unalterable law. Following this tradition, the Greek New Testament also used nomia to signify the Torah." One teacher has written that, "The Hebrew word "torah," literally "teaching, doctrine," is rendered in both the Septuagint and the New Testament by the Greek word "nomos," which means "law." Greek has had a more direct and pervasive influence on English and other modern languages than Hebrew has, and this is why in most languages one speaks of the "law" of Moses rather than the "teaching" of Moses. What does this mean to you?

January 15

In Genesis 3, Adam and Eve were tempted with desires and thoughts by an independent force called the "serpent." It was not their own idea to violate the Almighty's commands. Nor did the first couple bring sin into the world. The Scriptures record that the original sin was actually committed by an angel that led a rebellion against the Most High. Since creation the accuser (satan in Hebrew) and his minions have led a spiritual war against mankind. The adversary comes as an angel of light and tempts through desires and thoughts that may at first seem pleasing, but in the end will result in disaster. Big sins (like adultery) and little sins (like stretching the truth) both welcome the presence of the kingdom of darkness.

Simply because something seems good and feels good, doesn't mean it is for the good. Plus, when a person agrees with satan to disobey the scripture, a door to the enemy is opened. With rebellion, the entity of sin is empowered within the flesh to act as it independently desires. The Apostle Paul wrote of this when he said, "We know that the law is spiritual; but I am unspiritual, sold as a slave to sin. I do not understand what I do. For what I want to do I do not do, but what I hate I do and if I do what I do not want to do, I agree that the law is good. As it is, it is no longer I myself who do it, but it is sin living in me," Romans 7:14-17. Sin is more than just an act. It is a living spiritual power that can actually overcome individuals. Sin has influence, but it doesn't have to win.

You can prevail over lust and not allow sin in your flesh to manifest if you apply the principle of James 4:7. This passage teaches that the enemy is defeated when a person submits to the Words of the Bible and then resists and renounces the tempting thoughts of sin.

Henry Wright of "Be In Health Ministries" teaches these steps to freedom from the power of sin:

- Recognize -You must recognize what it is
- Responsibility - You must take responsibility for what you recognize
- Repent - Repent to YHWH for participating with what you recognize
- Renounce - You must make what you recognize your enemy & renounce it
- Remove - Get rid of it once and for all
- Resist - When it tries to come back, resist it
- Rejoice - Give YHWH thanks for setting you free
- Restore - Help someone else get free

January 16

Is the return of the Messiah really imminent? Could the eastern sky really part any day now?

Many who believe in the "any day" return of Christ also teach that the rapture will occur before the Great Tribulation. Such is blatant error. There will not be rapture or catching away in the sky and then a second coming. That would equal three comings of Christ, which is never spoken of in the Bible. It's not until after the tribulation that the Savior comes. "Immediately after the tribulation of those days the sun will be darkened, and the moon will not give its light; the stars will fall from the sky, and the heavenly bodies will be shaken. At that time the sign of the Son of Man will appear in the sky, and all the nations of the earth will mourn. They will see the Son of Man coming on the clouds of the sky, with power and great glory. And he will send his angels with a loud trumpet call, and they will gather his elect from the four winds, from one end of the heavens to the other," Mathew 24:29-31.

Anyone who suggests that time is short should remember Mark 13:32 which says "of that day and that hour knoweth no man, no, not the angels which are in heaven, neither the Son, but the Father." Don't be misled into fear regarding the appearing of Y'shua in the next few days or months. And don't allow yourself to be captivated by the innumerable conspiracy theories regarding the soon end of life as we know it. Study the Scriptures for yourself and find that there are many more prophecies that must be fulfilled before the Savior's return. Our mission as believers is to be a light to the nations through our love of YHWH and each other. An unhealthy focus on apocalyptic events stops this type of devotion from flowing properly. Instead of spending hours on eschatology so we can argue with those who do not agree with us, perhaps we should each be seeking to walk in Spirit and share the gospel of the Kingdom. And the, when things really begin to happen we can "we can stand up and lift up our heads, because redemption draweth nigh," Luke 21:28.

January 17

An honest survey of the Bible will reveal that Y'shua isn't returning in the next few days or any time soon. Ironically, while the Bible tells us to pray for His soon return, The Bible doesn't agree with the idea of the imminent return, a theory that states that the Messiah could return at any moment. This belief in an imminent return ignores many events that are yet to come on the prophetic calendar of the Bible. Many things must happen before Y'shua comes back for His bride.

Further, Daniel 12:11, Revelation 11 and Second Thessalonians 2:4 tell us that before the Messiah can return, the holy temple in Jerusalem must be totally rebuilt, and must be fully functioning. Some end times teachers have tried to get around the idea of a fully functional temple by stating that only a corner portion of the temple will have to be rebuilt, and that this will accomplish the task. This is in a vain effort to make their timelines work for an upcoming apocalypse. Sorry, but the Scriptures are clear that the red heifer, priesthood, holy menorah and all elements must be functioning during the end of days. Today there are many efforts being made to restore the holy of holies but one big problem stands in the way: sitting on the exact spot of where the temple should be is the Muslim Dome of the Rock. Perhaps the Al Aqsa Mosque will be destroyed as part of the seven year peace treaty with Israel that is yet to come? Even if that is the case, it will take many years to build the next Temple according to the specifications given in Ezekiel 40-46, perhaps even decades. According to Scripture, the Messiah cannot return before this is done.

The sun, moon, and stars are still in place, which is an obvious sign that the end isn't near. Luke 21:25-33 states that the heavenly bodies will fall from the sky when the Savior returns and the Day of YHWH comes. The Bible also states that there must be a great falling away from the truth and the unveiling of the anti-Christ. "Concerning the coming of our Master Y'shua and our gathering together to Him, we ask you, not to be soon shaken in mind or troubled, either by spirit or by word or by letter, as if from us, as though the day of Messiah had come. Let no one deceive you by any means; for that Day will not come unless the falling away comes first, and the man of sin is revealed, the son of perdition," 2 Thessalonians 2:1-3. Some will say that the great falling away has already occurred, but the Anti-Messiah is not yet revealed. Sorry, but Obama is not the Ant-Christ. Nor is he Prince Charles or Bashar Al Asad. Scripture tells us Anti-Christ can't come on the scene until after the anti-Messiah is revealed, but as we saw earlier, we are nowhere near having a completed temple in which such an anti-Messiah could serve.

Instead of focusing on Messiah's return, try working out your own salvation with fear and trembling.

January 18

Ever heard of the Hebrew word "Elohim?"

"Elohim" is the plural Hebrew term found throughout the Bible for "gods." Most English Bibles translate this same Hebrew statement as "God," "god," or "gods." While the Hebrew word Elohim is unchanged, the only difference in the English is the capitalization by the publisher. This is because the Hebrew word "Elohim" is a general term used throughout the Scriptures to describe spiritual beings or "mighty ones." "Elohim presides in the great assembly; he gives judgment among the gods," Psalm 82:1.

The Egyptians, for example, had many elohim or "gods." According to Strong's Exhaustive Dictionary the word "elohim" carries with it the connotation of judgment and literally means "gods in the ordinary sense; but specifically used of the supreme God; occasionally magistrates." Elohim comes from the root word prefix "El" meaning "strength; as an adjective mighty; especially the Almighty (but used also of any deity):-God or god, goodly, great, idol, might (-y one), power, strong." The term Elohim appears over 1,100 times in the Bible as a "title" describing YHWH.

The pagans, like the Egyptians, worshipped many elohim, or spiritual beings. Even Pharaoh was considered a god. Pharaoh himself said, "Who is YHWH that I should obey when he says to let Israel go? I don't know YHWH, and I also won't let Israel go." Well, Pharaoh and all of Egypt would soon found out exactly who YHWH is by the plagues upon the land. YHWH judged the gods / elohim of Egypt with His plagues, proving Psalm 82:1 - "Elohim presides in the great assembly; he gives judgment among the "gods," Tehillim 82:1. Today, like yesteryear, there are many elohim. These false gods steal worship from YHWH and will one day be judged. YHWH is THE elohim of Israel and the only elohim worthy of worship. Have you allowed false elohim (like the media, knowledge, or entertainment) to steal your time or attention?

January 19

Numbers in Scripture aren't just numbers, they are also symbols. With the Hebrew alphabet letters are numbers and letters are signs. The study of Hebrew letters is called "gematria." In gematria each Hebrew letter is assigned a number. An interesting insight about gematria is that if two words have the same number, there is a connection. One web site says "gematria is the calculation of the numerical equivalence of letters, words, or phrases, and, on that basis, gaining, insight into interrelation of different concepts and exploring the interrelationship between words and ideas."

Even with numbers and letters, what happens in the natural is a reflection of the supernatural. For example the number one speaks of unity and sovereignty. Seven is the numeral of divine completion, perfection, and wholeness. And the number ten is the number of law and establishment. It should be no surprise to the Bible student that something special happens on day number throughout the Scriptures. The number eight, shemini, is the symbolic number of new life.

Shemini is associated with newness, regeneration, and order. When the world was covered by the flood of water, it was Noach who was the "eighth person" (2 Kefa / Peter 2:5) who stepped out on to a new earth to commence a new order of things. "Eight souls" (1 Kefa 3:20) passed through it with him to the new or regenerated world. Also, on the eighth day of the life all Hebrew boys are to be circumcised as found in Beresheet / Genesis 17:12. Eight is also the first cubic number, pointing to the new life found in the holy of holies and the New Jerusalem / Yerushalayim.

The point is that numbers are more than just numbers. The Creator did not just haphazardly allow things to happen or allow things to be written in the Scriptures. There is certainly a method and symbolism to the use of numbers in scripture. Volumes more could be written about numbers, numerology, gematria, and their profound impact upon Biblical understanding. What is important to remember is that accidents just don't happen. If there is great learning and insight to be found in just the numbers and letters of the Torah, how much more then its message as a whole.

There are no such things as coincidence whether you are speaking of numbers in the Bible or events in your life. YHWH has a special and unique plan for you. What numbers are special to you?

TRUTH FOR TODAY

January 20

"But every man is tempted, when he is drawn away by his own desires, and is taken away. Then when desire has conceived, it births sin: and sin, when it is spread, brings forth death," Ya'acov / James 1:15-17. Psychologists tell us that an average person has 10,000 thoughts a day. That is 10,000 choices to walk in the spirit or give in to our lusts and sinful desires.

It is NOT sin when the thought FIRST comes to mind or when we are FIRST tempted by the adversary. Sin occurs when we make that thought our own by EITHER dwelling on the idea OR acting on the idea. When the door is opened to ha satan, the negative forces grow until the desire becomes normal behavior.

Because of the strongholds in your life, you may be TOTALLY saved from eternal damnation BUT you may also be TOTALLY bound up by the enemy. The adversary and his shadim / demons want to keep us defeated, oppressed, repressed, and in a mess. He wishes to render every believer to be so bound up with strongholds that we resemble a lunatic in a strait jacket fighting for freedom. The battle for freedom begins in the mind!

Every single scripture in the Newer Testament that deals with Spiritual Warfare is in context to the thought process of the believer. Biblically, the subject and place of spiritual warfare is in the mind! If we could just have our minds renewed to the truth of Torah then we could experience freedom from demonic oppression. It's that simple.

The Bible says, "we war not against flesh and blood." We are in a spiritual battle. When Y'shua died on the tree, Y'shua "Spoiled principalities and powers, He made a show of them openly, triumphing over them in it," Colossians 2:15. Each believer has authority and power over the enemy. Ha satan has been defeated by the work of Y'shua on the tree. We, the army of YHWH, must exercise our authority and not allow the evil one to conquer us.

The emet / truth is that the only power Ha Satan has over us is what we give him. The adversary takes his power through deception. Indeed, the ONLY power the adversary has is the power of deception. Yet, when he deceives; he controls. Will your through today be in line with the satan or with YHWH?

TRUTH FOR TODAY

January 21

"Sha'atnez" is the Hebrew term for counterfeit, false, or unholy mixtures prohibited by YHWH's Torah. The wearing of mixed fabrics is just one of three Sha'atnez that are to be avoided. The context of Vayikra / Leviticus explains this a little further. "Keep my decrees. Do not mate different kinds of animals. Do not plant your field with two kinds of seed. Do not wear clothing woven of two kinds of material," Vayikra / Leviticus 19:19. We are not to mix: plants with other plants and create a hybrid; animals with other animals and create a mongrel; plant based fabrics with animal based fabrics and create a garment.

"You are not to wear a garment with two kinds of thread, wool and linen together," says Devarim (Deuteronomy) 22:11. This command is a definite "chok" commandment. These types of instructions seem to have no apparent reason other than expressing the Divine will of YHWH. Linen is a plant-based material and wool of course is an animal based material and the two should not be mixed for attire. If linen and wool appear in the same garment then you should not wear that item of clothing.

The Rabbis have concluded that it is wrong to wear anything when these elements are sewn, tied, pasted together, weaved, twisted or carded. The Talmud even prohibits sitting on a fabric with Sha'atnez! How does all of this relate to life today? Well, if you believe the Bible then not much has changed.

A simple look through your closet with a fast examination of clothing tags will reveal if you own any Sha'atnez. Be careful though! Many suits of wool have linen liners or pockets and many items with padding may mix the two threads. Also, "lano/lino" is Spanish for wool/linen so it's very easy to get confused with this subject. You don't have to discard of the garment if it is Sha'atnez, just don't wear it. (The Torah only prohibits "wearing" these – not making them or owning them.) Or you can donate the clothing to a local thrift store or trash the clothes if you so choose. It is much easier to not wear something if you don't have it in your closet or dresser.

What is the meaning behind the mitzvot of Sha'atnez? Jewish rabbis and students have pondered this question for literally thousands of years. Some say not to wear Sha'atnez because only the garments of the Cohen Hagadol (high priest) could be made of linen and wool. Many Sages teach that Sha'atnez has its origins in pagan cults of old. Others point out that Sha'atnez completes the set of forbidden combinations and man should not change creation to "improve" upon it. For various teachers Sha'atnez is a reminder of the story of Kayin and Hevel (Cain and Abel). Kayin's offering was from the produce of the ground and Hevel's was from his flock. Keeping wool and linen separate in garments reminds us of this episode and its lessons. How can you keep this commandment today?

January 22

"And Elohim spoke to Moshe in the desert of Sinai," Bamidbar / Numbers 1:1. From the sunny land of sand came forth Torah. It wasn't in the land of Mitzrayim / Egypt that Torah was given. It was in the land of desperation, in the land of the desert that YHWH gave His divine will. In the midst of the desert a flower bloomed for the teachings of Torah are a "tree of life to them that lay hold upon her: and happy is every one that retaineth her," Mishlei / Proverbs 3:18. Who would have thought that such greatness could come from a desert? Selah.

The English word "desert" is a translation of the Hebrew term "midbar." Strong's Exhaustive Concordance defines midbar as "in the sense of driving; a pasture (that is, open field, whither cattle are driven); by implication a desert; also speech (including its organs): -desert, south, speech, wilderness." Midbar comes from the root word "dabar" which means to "say, speak, be spokesman, subdue, talk, teach, tell." Learning from the root word "dabar," to speak, and the word "Bamidbar," in the wilderness, quickly shows that the Torah was spoken in the wilderness or desert! This lesson can be learned just from understanding the Hebrew word "bamidbar" or reading Numbers 1:1.

"Bamidbar" or "in the desert" is the Hebrew name of the book of Numbers. "Numbers" is an English moniker derived from the Greek Septuagint and counting of Israel that takes place in the book. "Why was the Torah given in the desert? To teach us that if a person does not surrender himself to it like the desert; he cannot merit the words of Torah. And to teach us that just as the desert is endless, so is the Torah without end," says one Rabbi.

The desert is a place of desolation. Throughout the Bible the dangers of the midbar are mentioned. Hunger, thirst, wild animals and enemies lead to the midbar being described as wilderness, as "land of deserts and of pits, a land of drought, and of the shadow of death, a land that no man passed through, and where no man dwelt," Yermi'yahu / Jeremiah 2:6. YHWH took Israel through these dangers to teach them some lessons. Bnai Israel / the children of Israel had to learn to trust Abba, to obey His mitzvot, and depend totally upon Him. "For YHWH's portion is his people; Ya'acov is the lot of his inheritance. He found him in a desert land, and in the waste howling wilderness; he led him about, he instructed him, he kept him as the apple of his eye. As an eagle stirreth up her nest, fluttereth over her young, spreadeth abroad her wings, taketh them, and beareth them on her wings: So YHWH alone did lead him, and there was no strange god with him," Devarim / Deuteronomy 32:9-11. It seems that the midbar, the desert, is some type of training arena for the Almighty where He prepares them for The Promised Land. Wasn't Moshe too found in the desert? Did not Y'shua spend time in the desert before His ministry began?

TRUTH FOR TODAY

January 23

To bear fruit is one primary purpose of man. In the beginning, Adam was told to be fruitful and multiply. However, Adam failed in his mission as a gardener. He ate from the wrong tree and tasted the forbidden fruit. Because of his sin, Adam produced the rotten fruit of the flesh. All of mankind has inherited the Adamic nature. This impulse will easily give in to fleshly desires and selfish actions. Today each person follows in the footsteps of Adam and must choose between the two trees of Eden. One can follow the sin of Adam and harvest spoiled fruit. "The works of the flesh are well known, among which are these; Adultery, fornication, uncleanness, indecency, idolatry, witchcraft, hatred, quarrels, jealousies, rage, strife, selfish ambition, stubbornness, heresies, envy, murder, drunkenness, wild indecent parties," Galatians / Galutyah 5:19-21.

Or instead of satisfying the ego, a person can choose to eat from the Tree of Life and bear the fruit thereof. The tree of life isn't really a tree, but a book containing instructions for every part of life. The Creator's plan for man is found within the first five books of the Bible. This blueprint for living is called "Torah" in Hebrew. The Torah is "a tree of life / ẹytz chayim to them that take hold of her: and happy is everyone that takes hold of her," Mishlei / Proverbs 3:18. To walk in the Spirit is to eat from the Tree of life and produce a fruitful life. Torah explains how we abide in the Savior and produce the fruit of the Spirit.

"The fruit of the Ruach HaKodesh / Holy Spirit is love, joy, shalom, patience, chesed / kindness, rachamim / goodness, trustworthiness, gentleness, self-control: there is no true Torah that is against this kind of fruit," Galatians / Galutyah 5:22, 23. In the list of Spirit fruit, the word joy is found. Many preachers say that joy is directly linked to service. They say to show up whenever the church doors are open and a person will be joyful. Many Sunday school teachers believe JOY is an acronym for serving Jesus first; Others second, and Yourself last. However, in ancient text j-o-y cannot be found. Instead, throughout the Scriptures over ten different Hebrew words are translated "joy."

Joy is a fruit that is either eaten or spoiled. It can also be stolen by others if you do not guard it carefully. The thief comes to "steal, kill, and destroy" us by demolishing our joy. Will you allow the enemy to take your

January 24

One word for "joy" in Hebrew is "oneg," spelled in Hebrew ayin – nun – gimmel. The dictionary defines oneg as "luxury, delight, enjoy, pleasant." Oneg is often associated with the Sabbath day of rest. The scripture tells us to "oneg in Shabbat." The concept of oneg or delighting in Shabbat proves that the Sabbath is not a day of restrictions but a day of relief. It is not a day to endure but enjoy. Shabbat is not a day of sadness but joy according to Jeremiah 58:13, 14.

In the book of Tehillim / Psalms we are told to, "Delight yourself in YHWH and He will give you the desires of your heart," Tehillim 367:4. The word for delight here is "oneg," which once again means to "enjoy and treat as a delicacy." When we begin to oneg in the Shabbat, YHWH will give us the desires of our heart. This doesn't mean Ed McMman will show up at the front door with a million dollar check. Instead, YHWH will give you HIS desires. HIS desires will become YOUR desires. As a person onegs Shabbat, he is brought closer to YHWH, and his desires are changed from worldly passions to spiritual desires. Perhaps this verse could read, "Oneg yourself in the Shabbat of YHWH and His desires will become your desires."

In Modern Hebrew, oneg is used to describe a meal or fellowship time. A covered dish dinner after a worship service is often called an "oneg." This again shows us that one should experience the same pleasure in Shabbat that one feels when enjoying a freshly prepared meal. Just think about it. After you have grilled a choice cut of steak, do you rush to eat it? Or do you slowly chew each bite and savor the flavor? A perfectly prepared steak and the Shabbat are both for our pleasure.

YHWH rested on the Shabbat and enjoyed His creation. He took oneg in Shabbat and expects us to do the same. Shabbat is not to be a day of deeds but a time of renewal and relaxation. It isn't a day to experience "new" joy by creating but revel in what has already been done. The Sabbath is a gateway to oneg and the appreciation of life.

The most common Hebrew word in Scripture for joy is "simchat." This term is used over 97 times and means, "mirth, gladness, gaiety, pleasure." While oneg is an inward awakening of appreciation, simchat is an outward response. Oneg delights while simcha shouts for joy!

Simcha is felt as a person does something. It is dependent upon the exterior factors of a worshiper's response. In other words, the fruit of simchat is a believer's outward response to YHWH's greatness. This fruit doesn't just magically appear. It has to be produced by the believer. For example, simchat is felt when a person gives an offering, blows the shofar, builds a sukkah, eats matzah, or wears tzittzit. This word is used in reference to many of the Biblical Holy Days including Passover, the Feast of Trumpets, and Purim.

TRUTH FOR TODAY

January 25

Simchat is a gift from YHWH that is to be manifested. Simchat is like a seed planted inside the soul that must be watered and cared for until it grows. It's a fruit that should be enjoyed like a fresh apple plucked from a tree. But, watch out for worms!

The worms of the adversary will try to corrupt the fruit of joy. Everyone knows that one bad apple spoils a bunch; so don't be let the enemy steal your joy even in one area. Y'shua said, "The thief comes not, but to steal, and to kill, and to destroy: I am come that they might have chayim / life, and that they might have it more abundantly," Yochannan / John 10:10. This verse describes the three main ways the adversary tries to take our simcha.

First, he wants to steal our joy. He does this by tricking us to live life in the past. A person can't experience life in abundance if he walks around with regret. Too many believers are defeated because of yesterday's sins. The concerns, pains, and hurts of the past will stop simcha from flourishing. Through away the poisoned apple of regret.

The enemy also wants to kill our future. He does this by whispering to us about what might happen. Fear grips the weary heart and paralyzes the saint not walking in the fruit of joy. The enemy knows he can defeat us if we are uptight and worrisome. However, YHWH says, "I know the plans I have for you, plans to prosper you and not harm you,"

The enemy understands that if he can keep us uptight and fearful of tomorrow or living in the regret of yesterday then he can DESTROY our present. If we are gripped by fear or pain we cannot experience the abundant life of Y'shua. He tries to DESTROY our present by KILLing our STEALing our future. Y'shua came that we might experience LIFE! The enemy has been defeated. "For this purpose the Son of YHWH was manifested, that He might destroy the works of the adversary," 1 John / Yochannan 3:8.

Y'shua came that we might have chayim – life and life to its fullest. The connection is clear. Life comes through walking in the simcha of YHWH. On Purim we are told that each person should become intoxicated until the reality of good and bad is distorted. The traditional toast to any Hebrew cup of wine is "l'chaim" – to life! This shows that one can experience the simcha of YHWH when one is filled with the life of YHWH. L'chaim! Be filled with the Ruach to life and to life abundant!

Truth For Today

January 26

Doomsday naysayers proclaim that we at the end of the end. TV preachers say the imminent return of Jesus in the clouds. Earthquakes are on the rise, wars are everywhere, and evil continues to mount. Is there any validity to the claim that we are living in the end times? What does the Bible have to say about such? How should we be preparing for events to come? Should we trust the religious TV preacher? How does Judaism regard the end of days? What did our Messiah say about the end time events?

The signs are obvious that we are living in a special time. But are we in the end times?

In Hebrew, the phrase "acharit-hayamim" literally means "end of days." This is when the "olam hazeh" or present world is coming to an end and the "olam haba" or "world to come" is about to begin.

The term stems from Beresheet / Genesis 49:1 and Micah 4:1: "Then Ya'acov called for his sons and said, "Assemble yourselves and I will tell you what will befall you in the End of Days / b'acharit ha-yamim."

"It will be in the end of days (b'acharit ha-yamim) that the mountain of the Temple of YHWH will be firmly established as the most prominent of the mountains, and it will be exalted up above the hills, and people will stream to it." Note that the Hebrew phrase "acharit hayamim" appears 7 times throughout the Tanakh / Old Testament.

One verse from the Scriptures that includes this phrase explains how we should view these dark days. In Hosea 3:5 it is written, "they will come trembling to YHWH and to His blessing in the last days." This is what we need – a balanced picture and understanding of the acharit hayamim.

Yesha'yahu / Isaiah 48:3 shows us that YHWH declares the end from the beginning. If we want to understand the end of days then we should understand the start of days. "I have declared the former things from of old; yea, they went forth out of My mouth, and I announced them; suddenly I did them, and they came to pass." In the beginning YHWH created the heavens and the earth in six days and rested on the seventh day – Shabbat day. As we look to the scriptures for answers we can clearly see a 7,000 plan for man. In Hebrew this is called "Yom SheKulo Shabbat" – the day when all will be Shabbat. Each day of creation corresponds to a millennial period. "One day with YHWH is as a thousand years, and a thousand years as one day," 2 Kefa / Peter 3:8-10. There are many more a parallels in Genesis and Revelation.

Does your understanding of the End Times match Matthew 24:14? Look up that verse and pray about this subject today. Time is short so it's necessary we are balanced in this subject.

January 27

Acts chapter 5 tells of Ananias and his wife Sapphira who knew about the Almighty but evidently didn't know Him. This couple was a vital part of the early body of believers and planned to prove their allegiance by selling a possession and giving the proceeds to the apostles for ministry. Ananias and Sapphira sinned though by giving most of the profit to the leaders. They had vowed to give all of the proceeds to the apostles but didn't. Because of this sin they were struck dead.

Perhaps Ananias and Sapphira knew about the Creator, maybe they even knew about the principle of sowing and reaping. They were a part of the early community of believers it seems but how could two people be so close but yet so far away? How could two people who know how serious a vow to the Almighty is not fulfill their part? How could someone who claims to love the Most High not be faithful to him? Maybe they were too satisfied with their relationship with the Savior or maybe they really didn't know Him at all. Maybe they just knew of him.

You see, the more familiar you are with a person the more comfortable you are being around that person. Think back to when you were in school and wanted to impress someone of the opposite sex. You were probably on your best behavior because you wanted to make a good impression. You were most likely courteous and charming. But, as time went on your desire to impress was exchanged for a desire to be comfortable around your friend. In the same way, when we become too familiar with the Most High, we are breeding a lackadaisical attitude that produces an awful way of thinking and acting. Many people trade their passion for comfort as Bible stories lose their dazzle and ministry leaders let them down.

Just because you know the Bible from cover to cover or pound the pulpit with authority, it doesn't mean know the Redeemer. The abundant life is a matter of intimacy not familiarity. Many believers have become so familiar with their religious' ways that they are content with what they have always been taught and don't care to search the scriptures themselves. "Don't confuse me with the facts, I'm happy being ignorant," is a statement that describes countless individuals who warm pews every week. Today the Father is calling His people to know Him intimately. We are to pursue Him and Him alone. This pursuit is accomplished through knowing Him, not just knowing about Him.

How can you deepen your relationship with Y'shua today?

TRUTH FOR TODAY

January 28

"Therefore, O house of Israel, I will judge you, each one according to his ways, declares the Sovereign YHWH. Repent! Turn away from all your offenses; then sin will not be your downfall. Rid yourselves of all the offenses you have committed, and get a new heart and a new spirit. Why will you die, O house of Israel? For I take no pleasure in the death of anyone, declares the Sovereign YHWH. Repent and live," Ezekiel 18:30-32.

Notice that it is only after repenting and turning from "all your offenses" or doing "teshuvah" that man receives "a new heart and a new spirit." This renewal or rebirth, a return to the Torah and to YHWH, is THE message of the Messiah. "From that time on Y'shua began to preach, "Repent, for the kingdom of heaven is near," Matthew / Mattitiyahu 4:17. Teshuvah is the end time's message.

The early followers of Y'shua's teachings continued spreading this timeless message, "First to those in Damascus, then to those in Jerusalem and in all Judea, and to the Gentiles also, I preached that they should repent and turn to Elohim and prove their repentance by their deeds," said Sha'ul / Paul in Acts 26:20. Even in the book of Revelation Y'shua echoes these words:

"Remember the height from which you have fallen! Repent and do the things you did at first. If you do not repent, I will come to you and remove your lamp stand from its place," Revelation 2:5.

"Remember, therefore, what you have received and heard; obey it, and repent. But if you do not wake up, I will come like a thief, and you will not know at what time I will come to you," Revelation 3:3.

The power of Teshuvah is an amazing thing, for it enables sinful man to fellowship with holy YHWH because teshuvah actually wipes out all memory and stain of the sin. "Come now, let us reason together," says YHWH. "Though your sins are like scarlet, they shall be as white as snow; though they are red as crimson, they shall be like wool," Yesha'yahu / Isaiah 1:18.

How can you make teshuvah today? Don't just say you are sorry when you offend. Take the time to turn from the action and make restitution for the pain you have caused.

TRUTH FOR TODAY

January 29

In Beresheet / Genesis, YHWH blessed the Shabbat day and made it holy/kadosh/set apart. What this means is that YHWH put Himself into the Shabbat day. YHWH made the day holy; therefore He invested part of His power and glory into this day. Friday night to Saturday night is a span of hours unlike any others. Each second of each minute holds a divine spark of YHWH's power. We experience this power by simply experiencing the day of Shabbat. YHWH empowers us as we rest in Him. "Those who wait/rest upon YHWH shall mount up with wings as eagles," says Isaiah.

Shabbat is a day to become more and more like Him. Exodus / Shemot 31:13 says, "I am YHWH that makes you kadosh / holy." On all other days you strive to be holy and set apart by prayer and the mitzvot. On Shabbat we are to rest in Him and allow Him to make us set apart. On the Sabbath we should totally rest in Him and allow Him to make us set apart/holy.

The moment we were saved YHWH could have taken us out of this world. He could have told us to go and wait on a church pew for the rapture bus to take us to heaven. But, He did not. He has left us here to be His voice; His representatives to the world, to continue in our heavenly education, being made through testing and trials more like our Master. YHWH left us here to shine forth His Light.

The mitzvot / commandments shine light in the darkness. They illuminate the truth of what is really going on. They bring glory to YHWH. "Let your light shine before men so that they may see your good works and glorify your Father who is in Shamayim / Heaven," said Y'shua. Shabbat is a day to do good and obey the mitzvot of the Word.

The story is told of one man who challenged another to an all-day wood chopping contest. The challenger worked very hard, stopping only for a brief lunch break. The other man had a leisurely lunch and took several breaks during the day. At the end of the day, the challenger was surprised and annoyed to find that the other fellow had chopped substantially more wood than he had. "I don't get it," he said. "Every time I checked, you were taking a rest, yet you chopped more wood than I did." "But you didn't notice," said the winning woodsman, "that I was sharpening my ax when I sat down to rest." Shabbat is a time to sharpen our ax as we rest in Him!

January 30

We are Israel. We are part of the olive tree of Israel. We have a rich heritage and an identity. With this knowledge we must begin to learn how an Israelite it so act, talk, worship, love, eat, dress, and more. This, in essence, is the Hebrew Roots movement in a nutshell. However, too many times we think that our faith is all about Judaism OR we consider that our faith is all about being ANTI-Christian. NO! Our faith is about Hebrew Roots – SPECIFIALLY – our faith is about THE Hebrew Root. Our relationship with THE Hebrew root is most important!

Y'shua is the "root of Jesse" and a study of Hebrew roots must be focused on Him. Isaiah 11:1, 2 "A shoot will come out of the stock of Jesse, and a branch out of his roots will bear fruit. The Spirit of YHWH will rest on him: the spirit of wisdom and understanding, the spirit of counsel and might, the spirit of knowledge and of the fear of YHWH." The book of Revelation agrees, Revelation 5:5, "Don't weep. Behold, the Lion who is of the tribe of Judah, the Root of David, has overcome; he who opens the book and its seven seals."

Know this - a study of the Jewish Roots of Christianity; a study of the Hebrew Roots of the Bible is a study of Y'shua. A study of the Torah is a study of Y'shua. It's all about Y'shua. We must be cautious to guard our faith from being focused on anything other than Messiah Y'shua. HE is the root! We are the branches. By faith in Y'shua we are grafted into the Y'shua. That indeed is the beauty of the Hebrew roots movement. However, that's also the danger of our faith.

The commandments in the Torah, first five books of the Bible, speak of every facet of life. There are guidelines for everything from when we are to worship (seventh day) and even guidelines to farmers about how they plant their garden. ALL of the commandments were given to influence our relationship with Messiah Y'shua. They weren't just given for obedience to see if we would obey the Bible or not. The Torah is given as a blueprint to Y'shua and about Y'shua. Leviticus 19 gives us many specific commandments from not having a tattoo to keeping the Sabbath. Verse 19 of this chapter says, "You shall not sow your field with a mixture of seeds, and a garment which has a mixture of sha'atnez shall not come upon you."

We must take time to uproot the fear, rejection, and oppression of the enemy before we dig deep into our Hebrew roots. Otherwise all we are doing is throwing seeds of Torah knowledge upon the top soil of our broken and tattered lives. Take a few minutes today and ask YHWH to reveal how you have put other things before the Root of Jesse. Exalt Y'shua and seek first his kingdom.

TRUTH FOR TODAY

January 31

In the Bible, there are two main commandments concerning the Shabbat. The first is a negative command which tells us not to work. "Remember Yom Ha-Shabbat / Sabbath day, to keep it as kadosh / set apart. Six days shall you labor, and do all your work: But the seventh day is the Shabbat of YHWH your Elohim: in it you shall not do any work, you, nor your son, nor your daughter, your male eved / slave, nor your female eved, nor your cattle, nor your stranger that is within your gates: For in six days YHWH made the Shamayim and earth, the sea, and all that is in them, and rested on the seventh day: therefore YHWH blessed the Shabbat day, and set it apart," Exodus / Shemot 20:8-11. The second main mitzvot is a positive commandment to simply rest. "Six days you shall do your work, and on the seventh day you shall rest," Shemot / Exodus 23:12. There is a difference between not working and resting. Shabbat calls us to refrain from influencing the world AND simply enjoy the world. To experience this type of Shabbat one must finish what he started. Bring your labors to an end and remind yourself that you are a "human being" and not a "human doing." Such thinking is foreign to us.

We are so programmed to operate as a robot that it's difficult to stop and just "be." We wake up, have our coffee, head to work, labor all day, come home, eat dinner, watch the TV, check our email, say our prayers, and then go to bed only to repeat the process on the next day. We are so used to life in the fast lane that we struggle with Shabbat. We live between the distant hope of heaven in the windshield and hell in the rear view mirror. We strive to keep Shabbat but too many times our observance goes from "Shabbat Shalom" to "Shabbat Sheol." Our thoughts are filled with things to do and people to see instead of rest and peace. Some even look for ditches to throw oxen into. Sadly, many people view Sabbath as a burden instead of a release. The worries of life and the cares of the world cause us to loose site of Heaven. We have forgotten what it feels like to really rest in Him!

The book of Hebrews states that "there remains a Sabbath rest" for us today. To truly experience this peace this week, finish your work and seek YHWH on the seventh day. Cut off your cellular phone, sleep in, or spend the day reading the Scriptures and praying. Make this coming Shabbat special.

February

February 1

The olive tree is very different than the grape vine. The vine grows horizontally while the olive tree grows vertically towards Heaven / Shamayim. The olive tree is used throughout the Bible in reference to the nation of Israel. The first mention of the olive tree in the Scriptures is in reference to a restoration after the flood of Noach. In like manner, the Olive Tree of Israel will be restored during the day of Noach as seen in Matthew 24:37.

The Mount of Olives, located just east of the Old City of Jerusalem, attests to the prevalence of olive trees around the city. Also, it was in the Garden of Gethsemane (Gat Shemen in Hebrew, literally, the place of the "olive press"), where Y'shua spent much of His time in Jerusalem with His disciples. "Coming out, He went to the Mount of Olives, as He was accustomed, and His disciples also followed Him," Luke. 22:39.

Gat or Geth is Hebrew for press and Shemen in Hebrew means "oil." The word "zayit" is Hebrew for olive. Gat Shemmon is at the western slope of the Mount of Olives. This land was covered with olive groves. Y'shua went to the Garden of Olive groves. The process that took place here is symbolic to what happened to our Master and to what happens to us in the Spirit realm.

At Gat Shemmon, the air would be filled with the pungent odor of the fresh oil. A huge stone pillar needed to be lifted onto the olives. This was turned for the first pressing for the finest virgin oil – that used for anointing. For the second pressing, the remaining pulp was placed on baskets. (If olive oil comes from crushed olives, where does baby oil come from?)

The place of the olive crushing is the place that we must visit as we are made more like Y'shua. It is a time and place in our lives that we must pray, "may your will be done." It is here that abiding in the true vine comes to fruition. The progression is simple - We obey and we pray and then we yield to the Father's will!

No matter what the conditions: hot, dry, cold, wet, rocky, or sandy, the evergreen olive tree will live and produce fruit. It is said that you can never kill an olive tree. Even when cut down or burned, new shoots will emerge from its roots. Israel may have looked as if it was destroyed but a remnant of the nation has always remained. The tenacity of the nation of Israel is beautifully illustrated in the olive tree.

"The YHWH called your name, Green Olive Tree, Lovely and of Good Fruit....For YHWH of hosts, has planted you," Jeremiah 11:16, 17.

February 2

"I will be like the dew to Israel; he shall grow like the lily, and lengthen his roots like Lebanon. His branches shall spread; his beauty shall be like an olive tree, and his fragrance like Lebanon," Hosea 14:5, 6.

The physical attributes of the olive tree mirror many characteristics the Israelites have displayed throughout the ages. Their history in the Exile / Diaspora / Galut (all the nations of the world outside Israel) testifies of their enduring nature in hostile, foreign lands: Its branches are gnarled and twisted and will grow where other trees cannot survive. It clings to life and is enduring. Some olive trees live as long as 3000 years. Only one flower in 100 bears fruit as the others fall off. Cultivated olive tree branches can be grafted into wild olive trees to improve the wild olive tree; but rarely are the branches of the wild olive ever grafted into a cultivated olive tree.

Romans 11:24-25: "For if you were cut out of the olive tree which is wild by nature, and were grafted contrary to nature into a cultivated olive tree (Judah) how much more will these, who are natural branches be grafted into their own olive tree (be returned to YHWH's privilege.)"

One author has written, "We are going to see individuals within many Christian congregations learn they are the lost sheep of the House of Israel in the coming years, as they move toward the Torah, learn the Name, and realize who they are in Y'shua. They will receive a love for the Torah (the Truth, YHWH's Word), which is inviting Y'shua to write the 10 Commandments on their heart, which is the New Covenant (or re-newed Covenant). They will engraft into Israel, by being immersed into the New Covenant (or re-newed Covenant), and know they are branches (Natsarim) in the olive tree (the natural olive tree, ISRAEL - Romans 11 - we don't remain "wild" olive branches, but are engrafted into the natural one."

You are the olive tree of Israel. How can you learn more about your faith today? Who can you share this message with today?

TRUTH FOR TODAY

February 3

The 15th of the Hebrew month Shevat is a special day. This day is called "Rosh Hashanah L'llanot" or the "New Year of the Trees." This special time was set aside as the start of the season to tithe the harvest of plants. "And all the tithe of the land, whether of the seed of the land, or of the fruit of the tree, is YHWH's: it is holy unto YHWH," Exodus 27:30. On this day, in Eretz Yisrael / the Land of Israel, the tithing year for plants begins and ends. It is during Shevat that the heavy rains in Iisrael begin to end and in comes spring. With the change in seasons the sap in the fruit trees starts to rise. It is customary for farmers in Israel to set aside a small part of their crops for holy purposes. The new crop starts each year on Tu B'Shevet. It has also become tradition to plant trees in Israel on Tu B'Shevat as a type of "Arbor Day" celebration.

Is there really a New Year for the trees? The Talmud says, "There are four new years. On the first of Nisan is the new year for kings and for festivals. On the first of Elul is the new year for the tithe of animals. R Eliazar and R Shimon say on the 1st of Tishrei. On the 1st of Tishrei is the New year for the years, for the shmitta (Sabbatical) and Yovel (Jubilee) years, for the sapling and for the vegetables. On the 1st of Shevat is the New Year for the tree according to Beis Shammai, Beis Hillel say on the 15th."

To learn moreabout trees and the faith consider these verses:

- Leviticus 19:23-25, "When you enter the land and plant any kind of fruit tree, regard its fruit as forbidden. For three years you are to consider it forbidden; it must not be eaten. In the fourth year all its fruit will be holy, an offering of praise to YHWH. But in the fifth year you may eat its fruit. In this way your harvest will be increased. I am YHWH your Elohim."

- "A land of wheat, and barley, and vines, and fig trees, and pomegranates; a land of oil olive, and honey; A land wherein thou shalt eat bread without scarceness, thou shalt not lack any thing in it; a land whose stones are iron, and out of whose hills thou mayest dig brass. When thou hast eaten and art full, then thou shalt bless YHWH thy Elohim for the good land which he hath given thee," Deuteronomy 8:8-10.

- "And all the tithe of the land, whether of the seed of the land, or of the fruit of the tree, is YHWH's: it is holy unto YHWH," Exodus 27:30.

- "The Land must not be sold beyond reclaim, for the land is Mine," Leviticus 25:23.

- "The earth is the Eternal's and all that it holds," Psalms 24:1.

February 4

Study will reveal that calendar keeping is truly an issue of personal conviction. We are to study to know what the Scriptures say about this and other subjects. If you are convinced the Rabbinic calendar is right, then follow it. If you are convinced the Aviv barley matters today, then take such into your calendar consideration. Romans 14:5 makes this clear – "One man considers one day more sacred than another; another man considers every day alike. Each one should be fully convinced in his own mind."

We are to study to show ourselves approved. And we should know what we believe regarding the precepts of Torah, Hebrew names, and dates. This knowledge must be accompanied with patience and acceptance of those who may be different.

Instead of arguing with others, why not to lay aside your "correct" interpretation of Scripture and trust the Creator to correct His chosen people. Submit to local leadership in love and accept that each person is at a different place in their faith. Time will allow the Ruach HaKodesh / Holy Spirit to bring the believer into truth. We need to leave the judgment of sin and error to the Spirit of YHWH. "Let no man therefore judge you in meat, or in drink, or in respect of an holy day, or of the new moon, or of the Sabbath days," Colossians. This verse clearly shows that it is the Almighty's job to judge between the intentions of the heart and the actions of the person. We are to love and pray for those who may be different in their walk of faith.

If you know you are right about an issue and you know that your friend or spiritual leader is wrong, then you are to intercede for them. Don't try to explain your way as right. Stop your tongue from wagging with verses, facts, and history. Resist the urge to send an email which explains your side of the issue. Unity and love is much more important than totally correct doctrine. For such arguments over the commandments go unheeded unless the other person is open to correction.

Know that a person will be willing to change only if he shows an attitude of change. Truthfully, we should only give advice or information IF the person is open to such correction. When it comes down to it, there are only two types of people that you can help – those that ask and those that are in immediate danger. You can only help a person who is genuinely interested in your opinion. Or you can only help a person who is in sudden danger. All other people will simply ignore your words. We are not to cast our pearl of Torah before many people who act like swine through wallowing in their error.

What is most important is that a person is trying to obey Torah instead of following man made religions and customs of the popular society. It is through our "ahava" or "love" that the world should tell that we are disciples of our Master. Ahava should offer acceptance and compassion to those with different doctrines, ideas, and convictions.

TRUTH FOR TODAY

February 5

The mitzvoth or commands of the Torah are an intermediary tool used to break down the flesh and beat down the power of sin. The mitzvoth are not just to bring blessings to Yah's people. They are to prepare us for eternity and establish the Malchut Shamayim / Kingdom of Heaven here on earth. Following the Torah makes conditions right for "deveikut" or "clinging to YHWH." This is because the mitzvoth bring Light.

Light is symbolic of YHWH. Light is His presence, His essence, and His power. Remember that Adam and YHWH were connected until Adam broke the Divine Will and sinned. "All have sinned and fallen short of the glory," says the Brit Chadasha / New Testament. Perhaps Adam and Chava were created like YHWH in the idea that they were originally 'light beings.' When Adam fell he gave into the darkness and moved away from the glory or Light of YHWH. When Adam fell, Adam lost his light. It wasn't until after the fall that YHWH covered mankind with skin. Before the fall Adam was full of Light, he had perfect relationship with the Creator, he exhibited dominion, and was sinless. "This is the verdict: Light has come into the world, but men loved darkness instead of light because their deeds were evil. Everyone who does evil hates the light, and will not come into the light for fear that his deeds will be exposed. But whoever lives by the truth comes into the light, so that it may be seen plainly that what he has done has been done through Elohim," Yochannan / John 3:19-21.

The mitzvoth allow us to give pleasure to YHWH and at the same time receive pleasure from YHWH. At creation "Elohim took Adam and placed him in the Gan Eden, to work it and to guard it," Beresheet / Genesis 2:15. One ancient Jewish writing says that "the word 'work' alludes to the two hundred and forty-eight positive commandments; 'guard' hints to the three hundred and sixty-five Torah prohibitions." So, if this is true then Adam's working and guarding the Gan Eden shows that Adam's purpose in life was to obey Torah and thus bring Light to the world. When Adam sinned he allowed darkness to reign. Since the fall mankind has been struggling to regain the Light of creation.

"If you fully obey YHWH your Elohim and carefully follow all his commands I give you today, the YHWH your Elohim will set you high above all the nations on earth. All these blessings will come upon you and accompany you if you obey YHWH your Elohim," Devarim 28:1-2. YHWH wants to give His goodness to mankind. He desires to restore us to the fellowship of the Garden of Eden. Out of His great love He has allowed us to choose our own path towards fulfillment. Either we cling to YHWH or we cling to our flesh. Either we run to the Light or we run to the darkness. "In him was life; and the life was the light of men. And the light shineth in darkness; and the darkness comprehended it not," Yochannan / John 1:1-2. What does this word mean to you today?

February 6

Mel Gibson's movie, "The Passion of the Christ," detailed the last hours of the life of Messiah. The film was recorded totally in the ancient languages of Latin and Aramaic. Throughout the blockbuster, the Savior is called "Y'shua" in Aramaic. This further shows that Jesus is not the Savior's name. Just think about it, how could the Jewish Messiah have an English name?

When the angel spoke to Mary and Joseph about the pregnancy, the Hebrew-speaking couple was told that the Savior's name was "Y'shua," meaning "Salvation is of YHWH."

One basic reason that the name Jesus is not correct is that the English language is not that old. Moses did not speak King James English. And the Savior's name could not start with a "j" because it simply did not exist. There isn't even a Hebrew letter sound similar to "j."

The King of the Jews was given a Jewish name. Religious groups have used the name of Jesus for so long, that few people stop to question how a Hebrew Messiah could have a Greek/English name. When the Messiah walked this earth, He was never called "Jesus." His name was, and is, Y'shua.

The name "Jesus" is derived from the Greek name "Ieasus," which actually could mean "son of Zeus." Sadly, when people call upon the name of Jesus they are actually speaking of Greek mythology. The Bible clearly reveals that salvation is available in only one name: "Neither is there salvation in any other: for there is none other name under heaven given among men, whereby we must be saved," Acts, chapter 4:12. What is found in English Bibles is a fake name. Mel Gibson was right after all.

Which name of the Messiah do you use? Which should you use?

Truth For Today

February 7

If we don't guard our heart, we'll soon begin to doubt our actions and become trapped by doing only what is required of us. There are those in the faith that use the excuse that they will do "only what is required in the Torah" before they move on in their faith. These people won't follow traditions like lighting Shabbat candles because the "Torah doesn't command it." And they equate not working on the Sabbath to spending a day in the Dentist's waiting room. These attitudes are dangerous because of how they clog our heart.

Again, YHWH doesn't want just our actions. He wants our life. He wants us. The Scriptures have an answer for those who would question what is required of believers. "Israel what does YHWH your Elohim require of you, but to fear YHWH your Elohim, to walk in all his ways, and to love him, and to serve YHWH your Elohim with all your heart and with all your soul," – Devarim / Deuteronomy 10:12. Notice that walking in his way, observing the mitzvoth, and loving YHWH with all of the heart are equal. What does YHWH require? He requires all that we are.

"What does YHWH require of you, but to do justly, and to love mercy, and to walk humbly with your Elohim," Mica'yah / Micah 6:8. If our heart's condition is right before YHWH, it is as if we are obeying all of the mitzvoth, because we will be obeying the mitzvoth. Y'shua said, "'You shall love the YHWH your Elohim with all your heart, with all your soul, and with all your mind. This is the first and greatest commandment. And the second is like it: 'You shall love your neighbor as yourself. On these two commandments hang all the Law and the Prophets," Mattitiyahu / Matthew 22:38-40. This verse corresponds with the previous pasuk / passage in Micah.

When we love YHWH with all our heart, we will do justly. When we love Him with all of our soul, we will view others in compassion and so we will love mercy. And when we love Him with all of our mind, we will keep our mind upon Him and walk humbly in His Spirit. One Jewish writing says, "when a man's love to the Holy One is roused, the "right hand" is moved only by a threefold impulse, by "heart", "soul", and "might", for it does not say, "with all thy heart or with all thy soul", etc., but "and with all thy soul", etc.: all three are essential and necessary. Then does the Holy One respond and stir up His Right Hand towards that man."

YHWH wants our heart. He wants all of us. His desire is for His people to submit to His will for their lives. This will is revealed throughout the Torah. To obey the Torah without giving our heart to YHWH is great loss. To submit to the Almighty and seek to walk in obedience to the Torah is great gain.

February 8

Through His Shalom / peace we can make it through a bad day or a string of terrible events. The book of Ephesians proves how this is possible. "He is our Shalom, Who hath made both one, and hath broken down the middle wall of partition between us," Ephesians 2: 14. Our shalom is the presence of Master Y'shua. It is Him. Nothing more and nothing less. He is our peace. The Prince of Peace is our wholeness. He is the one that completes us. To illustrate this, a Jew who accepts Y'shua as Messiah is often called "completed Jew." Rav Sha'ul wrote, "For YHWH was pleased to have all the fullness dwell in Him, and through Him to reconcile to Himself all things, all things, whether things on earth or things in heaven, by making shalom though His blood, shed on the execution stake," Colossians 1:19, 20.

Every time we use the word "shalom," we should be reminded that we are speaking about Y'shua. He is our peace. Now, apply this idea to Tehillim / Psalms 122: 6 where we are told to "pray for the peace of Jerusalem." When we do this, we are actually praying for the salvation of Jerusalem. As we pray for the peace of Jerusalem, we are praying that all Israel comes to know Y'shua as their Master and Savior! The Talmud confirms this in Megillah E: 33-35, "And where is the horn of the righteous exalted? In Jerusalem, as it says, Pray for the peace of Jerusalem, may they prosper that love thee. And when Jerusalem is built, David will come, as it says." The Jews have this truth, yet many are so blind that they don't see it and accept Y'shua as their Messiah!

As we walk in Shalom we are walking as Y'shua walked and thus replicating His life. "My covenant was with him of life and shalom; and I gave them to him for the fear wherewith he feared me, and was afraid before my name. The law of truth was in his mouth, and iniquity was not found in his lips: he walked with me in shalom and equity, and did turn many away from iniquity," Malachi 2. Y'shua was never in a hurry nor did he ever worry about life. He lived in total shalom. Y'shua focused on YHWH, brought forth the Kingdom of Heaven. Having Y'shua's focus is what enables us to have the Shalom promised in the Scriptures. "He wilt keep him in perfect peace, whose minds is stayed on Thee." Isaiah 26: 3

TRUTH FOR TODAY

February 9

Anti-Semitism is the ugly hatred of anything Jewish. "Anti-Semitism has its roots planted deep in the soil of the world religions of Christianity and Islam. Both of these claim to be the "true" religion of the Scriptures and claim to have replaced Judaism. Mainstream Christianity, as it now exists, claims to be the "New Israel" and they claim the "New Covenant" has replaced the inferior "Old Covenant." The "New Testament "god is one of love and grace, while the god of the "Old" is judgmental and shows no mercy to the sinner. The Torah is bondage and their anti-Torah teachings are called freedom in "Christ". Their Messiah came to free the Jews from the law and to put an end to their legalistic religion. According to their doctrines, Y'shua came to stop all tradition and Torah observance. In their mixed up world, the "Church" replaces Israel and the Jews are destined for hell-fire unless they convert to their brand of Christianity. The Christian religion claims to love the Jewish people, yet their history only proves their distain and persecution of the Jews," wrote one rabbi.

Sadly, for many years anti-Semitism has been taught by religion by suggesting that the Jewish people killed the savior. This idea breeds dislike and disgust of the Hebrew people.

The Jews did not kill Y'shua. Nor did the Romans. No one took Y'shua's life from Him. He gave up His life freely for all mankind. "I lay down My life that I may take it again. No one has taken it away from Me, but I lay it down on My own initiative. I have authority to lay it down, and I have authority to take it up again," John 10:17-18. Don't blame the Jews! Don't harbor anti-Semitism. The Hebrew people were and are the chosen people of YHWH.

We do not support the root. The root supports us. Pray about this reading today.

Truth For Today

February 10

Biblical love is more concerned about giving than receiving. Giving is the vehicle of love. "For YHWH so loved the world that He gave His only Son," John 3:16. True love is not even based on feelings, as feelings can actually stop someone from giving love to others. We treat people the way we feel. Therefore, if we feel loved of the Almighty then we will treat other people with that same love. When you treat others rudely, it's simply because you are not feeling loved. Feelings are symptoms of thought. The problem is that most of people think that they are unlovely. Masses think that God doesn't love them. When we have these thoughts we then are inclined to act unloving to others. Understand that if you are not feeling the love of the Almighty, then it is your emotions that are stopping His ahava / love from filling your life. But, if you meditate, think, sing, or pray about YHWH's ahava / love then your emotions and actions will reflect His love. Your actions go along with what you think about. "Beloved, if YHWH so loved us; we also should love one another," 1 John 4:11.

Don't allow bad problems or emotions to convince you that YHWH doesn't feel compassion towards you. Regardless of what you have done in the past, YHWH loves you and you are special to Him. His love is unconditional because it is His nature to love. "But anyone who does not love does not know YHWH, for YHWH is love," 1 John 4:8.

A person of faith should overflow with the love of Messiah; a love that constantly gives to others. "He that has my commandments, and keeps them, he it is that loves me," John 14:21. Notice the pattern in this verse – first you do love and then you feel it and receive it. For faith to be effective, each religious action, each prayer, and each good deed must be from the motivation of showing love. Biblical love is an unconditional gift that is freely offered from the heavens. The Savior said, "My command is this: love each other as I have loved you," John 15:12.

Truth For Today

February 11

Have you had a heart transplant? If you are born again then your heart has been changed!

The heart is made new at salvation. We are no longer "sinners saved by grace." We are now a new creation that has been given "a new heart," Ezekiel 36:26. We have been changed on the inside. If we truly believe this then we have to have our mind renewed about many issues and pet theologies that we have learned over the years. The revelation of the mystery of Colossians 1:27 changes a lot. Teachers in the Messianic movement like to say that "if it's in the Bible then it's for us today." We believe that since we are the commonwealth of Israel then all that happened to Israel was written for our application and our identification. While all of this is true to some extent, we seldom recognize and often fail to realize exactly what Y'shua did when He died and rose from the dead.

Remember that Messiah's work ripped the Temple veil from top to bottom. The Temple of stone was no longer the main attraction as YHWH's Spirit now resides in the temple of each and every believer. The Ruach HaKodesh is not just resting "on" people as the Spirit did in the Old Testament because the Spirit is "in" people today. May we pray as Paul did in Ephesians 1:18, "I pray that the eyes of your heart may be enlightened in order that you may know the hope to which he has called you, the riches of his glorious inheritance in his holy people." Notice that verse is a prayer that the eyes of our hearts would be opened so that we could see the "glorious inheritance "IN" us today.

Take a few minutes today to study and pray about the "riches of his glorious inheritance in" you today. As you do, your mind will be renewed to the power of YHWH to transform you from the inside. Philemon 1:6 says, "may your faith become affective through the acknowledgment of every good thing in you in Y'shua."

Your heart is not sinful because your heart is now Y'shua's heart. How can this truth set you free?

Truth For Today

February 12

YHWH's love is His power to reach into this world and give hope. Today, take some time and think on these verses:

- "For YHWH so loved the world that he gave his one and only Son, that whoever believes in him shall not perish but have eternal life," John 3:16
- "I have been crucified with Messiah and I no longer live, but Messiah lives in me. The life I live in the body, I live by faith in the Son of YHWH, who loved me and gave himself for me," Galatians 2:20
- "Know therefore that YHWH your Elohim is Elohim; he is the faithful Elohim, keeping his covenant of love to a thousand generations of those who love him and keep his commands," Deuteronomy 7:9
- "For YHWH loves the just and will not forsake his faithful ones," Psalm 37:28
- "I love those who love me, and those who seek me find me," Proverbs 8:17
- "This is how YHWH showed his love among us: He sent his one and only Son into the world that we might live through him. This is love: not that we loved Elohim, but that he loved us and sent his Son as an atoning sacrifice for our sins. Dear friends, since YHWH so loved us, we also ought to love one another," 1 John 4:9-11
- "And so we know and rely on the love Elohim has for us. Elohim is love. Whoever lives in love lives in YHWH, and Elohim in him," 1 John 4:16
- "We love because he first loved us. If anyone says, "I love YHWH," yet hates his brother, he is a liar. For anyone who does not love his brother, whom he has seen, cannot love YHWH, whom he has not seen," 1 John 4:19-20
- "This is how we know who the children of YHWH are and who the children of the devil are: Anyone who does not do what is right is not a child of YHWH; nor is anyone who does not love his brother," 1 John 3:10
- "So be very careful to love YHWH your Elohim," Joshua 23:11

February 13

Valentine's Day seems harmless and wonderful but dangers lurk in this pagan love feast. The Encyclopedia Britannica explains, "This holiday has its origin in the Roman festival of Lupercalia, held in mid-February. The festival, which celebrated the coming of spring, included fertility rites and the pairing off of women with men by lottery." Thousands of years ago, On February 15, Romans celebrated Lupercalia, honoring Faunus, god of fertility. Men would go to a grotto dedicated to Lupercal, the wolf god, located at the foot of Palatine Hill. Here, the Romans believed that the founders of Rome, Romulus and Remus, were suckled by a she-wolf. These men would sacrifice a goat, wear its skin, and run around, hitting women with small whips, an act which was supposed to ensure fertility. The Encyclopedia Americana states the custom of exchanging valentines was "handed down from the Roman festival of the Lupercalia, celebrated on the 15th of February, when names of young women were put into a box and drawn out by men as chance directed."

Later, the Catholic Church replaced Lupercalia with St. Valentine's Day. History shows that early church policy was to incorporate pagan celebrations. Instead of just banning these ancient satanic religions, the Catholic Church adopted evil practices into the religious Christian faith. A story was fabricated about a martyred Catholic priest who would sign his letters, "with love from St. Valentine." Today, we have the mixture of a Roman festival, savvy retail marketing, and a false story of a patron saint. Valentine's Day is no longer part of the liturgical calendar of any church. This day was dropped from the Catholic calendar in 1969 and not surprisingly has returned to its original pagan roots of unbridled love making. The Bible says to "take no part in the worthless deeds of evil and darkness; instead, rebuke and expose them," Ephesians 5:11.

Mythology teaches that Venus was the mother of Cupid, whose name means "desire." Nimrod's mother, Venus desired / lusted after her own son. That is why she is called the goddess of sexual immorality - she had relations her own son. Their twisted sexuality is the object of Valentine's Day as their relationship was consummated on February 14. Cupid can also be traced back to the evil man Nimrod, who built the tower of Babel in Genesis 10. Nimrod / Cupid was a mighty hunter with bow and arrows. His vicious rebellion against the Almighty continues with Valentine's Day.

The history and origin of modern practices and holidays should be an issue to Bible believers. Pagan holidays, like the love feast Valentine's Day, should be avoided. Zephaniah 1:8 says, "On that day of judgment," says YHWH, "I will punish the leaders... and all those following pagan customs." Love is wonderful but Valentine's Day is like a tainted candy with deadly poison.

TRUTH FOR TODAY

February 14

Love is a basic but often misunderstood subject. We may think we know all about love, but the love spoken of in the Scriptures is different than that in the world. The love YHWH has shown us is better than the bond between husbands and wives. The love of YHWH is greater than anything that has been presented in the church or the synagogue. "O the depth of the riches both of the wisdom and knowledge of YHWH! How unsearchable are his judgments, and his ways past finding out!" Romans / Romiyah 11:33.

If we really understood YHWH's love and if we really experienced His love then our lives would be different. Do you remember the day when YHWH's love broke through the darkness of sin in your life? That same love is available today. In Hebrew, the word translated "love" is "ahava." It is YHWH's ahava that brings us to the good news, allows us to experience life, and calls us to help others. "For the ahava / love of Moshiach compels us; because we have judged this to be truth," Second Corinthians 5:14.

The ahava / love of YHWH is unconditional. The Merriam Webster definition of "unconditional" is: "not conditional or limited: absolute, unqualified." YHWH loves the world even though the world is absolutely unqualified and unconditioned for love. Romiyah / Romans 5:8 states, "YHWH showed His great love for us in this manner, while we were still sinners, Y'shua died for us."

YHWH demonstrated His ahava before any good deeds of Torah were performed. Y'shua is the lamb of YHWH slain from the foundation of the earth. This is unconditional ahava. YHWH showed this ahava to His son. At his mikvah / baptism, before a single miracle of Y'shua is recorded in the Scriptures, YHWH declares from the heavens / shamayim "this is my beloved son in whom I am well pleased." YHWH felt that way about His son Y'shua and He feels the same way about YOU today! YHWH loves YOU regardless of what you do or don't do!

We have been called to walk in the fruit of love and demonstrate His ahava to the world. For us to walk in ahava we must FIRST better understand and then focus on His ahava / love. Psychologists tell us that the average person has 60,000 thoughts per day. If you were to categorize your thoughts from the past 24 hours, what would they include? What have you been thinking upon? Our thoughts should be on and about the love of YHWH.

We shall know the truth of YHWH's love and the truth of His ahava / love will set us free! As we walk in His love YHWH purifies us from demonic attacks, sin, and shame. We are to focus FIRST on YHWH's love and THEN all other thoughts, issues, obedience, or study should flow from His ahava.

February 15

The Scriptures declare that "YHWH declares the end from the beginning" in Isaiah / Yesha'yahu 46:10. When the Nile River was first turned to blood, YHWH was warning Pharaoh of a coming disaster. YHWH was offering Pharaoh an escape. You can read more about this in the book of Exodus. YHWH was telling Pharaoh that "life is in the blood," Leviticus / Vayikra 17:11. Pharaoh ignored the blood and brought death upon his entire family and people.

The wages of sin is death but the blood offers life!

The blood remained for 7 days giving the leader and his people plenty of time to repent. YHWH is so gracious that he always gives us time to turn to Him. During the time YHWH gives, man will either grow sorry for what he has done or he will allow his heart to harden. Pharaoh chose the latter. Notice too that Pharaoh turned to his magician's to see if they could duplicate the blood. Through the power of shadim / demons the enchanters were able to seemingly copy the miracle of YHWH. However, they were not able to make the blood leave and allow the Nile to return to normal. The occult and the world have many false promises and false manifestations that seem to mirror moves of YHWH. The evil powers may be able to duplicate some of YHWH's miracles BUT the dark side cannot stop YHWH's judgment. Life is not found in false fabrications but in the blood of the lamb of YHWH. Today, millions know the message of the gospel but turn to mediums, horoscopes, and witchcraft. Even Messianic believers have to battle the demonic powers behind the teachings of reincarnation and "practical" Gnostic kabbalah. The Messiah's message is pretty simple - life is in the blood!

When Y'shua celebrated Passover he lifted the cup and said "this is the blood of the brit / covenant, unless you drink my blood and taste my flesh you cannot enter the kingdom of YHWH." Again, He was proclaiming that life is in the blood. His blood was the fulfillment of the prophetic blood of the Nile and the lamb's blood on the doorposts. We read in the book of Mattitiyahu / Matthew that the disciple that betrayed Y'shua dipped his hand in the dish before the cup was offered. Even in the face of death, Y'shua offered eternal life to those at his table, including the one who would trade his life for silver. The blood covers all sin and all reproach, no matter what you have done, said, or thought. "And the dahm / blood of Y'shua ha Moshiach His Son cleanses us from all sin," Yochannan Alef / 1 John 1:7. Forgiveness is found in the blood.

In view of the life and death offering of Y'shua may we present Him our lives as a spiritual act of worship. Read Romans 12:1-2 to learn more about what our response should be to YHWH's mercy.

February 16

Throughout the Scriptures are many admonishments to remember -- "forget not" eight times, remember" 214 times. He's not telling us to recall our spouse's social security number or our anniversary, though. We are to "forget not all His benefits" and to "remember the Sabbath day". We are to live in constant awareness of the Almighty and all His ways, "forget not my Torah / instructions; but let thine heart keep my mitzvoth / commandments," Mishlei / Proverbs 3:1.

The Hebrew term for remember, is "zakar." Zakar is a verb that means "to mark (so as to be recognized), i.e. to remember; to mention; to burn incense, earnestly, be mindful, recount, record, make to be remembered, bring (re)call, come, keep, put (in) to remembrance." This phrase is used many times, all in connection with us turning our thoughts and deeds towards the Light.

Remembering the Almighty can-and-should become an important dynamic; an habitual behavior in the life of every Bible believer. This idea is repeated over and over again by the Biblical authors, to help us to develop the habit, as they instruct readers on how to live. Yet, we are not to just mentally meditate about heaven. We are told to actually do certain things, actions that will develop habits, to bring about remembrance. To grasp this concept, just realize that Zakar is a verb. Verbs in speech promote action. To Zakar is to turn our thoughts towards Heaven, which will bring about earthly actions. These actions will bring us out of this physical realm and guide us onto a spiritual plane.

For example, we are not to just mentally think about the Sabbath day, but deliberately do what will keep our mind focused on rest and on the Creator. This is part of the Ten Commandments. To remember and to keep the Sabbath is actually two-commandments-in-one. We are to first Zakar, or remember the Shabbat day. We do this by accomplishing the second part of the commandment, guarding or keeping it as set apart. "Remember Yom Ha-Shabbat, to shomer / keep or guard it as kadosh / set apart. Six days shall you labor, and do all your work: But the seventh day is the Shabbat of YHWH your Elohim: in it you shall not do any work," Shemot / Exodus 20:8.

Shabbat is a day to remember and worship. It's a day to guard and believe. Make the next Sabbath one to remember.

February 17

The word "church" originally comes from an Old English term "kirke." Long ago, the Anglo-Saxons used to refer to their pagan places of worship as a "kirke." When the Anglo-Saxons accepted Christianity, they simply continued to call their worship centers kirkes, which eventually evolved into "churches." The word "church" is in fact a pagan term that describes a worship system founded by man.

Early believers were never called "church goers" or even "Christians." The faith in Messiah was originally just a sect of Judaism. The first believers were called "Nazarenes" or "Followers of the Way." In Paul's trial before Felix, the lawyer for the prosecution said, "We have found this man to be a troublemaker, stirring up riots among the Jews all over the world. He is a ring leader of the Nazarene sect," Acts 24: 5.

So when did the church start? Catholics proclaim that the church began when the Savior commissioned Peter to become the first Pope. They believe the apostles were the original Catholics who lead the early believers to start the new religion of Christianity. They reasoned that since the Jews killed, God had now turned his attention to the rest of the world. "After the crucifixion, the apostles passed to the Early Church Fathers, the Faith. Later Emperors, like Constantine, and Monarchs accepted the Creed; their subjects followed. That's how it started," says one web site. It was Roman Emperor Constantine who mandated Catholic Christianity to be the universal religion. Before he did this though, he made huge changes in the faith. Constantine gave several edicts that would separate the church from the Bible faith. These decrees mandated ancient pagan practices, like Christmas, Communion, Easter, and Sun day worship, as "Christian."

In the preface to Edward Gibbon's History of Christianity, we read: "If Paganism was conquered by Christianity, it is equally true that Christianity was corrupted by Paganism. The pure Deism of the first Christians; was changed, by the Church of Rome, into the incomprehensible dogma of the trinity. Many of the pagan tenets, invented by the Egyptians and idealized by Plato, were retained as being worthy of belief."

What in your faith actually has a foundation in paganism and falsehood?

February 18

In the book of Isaiah, chapter 53, the Word says, "To whom has the arm of YHWH been revealed?" This quick quote is a reference to the Book of Esther and the story of Purim. The festival of Purim is about the power and protection of YHWH.

The arm of YHWH is a metaphor...it's a picture of salvation. It's a picture of Y'shua. Whenever the Scriptures talk of the "arm of YHWH" this is a direct reference to the Messiah. Who has the salvation of YHWH been revealed? Now we see the arm of YHWH. We can see in the story of Esther, the redemption of YHWH. To whom has it been revealed? It has been revealed to us if we will have eyes to see.

Now what's interesting here is that though the arm of YHWH has been revealed to us in the book of Esther, as we can see Him working and protecting the Hebrews and keeping them, we don't see the name of YHWH. In fact, the book of Esther is the only book in the entire Bible that does not contain the name of YHWH. It's never mentioned. Not even once. The Book of Esther hides His name, yet YHWH is there and His arm is present.

The truth is the arm of YHWH is there in Purim and the book of Esther. Because if it was not for Esther and the events of Purim then Y'shua could not have been born. Y'shua was born the tribe of Judah. The Jewish people and the tribe of Judah would have been annihilated and destroyed if Haman would have had his way, and Y'shua could not have come. So when we celebrate Purim, when we celebrate what's in the book of Esther, we're celebrating the arm of YHWH. And though YHWH's name is not present in the book, we can sense His might. We can experience His salvation.

YHWH has revealed His arm to us in the story of Esther and the holy day of Purim. Are you prepared to party this Purim?

February 19

The doctrine of the trinity just doesn't make any sense. Many different Trinitarian ideas exist, which generally present the Godhead as three persons. This doctrine says that the Father, Son, and Holy Ghost are separate but each equally "god." This is very confusing! Even the Encyclopedia Americana notes that the doctrine of the Trinity is considered to be "beyond the grasp of human reason." When questioned about this doctrine, most preachers respond that we should "just believe" and that we might not every really understand the trinity.

Not surprisingly, the word Trinity cannot be found in the Bible. And it wasn't formally a part of church doctrine until the 4th century, when the Catholic Church first began teaching god as being in three separate persons. The New Catholic Encyclopedia says, "the Trinity is not directly and immediately the word of God. The doctrine of the Holy Trinity is not taught in the Old Testament." The Savior himself said, "Eternal life is this: to know you, the only true Elohim, and Y'shua whom you have sent," John 17:30. It is pretty clear that Messiah didn't believe in the Trinity.

The truth is that the Bible doesn't teach the trinity. What the Bible teaches is Unity. The Father, Son, and Spirit are One. Devarim 6:4, "Hear O Israel YHWH our Elohim is the one, the only YHWH." Paul wrote that "Elohim is only one," in Galatians 3:20. "I am YHWH your Elohim; You shall have no gods except me," Exodus 20: 2, 3. The Father, Son, and Holy Spirit are not three separate persons with different personalities. The Father is not some upset parent ready to strike disobedient people with a lightning bolt. The Son did not come to save us from His angry Father. The Savior came, as an expression of the Father's love, to save us from our sins.

While the trinity is difficult to understand, unity makes sense. YHWH is one with His Son, His Word, and His Spirit.

What about this teaching upsets you? What from this reading can you share with others?

February 20

Sadly, much of what is called "spiritual warfare" in religion is actually vain actions that only empower the adversary. Instead of stopping him, most religious people actually give him glory and power that he does not deserve. We actually empower him when we focus on him. You empower the adversary when you learn demon's names, give him more credit than he is due, and spend more time rebuking him than praying to YHWH.

The adversary / ha satan does not have the power and authority to stop us from walking in the abundant life Y'shua promised. But he sure does try through his power of deception. He blinds people to the commandments in the scripture and from submission to their spiritual leaders. Yet, the Torah says that Y'shua gave his life's blood and redeemed us from the curse of sin so that we could have eternal life now and not just in the sweet bye and bye

The salvation power extended to us when we were born again is still available for us to walk out our faith TODAY. We are more than conquerors through YHWH. No weapon that is formed against us shall prosper. If YHWH is for us then who can be against us? Qolesayah / Colossians 2:6 clarifies this, "As you have therefore received Moshiach Y'shua the Master, so have your halakha / walk in Him." The New American Standard Bible says, "Therefore as you have received Y'shua Ha Moshiach the Master, so walk in Him."

We were born again by grace through faith – we were saved from our sins AND FROM the bondage of sin. This verse is telling us to walk out our salvation and to walk out our freedom. Just as we were saved by faith we should live by faith!

Y'shua died to set us free from the vices and influence of the evil one. "The thief comes not, but to steal, and to kill, and to destroy: I am come that they might have chayim / life, and that they might have it more abundantly," Yochannan / John 10:10

YHWH wants us free from demonic oppression and demonic attacks. Ha Satan wants to put you in bondage, deception, oppression, depression, worry, fear, doubt, lust, wickedness, negativity, unforgiveness, pain, pity parties, hurt feelings, loneliness, grudges, and the like. "Stand fast therefore in the liberty in which Moshiach has made us free, and be not harnessed again under the yoke of slavery," Galutyah / Galatians 5:1.

February 21

The great commission from Mark 16: 15-20 says, "And He said to them, Go into all the olam hazeh / world, and proclaim the Besorah / Good News to every creature. He that believes and is immersed shall be saved; but he that believes not shall be condemned. And these signs shall follow them that believe; In My Name shall they cast out shadim / demons; they shall speak with new tongues; They shall take up serpents; and if they drink any deadly thing, it shall not hurt them; they shall lay hands on the sick, and they shall recover. So then after Y'shua had spoken to them; He was received up into the third shamayim / heavens, and sat down on the right hand of YHWH. And they went out, and proclaimed everywhere, YHWH working with them, and confirming the word with signs following. "

Y'shua's final command included the proclamation to go and proclaim the good news of YHWH; repent and receive the forgiveness promised in the Scriptures; and be immersed in water for salvation from destruction. And then as a person accepts Y'shua they should continue on with their faith. The true gospel is NOT just about salvation but walking in freedom and deliverance.

"And these signs shall follow them that believe; In My Name shall they cast out shadim / demons; they shall speak with new tongues. They shall take up serpents; and if they drink any deadly thing, it shall not hurt them; they shall lay hands on the sick, and they shall recover." The order in this text is important and not listed haphazardly. First there is the proclamation and reception of the gospel / besarot. Then with water baptism, the body comes under subjection to the Word. Sadly, this is where most people stop. The next part of salvation includes casting out demons for deliverance and spiritual freedom. Speaking with "new tongues" is symbolic of the baptism in the Ruach Ha Kadosh. Taking up serpents, drinking deadly poison, and laying hands on the sick is a description of our daily walk with Y'shua after salvation and baptism.

Our call as believers is to cast out demons and walk in freedom of Y'shua. Deliverance ministry is simply coming face to face – confronting patter of thoughts, attitudes, behaviors, sin and proclaiming the emet / truth of the Torah. "Submit yourselves, then, to YHWH. Resist the devil, and he will flee from you. Come near to YHWH and he will come near to you," James 4:7-8.

Deliverance ministry is to be a part of our effort to spread the good news of Y'shua and to disciple others. The gospel sets people free from the power of sin yet salvation is more than just stating a prayer and hoping for heaven. The darkness is cast out with salvation and is replaced with Light with deliverance. Let Y'shua set you free today.

February 22

Y'shua the Messiah is the Torah or Law alive. "And the Word was made flesh," John 1:4. Y'shua actually walked fully in the Torah commands and never broke the law or sinned. Or to put it plainly Y'shua kept the Torah in its entirety. And therefore to follow Y'shua we must follow the Old Testament Law. A life patterned after Y'shua, or after the Torah, will be a life absent of sin! For Y'shua never broke the law. Remember it says in 1 John 3:4 that "sin is lawlessness." Therefore, if Y'shua kept the law or obeyed the law He never sinned.

If you believe the scriptures then you must agree that sin is "lawlessness" and that to be sinless one must obey the Law. Well that's exactly what Y'shua did and commands also to do.

1 John 3:5, "But you know that he appeared so that he might take away our sins. And in him is no sin." If no sin was in Y'shua then no lawlessness was in Him. And yes, Y'shua would often defend the Torah saying, "You have heard it said..." and then would say "but I tell you..." These words were directed not towards the Torah but towards religious leaders who taught anti-torah wisdom. These piercing words of Y'shua found in Matthew 5 and other places were spoken to those who had perverted the Torah / law: the Pharisees, Sadducees, and Scribes. Matthew 5:27 & 28, "You have heard that it was said, 'Do not commit adultery.' But I tell you that anyone who looks at a woman lustfully has already committed adultery with her in his heart." Here Y'shua again brings the attention to the heart motive, from which words and actions flow. Romans 7 specifically state that the Torah is "holy, righteous and good." Part of Y'shua's ministry was to call people back to a right interpretation and understanding of the Torah, and he would never teach against it.

Ask yourself, if the Savior is the living word would he teach others not to follow the Torah?

TRUTH FOR TODAY

February 23

John 10:10, now that's a verse that clearly shows the hope of our faith. Here, Y'shua said, "the thief comes to steal, kill, and destroy but I have come that you might have life and life in abundance." When you read this passage in the context of chapter 10 we can see that the abundant life Y'shua promised is ONLY when we hear His voice and trust our Shepherd. Go ahead. Read John 10. We are the sheep. He is the shepherd. And our Shepherd wants to lead us beside still waters and calm our souls. Our Good Shepherd says that goodness and mercy follow us all the days of our life – even if our days are during the time of tribulation. As we trust the Shepherd our head will be anointed with oil and our cup with overflow.

Sheep don't fret about conspiracy theories. Sheep don't worry about what some rogue Planet X may do. Sheep trust their shepherd and obey his voice. The Shepherd is still speaking to His sheep and if you are born again then you should be hearing his voice daily.

YHWH speaks primarily through His word. He also speaks through events, other people, our spirit, His voice, and even "checks" in our spirit. We can hear his voice today. We must hear his voice. John 4 says that "YHWH is Spirit and those that worship Him must worship in Spirit and in truth." This passage expresses how YHWH communicates with us. He is Spirit and therefore will communicate with us through our spirit. As we read the Bible, YHWH's Spirit will make certain passages jump off the page. As we go through our day, YHWH's Spirit will lead us to make certain decisions through the presence or absence of peace. As we pray, YHWH's Spirit will bring things to our remembrance and comfort our hearts. Walking "in the Spirit" means to "walk in step with the Spirit" and living in constant awareness of YHWH's abiding presence.

Decide right now to live in step with YHWH's Spirit today.

Truth For Today

February 24

"These are the words YHWH spoke concerning Israel and Judah: "This is what YHWH says: "'Cries of fear are heard— terror, not peace. Ask and see: Can a man bear children? Then why do I see every strong man with his hands on his stomach like a woman in labor, every face turned deathly pale? How awful that day will be No other will be like it. It will be a time of trouble for Jacob, but he will be saved out of it," Jeremiah 30:4-7.

There is much said about "Jacob's Trouble" today yet most people have never studied it in relation to the Jacob of the book of Genesis. What was the "real" Jacob's trouble?

Jacob had trouble discerning the Spirit of YHWH. Beresheet / Genesis tells of a time when Jacob slept on a stone and saw a vision of angels. He woke up and said "Surely YHWH is here and I didn't know it." Jacob's trouble was that though he was familiar with YHWH he didn't walk in YHWH's presence and perceive His power. Later in Genesis we read that he did learn from this trouble.

Jacob indeed learned the importance of walking with YHWH and we need to do the same. In Genesis 28 Jacob perceived the presence of YHWH and wrestled for a blessing. This time he wasn't going to encounter YHWH's presence and leave the same way. This is the heritage of our ancestor Ya'acov. We can walk in YHWH's presence, blessing, and power. If we are focused on walking with YHWH; if we are addicted to hearing His voice over the little things in our lives; if our average day is friendship with Y'shua then the end times will take care of themselves. YHWH will lead us on how and when to prepare for the end times we are walking after Him.

Start talking to Him about the small things. Ask YHWH about the tiniest details of your life and trust Him when you feel a leaning in one direction or another. Ask the Holy Spirit / Ruach HaKodesh to speak to you daily. Make sure your heart is humble and that you are willing to obey, regardless of how you are lead. Get quiet and then listen to the gentle whisper of the Ruach. Maybe even keep a journal of your life and the things YHWH shows you. As you are faithful in the small things it will be easier to discern His voice in the major decisions in life.

Jacob didn't practice the presence of YHWH and that was his trouble. Today, we can learn from him and be ever mindful of the actual attendance of YHWH inside of us. Y'shua will never leave us nor forsake us because he is the Good Shepherd. Jeremiah 30:7 is true, we will be safe as we learn to hear His voice and discern the very presence of YHWH.

February 25

Too many times we belittle the work of Y'shua by focusing on the many other issues of our faith. We spend hours discussing end times ideas, conspiracy theories, and even the commandments without recognizing the effect of the Messiah on these issues. As Messianic believers we glean much as we review the Torah portion each week to learn of Moshe, the Torah, and the Prophets. Sadly though, we seem to show disregard to how Y'shua affected our observance of the Torah. Because of Y'shua's life and the indwelling Holy Spirit we each have a greater advantage than those in the times of Tanakh / Older Testament. Let's make this clear. Each and every born again person today has more power, anointing, and ability than all of the Old Testament prophets put together because we have Y'shua in us!

Before Y'shua the Temple was the place of worship and the Ruach Ha Kodesh would come for a visitation when the people walked in covenant with YHWH. Today, we ARE the temple of YHWH and His Spirit has come for habitation!

"Whereby are given unto us exceeding great and precious promises: that by these ye might be partakers of the Divine Nature, having escaped the corruption that is in the world through lust," 2Peter 1:4.

At creation we received the very breath of life from YHWH. "Then YHWH formed the man from the dust of the ground and breathed into his nostrils the breath of life, and the man became a living being," Genesis 2:7.

YHWH Elohim breathed His life into us. In the Hebrew the word for "being" in this passage is the phrase "ruach." This is an important term to consider for in the ancient tongue the word "ruach" literally means "breath" or "spirit." YHWH breathed upon man and imparted his "breath" or "spirit" to us. From Adam until today each person in the entire world has this "breath" or "spark" of YHWH in them. This is the part of man that is eternal. Understand that this doesn't mean that we are little "gods." Instead, what we can learn from this the potential life of YHWH is in your family, your friends, and even your enemies.

This shows us why it is so important to love our neighbor. When we are showing compassion and kindness to other people we are actually showing compassion and kindness to YHWH. We show our love to YHWH by showing love to people. What did you learn from this reading that you can apply to your life?

February 26

Sin has caused mankind to "loose" or "fall short" of the glory. The fall of Adam affected the spiritual DNA of mankind as we who were meant to be eternal can now experience death. The original temptation was to question the Almighty's warning of death. "Ye shall not surely die?" questioned the serpent. But die they did. As sin and the curses of sin entered humanity Adam and his sons would no longer have eternal life. Their spirit would be inclined towards evil. Noah's generation experienced this so much that they had to be washed away from the face of the earth.

Adam's sin created a rift of death in the spirit of man. No longer would mankind enter the world as perfect. Instead, we are each born with an inclination to sin because our spirit is first dead to YHWH and alive to sin. Our heart is "evil" and inclined to sin. Judaism calls this desire to receive for self alone the "yetzer hara" or the "evil inclination." Judaism though only provides the Torah as a remedy for the evil sinful nature. Torah does many things but it can't transform a person's spirit. Changing behavior through obeying the Torah does NOT change the spiritual DNA makeup of a person. Even the Pharisee Nicodemus was told that he "must be born again." Nick's obedience to the Torah couldn't bring him eternal life because it didn't change his spirit. Nicodemus, like all other Old Testament saints, didn't have the Holy Spirit inside of them and therefore did not experience the regeneration of YHWH. Colossians 1:13 says that at salvation a person is "translated from the kingdom of darkness into the kingdom of light."

According to Romans 10:9 and 10, a person is delivered from darkness (or "saved") when they "believe in their heart that Y'shua is their Master and confesses with their mouth that YHWH raised Him from the dead." A person who earnestly repents of their sins and turns from their wicked ways by calling upon the name of YHWH Y'shua is instantly born again in their spirit (and not their mind or body).

What happens in the spiritual realm is that the evil inclination or sinful nature instantly and completely is crucified and resurrected with Y'shua. The "yetzer hara" is replaced with a "yetzer tov" or "good spirit" that is joined completely with YHWH's Holy Spirit. And at this moment all of the Ruach Ha Kodesh comes into man. Salvation is when the glory of creation is restored because your spirit is joined to YHWH's Spirit. We are now sons and daughters of YHWH, joint heirs with Y'shua, and the temple of the Holy Spirit.

February 27

There are many covenants in the Bible. The rainbow is a sign of the covenant with Noah. The Torah is a sign of the covenant with Moses and mankind. Abraham was given the covenant of circumcision or "brit milah" in Hebrew. This was a physical action that symbolized the change that took place inside of Abraham. Brit milah is a cutting of the flesh and is symbolic of how we are to cut off the flesh and its desires if we are to truly follow YHWH. Abraham believed the word of YHWH and it was accounted to him as righteousness. That was the covenant that was made with Him. As Abe believed he would be blessed with physical descendants and so much more. Abe was circumcises as well as the men in his household. Brit Milah is a picture of salvation. The Savior doesn't just come to live in our heart when we are saved. Instead, our hearts are circumcised as we believe YHWH and we are accredited righteousness.

We need to realize that Y'shua just didn't do something FOR us with his death and resurrection; Y'shua did something IN us. There is a difference. By His covenant Y'shua changed so much. Romans 2:28-29 explains, "A person is not a Jew who is one only outwardly, nor is circumcision merely outward and physical. No, a person is a Jew who is one inwardly; and circumcision is circumcision of the heart, by the Spirit, not by the written code. Such a person's praise is not from other people, but from YHWH." Here we see that a true "Jew" or descendant of Abraham is one that has been changed and circumcised in the heart. When we are born again our innermost being is radically transformed. Colossians 2:11, "In him you were also circumcised with a circumcision not performed by human hands. Your whole self-ruled by the flesh was put off when you were circumcised by Messiah."

Y'shua did this for us and in us. We get much more than forgiveness and redemption with salvation. The true faith transcends laws and commands because the Biblical faith first establishes the fact of a covenant change on the inside. Like the Tin Man in "The Wizard of Oz" we have had a full and complete heart transplant. Our old heart has been cut away, or circumcised, and replaced with THE heart of YHWH. Much of Evangelical Christianity mistakenly teaches salvation is asking "Jesus to come into your heart." That's not true. Salvation is not asking him into our sinful heart BUT asking him to replace our sinful fleshly heart of stone with His heart of love. Instead of praying for Jesus to "come into our hearts" we should be asking the Messiah to "circumcise and replace our hearts." By his life, death, and resurrection His very presence can come into us and change us. Has your heart been circumcised?

February 28

We are now the Temple of the Holy Spirit and our heart is the holy of holies. Our heart is the Ark of the Covenant. YHWH is not out "there" somewhere. YHWH is in us and wanting to be released through us. Ephesians 3:17, "so that Messiah may dwell in your hearts through faith. And I pray that you, being rooted and established in love."

Now, please understand that YHWH's Holy Spirit is indeed just that – holy. YHWH can not dwell where there is sin or evil. Psalm 5:4, "You are not an Elohim who takes pleasure in evil; with you the wicked cannot dwell."

So, for YHWH to dwell within us then something drastic must take place. What happens is that each and every believer has had a heart transplant. This isn't an upgrade or a change in behavior. YHWH doesn't just want us to obey a set of rules or make a mental decision to follow some creed. Now, YHWH wants to give us a new heart; YHWH wants to give us His heart.

Jeremiah 24:6-7, "My eyes will watch over them for their good, and I will bring them back to this land. I will build them up and not tear them down; I will plant them and not uproot them. I will give them a heart to know me, that I am YHWH. They will be my people, and I will be their Elohim, for they will return to me with all their heart."

Ezekiel 36: 24-29, "'for I will take you out of the nations; I will gather you from all the countries and bring you back into your own land. I will sprinkle clean water on you, and you will be clean; I will cleanse you from all your impurities and from all your idols. I will give you a new heart and put a new spirit in you; I will remove from you your heart of stone and give you a heart of flesh. And I will put my Spirit in you and move you to follow my decrees and be careful to keep my laws. Then you will live in the land I gave your ancestors; you will be my people, and I will be your Elohim. I will save you from all your uncleanness. I will call for the grain and make it plentiful and will not bring famine upon you."

The heart is made new at salvation. We are no longer "sinners saved by grace." We are now a new creation that has been given "a new heart," Ezekiel 36:26. We have been changed on the inside. If we truly believe this then we have to have our mind renewed about many issues and pet theologies that we have learned over the years. The revelation of the mystery of Colossians 1:27 does indeed change a lot. Teachers in the Messianic movement like to say that "if it's in the Bible then it's for us today." We believe that since we are the commonwealth of Israel then all that happened to Israel was written for our application and our identification. While all of this is true to some extent, we seldom recognize and often fail to realize exactly what Y'shua did when He died and rose from the dead.

March

TRUTH FOR TODAY

March 1

The month of March is the time of the holiday of Purim. "On the thirteenth day of the month Adar; and on the fourteenth day of the same month they rested, and made it a day of feasting and joy / simcha. As the days in which the Hebrews rested from their enemies, and the month which was turned from sorrow to joy, and from mourning into a Yom-Tov / feast day: that they should make them days of feasting and simcha, and of sending portions one to another, and gifts to the poor," Esther 9:17, 22.

For obvious reasons, Purim is called "the feast of happiness." It is a time of gift giving, costume parties, and celebrating the victory YHWH gives against oppression. When the story of Esther is read on Purim, it is customary to interrupt the reading with celebration. When Haman's name is read in the story, the congregation erupts in a deafening chorus of noise-makers, clanging pots, cap-guns, clapping, booing, and sirens. The congregation also applauds and celebrates when the hero, Mordechai is mentioned.

One strange, yet, traditional way to celebrate Purim is to drink wine. The Talmud says that "on Purim a person is obligated to become intoxicated to the point where he can no longer tell the difference between 'cursed be Haman' and 'blessed be Mordechai." Yes, on this one date, Judaism encourages drunkenness. Or does it?

A careful reading of the Talmudic quote will reveal that the mitzvah is not to drink wine. The commandment is to become intoxicated. Don't be mistaken. A person can be drunk without taking a drink! The joy of Purim is not found in drinking alcohol, but in elevating the Spirit! "Do not be drunk with wine, but be filled with the Ruach HaKodesh," Ephesians 5:18.

During the first Purim celebration, the scroll says the Hebrews had "simchat" or "joy." It never says they drunk Manashevitz kosher wine. No wine was needed. They were simply intoxicated with YHWH's joy!! This is the real meaning of simchat. "And Mordechai went out from the presence of the melech / king in royal apparel of blue and white, and with a great keter /crown of gold, and with a garment of fine linen and purple: and the city of Shushan rejoiced and was in simchat. The Hebrews had light, and gilah / rejoicing, and simcha, and kavod / glory," Esther 8:15, 16.

To have the joy of YHWH is to blur the lines of reality as a drunkard. True simchat is viewing the evil actions of Haman as equal to the righteous actions of Mordechai. Simchat / joy sees through the "good" and the "bad" events in life to agree that YHWH is in control. "What shall we then say to these things? If YHWH be for us, who can be against us?" Romans 8:31.

TRUTH FOR TODAY

March 2

In a sober state, we view the events in the book of Ester like Mordechai's righteousness as more beneficial than Haman's wicked plans. A drunken person though, cannot tell the difference between Mordechai and a monkey. As believers filled with the Ruach, we, too, should have our vision blurred. The events of life should not lead us to worry. Instead, we should agree that what may begin as evil will turn out for the good. Sober-minded people only see facts, doctor's charts, and negative bank balances. Those drunk with joy know that all things work together for the good of him that loves YHWH. This isn't a blissful existence, but an awareness that YHWH is in control. "And we know that all things work together for good to them that love God, to them who are the called according to his purpose," Romans 8:23.

Remember too, that Purim occurs during the month of Adar, the 12th month in the Biblical calendar. The Sages have said that "our joy increases in Adar." In Hebrew, "adar" means "power, force, or strength". This proves once again the joy of YHWH is our adar strength! Just as YHWH rescued Israel from impending danger, He protects and keeps Israel today.

Simchat / joy is a gift from YHWH that is to be manifested. It's like a seed planted inside the soul that must be watered and cared for until it grows. We are told to serve YHWH with simcha in Tehillim / Psalm 100. The dangers of not doing so are treacherous. The 27th and 28th chapters of Devarim / Deuteronomy describe the Torah and the blessings and curses presented to the nation of Israel. The curses for Torah disobedience were centered on the fact that the nation did not serve YHWH in joy. "Because you did not serve YHWH your Elohim with simcha, and with gladness of lev / heart, for the abundance of all things; Therefore shall you serve your enemies that YHWH shall send against you, in hunger, and in thirst, and in nakedness, and in want of all things: and He shall put a yoke of iron upon your neck, until He has destroyed you," Devarim 28:47. Clearly, joy is no laughing matter. It's a subject that needs to be taken seriously. It's a fruit that should be enjoyed like a fresh apple plucked from a tree. But, watch out for worms!

The worms of the adversary will try to corrupt the fruit of joy. Everyone knows that one bad apple spoils the bunch. Let us guard against the enemy stealing our joy. How can you view the good and the bad that happens to you today as a way for your joy to increase?

TRUTH FOR TODAY

March 3

Y'shua said, "The thief comes to steal, and to kill, and to destroy: I am come that they might have chayim / life, and that they might have it more abundantly," Yochannan / John 10:10. This verse describes the three main ways the adversary tries to steal our simcha.

First, he wants to STEAL our joy. He does this by tricking us to live life in the past. We cannot experience life in abundance, if we walk around with regret. Too many believers are defeated because of yesterday's sins. The concerns, pains, and hurts of the past will stop simcha from flourishing.

The enemy also wants to KILL our future. He does this by whispering to us about what might happen. Fear grips the weary heart and paralyzes the saint not walking in the fruit of joy. The enemy knows he can defeat us, if we are uptight and worrisome. However, YHWH says, "I know the plans I have for you, plans to prosper you and not harm you," Jeremiah 29:11

The enemy knows that if he can keep us uptight and fearful of tomorrow or living in the regret of yesterday, then he can DESTROY our present. If we are gripped by fear or pain, we cannot experience the abundant life of Y'shua. However, the enemy shouldn't defeat us because Moshiach defeated him! "For this purpose the Son of YHWH was manifested, that He might destroy the works of the adversary," 1 John / Yochannan Alef 3:8.

Y'shua came that we might have chayim – life and life to its fullest. The connection is clear. Life comes through walking in the simcha of YHWH. On Purim we are told that each person should become intoxicated until the reality of good and bad is distorted. The traditional toast to any Hebrew cup of wine is "l'chaim" – to life! This shows that one can experience the simcha of YHWH when one is filled with the life of YHWH. L'chaim! Let us be filled with the Ruach to life and to life abundant! Trust YHWH no matter what happens. He came through for Mordechai and the Hebrews and He will come through for us!

March 4

Do you know how simple our faith can be? Here's the bedrock of our belief system in a nutshell: The first five books of the Bible are called the Torah. These are the books of Genesis, Exodus, Leviticus, Numbers, and Deuteronomy. The Torah is the story of creation and YHWH's plan for man as revealed through the nation of Israel. In the Torah is the story of how Israel came out of the slavery of Egypt and was called to be the light to the world.

We read and study a little bit of the Torah each week. This reading is called a "portion" or "parasha." Each parasha of the Torah helps us know YHWH better.

The Torah is followed in the Bible by the books of the Prophets. The prophets were people who called people to keep the Torah and worship YHWH. In Hebrew the word for "prophets" is "Nevi'im." The books of the Prophets are called the Nevi'im.

The Prophets are followed by writings or "Ketuvin." The Ketuvin are the writings like the book of Proverbs and Psalms. These parts of the Bible reveal wisdom through the Torah.

Together the Torah (T) and the Nevi'im (N) and the Ketuvin (K) make the TNK or the TaNaKh. The Tanakh is one way to say "Old Testament." The Tanakh was originally written in Hebrew. It is important that we learn to read and speak the Hebrew language so we can better understand the culture, people, and writings of the Bible.

After the Prophets comes the "Brit Chadasha." This part of the Bible is often called the "New Testament." In the Brit Chadasha we learn about Messiah Y'shua's life, ministry, death, and resurrection. We also learn about the first believers in Y'shua and the book of Revelation.

The Tanakh and the Brit Chadasha combine to make the Bible. There are 66 books or separate writings in the Bible. Each of these books tells the story of how we are to live in this world and how we are to worship YHWH.

We can trust the Bible because it is YHWH's word. Every promise in the Bible is true and every prophecy is right. Our life is found in the Word of YHWH.

March 5

Here's the Gospel in a nutshell:

If you have a dirty face you don't know this until you look into a mirror. In the same way, we don't realize what a bad state we are in until we look into the "mirror" of the Ten Commandments. When we disobey the commandments in the Bible we "sin." To "sin" means to not follow the Torah and the Ten Commandments. Have you ever sinned?

"Have you ever told a lie? What does that make you? Have you ever stolen something, even something small? What does that make you? The standard of Torah acts as a mirror for people to compare themselves to. The bible says that having hatred in your heart is equal to committing murder. "Whoever is angry with his Neighbor without a cause shall be in danger of the judgment," Matthew 5:22. And the Bible says, "No thief will inherit the kingdom of Heaven," 1 Corinthians 6:10. Revelation 21:8 states, "All liars will have their place in the lake of fire." The Bible declares that if we have broken one commandment then we are guilty of breaking them all. One sin makes us sinful and separated from the Almighty. "Cursed is everyone who does not continue in all the things written in the Torah to do them," Galatians 3:10.

Have you ever done these things? Have you ever told one lie? Or stolen anything in your life, even something small? If so then you are a liar and a thief and you are in danger of judgment.

By your own admission you are a lying, stealing, adulterer at heart and will face the Almighty on judgment day. As you face judgment day, will you be guilty or innocent? Are you going to Heaven when you die? Or will you perish? Are you concerned about this?

The Bible says that the wages of sin is death but the gift of YHWH is eternal life. Can you see the Ten Commandments are like the mirror -- they show us how bad we are, and how we need to be clean before the Day of Judgment? That is the Day of YHWH will punish people who have broken the Ten Commandments. YHWH doesn't want you to be punished.

He loves you so much that He made a way for you to be clean before Judgment Day.

By repenting of your sins and calling upon the name of YHWH Y'shua, you can receive the gift of eternal life and be born again. "YHWH showed His great love for us in this manner – while we were still sinners Y'shua died for us," Romans 5:8. So, what should you do? Ask YHWH to forgive you for the Commandments you've broken (called "sin"), and then give your life to Y'shua. The Bible calls this being "born again." When you are "born again" it is like you die to your sins and you begin to live for YHWH Y'shua by following the Torah and listening to His Spirit.

TRUTH FOR TODAY

March 6

We all like to celebrate good times, don't we? Well, YHWH has given us many reasons and many special days to celebrate. Throughout the Bible YHWH set apart certain days that is unique and important to Him. Because they are important to YHWH they should be important to us too!

These are holy days, not holidays, because of the lessons that we learn. You can turn to Leviticus 23 and learn about the party calendar of YHWH. First, we read about the weekly day of rest, called the Sabbath or Shabbat. The Shabbat is the seventh day and it during this day to we come for worship, we rest, and we spend time with our family. Shabbat is a wonderful time to learn of YHWH and fellowship with other people.

YHWH loves us so much that we get one Shabbat a week! And, He has given us seven MORE Shabbats during the year. These "Shabbats" are called "feasts" or "festivals" or in Hebrew they are called "moadim." The moadim are seven times that we are to stop what we are doing in our lives, learn of YHWH, and seek Him. The moadim are separated into two sets. There are the Spring moadim and the Fall moadim. Are you familiar with Passover? What about Sukkot? Do you remember the "Feast of Trumpet?" How about Yom Kippur? These are all the moadim of YHWH. We often call them "feasts" because we usually feast or eat when we celebrate.

The Spring moadim start with Passover and the Feast of Unleavened Bread. We then have First Fruits and after a few weeks comes the day of Pentecost or Shavuot. In the fall there is the Feast of Trumpets, Yom Kippur, and finally Sukkot or the "Festival of Tabernacles."

We call these the Spring moadim because they occur in the Spring. The Bible shows us that these events take place around the Hebrew month of Aviv, which is around this time of the year. Every year at this time we are to recall the power of YHWH to rescue Israel from the slavery of Egypt and the wicker ruler Pharaoh. We also remember that it was during this time that our Messiah Y'shua gave His life to be the Passover Lamb. Are you planning on keeping the Spring feasts this year?

TRUTH FOR TODAY

March 7

Romans 3 say that we "all have sinned and fallen short of the glory of Elohim." Sin is a "self-centered" act. It is a state of rebellion against YYHWH. It is the exact opposite of love. The scriptures state in Romans "where sin increased, grace increased all the more, so that, just as sin reigned in death, so also grace might reign through righteousness to bring eternal life through Y'shua our Messiah." Through these verses a person can understand the effects of sin. Sin has affected everyone that has lived since the beginning of time. Sin separates man from the Heavenly Father. Sin makes mankind in need of forgiveness. Without forgiveness there is no eternal life, no grace, and no righteousness. This is all because of sin. To remedy sin is one of the reasons why the Messiah came.

Y'shua actually walked fully in the Torah commands and never broke the law or sinned. Or to put it plainly Y'shua kept the Torah in its entirety. And therefore to follow Y'shua man must follow the Old Testament Law. A life patterned after Y'shua, or after the Torah, will be a life absent of sin! For Y'shua never broke the law. The Bible says in 1 John 3:4 that "sin is lawlessness." Therefore, if Y'shua kept the law or obeyed the law He never sinned.

Sin or torah-less-ness separates man from YHWH. Sin also hardens a person's heart to the things of YHWH. When a person sins, that person is putting a layer between their heart and YHWH. The more a person sins, the greater the layers become. Unless dealt with through the blood of Y'shua, sin will bring condemnation and death. The Old Testament has a rich vocabulary for sin. The Hebrew word Chata means, "to miss the mark." The word could be used to describe a person shooting a bow and arrow and missing the target with the arrow. When it is used to describe sin, it means that the person has missed the mark that Elohim has established for the person's life. The Hebrew word Aven describes the crooked or perverse spirit associated with sin. Sinful persons have perverted their spirits and become crooked rather than straight. It also has the connotation of the breaking out of evil.

What sin is holding you back from YHWH's best? You can overcome because Y'shua dealt with sin once and for all.

TRUTH FOR TODAY

March 8

"He is the Rock, his work is perfect: for all his ways are right: a Elohim of truth and without iniquity, just and right is he," Devarim / Deuteronomy 32:4. Before everything else, the Creator YHWH was. The universe, and all it holds, came forth from Elohim.

Creation and the Creator are "Echad," are one. "For by him were all things created, that are in heaven, and that are in earth, visible and invisible, whether they be thrones, or dominions, or principalities, or powers: all things were created by him, and for him. And he is before all things, and by him all things consist," Colossians 1:16-17. Everything that is in creation was made for His good will and pleasure, to accomplish His will.

Everything that is in creation is loved, wanted and sustained by the Creator, or else it would not, and could not exist. "We, who are a conscious part of that creation, are inspired by the Creator's love, which creates and sustains us. Love is the ultimate source of energy of all creation," wrote one unknown source. This energy of love restores Creation to its intended purposes and wipes out the effects of sin and evil. The curses of the fall are broken by the love of the Creator.

In the Messianic writings, when Y'shua said that he was one with the Creator, He was also saying that He was one with creation. Because of the power of oneness or "echad" He could perform what, to others, seemed to be miracles. Y'shua wasn't really doing "miracles" or "impossibilities," He was just reconciling the creator to the Creation.

When Y'shua was healing the sick and raising the dead, He was just establishing the Malchut – His Kingdom. He was bringing heaven to earth and rectifying the world. Y'shua was restoring life, to the way it was meant to be, and to the way it currently is in the spirit realm. He revealed the enlightening truth that, as we acknowledge Elohim and understand our oneness with him, then, we can also unite creation. "Believe me when I say that I am in the Father and the Father is in me; or at least believe on the evidence of the miracles themselves. I tell you the truth / emet; anyone who has faith in me will do what I have been doing. He will do even greater things than these, because I am going to the Father," Yochannan / John 14:11-12. This does not mean that we become 'little gods.'

What this message does mean is that through the Moshiach, the Living Torah, we are actually one with the Creator. We who follow Moshiach are an active part in the restoration of creation, back to the creator. We are part of the "restoration of all things," Acts 3:21. We have to trust and obey the Creator, the psalmist prayed, "Into thine hand I commit my spirit: thou hast redeemed me, O YHWH Elohim Emet," Tehillim / Psalms 31:5.

What does this mean to you today? How can you be echad / one with YHWH?

TRUTH FOR TODAY

March 9

Think of one area in your life where you have a need – finances, family, or your future? Have you considered that doubt could be stopping you from receiving YHWH's best in that area? The truth today is that doubt will kill your faith. Doubt will stop your prayers from being answered and doubt will hinder you from walking in the abundant life.

Doubt is worry, fear, anxiety, stress, or thinking twice about the Bible. Mark 11:23 says, "Have faith in YHWH. For assuredly, I say to you, whoever...does not doubt in his heart, but believes that those things he says will be done, he will have whatever he says." Notice the phrase "have faith in YHWH" precedes the other, "have faith in the promise of an answer to prayer."

You might doubt that you have doubt, but doubt is a spiritual disease that everyone fights. It is highly contagious and it will render you unclean and sick. Take a hospital for example. Hospitals are full of doubts. Just walk through the halls of a hospital and you can feel the doubt in the air and you can hear the bad news as it's whispered from the doctors to the patients and their families. Remember that Y'shua cast out the doubters. Before He raised Jarius' child from the dead in Mark 5 he kicked the doubters into exile and surrounded himself with those who had faith. This is a Torah concept. Those who do not put their trust in YHWH will not receive from YHWH. You must get the doubt out. Your level of revelation and blessing from YHWH is equal to the faith you have in YHWH. Matthew 7:7 says to "ask you shall receive."

Today, think about this statement: "your level of blessing from YHWH is equal to the faith you have in YHWH."

TRUTH FOR TODAY

March 10

John was no ordinary Southern Baptist. No, he was an amazing man whom the Bible calls "great." John was a bony fingered prophet that came before Y'shua began his ministry. He was mightily used of YHWH and even filled with the Holy Spirit at birth. (John is the only person that the Bible says was filled with the Spirit at birth!) He had amazing faith that led him to lead a renowned ministry. He put his entire life on the line that Y'shua was the Messiah. He knew this so much that He dedicated his life to calling people to repent for the kingdom of heaven was at hand. He was a true fanatic, who lived off of locusts and honey and even wore camel skin in the dessert. Matthew 11 states he was greater than Moses and even more important than Paul.

John was an amazing person but he suffered for His faith. He was thrown in prison and probably harshly treated and beaten. The negative circumstances over a long period of time beat the faith out of John and even he began to doubt. Proverbs states that "hope deferred makes the heart sick."

Do you have hope for something that hasn't happened yet? Do you feel frustrated over the issue? Are you sick about waiting for the manifestation of healing, or a house, or a child, or salvation of a loved one, or a job, or a blessing, or whatever? John knows how you feel. You know how John felt. This man was at one time absolutely certain that Y'shua was the Messiah but in Luke 7:4 we see that he had some doubts.

John sends his disciples to just make sure Y'shua was the Messiah. His time in jail had caused him to doubt and weaken in faith. Now, remember that this is the same John that had baptized the Messiah and saw the Holy Spirit descend like a dove upon Y'shua. The Bible states that John even heard an audible voice from Heaven that Y'shua was set apart. And after all of this John still doubted? Why did he doubt? How could he doubt? The negativity of jail had most likely caused Him to wonder. Hope deferred makes the heart sick. What is your heart sick of right now? What do you hope for and pray for and want? The way to deal with doubt is to get into the Word.

If you are battling doubt today then you need fight fire with fire. Let's the Word of YHWH burn into your soul and cleanse you. Spend a few extra minutes reading and praying the Scriptures. Faith comes by hearing the Word of YHWH and your faith can overcome the doubt.

Truth For Today

March 11

Hearing the word of YHWH is the best way to get doubt out. We need to be in love with the word. To get the doubt out you must get the word IN. If you have doubts about the resurrection then you should read where Y'shua rose from the dead and when he said "I am the resurrection and the life." If you have doubt about YHWH's provision then you should read in the Psalms where it says that YHWH delights in the prosperity of His servants. If you have doubts of YHWH's love then you should read Romans 5 where it says that he has shed his love abroad in our hearts and that out of His great love He sent Y'shua. You must get the word in to get the doubt out.

How much time do you need in the word? Doubt leaves with quantity Scripture time. How much time are you in the Scriptures – not on websites or learning of conspiracies but in the Torah of YHWH?

Getting into the Word is more than just random reading or even skimming through the Torah portion. To have spiritual power to defeat the demon of doubt we must think on the word, meditate on the word, and get the word in us!

The following verse can change your life...Joshua 1:8, " Do not let this Book of the Law depart from your mouth; meditate on it day and night, so that you may be careful to do everything written in it. Then you will be prosperous and successful."

Here we see that success comes from chewing on the Word. We are to study it but this passage speaks more about taking a verse or idea and grabbing it and making it your OWN through considering it all day.

Grab onto the word, meditate on it and then confess it.

TRUTH FOR TODAY

March 12

The holy day of Passover is a Biblical worship experience that celebrates the deliverance of the Hebrew people from the harsh slavery of Pharaoh. Passover recalls how ten horrible plagues pronounced judgment upon Egypt and pagan gods. On the night of the final plague, the Israelites were commanded by the Almighty to take the blood of a lamb and smear it on the doorposts of their home. The death of the firstborn would "pass over" the houses marked with blood. This of course foreshadows the Lamb of YHWH, the Messiah, whose blood would be shed to cover the sins of the world on a future Passover.

Since that dark night in Egypt, the Jewish people have faithfully kept the Passover. John 2:13 shows that from His childhood, the Savior celebrated the festival. Much can be learned as a person follows the Savior's examples of life and culture. "For here unto were ye called; because Messiah also suffered for you, leaving you an example that ye should follow his steps, 1 Peter 2:21. In the Gospels, the disciples participate in the iconic "Last Supper," which was actually a Passover teaching.

Even today, the Passover story is told through an interactive meal called a "Seder." The Seder menu includes bitter herbs, unleavened bread called "matzah," wine, and lamb. These foods have specific meaning to convey the divine message of slavery, liberation, sin, and blood sacrifice. The meal is then followed by a 7 day fast of all food products that contain yeast. "That same night they are to eat the meat roasted over the fire, along with bitter herbs, and bread made without yeast," Exodus 12:8.

Have you made plans to celebrate Passover this year?

TRUTH FOR TODAY

March 13

The pearly gates or doorways into Heaven are each named after one of the twelve tribes of Israel. Revelation 21:12, "And had a wall great and high, and had twelve gates, and at the gates twelve angels, and names written thereon, which are the names of the twelve tribes of the children of Israel." To enter into the gates, one must associate with a tribe of Israel. The Scriptures clearly indicate that there is not a Baptist, Lutheran, or even a Christian door to Heaven.

The picturesque mansion over the hill top is really the Holy Temple on the mountain top of Jerusalem. The New Jerusalem (mistakenly called "heaven") is the realm in which YHWH's presence is manifest. It is more magnificent than any person can imagine and is the place where the angels and all believers who have departed because of death now live, Hebrews 12:22-24. In the New Jerusalem, people will be occupied with living and enjoying the best things in life. Believers will recognize loved ones and fellowship with others, Luke 23:42-43.

The Messiah is now in Heaven preparing the place for future events according to John 14:2. At the end of the Great Tribulation there will be a 1,000 year reign of YHWH upon the earth. Isaiah 66 states that during this time, all nations will keep the Law of Moses, celebrate the seventh-day Sabbath and New Moons. Then, the universe will be transformed as Heaven descends to earth. Revelation speaks of a huge squared city of the New Jerusalem that will come down from the sky to rest upon the planet. Clearly, heaven is not some place in a faraway galaxy but is actually very earthly. Revelation 21:2, "And I saw the holy city, New Jerusalem, coming down from YHWH out of heaven." The New Earth will have no sea, sun, or moon because the Lamb will be the light. The paradise of the Garden of Eden will also be restored. "He will dwell with them, and they shall be His people, and YHWH Himself will be with them and be their Elohim. And YHWH will wipe away every tear from their eyes; there shall be no more death, nor sorrow, nor crying; and there shall be no more pain, for the former things have passed away," Revelation 21:3-4.

The final destination for those who put their trust in YHWH and His Messiah isn't an eternal church service, but the New Jerusalem. Such knowledge of Heaven demands a paradigm shift in the mind of the believer. For if Jerusalem and Israel will be important in the world to come; perhaps it should be a priority today. The promise of Heaven is in reality the promise of the restoration of the nation of Israel. "On that day living water will flow out from Jerusalem. The YHWH will be king over the whole earth. On that day there will be one YHWH, and his name the only name," Zechariah 14:8-9.

March 14

The Trinity was first introduced to the faith to appease polytheistic converts during the Nicene Council of 325AD. The Egyptians had their trinity of Osiris, Horus, and Isis and the Babylonians used the triangle to symbolize their triune deity. Early church leaders Tertullian and Origen spoke of the trinity and the notion formally became part of church doctrine in the fourth century. It was then that the Catholic Church first began teaching god as being in three separate persons. The New Catholic Encyclopedia says, "the Trinity is not directly and immediately the word of God. The doctrine of the Holy Trinity is not taught in the Old Testament."

Many different Trinitarian ideas exist, which generally present the Godhead as three distinct persons yet each equally "god." Those who defend the trinity will often take segments of Scripture, of an incident, or of a text and try to make them say what the entire Bible refutes. One major problem with the trinity is that leads to a separation of the godhead. People envision Jesus the Son being sent to rescue the world from an angry Old Testament God the Father. The Holy Spirit is considered to be a flighty personality that rests on some but not on others. Such ideas could not be farther from the truth. Paul wrote that "YHWH is only one," in Galatians 3:20.

What the Bible does teach is "unity." This is the idea that there is one Elohim who may choose to be revealed in various ways such as the burning bush or the voice from heaven. The Messiah alluded to this when He quoted Deuteronomy 6:4 as He was asked which commandment was the greatest. "Hear, O Israel; YHWH is our Elohim; YHWH is One: And thou shalt love YHWH thy Elohim with all thy heart, and with all thy soul, and with all thy mind, and with all thy strength: this is the first commandment," Mark 12:29-30. Notice that He didn't say that YHWH is three!

The original Hebrew of Deuteronomy 6:4 reads "YHWH echad." The Hebrew word "echad" is the word for "unified, unique, and special." This is also the numeric word for one. The Bible says that even the demons know better than to believe in a triune god. James 2:19 says, "you believe that there is one Elohim, good! Even the demons believe that and shudder." For the most compelling evidence against the trinity, simply consider the many words spoken by the Messiah on this subject. In John 10:30 He stated, "I and the Father are one." Truly, there is only one divine will. There is only one divinity. The Trinitarian idea of "god in three persons" doesn't pass the litmus test of the Scriptures. There exists the Father or "YHWH" as revealed in Exodus 3. The Messiah is certainly 100% divine yet is subject to the Father. The Holy Spirit is the Almighty's power at work. Do you believe in the trinity? Why or why not?

TRUTH FOR TODAY

March 15

There is a right way to say "I am sorry." Doing teshuvah / repentance is a part of life that requires us to turn from our sin and seek to do right. Read and meditate on these words today:

• Leviticus 26:40-42, "'But if they will confess their sins and the sins of their fathers--their treachery against me and their hostility toward me, which made me hostile toward them so that I sent them into the land of their enemies--then when their uncircumcised hearts are humbled and they pay for their sin, I will remember my covenant with Jacob and my covenant with Isaac and my covenant with Abraham, and I will remember the land."

• Luke 5:32, "I have not come to call the righteous, but sinners to repentance."

• Ezekiel 18:21-22, "If a wicked man turns from all his sins which he has committed, keeps all My statutes, and does what is lawful and right, he shall surely live; he shall not die. None of the transgressions which he has committed shall be remembered against him; because of the righteousness which he has done, he shall live."

• Acts 2:38, "Peter replied, 'Repent and be baptized, every one of you, in the name of Y'shua Ha Moshiach for the forgiveness of your sins. And you will receive the gift of the Holy Spirit.'"

• Joel 2:12-13, "Even now," declares the YHWH, "return to me with all your heart, with fasting and weeping and mourning. Rend your heart and not your garments. Return to YHWH, for he is gracious and compassionate, slow to anger and abounding in love, and he relents from sending calamity."

• Mark 1:15, "The time is fulfilled, and the kingdom of YHWH is at hand: repent and believe the gospel."

March 16

1 John 3:15 says, "Whosoever hateth his brother is a murderer." This means that anger, left unchecked and unbridled, is equal to the heinous murder and abuse of another person.

The Ten Commandments clearly state "thou shalt not murder." Most people would never willingly take the life of another. However, the Messiah made it clear that wishing someone dead is as bad as physically killing them. This was the original intention of the command to not murder. "You have heard that it was said to the people long ago, 'Do not murder, and anyone who murders will be subject to judgment.' But I tell you that anyone who is angry with his brother without cause will be subject to judgment," Matthew 5:22. This comment by the Savior expounds upon the true heart of the Law of Moses that goes way beyond the letter of the Law. There is a depth of application below even the most basic commandment in the Bible.

Anger is a sin that takes control until more pain occurs. Genesis 4:5-8 shows how Adam's son "Cain became very angry and rose up against Abel his brother and killed him." Anger causes families to divorce, churches to split, and people to have high blood pressure. The Journal of the American Heart Association has said that "anger-prone people are more likely to have heart attacks." Man's anger works in rebellion to the Holy Spirit. "Get rid of all bitterness, rage and anger, brawling and slander, along with every form of malice," Ephesians 4:31.

The Scriptures are clear that anger has no place in the life of the believer. Are you angry about something? How can you deal with that anger?

TRUTH FOR TODAY

March 17

Instead of joining the worldwide rescue mission to seek and save the lost sheep of Israel many individuals choose to focus on differences of opinion. These folks choose division over unity and shame the entire faith. The issue of the day doesn't matter. Just pick any topic and the problem will arise. People have their tight-nit ideas on calendars, diets, home schooling, music, moons, and marriage. Sway from a certain belief and be labeled a "heretic" or "cult." If you don't measure up to a certain standard or hold a different doctrine then you may be considered worse than a heathen. Can't you hear the voices now?

Throughout the world, there are many agents working against the truth which we teach. Sadly, the largest battle we seem to face comes from similar 'believers' who choose to push their personal convictions onto others. A personal conviction is just that - a unique and individual area in which a person is convinced to do or not do something. These are the "grey" areas of the scriptures that the Bible leaves open for believers to make their own decision. These are not commandments or areas of sin. These issues can become sin if they are pushed on to others as binding and necessary. Woe unto the man that pridefully exalts personal convictions as truth.

If YHWH leads you to not drink water on Tuesday then you should not do so. Nor should you push that belief on to other people. Envy and strife occur when you are so convinced that yours is the best way, so that you condemn others who do not agree. The longer you have had this personal belief the harder it is to allow others freedom in that area. Have you ever done this?

You will never find a ministry that is 100% doctrinally correct. Nor will you ever find a person that you agree with on every issue of Torah. It takes a mature believer to accept differences and strive for unity in the body. Immature believers find one issue of disagreement to focus, discuss, debate, and divide. Sadly, our faith is full of clanging cymbals who make a lot of noise but show little acceptance or love. Perhaps we should call these "personal condemnations" instead of "personal convictions." Take head coverings, wearing a tallit, drinking alcohol, calendars, the correct pronunciation of the name of YHWH, for example. There is Biblical freedom in these issues.

The Almighty shows His chesed / grace regarding feasts and dates in Numbers 9. Those defiled or unavailable to keep the Passover were allowed to celebrate the feast one month later. These folks were blessed as they celebrated YHWH's festival on a DIFFERENT date than others! Moses and the leaders of Israel didn't condemn them. Nor did the Creator strike them dead. Instead, their earnest worship was accepted. This doesn't mean that we can keep the feast days whenever we choose. The message of the second Passover is an example for us to love and accept those who are different in their heartfelt keeping of Torah.

March 18

Even school children can easily recognize the Easter math problem of Y'shua being in the tomb for three days if he died on Good Friday and resurrected on Easter Sunday. Y'shua Himself said, "A wicked and adulterous generation asks for a miraculous sign! But none will be given it except the sign of the prophet Jonah. For as Jonah was three days and three nights in the whale's belly; so shall the Son of man be three days and three nights in the heart of the earth," Matthew 12:40-41. There are not three days and three nights between Friday afternoon and Sunday morning. From this passage one must conclude that either the Bible is wrong or the traditions of a Good Friday death and Sunday morning resurrection are in error. No stretch of the imagination can create three nights between Friday afternoon and Sunday morning.

John 20:1 reveals the truth concerning the resurrection, "The first of the week cometh Mary Magdalene early, when it was yet dark, unto the sepulcher, and seeth the stone taken away from the sepulcher." Mary came to the tomb when it was dark and the Savior had already risen from the dead. This teaches us that Easter Sunrise services are not proper worship because the resurrection occurred before the sun rose on Sunday morning.

For the Messiah to be in the tomb three nights and resurrect before the sun rose on Sunday, then he must have been crucified on a Wednesday. Mark 15 recounts how Joseph of Arimathea wrapped Y'shua in a linen shroud and placed him in a borrowed tomb before sundown Wednesday night. He was buried late in the afternoon on Wednesday and then resurrected three days later about Saturday evening.

Do you really think the Messiah died on Friday and rose on Sunday? Can you prove it?

March 19

History reveals why people celebrate on Easter Sunday despite these Scriptural truth.

Thousands of years before 33AD the fertility goddess “Ishtar” was worshipped as people dyed eggs and arose early for sunrise services in the Spring. The Encyclopedia Britannica (1934) states: “Easter, Ostara, or Ishtar was the goddess of Spring in the religion of the ancient Angles and Saxons. Every April a festival was celebrated in her honor. With the beginnings of Christianity, the old gods were put aside. From then on the festival was celebrated in honor of the resurrection of Christ, but was still known as Easter after the old goddess.” Worship of the sun was a common practice of pagans who worshipped a pantheon of gods.

Neither the apostles nor the Messiah commemorated Ishtar/Easter Sunday. “Constantine the Great, Roman emperor, convoked the Council of Nicaea in 325. The council unanimously ruled that the Easter festival should be celebrated throughout the Christian world on the first Sunday after the full moon following the vernal equinox,” says the History Channel.

Indeed, the date of Easter has nothing to do with the Biblical account of the resurrection and everything to do with ancient earth worship. Easter always occurs on the first Sunday after the first full moon after the Spring Equinox. Sunrise services were actually held over a thousand years before Christ walked the earth as pagans would wake early to watch the sun ascend on the exact same date of Easter today. The New Book of Knowledge (1978) declares, "The custom of a sunrise service on Easter Sunday can be traced to ancient spring festivals that celebrated the rising sun." The accepted Christian teaching that Jesus died on Good Friday and resurrected three days later on Easter Sunday is really bad math that only leads to more error. Don’t be misled by these vain traditions that actually glorify pagan gods and not the resurrected Savior.

Who can you share this truth with today?

Truth For Today

March 20

In the beginning YHWH chose the seventh day as a day of rest. The very first thing that Adam and Eve experienced after their creation was the joy of the Sabbath. The seventh day was reaffirmed in the Ten Commandments and throughout the Prophets. Luke 4 shows that it was the custom of Y'shua to "enter the synagogue on the Sabbath." Even the Apostle Paul kept Saturday as holy. "And Paul reasoned in the synagogue every Sabbath, and persuaded the Jews and the Greeks," Acts 18:4. Notice in this verse that Jews and Greeks were worshipping together on the seventh-day Sabbath. Saturday isn't the "Jewish" Sabbath, but the Biblical one. Seventh day Sabbath observance is intended for all Bible believers.

Romans 14 states that any day can be a time of worship, yet there is only one Sabbath day that YHWH chose for His people. The Bible never grants man the authority to choose his own Sabbath day. "Remember the Sabbath day, to keep it holy. Six days you shall labor and do all your work, but the seventh day is the Sabbath of YHWH your Elohim. In it you shall do no work: you, nor your son, nor your daughter, nor your male servant, nor your female servant, nor your cattle, nor your stranger who is within your gates. For in six days YHWH made the heavens and the earth, the sea, and all that is in them, and rested the seventh day. Therefore YHWH blessed the Sabbath day and hallowed it," Exodus 20:8-11. Practically all churches recognize that the Messiah rose from the grave on Sunday - the first day of the week. These same religious institutions admonish their members to break the third commandment by worshipping on the very same first day of the week!

How do we know that Saturday is the Biblical Sabbath and not another day of the week? Well, for thousands of years the Jewish people have kept track of the days and regarded the true Sabbath. Even through the Holocaust, the millions of Jewish people didn't forget the seventh day from creation. History records that in 1582 Pope Gregory XIII made some calendar changes and actually dropped ten days from the year. It was Thursday, October 4, 1582, and the next day, Friday, should have been October 5. But Gregory made it October 15 instead. The same seventh day remained and the weekly cycle wasn't disturbed at all.

How do you keep the Sabbath?

TRUTH FOR TODAY

March 21

Passover is the celebration of the how the death angel executed judgment against the nation of Egypt and "passed over" the homes that had the blood of a lamb on their doorposts. It is also the exact time that Messiah Y'shua gave His life as a sacrifice for all mankind. Passover has been celebrated by Jewish people for thousands of years. However, the Bible commands all Bible believers to keep this feast in Leviticus 23. We know that the Messiah celebrated Passover. We are to follow His example and worship during this set apart time. The Passover events are traditionally remembered through a "seder" or memorial meal. The Seder includes dipping vegetables, singing, four cups of wine, and eating unleavened bread.

Whether or not you've ever celebrated the Biblical feast of Passover, the emotions of this time are contagious. And, the Passover message is applicable. With Passover (or Pesach in Hebrew) there is wonder, confusion, and excitement over the traditions and rituals. The Seder contains so many symbolic elements that it is easy to get lost in all the Matzah and bitter herbs, cups and questions. It is simply impossible to fully understand the full depth and meaning behind the search for leaven or counting the omer.

Yet as we learn to keep Pesach, we are to be on guard to just not "go through the motions." Passover should be more than just a religious ceremony. Our Passover service shouldn't be about yesteryear but about life today. We are reminded of this in the Haggadah, the booklet containing the order of service for Passover. The Haggadah says, "in every generation each person must look upon himself as though personally among those who came out of Egypt."

This teaches, that when it comes to Passover, we aren't supposed to be simple observers but participants. We are not to be an audience but involved. We aren't to just hear the Passover story but apply it. This year, make the effort to take Passover Personal. Let this festival of Freedom make a difference in your life so you don't just learn about Pesach but experience freedom; experience salvation; experience deliverance; experience the blood covering. Are you spiritually ready for Passover?

March 22

How often do you just think about the name of YHWH? The Bible has much to say about the blessed name of YHWH. Take a few minutes today and meditate on these verses...

- Psalm 135:13, "YHWH is Your name forever; YHWH is Your Remembrance from generation to generation."
- Psalm 116:13, "I will lift up the cup of salvation and call out in the Name of YHWH!"
- Psalm 122:4, "For there (i.e. in Jerusalem) the tribes ascended, the tribes of Yah, a testimony for Israel, giving thanks to the Name of YHWH."
- Psalm 105:1, "Give thanks to YHWH, call out in His name, make known among the peoples His deeds."
- Psalm 124:8, "Our help is through the Name of YHWH, Maker of heaven and earth."
- Psalm 33:21, "In Him our heart rejoices! In His holy name we trust!"
- Jeremiah 3:17, "At that time they will call Jerusalem "The Throne of YHWH" and all the nations will be gathered unto her for the Name of YHWH and for Jerusalem and they will no longer walk in the stubbornness of their evil heart."
- Jeremiah 10:25, "Pour Your wrath on the nations who knew You not, and on families who called out not in Your Name -- for they consumed Jacob and ate him up completely and laid waste his habitation."

March 23

The very first followers of the Messiah kept the Sabbath on the seventh day of the week as eternally commanded in the book of Genesis. "Thus the heavens and the earth were completed in all their vast array. By the seventh day Elohim had finished the work he had been doing; so on the seventh day he rested from all his work. And Elohim blessed the seventh day and made it holy, because on it he rested from all the work of creating that he had done," Genesis 2:1-2. The importance of a specific day for worship is repeated with the giving of the Ten Commandments as well. The specific day of our worship and rest does indeed matter to the Almighty.

The modern calendar clearly shows what day is what. Plus, in the latest edition of Webster's Unabridged Dictionary, the definition for 'seventh day' references: "Saturday, the seventh day of the week."

The Sabbath wasn't changed in the New Testament. Messiah Himself, kept the true Sabbath, "And he came to Nazareth, where he had been brought up: and, as his custom was, he went into the synagogue on the Sabbath day, and stood up for to read," Luke 4:16. Even the Apostle Paul kept Saturday as holy. "And Paul reasoned in the synagogue every Sabbath, and persuaded the Jews and the Greeks," Acts 18:4. Notice that Jews and Greeks were worshipping together. Saturday isn't the "Jewish" Sabbath, but the Biblical one. Seventh day Sabbath observance is intended for all Bible believers.

History shows that the day of worship wasn't changed by the Creator, but by man. Believers must make the choice to keep the Biblical seventh-day Sabbath. Will you honor YHWH or man on this upcoming seventh day?

TRUTH FOR TODAY

March 24

From creation, the Almighty considers a day to begin and end at evening. "And the evening and the morning were the first day," Genesis 1:5. Even today the Jewish people regard Friday evening to Saturday evening as the seventh day Sabbath. The Biblical week begins and ends on Saturday night. Leviticus 23:32, "from evening unto evening, shall ye celebrate your Sabbath."

John 20:1 reveals the truth concerning the resurrection, "The first [day] of the week cometh Mary Magdalene early, when it was yet dark, unto the sepulcher, and seeth the stone taken away from the sepulcher," KJV. The word [day] is in parenthesis as the translators added this word to the Bible. The verse accurately reads that Mary came to the tomb as the first day of the week began, near 8pm on Saturday night. The Savior had already risen from the dead before dark! Matthew 28:1-2 shows two women visiting the tomb shortly after sundown on Saturday night. Again, the tomb was empty at the end of the Sabbath on Saturday night.

The scriptures are clear that Y'shua spent three days and three nights in the tomb before rising from the dead slightly before sundown on Saturday night. This means that Y'shua's' triumphant entry in Jerusalem occurred on a Saturday and that the Savior was killed on a Wednesday afternoon. So much for Good Friday!

Celebrating the resurrection on Sunday morning is at best bad timing and at worst a violation of Ezekiel 8:15-18. If the timing of the death of Messiah is incorrect, then what other errors can be found within traditional Christianity? "Beware lest any man spoil you through philosophy and vain deceit, after the tradition of men, after rudiments of the world, and not after Messiah," Colossians 2:8.

What does this reading mean to you?

Truth For Today

March 25

Each person has been "fearfully and wonderfully made" to enjoy the best of life. Laziness and disease stop people from experiencing true abundance. This is not the Almighty's will! The Bible clearly indicates that YHWH wants His children to be healthy in spirit and in body. 3 John 1:2 "Dear friend, I hope all is well with you and that you are as healthy in body as you are strong in spirit."

Sadly, religious people are is just as obese and just as sick as the rest of the world. Physical and spiritual corruption has continued to fester since perfection was lost in the Garden of Eden. Adam and Eve were given a diet from the best of the earth which included fresh fruits, vegetables and no meat. The couple was tempted to eat the forbidden as the original sin came in the form of food. The wrong diet was chosen and the result of their disobedience brought sickness, pain, and death into the world. In Genesis 7, Noah is permitted to eat the meat of certain animals that were designated as "clean." Later in Leviticus 11, Moses reviews which animals are to be considered "food" and are fit for human consumption. And though mankind is allowed a lifespan of 120 years in Genesis 6:3, this potential for a long vibrant life is seldom experienced. Unhealthy personal choices and dangerous habits rob people of the physical fullness the Bible offers. "Do not join those who drink too much wine or gorge themselves on meat, for drunkards and gluttons become poor, and drowsiness clothes them in rags," Proverbs 23:20-21. Most sickness can be attributed to overeating, consuming unhealthy items, and not having enough physical activity. "One who is lazy in his work is a brother to one who destroys," says Proverbs 18:9.

The Bible indicates that the assembly of believers was to be an example to the world in all areas of life. From their abundance, believers should be caring for the needy and unfortunate. There would be no need for Government welfare or healthcare if the Church cared for the poor and regularly taught personal responsibility. "Religion that YHWH our Father accepts as pure and faultless is this: to look after orphans and widows in their distress and to keep oneself from being polluted by the world," James 1:27. If the people of YHWH would rise up in holiness to cleanse their bodies and commit themselves to providing for the needy, the government handout lines would soon turn to places of faith that can offer more than a meal or a prescription.

Who can you personally help today?

March 26

The Apostle Paul spoke of the importance of commemorating Passover when he wrote, "Messiah, our Passover lamb, has been sacrificed. Therefore let us keep the festival (of Passover)," in 1 Corinthians 5:8. History shows that the commandment to keep Passover was repealed by the Roman Catholic Church in 325AD. The Bible never abolishes this memorial.

Many dismiss Passover as an outdated Jewish festival. Yet to do so is to reject a set apart time of blessing and rich meaning. It was during a special Passover meal the Savior said, "This is my body which is given for you: This do in remembrance of me," Luke 22:19.

On the night before his death, that the Savior commemorated the Passover with His disciples as seen in Matthew 26:17-24. During this meal the Savior said, "This bread is my body," and "this cup is the new testament in my blood," Luke 22:7, 19-20. The Messiah wasn't instituting the service of "communion" at this point. These words were spoken during and about the Passover meal. Bible believers are to keep Passover in remembrance of the Messiah.

The bread and the wine were later removed from the Passover and developed into the weekly Eucharist by the Roman church. The idea of transubstantiation was then adopted into communion to appease the nations that were accustomed to offer goblets of human blood to acquire the virtues of the dead person. Christians everywhere now partake of wafers and wine without truly recognizing the meaning behind the service. Sadly, the message behind the meal is lost as communion is accepted and Passover is ignored. The main point of Passover is for each Bible believer to actively reflect upon their faith and seek true holiness. The communion table is only part of the meal, which is often taken at the wrong time. Are you ready for Passover this year?

March 27

The true origin of Easter is more about fertility and mother earth than the Bible. "The egg was a sacred symbol among the Babylonians. They believed an old fable about an egg of wondrous size which was supposed to have fallen from heaven into the Euphrates River. From this marvelous egg - according to the ancient story - the Goddess Ishtar (Semiramis), was hatched. And so the egg came to symbolize the Goddess Easter," The Jewish Encyclopedia, Vol. 9, p. 309. Three month old infants were sacrificed to Ishtar and their blood was used to dye eggs in honor of the false god. To imbue fertility upon their growing season, Pagans would roll these eggs on their fields. The eggs were then hidden from evil spirits to later be collected in baskets.

The word "Easter" appears only once in the King James Version of the Bible (and not at all in most other translations). From this one appearance a true concern arises. Here, the King James translators mistranslated the Greek word for Passover as "Easter." Acts 12:4, "And when he [King Herod Agrippa I] had apprehended him [the apostle Peter], he put him in prison, and delivered him to four quaternions of soldiers to keep him; intending after Easter to bring him forth to the people." The Greek word for "Easter" in this verse is "pascha." This term is properly translated over 28 times in the Bible as "Passover." Passover is a yearly festival that recalls Israelite's exodus from Egypt. This holy day was given to mankind (and not just the Jewish people) as an everlasting commandment. Passover was part of the original faith of the Apostles and the Savior. Sadly, the mistranslation in the book of Acts is just one example of how the true festival of Passover has been replaced with the idolatry of Easter.

Neither the apostles nor the Messiah commemorated Easter. "Constantine the Great, Roman emperor, convoked the Council of Nicaea in 325. The council unanimously ruled that the Easter festival should be celebrated throughout the Christian world on the first Sunday after the full moon following the vernal equinox," says the History Channel. For the first 300 years after the Savior's crucifixion, the early church kept the festival of Passover as commanded in Leviticus 23. The holiday of Ishtar/Easter is problematic for a person who seeks undefiled worship. The mixture of bunnies, baskets, and the Bible believer certainly is perplexing. "YHWH is spirit and those that worship him must worship in spirit and in truth," John 4:24.

Which Spring holidays or holy days will you celebrate this year?

March 28

The Ten Commandments clearly state "thou shalt not murder." Most people would never willingly take the life of another. However, the Messiah made it clear that wishing someone dead is as bad as physically killing them. This was the original intention of the command to not murder. "You have heard that it was said to the people long ago, 'Do not murder, and anyone who murders will be subject to judgment.' But I tell you that anyone who is angry with his brother without cause will be subject to judgment," Matthew 5:22. This comment by the Savior expounds upon the true heart of the Law of Moses that goes way beyond the letter of the Law.

Anger is a sin that takes control until more pain occurs. Genesis 4:5-8 shows how Adam's son "Cain became very angry and rose up against Abel his brother and killed him." Anger causes families to divorce, churches to split, and people to have high blood pressure. The Journal of the American Heart Association has said that "anger-prone people are more likely to have heart attacks." Man's anger works in rebellion to the Holy Spirit. "Get rid of all bitterness, rage and anger, brawling and slander, along with every form of malice," Ephesians 4:31.

It has been taught from the pulpits that "holy anger" is an acceptable way to deal with spiritual problems. This is a lie. "The anger of man does not achieve the righteousness of Elohim," James 1:20. The Bible never uses the phrase "righteous indignation." Nor is anger justified by the account of an upset Y'shua turning the tables on the unfair money-changers in the Temple. A careful reading of Matthew 21 shows that Y'shua was never angry. Instead, he was full of "zeal for the house of Elohim." Y'shua never let anger take control as His actions were motivated by love. Everything the Savior did showed that he was gentle and humble of heart. The Gospel of Luke records that "the chief priests and the scribes and the leading men among the people were trying to destroy Him, and they could not find anything that they might do, for all the people were hanging upon His words." The actions of Y'shua in the Temple show us that zeal and passion for righteousness is perfectly ok but all anger is wrong.

Ephesians 4:26-27 in the New Living Translation says: "And don't sin by letting anger gain control over you. Don't let the sun go down while you are still angry, for anger gives a mighty foothold to the Devil." The Greek word for "anger" in this verse literally means "impulse." So, how does a person deal with this deadly emotion? "The best way of dealing with the anger habit is to prevent it occurring in the first place. This means getting to know the triggers that evoke angry feelings and systematically defusing each trigger situation's ability to affect you," wrote Ernest H. Johnson in the book The Deadly Emotions. Anger must be avoided and prevented before it leads to pain or even death. Proverbs 29:11, "A fool vents his feelings, but a wise man holds them back."

March 29

The power of the Gospel is vividly illustrated through a Hebrew word Y'shua often used. Messiah spoke on countless occasions about "eating His flesh." The word in Hebrew for flesh is "besar." During His last Passover meal, often called the Last Supper, Y'shua lifted the matzah and said, "this is my besar / body that is broken for you." He said unless you "eat of my besar / flesh and drink of my blood, you have no life in you," John / Yochannan 6:53. Even in Isaiah 9:19, the Hebrew word "besar" is translated "flesh."

What is interesting is that like most Hebrew words, "besar" has several meanings. The word besar not only means "flesh" but also "good news" or "gospel." Besar is translated "good news" in Isaiah 52:7, "How beautiful on the mountains are the feet of him who brings good news / besar, who publishes peace, who brings good news / besar of good, who publishes salvation, who says to Zion, "Your Elohim reigns!"

The besar, the good news of Y'shua, is that YHWH has come in His flesh to offer salvation. So, to eat of His flesh is to eat of His besar. To eat Y'shua's besar is to believe His good news and experience life eternal! "If you shall confess with your mouth the Master Y'shua, and shall believe in your lev / heart that YHWH has raised Him from the dead, you shall be saved," Romans 10:9.

Make a list of people you can share this message with today. Take a few minutes and share your testimony with other people. Praise YHWH for the besar / good news of Y'shua.

March 30

Remember too that one Passover Lamb was killed for an entire family. If a family was too small to eat the entire lamb, then they could share with another family. The besar - good news of YHWH isn't just for you alone! The besar is to be shared with our friends and family! This is how we overcome - by the blood of the Lamb and sharing our testimony of the Lamb.

The Passover Lamb saved the Hebrews from slavery and bondage thousands of years ago. The blood of the Passover Lamb Y'shua still saves today. Like the ancient Israelites we need take the dahm / blood and apply it to our doorposts. And we need to share the Lamb. Passover is about more than a historical event or a special meal. Pesach recounts how Y'shua's blood protects us from sin and death.

In all the preparations for Passover, don't forget about the blood of Y'shua. Take this message of freedom and apply it. Share testimony with others. Forward this teaching to friends. This year during Pesach make it personal. Don't just learn about Hebrew roots. And don't just attend a Seder. Apply the blood of Y'shua. Experience freedom from the death angel and deliverance from sin. Recommit your life to YHWH and thank Him for the blood covering.

April

Truth For Today

April 1

The religious holiday of Lent is a horrible April Fool's joke. Neither the Messiah, the Apostles, nor the first church leaders spoke of Lent as an accepted practice. Lent officially became a "Christian" celebration at the Council of Laodicea in A.D. 360. Even the famed Catholic Saint Abbot John Cassian, the monk of Marseilles, admitted in the fifth century, "Howbeit you should know that as long as the primitive church retained its perfection unbroken, this observance of Lent did not exist." Today Lent is celebrated by most Catholics, Episcipals, Lutherans, and some Presbyterians who desire to be closer to the Almighty. Many unknowingly observe Lent without knowing its history or acknowledging its pagan past.

YHWH hates all pagan observances. Study these verses to understand the danger of participating in pagan practices: Jeremiah 10:2-3; Leviticus 18:3, 30; Deuteronomy. 7:1-5, 16.

What's wrong with Lent?

According to tradition Semiramis, the wife of Nimrod the King of Babylon, claimed she had been supernaturally impregnated by the Sun god and gave birth to Tammuz. One day while hunting, Tamuz was killed by a wild boar. Semiramis mourned for 40 days, at the end of which Tammuz was supposedly brought back from the dead. She proclaimed herself Queen of Heaven, founded a celibate priesthood to worship her son and declared its chief priest infallible, and memorialized her mourning in an annual 40 day period of denial. It was the world's first counterfeit of the Biblical story of the Redeemer and grew into a mother-child cult that was duplicated in almost every pagan mythology.

Lent, like many other religious holidays or practices has it's origin in mystery religion and not the Bible. It's easy to go along with such practices but the Bible has called us to "be in the world but not of the world." Instead of falling into the trap of Lent and Easter, follow the Scriptures and celebrate Passover and Unleavened Bread.

April 2

"And because law-less-ness increases in the world, the love of many will grow cold," Matthew 24:12. The Greek word translated "lawlessness" in this verse is "anomia." This word, according to Strong's Exhaustive Dictionary, means "illegality, i.e. violation of law, wickedness, iniquity, unrighteousness." Likewise, Thayer's Greek Lexicon defines anomia as "the condition of one without law - either because ignorant of it, or because violating it, contempt and violation of law, iniquity, wickedness." Anomia is exactly the same Greek term used in Matthew 7:23 where the Savior said, "And then I will declare to them, 'I never knew you; depart from Me, you who practice lawlessness (anomia)." Ouch!

Iniquity can be understood as law-less-ness or having no regard towards the Law of Moses. Iniquity causes the heart to grow cold to the arena of faith. 1 John 3:4, "Everyone who practices sin also practices lawlessness; and sin is lawlessness." To sin is to violate or break the law of the Almighty, called "torah" in Hebrew. This law is the eternal commandments that were given to Moses and then recorded in the first five books of the Bible. Today, the Torah is the entire Bible from Genesis to Revelation. The Torah reveals the expectations for all mankind. A person sins when the law is not kept. Sin is having lawlessness - having less of the law.

Blessings and purpose abound when a person walks in obedience to the whole of Scripture. On the contrary, violating the Torah dulls the heart. Like slow changes in the weather that go unnoticed, iniquity grows slowly in the hearts of many believers. Many act like super-market shoppers, picking and choosing what should be followed in the Bible while casting much of the "Old Testament" aside.

The opposite of law-less-ness is law-plus-ness, or having more of the Torah in life. Proverbs 4:23 says, "Guard your heart, for out of it flows the issues of life." Though iniquity increases in the world, believers have been called to not be affected by this chill factor. The Torah should clearly be studied, learned and become a part of everyday life. Have you studied the Torah this week? What part of Torah do you not understand?

TRUTH FOR TODAY

April 3

Have you ever run out of money before you ran out of month? Truth be told, most people live pay check to pay check and need to need. This is not how our life is meant to be. We are supposed to be overcomers. We are supposed to realize that's all of our needs are met. We're supposed to rest in the fact that everything you need has been done and given to you. "My Yah shall supply all of my needs according to his riches in glory," Philippians 4:19.

The creation account shows us how YHWH has already met all of our needs. From day one until the end of day six YHWH prepared for the needs of the entire world. Just think about it... all of the oxygen that was ever needed was made during those days. Today there are 6,000,000,000 people who share the same original oxygen YHWH made those first days. YHWH spent six days meeting or needs before he even made us. Everything we need in the physical realm was provided before we were created.

We also know that Y'shua is the lamb slain before the foundation of the world. This is according to Revelation 13:8. All of our spiritual needs were met before we were created. And then the first thing mankind does after creation is experience the Sabbath.

Immediately at the end of the sixth day Adam is commanded to rest. This instant rest before work showed him and shows us that YHWH is the source of all of our needs. Your job, Wall Street, retirement or your bank account is not your source. We simply need to do like Adam and rest in YHWH's provision. There remains a Sabbath rest for us today. This is true for the seven day worship and for trusting YHWH to provide for us.

Today, take the words of Proverbs 3:5 to heart, "trust YHWH with all your heart and lean not on your own understanding, in all your ways acknowledge Him and He will direct your path."

April 4

Y'shua is the Pesach lamb whose blood redeems us from the curse of death. He gave His life during Passover so that we might experience chayim / life eternal. Passover celebrations must not ignore the Messiah's sacrifice! Seders shouldn't just celebrate how YHWH saved the Israelites thousands of years ago. Passover should be a time to rejoice in how YHWH, through His son, continually saves us from bondage and slavery. With Passover this year, begin applying His blood to your gates, and experience true freedom from Pharaoh. Yes, we need to CONTINUALLY apply the blood of our Passover Lamb Y'shua.

His blood needs to be applied to our lives. But where? Read two verses from Exodus 12 and have your mind opened to a greater understanding of the blood covering:

• "And you shall take a bunch of hyssop, and dip it in the dahm / blood that is in the basin, and strike the lintel and the two side posts with the dahm that is in the basin; and none of you shall go out the door of his bayit / home until the morning."

• "And the dahm / blood shall be to you for a sign upon the houses where you are: and when I see the dahm, I will pass over you, and the plague shall not be upon you to destroy you, when I smite the land of Mitzrayim / Egypt."

According to these verses, the blood wasn't placed on the outside of the Hebrew homes! It was placed on the INSIDE! The Hebrews were to paint their doorposts and then lock the doors shut. The blood was a sign for the Israelites that no matter what happened outside their doors, they were safe inside. Now, a sign is something that is visible and seen. How could the blood be a sign if it was outside and they were inside? How could the blood remind them of YHWH's protection if they couldn't go outside to see it? We've always thought the blood was on the outside keeping the death angel out. BUT, it was on the INSIDE keeping the Israelites from going out into darkness. The blood was on the inside stopping them from opening the door to death. Sorry, but Cecil B. Demille got it wrong. The blood was applied to the inside door posts. Today, we are to apply the blood to the inside of our homes – our minds and our attitudes. Have you accepted the blood of Y'shua to cleanse you of all sin?

TRUTH FOR TODAY

April 5

It is during these weeks that we recall the agricultural and historical events of our past. We commemorate and celebrate YHWH's power and the freedom of His people. Keeping Passover, or Pesach in Hebrew, is to literally commemorate the protection from the blood of the Lamb with a festive meal called a "seder." To remember the exodus, we are to keep Chag Ha Matzoth, or the feast of Unleavened Bread. Though it overlaps with Passover, this is actually a separate celebration that lasts for seven days. These feasts are different, and have different laws, yet together they tell the story of our people and their release from bondage.

Thousands of years ago our ancestors were enslaved to the evil taskmaster Pharaoh in Egypt. Elohim sent forth a redeemer who cried the desires of YHWH's own heart, to "let my people go." The purpose of the Exodus was freedom for YHWH's people. His judgment upon Egypt poured down from the heavens as water turned to blood, infestations of frogs and swarms of lice descended, and death came to the firstborn of every home not protected by the dahm / blood of a lamb. After ten horrible plagues that showed forth the power of Elohim, the Hebrews were finally released from bondage. The Hebrews were told to leave Mitzrayim / Egypt quickly, to not even allow their bread time to rise. And so they began their journey towards the Promised Land and their history as a unified nation.

It is every year at this time that we are to remember the redemption and the liberation of our people. We do this by following the commandments, or mitzvoth, of the Scriptures that pertain to the feasts of YHWH. Within the Bible we are told, "Three times a year you are to celebrate a festival to me." Celebrate the Feast of Unleavened Bread; for seven days eat bread made without yeast, as I commanded you. Do this at the appointed time in the month of Aviv, for in that month you came out of Egypt. "No one is to appear before me empty-handed," Shemot / Exodus 23: 13, 14.

Concerning these issues, the scriptures teach that we are to:
- Celebrate Passover, Exodus 23: 14
- Remove leaven from our homes, Exodus 12: 15
- Remove yeast totally from our homes on the day before Passover, Exodus 12: 15
- Rest on the first and seventh days of Unleavened Bread, Exodus 12: 16
- Eat Matzah, or unleavened bread, on the first night of Passover, Exodus 12: 18
- Not allow leaven is to be found in our possession, Exodus 12: 19
- Eat no food with leaven for seven days, Exodus 13: 3
- Eat not leaven or leavening agents during the feast, Exodus 13: 8

TRUTH FOR TODAY

April 6

A Seder is a special commemorative meal that is held in the spring time and remembers the events surrounding the exodus from Egypt. Traditional Seders include bitter herbs, matzah, and four cups of wine. These four glasses of wine are each symbolic of statements. These cups tell the Passover story and vividly remind us that Y'shua is the Passover lamb.

The first cup consumed during the Passover Seder is the Cup of Sanctification. This cup of holiness originates from Exodus 6:6 when YHWH said; —I will take you out. The first cup is the Kiddush cup, or glass of holiness. With this juice, we remember the promise of YHWH to bring the people out of slavery and establish a holy nation. Similarly, Y'shua sanctifies us, "For them I sanctify myself, that they too may be truly sanctified," John 17:19.

The cup of deliverance is the second cup. It is with this cup that the Seder recalls the ten plagues of Egypt. Just as YHWH delivered the children of Israel, He still delivers His people from judgment. John 8:32 expresses the deliverance of Y'shua. "I will deliver you," is found in Exodus 6:6.

The third cup of wine during the Seder is the cup of redemption. This cup of blessing shows how YHWH redeems Israel from sin. Galatians 4:4-5, —4But when the time had fully come, Elohim sent his Son, born of a woman, born under law, 5to redeem those under law, that we might receive the full rights of sons.

Finally, the last cup is the cup of the Kingdom. This is also called the cup of praise or the cup of acceptance. YHWH says in Exodus 6:7, —I will take you as a nation. This is the cup of joy that we will experience fully in the coming kingdom. John 15:11 says, —I have told you this so that my joy may be in you and that your joy may be complete.

The pattern is simply: YHWH will bring, redeem, deliver, and take us as His people. In Luke 22 and Mathew 26 we can read of the Messiah partaking of the traditional Seder. He takes up the cup of redemption and offers it as a symbol of his covenant with believes. We were once in spiritual bondage to sin and Satan. Y'shua gave his life to deliver us from sin and the plague of death. The shed blood of Messiah paid the price to redeem us. And finally we are to live a life worthy of praise. Our actions should reflect the principles and practices of the cup of the Kingdom.

April 7

Sin has a powerful, magnetic pull. The members of the body are prone to seek satisfaction. The gates of the mouth, ears, and eyes only want what feels good. These gates are fed by the five senses of touch, taste, smell, sound, and sight. We must be careful not to allow these openings to rule us.

"Do not let sin reign in your mortal body, that you should obey its lusts," Romans 6:12. What gates are easy for you to open? Where is your problem area? Remember the Passover story and the fact that the blood of Y'shua was applied to the door posts of the believing Israelites. Pray for the blood covering over your gates. When you are tempted to sin, remember the power of the blood is on the inside. Let a nearby doorway in your home or work place be a reminder of the blood of Y'shua and take a stand.

The only way to conquer the sinful desires; the only way to lock the door shut to the adversary, is through the blood of the Lamb. Through his dahm / blood one can overcome this world and all its trials. "And they overcame by the dahm of the Lamb, and by the word of their testimony; and they loved not their lives even to the death," Revelation 12:11.

His blood gives us victory, no matter how hard the temptation is. Through His dahm we can overcome a troubled childhood, loss of friends, confusion, doubt, money issues, sickness, cancer, trials, enemies, bill collectors, and even death. You can defeat the problem or pain that beats you down like a slave. Remember this verse, "And they overcame by the dahm of the Lamb, and by the word of their testimony; and they loved not their lives even to the death," Revelation 12:11.

Whatever is enslaving you will lead to your freedom though His blood AND your testimony. You can overcome your Pharaoh through guarding your gates and sharing your story. What is your testimony? It is the account of how YHWH saved you from religion, self, sin, and death.

The word of your testimony is how the Lamb's blood gave you victory over darkness. Have you recently shared the faith with someone? Do you regularly witness to others about the Name of YHWH and His Son?

April 8

What exactly are we to do during the feast of unleavened bread? How are we to spring clean our lives for the Most High? What does all this talk of leaven, sin, and redemption really mean? Let's look behind the scenes and find some startling answers.

First, let's consider that these feasts are a time to cleanse and purge the soul. Judaism teaches there are two types of spiritual dynamics. It speaks of itaruta de-leylah and an itaruta de-letata, 'an awakening from above,' and 'an awakening from below.' When we are awakened from above, YHWH initiates a movement, miracle, or moment in which we can see the hand of YHWH. An awakening from below, a itaruta de-letata, is when we reach towards the Shamayim / heavens and reach out to YHWH.

Chag Ha Matzoth is a mixture of the two. It is when we can clearly see the hand of YHWH removing us from bondage, and we respond by allowing the Divine light to penetrate our souls and remove any trace of sin, symbolized by leaven. In the physical we eat unleavened bread, which greatly affects the spiritual realm. We must realize that during these days, YHWH is moving upon mankind urging us to become open vessels to receive from Him. It is at this time Y'shua gave His blood for us, and therefore we should accept life and blessing from Him. This is the season for taking a personal inventory of our life, accepting the fact that we do sin, and remove perversion from our being. We are to eat of the unleavened bread and stay away from yeast.

Matzah is the name of the unleavened bread eaten by our ancestors as they fled Egypt. It is usually flat, square, very crispy, and is more like a cracker than a loaf. Unlike sandwich or other types of bread, Matzah does not have yeast and therefore is not fluffy or puffed up. It is a pure food that reminds of the exodus. Eating Matzah is a sign of our connection to YHWH. "Eat unleavened bread during those seven days; nothing with yeast in it is to be seen among you, nor shall any yeast be seen anywhere within your borders. On that day tell your son, 'I do this because of what YHWH did for me when I came out of Egypt.' This observance will be for you like a sign on your hand and a reminder on your forehead that the law of YHWH is to be on your lips. For YHWH brought you out of Egypt with his mighty hand. You must keep this ordinance at the appointed time year after year," Exodus / Shemot 3: 7-10.

During the Feast of Unleavened Bread we are commanded to eat matzah and not to eat leaven. Make sure you are ready for this feast day.

April 9

The idea of pure bread symbolizing Moshiach is magnified as we consider that the words Matzah and mitzvoth / commandments are synonymous. In fact, the Hebrew letters used to spell Matzah and mitzvoth are exactly the same. The Hebrew word "mem, tzahdee, vav, tav" can either be read matzoth – which is the plural of Matzah with no vowel points, or it can be read mitzvoth – the commandments, the Torah. We can see by the word that Matzah in the plural – the mitzvoth – is symbolic of the pure, unadulterated teaching, the unleavened teaching of Torah as given by YHWH. Messiah is the "word/Torah made flesh," therefore as the "bread of life," Y'shua is the Matzah of the Torah! Also consider that the Sages of Judaism teach that, "when a mitzvah comes your way, do not all it to ferment." Or in other words, when we have the opportunity to do tov / good then we should do so quickly.

Matzah is basically a combination of wheat and water that is baked within 18 minutes of mixing. The Rabbis teach us that after eighteen minutes a chemical change of fermentation begins to take place within this mix. "This leavening occurs naturally as yeast bacteria, found in the air, invades the dough, multiplies by the millions, and then feeds on the sugar molecules in flour. As the yeast microorganisms multiply by the billions, they release the carbon dioxide gas that sours the dough, causing it to rise and become airy and light," says the book "Living Beyond Time." A short time is all that it takes for flour water to chemically sour and change the pure mixture. It doesn't take a yeast packet to make bread rise; it actually takes time. Time is the element that causes bread to ferment. Think about it, when mother makes bread, she mixes the ingredients, shapes the dough, and then allows the bread time to rise.

This is just one reason why the Israelites were commanded to leave Egypt in a hurry. They were not to allow their bread time to rise! "And the people took their dough before it was chametz, their kneading bowls being bound up in their clothes upon their shoulders. And the children of Israel did according to the word of Moshe; and they asked of the Mitzrayim / Egypt jewels of silver, and jewels of gold, and garments: And YHWH gave the people favor in the sight of the Mitzrayim, so that they gave to them such things as they required. And they plundered the Mitzrim," Exodus 12: 34-36

The Israelites weren't to think about it or weigh the pros and cons. They were to seize the moment and get out quickly; even on the very day of their liberation. "And ye shall observe the feast of unleavened bread; for in this selfsame day have I brought your armies out of the land of Egypt: therefore shall ye observe this day in your generations by an ordinance forever," Shemot / Exodus 12:17. Do you obey when you are told by the Holy Spirit or do you wait? How can you be more expedient to the Ruach's leading?

April 10

By accepting Y'shua as Messiah, a person's spirit becomes one with YHWH and "mercy triumphs over justice," James 2:13. The flood gates of Heaven are open to us as we walk in His ways. When we obey we put His blessings into motion. When we disobey we actively stop his blessings from reaching us and release curses to have power upon us. "Don't you know that to whom you yield yourselves slaves to obey, his servant you become? Whether a slave of sin unto death or obedience to righteousness," Romans 6:16.

When Y'shua died, He paid the price for forgiveness of all sins past, present, and future. Our sins have been charged to Y'shua's account. "But Moshiach has now become a Cohen Hagadol of tov things to come, by a greater and more perfect Tent of Meeting, not made with hands, that is to say, not of this creation; Neither by the dahm / blood of goats and calves, but by His own dahm / blood He entered in once into the Kadosh HaKedoshim, having obtained eternal geulah for us," Hebrews / Ivrim 9:11-12.

Disobedience doesn't break our relationship with YHWH. Sin is powerful BUT the blood of Y'shua is much more potent. Just think about it, if we had to confess every time we sinned then no one would be saved. But by entering into covenant with Y'shua we are saved from destruction. The Torah reveals that sin abounds around every corner. Y'shua through His mercy cleanses us from all unrighteousness so that we can build our intimacy with the Father. We are nothing without YHWH's rachamim.

Blessed are the merciful for they shall receive mercy! We all need a little more mercy. We are to accept His rachamim and show his mercy to others. Don't demand instant compliance of others. Don't look down and judge people. YHWH doesn't do that and neither should we. Instead, understand that WE are the ONLY person that WE can change.

All we can do is love others. By loving the people in our life, we can show the mercy of YHWH and allow The Spirit to convict them.

TRUTH FOR TODAY

April 11

Consider what the blood or "dahm" of Y'shua does for mankind...

The blood pays for our sins so we don't perish. Matthew 26:28, "For this is My dahm of the Brit Chadasha that is shed for many for the remission of sins."

The blood bought us. Acts 20:28, "Take heed therefore to yourselves, and to all the flock, over which the Ruach HaKodesh has made you overseers, to feed the congregation of Israel in YHWH, which He has purchased with His own dahm."

The blood justifies us before a holy Elohim. Romans / Romiyah 5:9, "Much more then, being made tzadik by His dahm / blood, we shall be saved from wrath through Him."

The blood redeems us. Colossians 1:14, "In whom we have geulah through His dahm, even the forgiveness of sins"

The blood brought us all into a relationship with YHWH that we didn't have before. Ephesians 2:11-16, "Therefore remember, that you being in times past gentiles in the flesh, who are called The Uncircumcision by those called the Brit-Milah in the flesh made by hands; that at that time you were without Moshiach, being excluded, aliens from the Commonwealth of Israel, as strangers from the covenants of promise, having no hope, and without YHWH in the world / olam hazeh: But now in Moshiach Y'shua you who sometimes were far off are made near by the dahm of Moshiach. For He is our shalom, who has made both echad, and has broken down the middle wall of partition between us; Having abolished in His flesh the enmity, even the law of commandments contained in human dogma; for to make in Himself from the two one renewed man, so making shalom; And that He might reconcile both to YHWH in one body by the law of commandments contained in human dogma; for to make in Himself from the two one renewed man, so making shalom; And that He might reconcile both to YHWH in one body by the execution stake, having slain the enmity through it."

Have you thanked Y'shua for the blood of Messiah today?

April 12

The blood of Messiah did so much for us that we can't discuss its power in just one day. Indeed, this entire book is about the blood of Messiah. Consider these thoughts today...

The blood brought us all (regardless of race or nationality) into a right relationship with YHWH. Revelation 5:9, "And they sang a renewed shir, saying, You are worthy to take the scroll, and to open its seals: for You were slain, and have redeemed us to YHWH by Your dahm out of every kindred and tongue and people and nation."

The blood brought peace. Colossians 1:20, "And, having made shalom through the dahm / blood of His execution stake, through Him to restore all things to Himself; whether they be things on earth, or things in the shamayim / heavens."

The blood purges our consciences from dead works. Hebrews 9:14, "How much more shall the dahm of Moshiach, who through the eternal Ruach offered Himself without blemish to YHWH, purify your conscience from dead works to serve the living YHWH ?"

The blood forges an everlasting covenant between the believer and YHWH. Hebrews 13:20, "Now the YHWH of shalom, that brought again from the dead our Master Y'shua, that Great Roei of the sheep, through the dahm / blood of the everlasting brit."

The blood sanctifies us. Hebrews 10:29, "Of how much worse punishment, do you think, he shall deserve, who has trampled underfoot the Son of YHWH, and has counted the dahm / blood of the brit / covenant, by which he was made kadosh as a common thing, and has insulted the Ruach of favor?"

The blood cleanses us from all sin. 1 John 1:7, "But if we walk in the Light as He is in the Light, we have chavurah / fellowship with one another, and the dahm / blood of Y'shua ha Moshiach His Son cleanses us from all sin."

The blood washes away our sins. Revelation 1:5, "And from Y'shua ha Moshiach, who is the Faithful Witness, and the Bachor / firstborn from the dead, and the Sar / prince of the melechim of the olam. Unto Him that loved us, and washed us from our sins in His own dahm"

The blood causes us to overcome this old wicked world. Revelation 12:11, "And they overcame him by the dahm of the Lamb, and by the word of their testimony; and they loved not their lives even to the death."

TRUTH FOR TODAY

April 13

Remember that Messiah's work ripped the Temple veil from top to bottom. The Temple of stone was no longer the main attraction as YHWH's Spirit now resides in the temple of each and every believer. The Ruach HaKodesh is not just resting "on" people as the Spirit did in the Old Testament because the Spirit is "in" people today. May we pray as Paul did in Ephesians 1:18, "I pray that the eyes of your heart may be enlightened in order that you may know the hope to which he has called you, the riches of his glorious inheritance in his holy people." Notice that verse is a prayer that the eyes of our hearts would be opened so that we could see the "glorious inheritance IN" us today.

The Messiah changed the way we relate to YHWH because Y'shua changed our hearts. If Y'shua didn't change our relationship with YHWH then we might as well get rid of the New Testament and only follow the Old Testament. Jude 1:8 says that we are "contend for the most holy faith that was delivered to the saints once for all time." We are to "ask about the ancient paths" and return to the original plan for man. This faith that was delivered once for all time was not given to Elijah or Moses. It was given to Adam and Eve. The original first couple walked with YHWH and heard His voice. They were given the right to eat from the tree of life. The restoration of all things is not back to Moses but to Adam and Eve and the fellowship of daily walking with YHWH.

Because Y'shua changed the way we relate to YHWH, because Y'shua changed our hearts, there are actually some things in the Bible that do not apply to us today. We slap YHWH in the face when we repeat certain scripture verses that were written from a relationship based on the hope of a new heart. We don't just have the hope for a new heart. We have a new heart with YHWH's word written upon it. Some things have changed! The relationship David dreamed of and the anointing Elijah emanated is now available to us today through Y'shua.

Because we think our heart is still evil or sinful then we agree with certain things in the Older Testament. Jeremiah 17:9 does state that the "heart is evil" and that's true before you are saved. When you are born again, your heart is changed and made good! But we forget this when we pray like David did in Psalm 51:10 "create in me a clean heart." Repeating that prayer isn't necessary. We already have a clean heart. Our hearts are now good. When we quote the Scriptures by saying "no man knows the heart" we are thinking from a pre-Messiah viewpoint. Such thinking tends to result in frustration and guilt. Again, we have been taught for so long that our hearts are evil and the Biblical faith is about denying our hearts, asking forgiveness, and waiting on heaven that it's hard to accept the truth about the new heart we have been given.

April 14

Many people continue in sin or excuse their sin because they reason that they are inherently sinful. This is like a person who is supposed to be on a diet but overeats during the day because of one small slip up. The thought is, "well I might as well give in to this sin and temptation since by heart is already evil and I'm already sinful." This is a scary mindset but it is found throughout much of the faith. We need to guard against such thinking.

When you were born again you were united with Y'shua and you are now the temple of YHWH. Like the Temple in Biblical times you have an outer court / body, and you have an inner court / mind, and you have a holy of holies / heart. All things have been made new in your spirit and you are a new creation in the spiritual realm. You have been blessed with every spiritual blessing in heavenly places. Because of the transformation in your spirit you now have victory over sin. Greater is he that is in you than he that is in the world.

The Greatest Commandment in the entire Bible is to hear YHWH and love Him with our "whole heart" as found in Deuteronomy 6:5. By understanding your heart is HIS heart; this verse takes a whole new meaning. To love YHWH with "all your heart" is to recognize what He has done in you and to release His heart in your life. To love YHWH with all YOUR heart is to love him with all of HIS heart because His heart is in you. First, we are to love Him and think on His power in us and then we are to obey His word. Every act of spirituality we show should flow from His heart.

Think on this short message today. What does it really mean to you to "love YHWH with all your heart?" How can you love Him more today?

April 15

It's easy to make the mistake and assume that everyone has to obey the Torah exactly as you do. This is probably one of the biggest error of our faith. The Torah is a liberal document of freedom that allows many various interpretations. We are accustomed to the tight knit theologies that tell us exactly what to believe and why. The Torah, on the other hand, allows people to come to various conclusions on their path of faith. This is the primary lesson we must learn in order to avoid other Torah mistakes.

Everything in the Torah and in life must be taken in perspective. Imagine you and a friend are at the coast of South Carolina. You are walking on a pier and your friend is snorkeling in the nearby ocean. You would both be viewing the ocean but the experiences would be very different. What you see and what your sees are different but similar. You may see waves and water and clouds. Your friends probably views fish, seaweed, and coral. You are both correct and you each have a unique perspective. The Biblical / Hebraic mind allows for people to see things differently.

Philippians 2:5, "Let this mind be in you, which was also in Messiah Y'shua"

Take for example the subject of keeping Shabbat. We are commanded in Exodus 20 to "Remember the Sabbath day and keep it set apart." How do you do this? What rituals or traditions does your family have? The Jewish rabbis have told us that the commandment is two-fold. First we are to" remember" the day with a service at the start of Shabbat and then we are to "keep" the day throughout and into the evening of Saturday. If someone keeps Shabbat different than you do, does that make them wrong?

James 2:14-17, "What good is it, my brothers, if a man claims to have faith but has no deeds? Can such faith save him? Suppose a brother or sister is without clothes and daily food. If one of you says to him, "Go, I wish you well; keep warm and well fed," but does nothing about his physical needs, what good is it? In the same way, faith by itself, if it is not accompanied by action, is dead."

What does this teaching mean to you?

April 16

It is interesting that in Luke 18:31 Y'shua said, "Everything must be fulfilled." Everything written about the Messiah and about the future must come to pass according to the words of the Bible.

Some people wrongfully assume that the Torah, or the writings of Moses, are obsolete, but did you know that the Torah, the law of Moses, is quoted over 245 times directly in the Newer Testament? Paul, who many people say, "Oh, well he taught against the law," quoted Torah 110 times himself. In fact, there are over 695 direct quotes from the Tanakh that are in the Newer Testament, the renewed covenant. Each and every book of the Tanakh can be found in the Newer Testament. We can even find the exact words of 1 Peter 2:9 in the Torah.

In Exodus 19, we see that the nation of Israel has been delivered with a strong and mighty hand from bondage of Pharaoh. They are at the mountain, they are preparing to receive instructions from YHWH, and they are told to approach the mountain with reverence and worship, and in Exodus 19:5-6 it says, "Now then, if you will indeed obey My voice and keep My covenant, then you shall be My own possession among the peoples, for all the Earth is mine. You shall be to me a kingdom of priests and a holy nation. These are the words that you shall speak to the sons of Israel." These same words, "a kingdom of priests, a set apart people, a holy nation" are repeated in 1 Peter.

The question is, who is YHWH speaking to? What nation is He speaking to? Israel, is He not? Not just the Jews, but He is speaking to the nation of Israel because there is a distinction between a Jewish person and an Israelite. We'll talk about that in a few minutes, but this was the mission and motto for the nation of Israel thousands of years ago, and this is our motto today. The words are repeated. The same words that were spoken to Israel apply to us because we are Israel. Everything written in the Torah must come to pass and as Israel we are destined to be a part of YHWH's work during these end times.

TRUTH FOR TODAY

April 17

"But you are not to be called 'Rabbi,' for you have only one Master and you are all brothers. And do not call anyone on earth 'father,' for you have one Father, and he is in heaven. Nor are you to be called 'teacher,' for you have one teacher, the Moshiach," Matthew 23:8-10. Y'shua was not banning people from being called 'dad,' or 'rabbi' here! The terms "rabbi" and "father" are perfectly acceptable for a believer to use in designation of relationship and authority. Y'shua was saying that the rabbi-talmid system culminated with Himself.

No longer were the disciples to make other disciples in their own names. The disciples were to proclaim the name and the teachings of Y'shua above their own. They were not to look to other Rabbis as the final source because Y'shua is our Rebbe! "You have one teacher, the Moshiach," He said. We are not to make talmidim of ourselves but talmidim of Y'shua. His halakha, or way to walk out the Torah, is what we are to proclaim - not our own personal interpretations in our own name. (Rabbi Sha'ul supported this when he talked about some believers being of Paul or Apollos in said in 1 Corinthians 1:12.)

"Provide yourself with a Teacher (of the Torah) and get yourself a companion, and judge all men in the scale of merit," says the Pirkei Avot 1:6. Today, believers are to submit to and ordain a leader to speak the Word into their lives. This leader should be submitted to in all areas and followed as the leader follows Messiah. "Remember those who led you, who spoke the word of YHWH to you; and considering the result of their conduct, imitate their faith," Hebrews / Ivrim 13:7. You shouldn't consider yourself a student of Rabbi Daniel or Rabbi Johnny-Come-Lately. As a follower of Y'shua, you are a talmid of Y'shua submitted to a local leader. The local leader provides accountability, teaching, fellowship, encouragement, and training.

Are you working with or against the leadership of your local assembly?

April 18

Thousands of years ago YHWH gave man specific instructions and directions called Torah. Sin is when we disobey Torah. First John 3:4, "Everyone who sins breaks the Torah." In fact sin is Torhalessness. When we break that sin the Bible says in Romans 3:23, "The wages of sin is death." We deserve to die. Yet teshuvah / true repentance is the bridge that YHWH has provided us to Him. Through the blood of the sacrifice of our Master Y'shua we can have forgiveness of sins totally and fully. Any sins we committed yesterday, today, or tomorrow are totally forgiven by His blood if we receive it.

The Bible says that "you are saved by grace through faith not of yourself that any man should boast. It is the gift of YHWH." But notice that it is by grace through faith; it's not just by grace that we are saved. If it was just by grace then everybody in the world would be saved.

But it says you're saved by grace through faith. You've got to have faith. You've got to do teshuvah / repentance to reach out and claim it and reach out and say, "Father, I'm sorry. Forgive me. Cleanse me with the blood of Y'shua." You must do teshuvah and turn from those sins. In Lamentations, chapter 5, verse 21, it says, "Turn to me / teshuvah, oh YHWH." Teshuvah is like restoring the relationship in the Garden of Eden.

YHWH is looking at the sincerity of the heart. In James chapter 4, verse 7 it says, "Submit to YHWH, resist ha'satan and He will flee from you." Too many times we forget that. Teshuvah submits to YHWH and then turns away from the enemy. What do you need to turn from today? How can you do teshuvah, submit to YHWH and turn from the enemy?

April 19

In 2008, the famed Time Magazine ran a cover story that listed the Top Ten Ideas that are changing the world. For the category of Religion, the magazine's editors chose the "Re-Judaizing of Y'shua" as the most life changing spiritual movement on the face of the earth. The article spoke of the Hebrew Roots movement as a growing force of Christians that forsake common Christian practices in search of the Bible based faith that is rooted in the Hebrew lifestyle and scriptures. Thus, we are called the "Jewish Roots" movement or the "Hebrew Roots" movement. These terms fit nicely. As we learn the customs, language, and lifestyle of the Biblical times we can more truthfully know our Messiah. Our movement is in search of the Hebrew Roots – a worship experience in spirit and in truth.

The word "root" has special meaning. A root is a deep foundation of a plant. Roots are hidden down below the surface are often hard to discover. Roots must be dug out and this takes effort. Our Hebrew roots are the same. We must look past the surface of the accepted ways of Christian and Jewish worship and dig into our Bibles to really get to the root of the issues. As we go deeper into the Scriptures we do indeed find that we are part of the Olive tree of Israel. This doesn't mean that we are Jewish! Remember that Israel is comprised of twelve tribes. The identity of the two tribes of Judah and Levi is known today as the Jewish people. This leaves 10 tribes that remain to be discovered and recovered. That's us! We can understand this clearly in Romans 11. The hidden root is an Israeli olive tree. This olive tree has vast importance and we must learn all about it! Understand this – if you are born again – if you have accepted the Messiah as your master and savior, then you are NOT just a New Testament Christian. You are not just a Baptist or Methodist or Pentecostal. No! All who call upon the Savior in true repentance and faith ARE ISRAELITES! Your identity is so important.

It is in Jeremiah 11:16, that YHWH identifies the Olive Tree as the symbol of Israel. "YHWH called your name Green Olive Tree, lovely and of good fruit."

Hosea prophesies that in the end-time Israel shall once again be restored and its "branches shall spread; his beauty shall be like an olive tree," Hosea 14:6.

Paul also in the new covenant uses this same analogy for Israel in Romans 11:16-21. Paul is explaining that because of their sin the ENTIRE nation of Israel were separated from YHWH. By faith we can ALL be grafted back into the common wealth of Israel. Praise YHWH today for His plan for your life!

April 20

The Ancient Hebrew word "Sheol" literally means the "underworld of the dead." The term speaks of an abode, thought to be deep within the earth (Psalms 88:6, Amos 9:2). Strong's Exhaustive Dictionary calls it a "subterranean retreat, grave, hell, or pit."

Korah rebelled and was swallowed alive by sheol / hell. The same is true for those who rebel against the Almighty's Law today. Romans 6:23 states that the "wages of sin is death." Spiritual death is separation from the Creator, which comes as a result of a lifestyle of sin.

The New Testament calls "hell" a place of "weeping and gnashing of teeth" where the "worm does not die, and the fire is not quenched." In the Bible, the word most often translated as "Hell" is derived from the Greek word "gehenna" or the "valley of Hinnom." The Messiah often referenced "gehenna" as He spoke about the eventual punishment for the wicked. His listeners understood exactly what and where He was referencing. The valley of Hennah was the trash dump for the nation of Israel. In Gehenna there was constant burning of waste, dead bodies, and trash until the items were totally consumed. Gehenna is a picturesque term used to describe the harshest of conditions for those who do not accept the gift of eternal life. Perhaps the only thing worse than eternal burning is being totally annihilated like burnt trash?

The Bible teaches that only those people who are "born again" will inherit eternal "life." All others will experience eternal "death" and cease to exist. This is worse than eternal burning! There will come a time when the lost souls will be annihilated. This is called the "Second Death" and is referenced throughout the book of Revelation.

Ezekiel 18:20 enforces this idea, "The soul who sins is the one who will die." In Matthew 10:28 the Messiah said, "Do not be afraid of those who kill the body but cannot kill the soul. Rather, be afraid of the One who can destroy both soul and body in hell." Finally, in John 3:16 the Greek word used for "perish" illustrates this point clearly. The verse says, "For YHWH so loved the world that whosoever would believe in Him would not perish but have everlasting life." This Greek word translated "perish" literally means "to destroy, put out of the way entirely, abolish, put an end, to kill." The idea of eternal punishment is not supported by the most popular Evangelistic verse! Those who do not accept the Messiah will face a time of torment in Hell/Sheol/Gehenna and will then be utterly destroyed along with Hell itself.

April 21

"Grace" is unmerited or undeserved favor. Though "grace" is often the subject of Sunday sermons, the term is usually misunderstood and misrepresented. Psalm 89:2 states that the world was formed upon the foundation of grace. The Hebrew word used in this verse and throughout the Old Testament for "grace" or "mercy" is "chesed." This term appears over 240 times in the Old Testament to explain how the Creator relates to His creation. Grace is not a New Testament idea! Somehow, it has become a mainstream Christian belief that God has changed to now accept people through grace when they were once accepted by obedience to the Law of Moses. The Elohim of grace has been incorrectly portrayed as dealing with people differently at different times. This demonic idea insinuates that what was wrong to do during the "dispensation of the law" is no longer a sin because Christians are now "under grace." The doctrine of "dispensationalism" was made popular by the Scofield Reference Bible and is now ingrained in the mind of most church leaders. The word "dispensation" appears only four times in the KJV and never to infer that there are different periods of YHWH's temperament. The Zondervan Pictorial Bible Dictionary says, "The modern theological use of the term is not in Scripture." There is no such thing as an "age of grace" or the "dispensation of grace."

Noah, Abraham, Moses and others all found "chesed" or "grace" in the eyes of YHWH. Their belief was accredited to them as righteousness. From creation, salvation has always been "by grace through faith," Ephesians 4:23. Those who put their trust in the Mighty One of Israel during Old Testament times were granted eternal life through chesed. The Law of Moses was not given as an instrument of salvation. Obedience to the Biblical commands cannot redeem anyone. The Law of Moses was given by the Almighty to explain how a person should relate to Him and other people. The Law defines sin and sets a standard for righteous behavior. According to Romans 3:23, a person who sins is under the death penalty of sin until the gift of amazing grace is accepted. This means that the entire world is "under the law" until they accept the Creator's chesed and are then placed "under grace." A person is saved by grace through faith in the shed blood of Messiah and then should live a life of obedience to the Law. "Sin shall not have dominion over you because you are not under law but under grace. What then? Shall we sin because we are not under law but under grace? Heaven forbid!" - Romans 6:14-15.

Grace doesn't replace the Law. The Law doesn't replace grace. The two work together to transform lives. Who can you share this truth with today?

April 22

The word "Shavuot" literally means "weeks." This is the festival of Pentecost which marks the completion of the seven weeks between Pesach and Shavuot, which are called the Sefirah Ha'Omer. Sefirah Ha'Omer means the "Period of Counting the Omer." During these fifty days the Israelites were and are to count a measure of grain each day in anticipation of the full fiftieth day, the full harvest of Shavuot.

The counting reminds us of the important connection between Pesach and Shavuot. Passover freed Israel physically from bondage, while the giving of the Torah on Shavuot redeemed Israel spiritually from the bondage of sin, idolatry, and immorality.

"And you shall count for yourselves from the morrow of the Shabbat, from the day that you bring the omer [offering] that is raised, seven complete weeks there shall be until the morrow of the seventh week you shall count fifty days," Vayikra / Leviticus 23:15, 16.

If you don't count the omer then you really don't know when to celebrate Shavuot, so you should make this a part of your days during this time.

Make it a practice to count the Omer as you count up to Shavuot/Pentecost. The Omer is counted every evening after nightfall (approx. 30 minutes after sunset), which is the start of the 'day.' Before counting, stand and say the following blessing:

Baruch ata YHWH, Eloheinu melech ha-olam, asher kid'shanu be'mitzvo'sav ve-tzivanu al sefiras ha'omer.

Blessed are You, YHWH our Elohim, King of the Universe, Who made us holy with His commandments, and commanded us on the counting of the Omer.

TRUTH FOR TODAY

April 23

Like the microscopic world of germs, there is an unseen world of the supernatural. Just because you can't feel it or see it, doesn't mean that it doesn't exist. The sickness of sin has been vaccinated and healed. In the spiritual realm, YHWH's chesed / grace has wiped out the plague of sin and death. Now, we must choose to walk in our spiritual healing. "This I say therefore, and testify in YHWH, that from now on you conduct your halacha / walk not as other gentiles walk, in the vanity of their mind, Having their understanding darkened, being alienated from the life of Y'shua through the ignorance that is in them, because of the blindness of their lev / heart: Who being past feeling have given themselves over to indecency, to perform all uncleanness with greediness. But you have not learned your life in Moshiach that way;" Ephesians 4:17-20.

To accomplish such a mighty task, one should cling to YHWH and His word. Study and meditate on the scriptures. Fast and pray. Believe that there is a world beyond what you can see, smell, touch, taste, or hear. And believe that in that spiritual realm, all of your needs are met in Y'shua our Messiah. In closing, when a person is born again, their spirit is transformed into a new creation. But, their mind and body are the same. If you were skinny before you accepted Y'shua, you were skinny right after you accepted Him. The old man that has died left behind a body! This body must come under control and subjection of the spirit of Y'shua.

The mind too must be renewed to Biblical pattern of thinking. Until the mind, or soul, is transformed an individual will continue to doubt, fear, lust, and sin. Romans 12:1 & 2 clarifies that there is a two step process to true holiness. "I beg you therefore, Israelite brothers, by the rachamim / mercies of YHWH, that you present your bodies a living sacrifice, set apart, acceptable to YHWH, which is your act of reasonable worship. And be not conformed to this world: but be transformed by the ongoing renewing of your mind, that you may discern what is that good, acceptable, and even the perfect, will of YHWH," Romiyah / Romans 12: 1 & 2.

The body must be presented to YHWH upon the altar and the mind must be renewed to YHWH's thought process. It is only when we fully offer ourselves to him and walk in emunah that we experience the true healing from sin and death. HIV is bad. Sin is worse. But, by chesed through faith in Y'shua we can have healing and deliverance.

TRUTH FOR TODAY

April 24

In Genesis chapters 6 through 11 we read a series of events that have shape the history of the world. First, Noach is commanded to build an ark to save humanity and the animal kingdom. Noach obeys the voice of the Almighty and brings glory to the name of YHWH through is obedience. Then Genesis tells the account of the evil Nimrod and the building of the tower of Babel. The people of the world construct their tower to build a name to themselves.

The similarities in these stories are amazing. Noach acts in righteousness and builds a saving ark to honor the name of YHWH. Nimrod and the nations act in unrighteousness and build an upward city to establish their dominance in the world. The same Hebrew word is used in both verses for "built." This is the Hebrew phrase "banah." From this information we can learn many spiritual truths.

From these stories we can learn the spiritual principle of building. This states that you dwell in the house that you build. You live in the life that you have created. Your life will be made of the walls of thought that you construct. First, we must first consider that our actions and thoughts either bring glory and honor to YHWH or shame Him. We can do good things and build kingdoms but that doesn't mean that we are working for the glory of YHWH. Similar building materials were used for both the ark and the tower but the motives were quite different.

From these stories we can also learn the spiritual principle of building. This idea states that "you live in whatever house you build." This is similar to the idea that "if you made your bed then you have to lay in it." What you think upon equals what you become. The actions you take develop the life you create. If you want your life to be different then you must be different. If you dream of being a teacher, trooper, or tinker then it's time to get busy! If you are happy with the status quo then keep doing what you are doing. If nothing changes then nothing changes. But if you change THEN everything changes!

Don't allow the simplicity of this message to sway your thinking. We all have complaints about our situations, our spouses, and our siblings. Instead of dwelling on the problem – change that negative energy into positive thoughts and then BE the change you want to see in this world. Agree with Y'shua and say, "not my will but thy will be done." Let go of the situation that demands your attention and stop trying to fix your problems. Trust YHWH to use you for His glory. "For I am confident of this very thing, that He who began a good work in you will perfect it until the day of Messiah Y'shua," Philippians 1:5-7.

Get a vision for your life and then take the necessary actions to accomplish your heart's desire. Today is the first day of your new life. Build your own house and then dwell in it for the glory of YHWH's name. What you face today, be it good or bad, will soon pass. All that will remain will be what was done by the Spirit of YHWH.

April 25

A pig is unclean for many reasons including the fact that it will eat anything, yet the animal lacks the proper digestive system to release poison from its body. Thus, the swine's sickness can be easily transferred to the person who eats the animal. Worms, called enzymes, also live inside the blood stream of swine and can be easily passed to humans. Such is also the case for shrimp, lobsters, vultures, and other scavengers. It is true that swine produce very little sweat from their skin. The inability to perspire keeps waste stored inside their body. The Center for Disease Control states that H1N1 cannot be caught from eating swine. Yet, there are no less than seventy different types of diseases including trichinosis that can be caused by eating pork.

The scriptures call many unclean animals "abominations" whose carcasses that should not even be touched. Mainstream Christianity teaches that the dietary laws of the Old Testament have been superseded by the New Testament. One misunderstood passage about this subject is Acts 10:9-19. In these verses Peter is said to have been extremely hungry. He is also confused about the acceptance of the Gentile believers. He then has a vision about various four-footed creatures. Peter is told to slaughter and eat as all are now made clean. When the vision concludes, Peter doesn't eat barbeque pork. Instead, he understands that the vision is not about unclean foods but unclean people. He proclaims, in Acts 10:28, "You know how that it is an unlawful thing for a man that is a Jew to keep company, or come unto one of another nation; but YHWH has showed me that I should not call any man common or unclean."

Another verse of confusion is found in the New International Version of Mark 7:19, "For it doesn't go into his heart but into his stomach, and then out of his body." (In saying this, Y'shua declared all foods "clean.") Here, the Savior is speaking about the tradition of religious hand washing. The words in parenthesis are found in most modern translations but not in the King James Version Bible. Nor are the parenthetical words found in the oldest manuscripts of the New Testament. This commentary was added by Bible translators in an attempt to free people from the dietary laws of Leviticus 11 and Deuteronomy 14. Regardless of such confusion, the precepts of the Bible are eternal.

Do you keep the clean and unclean laws found in the Scriptures?

April 26

The Bible speaks of the rise of a leader who will unite the world in an effort to establish peace and financial stability. This man will have a charismatic ability to powerfully influence people. The scriptures give him several names like "son of perdition" or the "man of lawlessness." Like the plot of a Stephen King thriller, the Bible lays out end time events which center upon the evil Antichrist.

His coming will climax a strong delusion of error. "For this reason YHWH sends them a powerful delusion so that they will believe the lie and so that all will be condemned who have not believed the truth but have delighted in wickedness," 2 Thessalonians 2:11-12. The man of sin will speak great things as he conquers the world through peace. Many will accept him as the Christ, the Messiah, sent from heaven to rescue the world from pain. His words and deeds will promise hope as he establishes himself as "anti" or "in the place of" the true Messiah.

Daniel 8:23-25, "In the end time, when evil men are at their worst state, a ruler with a fearsome face and who is able to understand mysterious sayings, shall rise up. And he will have very great power, but his power is not from himself: and he shall destroy terribly, and shall be successful, and accomplish, and shall destroy the mighty and the holy people. And through his policy also he shall spread deceit; and he shall exalt himself in his own heart, and in the name of peace he shall destroy many. He shall also stand up against Messiah; but he shall be destroyed by Him and not by human hands."

The phrase "antichrist" is only found in two chapters of the entire Scriptures. Here, Bible writers emphatically declare his presence. "The spirit of antichrist, of which you have heard is coming, is now already in the world." 1 John 4:3. Who is this man of sin? Some have suggested that he is Prince Charles of Wales, President Barack Obama, or even the Catholic Pope. His identity will be made known only to those living in truth. All others will believe his lies. Those whose names are written in the Lamb's book of Life will not fall prey to the deception.

Prepare now for the rise of the antichrist by living a faith of truth. Compare your beliefs to the whole of scripture and question tradition. Don't believe the strong delusions of humanism or religion. As you follow the truth you will know exactly who the man of sin is while the rest of the world follows after the beast of Revelation. In Luke 21:8 the Savior said, "Watch out that you are not deceived. For many will come in my name, claiming, 'I am he,' and, 'The time is near.' Do not follow them."

April 27

For thousands of years, the "w" shaped symbol of parted fingers has been used by the genealogical descendants of Jewish priests called "Kohanim" and other spiritual leaders in the synagogue. The Star Trek "Vulcan" gesture is a picture of the windows of heaven and the Hebrew letter "shin." It is raised high as a special blessing from Numbers 6 is proclaimed. The phrase "live long and prosper" could be considered a paraphrase of this special prayer. "May YHWH bless you, and keep you; May YHWH make His face shine on you, and be gracious to you; May YHWH lift up His countenance on you, and give you peace," Numbers 6:24-26.

For Christianity and Judaism this is the final benediction of many worship services. It is a prayer of mercy, protection, substance, and peace. This blessing calls for the Creator's favor and holy name to be upon all who follow the Scriptures. It is not some magical practice on the part of the priests, as they have no power over the divine. The text makes it very clear that while the priests may pronounce the words, it is the Almighty who does the actual blessing.

The Jewish people have a rich faith that is full of symbolism and Spiritual power. Such traditions have great meaning that can be lost if one is totally closed to the Hebrew roots of Christianity. "What advantage then has the Jew? Much in every way; chiefly as they were entrusted with the very oracles of YHWH," Romans 3:1-2. Judaism isn't all bad. Judaism isn't all good either. One must earnestly search for the true path of faith that hangs between the balance of our ancestor's practices and the Almighty's divine will.

The Almighty chose the Jewish people to preserve the Scriptures from error. Many of the traditions that surround their devotion, like the Vulcan hand symbol, bring added significance to life. Such traditions can be adopted by Bible believers if they are void of pagan origin, not prohibited in the Scripture, and if the action does not grieve the Holy Spirit. The Bible never bans tradition but it does speak against actions that make void the word of YHWH. There are many customs of Judaism and Christianity that are beneficial for the Believer. Which do you follow? Which should you follow?

April 28

The Messiah taught that true spiritual conversion begins with a proper use of the Law of Moses to point out the errors of sin. The wages of sin is death unless people repent of their law-breaking sins, trust the Almighty for forgiveness, and turn from their wicked ways. The Law of Moses, or Torah, is the instruction book for mankind that is found in the first five books of the Bible. These pages describe the righteous straight and narrow path a person should walk once they accept the Savior. The Torah also acts as a mirror to reflect mankind's sinfulness as compared to YHWH's high standards. The Torah defines sin but it itself is not sinful. A single violation of just one of the Old Testament commandments rendered a person sinful and deserving of eternal death. This strict death penalty was placed upon the Savior when he died at Golgotha. Those that confess their sins, change their behaviors, and submit to the Bible are born again through the Holy Spirit. Luke 24:46-47 states, "It is written, and thus it was necessary for the Christ to suffer and to rise from the dead the third day, and that repentance and remission of sins should be preached in His name to all nations, beginning at Jerusalem."

A person who has accepted the true gospel will bear the spiritual fruits of love, joy, peace, patience, kindness, goodness, faithfulness, gentleness, and self-control. A lack of this good spiritual fruit is a telltale sign that a person has accepted a false gospel and is perhaps a false convert. "Examine yourselves to see whether you are in the faith; test yourselves. Do you not realize that Christ Y'shua is in you—unless, of course, you fail the test?" 2 Corinthians 13:5. The full gospel of Y'shua is a message of repentance that produces real change. Do you share the truth of the Messiah Y'shua with others?

TRUTH FOR TODAY

April 29

Shavuot or Shavuoth is a special holy day of YHWH that occurs at this time. This holy day is the second of the three major festivals during which males in The Land of Yisra'el are to come to Yerushalyim / Jerusalem. Passover is the first and Sukkot is the third of the pilgrimage feasts. Shavuot comes exactly fifty days after Passover. Hence it being known as "Pentecost" by many. Pentecost means "fifty" in the Greek language.

Shavuot is both a historical and an agricultural day. Agriculturally, it commemorates the time when the first fruits were harvested and brought to the Temple, and is known as Hag Ha-Bikkurim the "feast of first fruits. Historically, this day celebrates the giving of the Torah on Mount Sinai. Shavuot honors the shift from spring to summer and the reaping of the first wheat harvest. Sometime during the Second Temple, Shavuot was formally declared as the anniversary of the giving of the Torah. Up to this point it was predominately kept as just an agricultural day.

On this day, YHWH gave the Torah to the Hebrew people on Mount Sinai over 3,300 years ago. It is on this day that believers should renew our acceptance of YHWH's word and commitment to His ways.

Shavuot has many names. It is also known as "Hag Matan Torateinu," meaning the Feast of the Giving of the Torah. Some call it "Chag Shavuot" which means the feast of weeks.

This day is also considered "Chag HaBikkurim" or day of first fruits and "Atzeret" – the day of "Being held back or close to YHWH."

Shavuot also means "oaths", with the giving of the Torah, the Hebrews and Elohim exchanged oaths, forming an everlasting covenant, not to forsake one another as a type of wedding vow.

Finally, this day is also called "Chag HaKatzit" – the day of the cutting of the crop. This name refers to the wheat harvest, which is the last of the crops to be reaped. This reaping took place at this time. There is also reference in the book of Ruth, which places the time of the events described in that book as occurring at Shavuot. Ruth says the events of the book happened "at the beginning of the cutting of the barley crop."

You can learn a lot about this holy day by studying and knowing the names of Shavuot. Are you getting ready for Shavuot?

April 30

One can search the entire Bible, from Genesis to Revelation, and not find a single verse proving the first day of the week as the prescribed day of worship.

In the beginning, with the Creation account, the seventh day of the week was made holy as a day of rest and worship. The importance of a specific day for worship is repeated with the giving of the Ten Commandments. “Remember the Sabbath day, to keep it holy. Six days shalt thou labor, and do all thy work: But the seventh day is the Sabbath,” says Exodus 20:8.

Now, compare this verse to a calendar. What day is the first day of the week? Sunday. What day is the seventh day? Saturday. Any questions? The point is pretty simple. The seventh day of the week is the Biblical Sabbath. The latest edition of Webster’s Unabridged Dictionary defines the ‘seventh day’ as “Saturday, the seventh day of the week.” So, how did the church get the days of the week mixed up? Is there a calendar crisis?

First, the Sabbath wasn’t changed in the New Testament. Messiah Himself, kept the seventh day Sabbath, “And he came to Nazareth, where he had been brought up: and, as his custom was, he went into the synagogue on the Sabbath day, and stood up for to read,” Luke 4:16. Even the Apostle Paul and the first believers in the book if Acts kept Saturday as holy, “And he [Paul] reasoned in the synagogue every Sabbath, and persuaded the Jews and the Greeks,” Acts 18:4. Notice that Jews and Greeks were worshipping together. Saturday isn’t the “Jewish” Sabbath, but the Biblical one. Seventh day Sabbath observance is intended for all believers. History shows that the day of worship wasn’t changed by the Creator, but by man.

From creation, the Seventh day of rest has been Saturday. Humanity has not lost track of time or confused which day is which. Man can’t pick his own personal seventh day. Nor did the Resurrection swap the days of worship. The Savior gave many sermons, but He never told us to change the Sabbath to Sunday. The church, be it Catholic or Christian, has no authority to add to or alter the Scriptures. The truth is that nowhere in the Bible is the day of worship changed from Saturday to Sunday.   How can you share this truth with someone today?

May

Truth For Today

May 1

Every May is the special celebration of Mother's Day for the women in our lives. The Bible has much to say about women and their place in the family. Proverbs 18:22, "He who finds a wife finds a good thing and obtains favor from YHWH."

Writing in the 14th century, Rabbi Israel al-Nakawa said: "If a man is fortunate enough to have found a good wife, he will never miss anything. Though he may be poor, he should consider himself rich. A good wife is one who manages her husband's affairs correctly, helps him to the best of her ability, gives him her honest advice, and does not urge him to spend more than is necessary. She intelligently supervises the needs of the home, and the education of their children; she does not act snobbish toward her husband's family even if she happens to come from a more refined environment. Marriage is not a one-sided affair. The man has obligations as well as the woman... A man should sacrifice his personal needs in order to provide more abundantly for his wife and children. Above all, he should treat his wife with love and sympathy, for she is part of him. He must never abuse her."

Indeed, an ancient Jewish proverb teaches that "YHWH could not be everywhere, so he created mothers." Many Mother's Day sermons are based on the Proverbs 31 "woman of valor." In Judaism, In Judaism, this section of scripture is not reviewed yearly BUT weekly. Each week during the traditional welcoming the Shabbat, the husband places his hands upon his wife and sings this portion. In fact, this blessing is given BEFORE the family even sits down to partake of the special Shabbat meal. In the Scriptures and in Judaism, these verses are known collectively as "Eshet Chayil" or in English "Woman of Valor." The woman described here is the spiritual manifestation of the perfect wife – the ideal bride. When we study the Proverbs 31 model woman we are also studying how the Bride of Messiah should act and become.

The word "Eshet" is Hebrew for wife or woman. The word "ima" is word for mother. The word "Chayil" has various connotations throughout the Bible. It means "an organized military, force, strength, valor, excellence, wealth, skills," In the Scriptures "Chayil" is translated as bravery (Psalm 76:6), capability (Proverbs 12:4), triumph (Psalm 118:15), and wealth (Proverbs 13:22.)

The month of May is a wonderful time to reflect on the gift of mothers and women. It's also a good time to study Proverbs 31 and begin reading this verse each time you welcome the Sabbath. If it wasn't for the women in our lives we wouldn't have life in the first place. Praise YHWH for your mother, sisters, daughters, or female friends.

TRUTH FOR TODAY

May 2

The Messiah said in John 4 that the Father seeks those who will "worship in Spirit and in Truth." For our worship to really be "in the Spirit" then it must be "in the truth."

Take some time today and tomorrow to study these special Hebrew words that deal with worship. Study these verses and these terms and ask the Holy Spirit to lead you into truth regarding worship according to the pattern of Heaven. Remember that it is best to let the Bible interpret the Bible.

Barak is a Hebrew word to "kneel or bow, to give reverence to YHWH as an act of adoration, implies a continual conscious giving place to YHWH, to be attuned to him and his presence." This verse is found in Psalm 34:1 when David wrote, "I will bless / barak YHWH at all times; His praise shall continually be in my mouth." In Psalm 95:6 this word for worship is explained as well, "Oh come, let us worship and bow down; Let us kneel before the YHWH our maker."

A second Hebrew word for worship is "guwl" which means to spin around, under the influence of any violent emotion. This word can be seen in a few verses:

Psalm 32:11, "Be glad in the YHWH and rejoice, you righteous; And shout for joy, all you upright in heart!"

Psalm 35:9, "And my soul shall be joyful in the YHWH; It shall rejoice in his salvation."

Psalm 118:24, "This is the day the YHWH has made; We will rejoice and be glad in it."

Another Hebrew word for worship is "hallal." This term means "to praise, to make a show or rave about, to glory in or boast upon, to be clamorously foolish about you adoration of YHWH." Psalm 22:23 says, "You who fear the YHWH, praise him! All you descendants of Jacob, glorify / hallal him, and fear him, all you offspring of Israel!" The term "hallal" is found in the word "halleluyah" which means "highest praise to YHWH." Psalm 44:8, "In YHWH we boast all day long, and praise your name forever."

Tomorrow you will learn of more Hebrew words for praise and worship. Today, use these phrases when you pray and seek YHWH. Read these verses and think on the greatness of our King.

May 3

Yesterday you read about worship in Spirit and in truth. The Hebrew terms barak, guwl, and hallal. These are ancient action terms that explain the Hebraic concept of worship. Another term to learn is "ranan" which actually means to "creak, to emit a stridulous sound, to shout aloud for joy." Worship isn't always to be silent! Psalm 7:17, "I will praise / ranan the YHWH according to his righteousness, and will sing praise to the name of the YHWH Most High." Psalm 33:1 and 98:4 also use this term

Shachah describes worship as homage or loyalty to YHWH. When you "shachah" you bow down or fall down flat. "Give unto the YHWH the glory due to his name; Worship the YHWH in the beauty of holiness," Psalm 29:2. The word "shachah" is clearly understood in Psalm 95:6, "Psalm 95:6 Oh come, let us worship and bow down; Let us kneel before the YHWH our maker.

Hebrew is an action language. In Hebrew the word for a sing or singer is "shir" or "shuwr." It is this special word that is used in Psalm 18:49, "therefore I will give thanks to you, O YHWH, among the Gentiles, and sing praises to your name." We are to shir to YHWH, "sing to him a new song; Play skillfully with a shout of joy," Psalm 33:3.

While "shir" is one term for singer, "tehillah" is a specific term meaning to "shir hallal" or to "sing praise." Psalm 34:1, "I will bless the YHWH at all times; His praise shall continually be in my mouth." In the plural form, "tehillah" is "Tehillim." In Hebrew the name of the book of Psalms is "Tehillim." The book of Tehillim/Psalms is an amazing look at praise and adoration of the Creator. Psalm 40:3, "He has put a new song in my mouth -- praise to our YHWH; Many will see it and fear, and will trust in the YHWH."

For some extra truth on worship, read a few chapters from the book of Tehillim and learn more about worship in Spirit and in truth.

May 4

Worship is more than just the 11am hour on Sunday morning. As worshippers of YHWH we are to totally give our time, attention, and focus to the Creator. The Bible, through the Hebrew language, gives great depth into the idea of worship activities. We've already discussed words like shir, tehillim, hallal, and barak. Today we will review a few final Hebrew terms and learn more about how to worship YHWH in truth and in the Spirit.

One of the most used Hebrew words in the Bible and in the Hebrew language today is "todah." This word basically means "thank you" but its full depth of meaning is much greater than a simple "thanks." The word "todah" is literally an "an extension of the hand, avowal, adoration, a choir of worshipers, confession, sacrifice of praise, thanksgiving." One of the greatest Tehillim/Psalms states "give thanks to YHWH for He is good, His mercy endures forever." In Hebrew this phrase is "hodu le YHWH key tov key lay olam chasdo." To say thank you to someone in Hebrew simply say, "todah." To say "thank you very much," you would say "todah rabbah." The Scriptures use the word "todah" in many verses, "offer to YHWH thanksgiving, and pay your vows to the Most High," Psalm 50:14 and Psalms 100:4, "enter into his gates with thanksgiving, and into his courts with praise. Be thankful to him, and bless his name."

Finally, "zamar" is a Hebrew phrase that describes a person making music with an instrument, celebrating with voice, and using praise to be loud. Psalm 66:2, "sing out the honor of his name; Make his praise glorious." Musical praise is also shown in Psalm 144:9, "I will sing a new song to you, O YHWH; On a harp of ten strings I will sing praises to you."

The Hebrew language gives many amazing terms to describe adoration to the Most High. By studying, understanding, and using these words we can better approach YHWH and worship him in His desired methods. John 4:24 says that YHWH seeks those who would worship in Spirit and in Truth. The Spirit of YHWH is seeking worshippers today. Will you worship Him through His word and His prescribed ways?

May 5

Your soul or mind is a type of filter that either allows or stops the Spirit of YHWH flowing in your life. The soul veils the spirit of YHWH. This is why we need the Spirit of YHWH to act as a knife to cut between spirit and soul.

The Hebrew word for soul is "neshamah." This term literally means, "breath or soul."

The neshamah is your thought process, emotions and feelings. As the temple of YHWH, your neshamah is the holy place or inner court where specially trained priests minister daily. The duties of the priest in the Holy Place included keeping the incense burning, the menorah lit, and the showbread fresh.

As a priest of YHWH in your own temple you must bring the neshama under the jurisdiction of the word of YHWH. Romans 12:1-2 speaks of this vividly.

You are transformed when your mind is renewed by the Word of YHWH. The Scriptures contain the power to change the way you think, feel, and act. When YHWH said, "love your neighbor as you love yourself" the Almighty was commanding us to control our emotions. We must take the Scriptures off the pages of the Bible and put them in our soul by acknowledging what is in our born again spirit.

2 Peter 1:4, "Through these he has given us his very great and precious promises, so that through them you may participate in the divine nature and escape the corruption in the world caused by evil desires."

Prayer, good deeds, obedience, and Torah observance do not transform your emotions. Your soul/emotions is changed when your mind is renewed. 2 Peter 1:4 states we share in the divine nature of YHWH by the knowledge or the renewing of the mind of the Messiah.

As you read, study, and think on the Word of YHWH, the Holy Spirit will bear witness with your Spirit and the soul will become one with the Spirit. This is called a "revelation." Your spirit witnesses that you are a son of YHWH and the Scriptures are true.

When your soulish mind agrees with the Mind of Messiah in you, there is unity, power, and transformation. You become a new man, a new creature, when your mind/soul agrees with the Holy Spirit in you. You can overcome temptation, trials, and the adversary through the acknowledgement of the Ruach in you.

May 6

In Mark 11:15-18 we read of Y'shua's house being used for something other than the original intention. The temple was not a house of prayer. It was something else. The money changers were amuck and the place of worship had been turned into a den of robbers. Now please understand that the Torah allowed for money changers to help those who brought offerings from lands of different currency. These "money changers" were actually doing the work of YHWH. The money changers were actually keeping Torah! But they had ulterior motives and reasons behind their work. Their obedience was selfish and rooted in something other than love. To these abusers Y'shua said "my house is to be a house of prayer." He disrupted their Torah observance (and abuse of the Torah) to remind them of what is most important – prayer. Y'shua said, "my house is to be a house of tefillah / prayer." He didn't say preaching, eating, singing, gossip, fellowship, study, debate, or even teaching. He said that the Temple was to be a place of prayer for all nations. The original intention of the tabernacle was to be a place for people to come from all walks of life and experience YHWH together. Revelation 3:15-17 explains the dangers of when we allow the Father's house to be something different than what was originally designed for.

Just as the physical temple was to be a place of prayer, our life is to be a house of prayer. We are the temple today and true prayer is our call. Tefillah / prayer is not just rubbing the genie in the bottle god that most of us grew up with in Sunday school. It's not exclusively talking about anything. Prayer is meeting him; it's praise, worship, thanksgiving, petition, and reception. True prayer is taking time out of our day and vocalizing our heart. Now, remember that your heart is not evil. Because you have been born again, your heart is good and your heart is the heart of YHWH. So, to vocalize your heart is to simply say the Words of YHWH. Praying the scriptures is one of the best practices we can learn.

When you pray the Bible you are not babbling like a hypocrite and you're not tossed from your ideas and desires. Praying the Scriptures is taking his message and confessing it as your own. This type of prayer will change you into His image and will place His words readily upon your lips. To pray the Scriptures simply personalize the passages. Pray like this, "by His stripes I am healed" or "by Yah shall supply all of my needs according to His riches in glory." Just insert yourself in the middle of the verse. Today can be a day of victory for you if you make your house (your life) a house of prayer.

May 7

Cain presented an offering of some produce from the land to YHWH. Abel as well gave an offering. But, Abel's sacrifice was from the best of His flock. Cain's offering was rejected. Abel's offering was received. Cain became furious at the situation and took out his anger upon his brother. The Scriptures recount the story of the first murder in Genesis 4:1-8. These brothers provide for us two anti-types of attitudes and actions that we face today. We make a choice each day and with each breath to either be like Cain or to be like Abel. No one forced either to give an offering or to give their best. The sacrifice was from their heart and therefore showed the essence of their heart. Cain's heart was full of wickedness and jealousy. Abel's heart was one of love towards YHWH.

The book of James says that "where there is envy and strife, there is confusion and every evil work." We may not physically murder our brothers when we are upset with them. However, the words that we use against other people and the actions we take are truly precursors to murder. They may even be types of murder as slander or gossip murders another person's reputation. Jealousy or hatred murders another person's potential for relationship. 1 John 3:15 clarifies this, "Whosoever hateth his brother is a murderer: and ye know that no murderer hath eternal life abiding in him."

Every interaction with another human being is in essence a choice to respond like Cain or like Abel. Every time we come to YHWH in worship we too must make a choice to respond like Cain or like Abel. Will we bring our best and present our lives to YHWH totally and fully? Or will we half-heartedly obey the commandments and hope grace covers all of our sins? The account of Cain and Abel reminds us of the daily decision to "uvacharta bachayim," which is Hebrew for "choose life."

We must also deal with the issue of hate. As believers we should despise or hate no one. There are to be no grudges in our hearts.

Hatred usually comes after hurt or disappointment. When hatred begins to take hold we must remember the words of Matthew 5:44, "But I say unto you, Love your enemies, bless them that curse you, do good to them that hate you, and pray for them which despitefully use you, and persecute you." Decide today to be like Cain or Abel. Don't murder your brother any longer.

May 8

Ever wanted to pass judgment on someone?

Moshe gives a repetition of words of the Torah in our last book of the Torah. In the book of words, or Devarim, Moshe says, "I charged your magistrates at that time as follows, "Hear out your fellow men, and decide justly between any man and a fellow Israelite or a stranger. You shall not be partial in judgment: hear out low and high alike. Fear no man, for judgment is YHWH's. And any matter that is too difficult for you, you shall bring to me and I will hear it." Thus instructed you, at that time, about the various things that you should do," Deuteronomy 1:16-18.

Here we see how judgment is YHWH's. It is interesting to note that Y'shua too left the judgment to YHWH the Father. Y'shua once said, "And if anyone hears My words and does not believe, I do not judge him; for I did not come to judge the world but to save the world. He who rejects Me, and does not receive My words, has that which judges him--the word that I have spoken will judge him in the last day," John 12.

The Messiah also said in Matthew 7:1, 2 "Judge not that you be not judged. For with the judgment that you judge, you shall be judged; and with the measure that you mete, it shall be measured to you." Here Y'shua made it clear that one must be careful how they judge others and do so without partiality. Y'shua went as far to state that how you express condemnation, correction, or high standards will be the same way such is given back. The actions and words of Y'shua judges each and every human being on the face of the earth. Either we see the example left by Y'shua and allow his word to conform us to His image or we will be judged by his word on the last day.

In the Heavenly court of YHWH Y'shua we are not called to be neither the judge nor the jury. We have been subpoenaed as "witnesses." Y'shua said "you shall be my witnesses in all the earth." Let's leave the judging up to the Father.

May 9

What is the main theme of the Bible? Deuteronomy 30 describes our times: "And it shall come to pass, when all these things are come upon thee, the blessing and the curse, which I have set before thee, and thou shalt bethink thyself among all the nations, whither YHWH thy Elohim hath driven thee, and shalt return unto the YHWH thy Elohim, and hearken to His voice according to all that I command thee this day, thou and thy children, with all thy heart, and with all thy soul; that then YHWH thy Elohim will turn thy captivity, and have compassion upon thee, and will return and gather thee from all the peoples, whither the YHWH hath scattered thee. If any of thine that are dispersed be in the uttermost parts of heaven, from thence will YHWH gather thee, and from thence will He fetch thee. And YHWH thy Elohim will bring thee into the land which thy fathers possessed, and thou shalt possess it; and He will do thee good, and multiply thee above thy fathers," 30:1-5.

It says in Jeremiah 29:14, "'I will be found of you,' says YHWH, 'I will turn away your captivity. I will gather you from all the nations, from all the places where I've driven you. I will bring you again into the place where I called you to be carried away captive.'" What did Y'shua say? He said, "I came to seek and save the lost sheep of the house of Israel." Why did Y'shua come?

Acts 3:19-20 says, "Therefore, repent and return so that your sins may be wiped away in order that the times of refreshing may come from YHWH that He may send Y'shua, the Messiah appointed for you, whom Heaven must receive until the period of restoration of all things which YHWH spoke about by the mouth of His holy prophets in the ancient times." It tells us here that Heaven must receive Y'shua until the restoration of all things spoken about by the prophets. Y'shua just can't come back tomorrow. He is being held in Heaven until certain things are restored on Earth today that the prophets talked about.

What did the prophets talk about? What is it we see that is important in the book of Acts and the Gospels?

They discussed the restoration of Israel. They kept calling them back, "Repent! Return to YHWH!" There are certain things that have to take place, and how does it take place? How was the nation of Israel restored? How were things going to take place? We are told to "repent and return." As we repent and return to Y'shua then He will be glorified as we are regathered.

No man can come to the Father unless Y'shua draws Him. This shows us that the current move of YHWH to restore the Torah and true righteousness is not about Hebrew roots or being "Jewish." What we are experiencing is a prophecy come true to glorify the Son of YHWH. Who can you share this teaching with today? What is holding you back from telling others about the King of Israel?

May 10

A believer can mature to great spiritual levels by grasping this simple message that what happened to the people of Israel in Biblical times is a picture of what happens to people today. History repeats itself. The times may have changed but the scenarios are still the same. Everything – everything – that occurs in your life is a message from the supernatural side. YHWH is speaking behind the details of the day. In every way the Creator is calling us closer.

Israel had forty years to work out their personal issues before they inherited the Promised Land. Can you imagine waiting through 40 years of tests and trials? Does it sometimes feel like you are in the middle of 40 years' worth of wandering? It took one night, the night of Passover, for YHWH to bring Israel out of Egypt. Yet, it took 40 years for YHWH to bring Egypt out of Israel. Let's not repeat the sins of the wilderness. Rather, let's learn from them and run towards the Promised Land. On the way, we'll no doubt see our fair share of trials and miracles.

One such miracle is the manna that fell from Heaven. This miracle type signifies the crux of the wilderness journey. YHWH was teaching His young nation to trust him for anything and everything. Call it "heavenly meals on wheels." Each day the people would rise from their sleep and find the ground wet with dew and covered with food.

"And when the dew that lay was gone up, see, upon the face of the wilderness there laid a small round thing, as small as the frost on the ground. And when the children of Yisrael saw it, they said to one another, It is manna: for they did not know what it was. And Moshe said, "This is the lechem / bread that YHWH has given you to eat," Exodus / Shemot 16:14, 15.

YHWH provided for Israel in the wilderness and YHWH will provide for you today. Don't allow unbelief to stop you from walking in His fullness.

Truth For Today

May 11

In the Hebrew language there are many different terms for "bread." While "lechem: is the usual bread eaten daily, Challah is the special food saved for special days. Traditional meals begin with the breaking of bread and a blessing of YHWH for His "bringing forth the bread from the earth." While it is usually the word "lechem" spoken during the blessing, it is usually Challah that is eaten after the blessing. This is to show that the simplest of blessings touch the most extraordinary aspects of life.

There are traditionally two loaves of Challah served at the Shabbat dinner table. The two loaves that are weekly baked are symbolic of many things including the showbread of the temple and the double portion of the manna received in the Wilderness before Shabbat. They can also represent the: two tablets of Torah, the two witnesses, the two people - Ephraim and Judah, the two commands to "remember" and "keep" the Shabbat.

The dough of Challah is traditionally twisted with three braids and these braids are even meaningful of the mitzvoth. The Rabbis teach that the "three braids are symbolic of the commands to observe Shabbat that appear in the Ten Commandments One braid represents the word 'Zachor' or 'Remember.' A second braid represents the word 'Shamor' or 'Guard.' The third braid is for 'b'Dibbur Echad' - that these commands of 'Remember' and 'Guard' were said by Elohim simultaneously and as one unit," says one source. The three rows can also point to the Creation, the Exodus, and the Messianic Era.

Even the way Challah is cut is a visible teacher for the Israelite. Most people serve Challah with a knife present but never use the knife at all! Just as the

Torah recounts that the patriarch Avraham, was tested by YHWH, and did not use the knife on his son Yitzchak. The bread is to be torn from the loaf, first by the priest or head of the household and then by everyone else.

Challah can have special ingredients added to it that add to the imagery. Enjoying Challah is a wonderful blessing of sustenance that YHWH gives us to reflect upon the bread of life Y'shua. Remember the Messiah when you enjoy Challah this week on Shabbat.

May 12

Mark Twain once said, "Don't complain and talk about all your problems – 80 percent of people don't care; the other 20 percent will think you deserve them."

There is a great deal of truth in Twain's words. Unfortunately Twain wasn't around to share this timeless wisdom with Beit Yisra'el / House of Israel during their wilderness wanderings. For forty years complaining and murmuring seemed to be an area that Israel excelled in. They were always fussing about something. In fact, the majority of the book of Bamidbar / Numbers is devoted to the reporting of the many rebellions of Israel and their consequences. Not perfect conditions and not perfect people led to complaining and rebellion. Are we really much different than the nation of Israel way back when?

Here are a few life lessons to reflect on about complaining. Don't fuss about it – just keep reading!

Talking about your ills just makes you more ill. Complaining never gets you anywhere but worse off. If all you do is talk about your problems then your problems will seem better. Sometimes it's best to remember that things are never as bad as they seem. Situations could always be worse and life is much better than it's opposite.

Complaining grieves the Ruach HaKodesh! When you bicker you enter the realm of the serpent and step out of the realm of the Spirit. Watch out or the snakes will bite you – —Do not let any unwholesome talk come out of your mouths, but only what is helpful for building others up according to their needs, that it may benefit those who listen. And do not grieve the Holy Spirit of Elohim, with whom you were sealed for the day of redemption," Ephesians 4:29 & 30.

It is the little things in life that often lead to murmuring...traffic jams, screaming kids, slow internet, old manna, and little water don't really matter. Before you fuss think about the subject of your mouth. Are you really making a point about your objections or are you just barking about wants, desires, and stuff? "Let us not become weary in doing good, for at the proper time we will reap a harvest if we do not give up. Therefore, as we have opportunity, let us do good to all people, especially to those who belong to the family of believers," Galatians 6:9-10.

May 13

The Torah makes it clear that some animals may be eaten by man for food while some are not to be eaten. What the Torah calls clean is clean and what the torah calls unclean is still unclean. The kosher commands did not pass away with the Savior or with Paul's letters. Romans 14:14 is another verse of confusion. It says "I am fully convinced that no food is unclean in itself. But if anyone regards something as unclean, then for him it is unclean." Most think that this verse means that all food is ok to eat, regardless of what the Old Testament. Through viewing this verse according to the Torah, one would understand that is means "that no food NOT MENTIONED IN THE TORAH is unclean in itself." The animals that qualify for "food" are the animals permitted for consumption. The pig, lobster, shrimp, or cockroach are not permitted in the Scriptures and therefore would never be considered food to the Rabbi Paul or his original audience.

There is another misunderstood passage in Acts 10:9-19. In these verses Peter is said to have been extremely hungry. He is also confused about the acceptance of the Gentile believers. He then has a vision about various four-footed creatures. Peter is told to slaughter and eat as all are now made clean. When the vision concludes, Peter doesn't eat barbeque pork. Instead, he understands that the vision is not about unclean foods but unclean people. He proclaims, in Acts 10:28, "You know how that it is an unlawful thing for a man that is a Jew to keep company, or come unto one of another nation; but YHWH has showed me that I should not call any man common or unclean."

The Messiah kept a strict kosher diet and we can actually see him in the foods that are permitted to be eaten. He is the first fruits from the earth and He is pictured in the spotless clean animals. These commandments to eat clean foods and stay away from unclean animals are considered to be a "chukim" or "rulings without known meaning." Though we think that we can understand the kosher diet from a basis of disease and cleanliness, these commandments truly are beyond our human understanding. In fact, all of the mitzvoth/commandments are indeed spiritual and must be followed by faith. "Now we see things imperfectly, like puzzling reflections in a mirror, but then we will see everything with perfect clarity. All that I know now is partial and incomplete, but then I will know everything completely, just as YHWH now knows me completely," 1 Corinthians 13:12.

YHWH said what animals are permissible for food and what animals are abominable. Our human reasoning doesn't match up to the unfathomable wisdom of YHWH that is found in Y'shua. "Oh, the depth of the riches both of the wisdom and knowledge of YHWH! How unsearchable are His judgments and unfathomable His ways," Romans 11:33. Eat good today!

May 14

Moshe, the Torah, the Prophets, and the Writings all speak of a coming Messiah. This "anointed one" would lead the human race back to the Garden of Eden to restore man's lost relationship with YHWH. These prophecies came to pass when a heavenly messenger visited a young Hebrew virgin named Mary / Miriam in Hebrew. The angel proclaimed that though Miriam had not known a man, she was going to give birth to a son. This child was to be named "Y'shua" which means "YHWH is salvation."

Mary was astonished by the possibility and said to the angel, "How can this be, since I do not know a man?" And the angel answered and said to her, "The Holy Spirit will come upon you, and the power of the Most High will overshadow you; therefore, also, that Holy One who is to be born will be called the Son of YHWH," Luke 1:34,35. (Notice that the Holy Spirit will "come upon" her and "power of the Most High" will overshadow her.) This, of course, is called the "virgin birth."

Something that is interesting about conception is that the mother contributes no blood to the baby. Blood is produced without contact with the mother's bloodstream, after the sperm meets the egg. "The mother provides the unborn developing infant with the nutritive elements for the building of that little body in the secret of her bosom, but all the blood which forms in that little body is formed in the embryo itself and only as a result of the contribution of the male parent. From the time of conception to the time of birth of the infant not one single drop of blood ever passes from mother to child," wrote Dr. M.R. Dehaan.

Miriam's spouse Joseph / Yosef physically had nothing to do with the conception of Y'shua. His sperm was not used and therefore his blood was not passed to Y'shua. Does this prove that the Savior had divine blood that had not been tainted by Adam's sin? That makes perfectly good sense.

Well, what about Mary? Did Y'shua get His humanity from her? Did He look like her? Wasn't it Mary's egg that was fertilized with a special seed? No. If that was the case, then Mary's sinful nature would have passed down to Y'shua. The truth is that Miriam acted merely as a surrogate mother of Y'shua. A surrogate mother is a woman who agrees to bear a child for a couple who are childless, usually due to wife being infertile or unable to carry a baby. The child grows inside the surrogate mother but has no biological relationship with the mother. This is exactly what we see with Y'shua and his earthly mother. YHWH bypassed human sperm and human egg to implant a heavenly body within Miriam. In doing so, Y'shua's flesh and blood was not tainted with the original sin of Adam. Think about this today. (learn more about this tomorrow)

May 15

Y'shua's flesh and blood - his temporary tent - was totally divine from YHWH. Y'shua said, "if you have seen me then you have seen the Father." Y'shua did NOT say, "if you have seen me then you have seen the virgin Mary." We've been told by our Pastors, Sunday school teachers, and church leaders that Jesus was 100% man and 100% god. What if that isn't true? What if Y'shua was more than just a man with a special anointing?

This message proves that Y'shua was not born a sinful sinner. He was not born with the physical traits of Mary. He was not born with "normal" human flesh. The scriptures clearly teach in Colossians 2:9 that in Y'shua "dwelt the fullness of YHWH in bodily form." Y'shua came to earth in the flesh but it wasn't earthly flesh. It couldn't have been earthly flesh because normal flesh had been polluted with sin.

The Messianic prophecies in Isaiah call Y'shua the "wonderful, counselor, everlasting Father, Prince of Peace." Y'shua was the exact image of Abba YHWH in an earth suit.

Y'shua's flesh, blood, and bones were all from YHWH in Heaven. "There is a natural body and there is a spiritual body. And so it is written, "The first man Adam became a living being." The last Adam became a life-giving spirit. The first man was of the earth, made of dust; the second Man is the Master Mar Yah from heaven. As was the man of dust, so also are those who are made of dust; and as is the heavenly Man, so also are those who are heavenly. And as we have borne the image of the man of dust, we shall also bear the image of the heavenly Man," 1 Corinthians 15:44-49.

Philippians 2 says that He "took on the form of a human." Hebrews 2 says that Y'shua appeared "like" his brothers but NOT in the nature of "angels or men." Y'shua came to earth with a perfect body just like Adam in Genesis. This truth totally rejects the Greek myth of a man-god coming to earth to rescue humanity. Can you share the truth about Y'shua's divinity with others today?

May 16

The more we are involved in this world, the more we are in darkness. The systems of economy, politics, and entertainment darkly cloud our memory of our true purpose. The world and all its cares cloud our memory, because they crowd our memory. As we fill our day with work and worries we block out the Light. However, with YHWH's reminders, we can function, despite our surroundings, with a mind that is steadfastly focused on Elohim.

Elohim has purposefully given us certain commandments like eating clean foods, to keep our mind alert and watchful. These reminders are like spiritual post it notes that remind us of YHWH and His Word. We can allow dirty diapers, fast food meals, deadlines, and car oil changes to fill our day. It is so easy to forget that what we see, touch, feel, taste, and experience in this world is only a small portion of what is really important.

Therefore, to help us remember that we are more than what we see, YHWH has filled our lives with small, yet significant, reminders. These prompts call us back to Him throughout our busy days. They help us zakar / remember and change our actions from being self-serving to YHWH serving.

"Zakar" is the Hebrew term for remember; it means "to mark (so as to be recognized), to remember; to mention; to burn incense, earnestly; be mindful, recount, record, make to be remembered, bring (re)call; come, keep, put (in) to remembrance."

When we don't remember our history, including the covenants made between our ancestors and the Creator, or disregard the words of Torah, we become stiff-necked and rebellious. This is spiritual amnesia at its worst. It is hypocrisy and exile.

"They stiffened their necks, and listened not to Your mitzvoth, and refused to obey, neither were mindful of Your wonders that You did among them; but hardened their necks, and in their rebellion appointed a leader to return to their bondage: but You are Elohim, ready to pardon, gracious and full of rachamim, slow to anger, and of great kindness, and forsook them not" -- Nehemiah 9: 16-17.

Read the Torah this week and zakar what you learn.

May 17

Haven't you struggled with certain commandments? Haven't you wondered 'exactly' how you should keep the mitzvoth? Doesn't the Torah go against every part of your surrounding family life, workplace, and world? Has your obedience to YHWH's will separated you from friends and loved ones? Does confusion or frustration ever make you want to give up and walk away? Have you ever felt alone in your life of Torah? If so, then good! Your frustrations just mean that the Torah is working! The word of YHWH is separating you from this world and its comforts. "For the word of YHWH (the Torah) is living and active. Sharper than any double-edged sword, it penetrates even to dividing soul and spirit, joints and marrow; it judges the thoughts and attitudes of the heart," Ivrim / Hebrews 4:12.

It is perfectly normal to struggle in Torah observance. Don't let anyone beat you down because you are trying. The Divine Will is directly opposite to every part of our society. The Torah is opposed to every bit of your fleshly nature. Yet, this is how your life was destined to be lived. The Torah lifestyle is how the Almighty purposed His people to exist. "When a person knows and grasps in his mind a Torah law... he thereby grasps and holds and encompasses with his mind the divine wisdom and will... while his mind is simultaneously enveloped within them. This makes for a wonderful union, like which there is none other and which has no parallel anywhere in the terrestrial world, whereby complete oneness and unity, from every side and angle, is attained," says the Talmud. Romans 2:13 says, "it is those who obey the law who will be declared righteous."

You must understand that YHWH is actually growing you when your faith is frustrated or when you doubt. When your ego is experiencing pain, you are very pregnant and about to give birth. Don't give up. Living Torah is a struggle, but it is worth it. The Torah itself declares some wise words on this subject. Write these words down. Memorize them and reflect upon them the next time you wrestle with the Mitzvot.

"Now what I am commanding you today is not too difficult for you or beyond your reach. It is not up in heaven, so that you have to ask, "Who will ascend into heaven to get it and proclaim it to us so we may obey it?" Nor is it beyond the sea, so that you have to ask, "Who will cross the sea to get it and proclaim it to us so we may obey it?" No, the word is very near you; it is in your mouth and in your heart so you may obey it. See, I set before you today life and prosperity, death and destruction. For I command you today to love YHWH your Elohim, to walk in his ways, and to keep his commands, decrees and laws; then you will live and increase, and YHWH your Elohim will bless you," Devarim 30:11-16. Take comfort in these words today.

May 18

Mercy is the sum description of our being of worship. He is merciful and gracious. Many times we gloss over the idea of YHWH being full of mercy as a weakness or temporary lapse of judgment. But this is not the case. It is through YHWH's mercy that the universe exists and we breathe.

"YHWH is merciful and gracious, slow to anger and abounding in steadfast love," says Psalm 103:8. In this verse as well as many others, the terms "merciful and gracious" are used together. In Hebrew this reads "rachum v'chanun".

This is YHWH! He has compassion and patience towards us at all times. To be merciful is to show empathy to a person. Empathy is the ability to recognize, relate, and directly feel the emotion of another person. To have empathy is to have rachamim. YHWH emphasizes with us.

It has been said that mercy is "not getting what you deserve." Well, that definition is just a small portion of the truth. Rachamim is so much more.

YHWH's mercy is the force that sustains creation and allows the world to spin on its axis.

Many describe the "God of the Old Testament" as an angry judge of the world that sent His son to save mankind from the religion of Judaism. This is not so. Such an idea of a bearded man with lightning bolts and a huge throne relate more to Greek Mythology than the Bible. The Scriptures state that "YHWH did not send His son into the world to condemn the world but that the world through Him might be saved," John 3:17.

Part of Y'shua's ministry on Earth was to restore the mercy and grace of the Torah. He did not come to start a new religion or write a second portion of the Bible called the —New Testament. John 1:17 states, "The Torah was given by Moses and its unmerited favor and truth were revealed by Y'shua."

Y'shua did NOT come to replace the Law with Grace. Our choice today is not mercy or torah but mercy and grace IN the Torah. This is a message we need to know, accept and share with others. Praise YHWH for his mercy today.

May 19

Genesis 49:18 is just one example of how we miss so much in the Scriptures because we don't read and study in the Hebrew. There are so many facets of truth that can only be discovered in the Hebrew texts. In this verse, the translation disguises the Messiah's name and prevents the casual reader from accepting the Savior's presence throughout the Old Testament.

Genesis 49:18 in English reads, "I have waited for Your salvation, O Lord." In Hebrew the verse is "Le Y'shua tehka keyoo eet'ee YHWH." Here, the word for "salvation" is the exact name of the Messiah as given to him by the heavenly messengers in Matthew 1:21. This verse could also be translated "To thy Y'SHUA I am looking, O YHWH." In this passage, Jacob is actually calling out the name of Y'shua and professing faith in the Moshiach before his incarnation. This isn't the only time the Savior's name is made known in the Tanakh / Old Testament. In Psalm 9:14, King David of Israel said "I will rejoice in thy salvation/Y'shua. The Prophet Isaiah agreed in 12:2&3, "Behold, Elohim is my Y'SHUA/salvation; I will trust, and be not afraid: for YHWH is my strength and my song; he also is become my Y'shua/salvation. Therefore with joy shall ye draw water out of the wells of Y'shua / salvation." Later in Isaiah 62:11 we read, "Behold, YHWH hath proclaimed unto the end of the world, Say ye to the daughter of Zion, Behold, thy salvation/Y'shua cometh; behold, his reward is with him, and his work before him." And in Habakkuk 3:13 we find a startling verse that actually call's Y'shua the anointed Messiah! "Thou wentest forth for the salvation / Y'shua of thy people, even for salvation / Y'shua with thine anointed / messiah..."

Y'shua is found throughout the pages of the Torah, Prophets, and Writings if we will just look. May YHWH open our eyes that we could behold wonderful things from His Torah.

May 20

Judaism remembers Pentecost, or "Shavuot" in Hebrew, as the exact day that Moses received the first five books of the Bible (called the Torah) on Mount Sinai. Observant Jewish people keep the day holy by attending special worship services, eating dairy products, and conducting an all-night vigil dedicated to study. On this night, it is said that the Holy Spirit will visit those waiting in worship to sweeten their tongues.

Celebrating Pentecost was nothing new for the first disciples of the Savior. They had regularly kept the "feast of weeks" in accordance to the Torah. The word "Pentecost" is from the Greek language as "pente" is a reference to a 50 day interval that starts with Passover. In Leviticus chapter 23 Bible believers are instructed to count 50 days until Shavuot. The traditional Jewish calendar starts this counting after the Sabbath day of Passover. This results in Shavuot occurring exactly fifty days after Passover, which could be on any day of the week. (Some Torah keeping groups wait until the seventh-day Sabbath after Passover to begin counting. This choice results in Pentecost always falling on a Sunday.)

"You shall count for yourselves from the day after the Shabbat, from the day when you bring the Omer of the waving seven Shabbats, they shall be complete. Until the day after the seventh Sabbath you shall count, fifty days... You shall have a holy convocation for yourselves on this very day; you shall do no laborious work; it is an eternal decree for all generations," Leviticus 23:15-16, 21.

At His ascension into heaven, the Savior instructed his disciples to go to Jerusalem and wait for the promise of the Holy Spirit. Acts 1 finishes with a small group of believers in the tiny upper room of a house. Then in Acts 2 the counting of 50 days was completed and the day of Pentecost had fully come. One hundred and twenty people were filled with the Spirit and began to speak in diverse tongues. The Bible clearly indicates that this did not take place in the upper room but at the Holy Temple in Jerusalem.

Acts 2:2, "And suddenly there came a sound from heaven as of a rushing mighty wind, and it filled the entire house where they were sitting." The upper room isn't mentioned. The phrase "house" is an idiomatic expression that indicates the "house of worship" or "temple." 120 people could not have fit into the tiny attic space of a first century house! Acts 2 then shows that many people at the temple heard the disciples speak in tongues as 3,000 accepted the Jewish Messiah. Such events taking place at the temple site further validates that Christianity was originally a sect of Judaism and was never intended to become a separate religion. Pentecost is important!

May 21

The book of Acts teaches that on Shavuot many believing Israelites from all over the world came together in worship at Jerusalem. These Hebrews were worshipping in submission to Leviticus 23 and as a result received the reward of a manifestation of YHWH. The events that took place in Acts 2 were exact fulfillment of words spoken by YHWH's holy prophets to the observant Hebrews that were keeping Shavuot.

"When the day of Pentecost came, they were all together in one place. Suddenly a sound like the blowing of a violent wind came from heaven and filled the whole house where they were sitting. They saw what seemed to be tongues of fire that separated and came to rest on each of them. All of them were filled with the Holy Spirit and began to speak in other tongues as the Spirit enabled them," Acts 2:13.

As we celebrate Shavuot we are to look to the past and see what happened on this unique day. The Torah was given at Shavuot and the Spirit fell at Shavuot. It is a wonderful time with agricultural, spiritual and historical significance. Indeed, we will be blessed as we keep Shavuot through the worship and the observance of YHWH's Torah. These are HIS set apart days on HIS calendar, that during which He is ready to meet with us. Aren't the holy days of YHWH great? We have Passover to remember the exodus from Egypt. We gather for Shavuot in remembrance of the gift of the Torah and the gift of the Holy Spirit. The feast of trumpets calls us out of our slumber and we can clearly see our high priest in Yom Kippur. Sukkot is a week-long blessing of fellowship, family, and dwelling in YHWH's presence. With all of the blessing and fun of the moadim / feasts of YHWH, it's hard to imagine how anyone could call these days "legalism." Yet these are also solemn assemblies and not just parties.

As we observe these days we are to remember the days of old, the nation of Israel, and YHWH's plan for man. BUT we are to do more than just remember how it was back then. Shavuot should not just be a history lesson for us. If we spend time just reminiscing of Acts 2 or Exodus 19 then we are not walking in all that YHWH has for us in His holy days. We shouldn't minimize this day of worship as just a historical event or something that happened long ago. Shavuot, the festival of Pentecost, should be a time of lasting change for our spirits.

As we look into the Scriptures we will see that the Shavuot after Y'shua ascended into heaven was life changing. We will also discover that YHWH wants US to experience the very same transformation the disciples encountered as they went PAST Pentecost. The believers in Acts 2 were changed by what took place at Shavuot. We too can be changed in the way we worship, pray, fellowship, and live as we allow YHWH's Spirit to move in our hearts and lives.

May 22

Whenever the symptoms of sickness begin to surface it's a good idea to check your temperature for a fever. The average fever doesn't hurt the body but indicates if something is amuck. YHWH created the body to warm up in an effort to destroy sickness. Body heat empowers the blood cells to fight off problems. A fever is reason to stay away from others, stay home from school, or stay in the bed.

Spiritually speaking we have many indications of health. Have you ever thought about what is the greatest indicator of your spiritual maturity? Most people think results are approval of a message. That idea sounds good but can also be twisted. Hitler led the masses and got results but those weren't good. Many ministries judge their effectiveness by the quality of the music, the response to the preaching, the outreach performed, or the tithes received. Perhaps the greatest indication of our spiritual health is not these outward actions but the inward awareness of the spirit realm called "prayer." The best preacher or teaching is no good if the audience is lifeless and in a spiritual coma. Prayer plows the ground of the mind and prepares the soil/soul to respond to the word. How's your prayer life doing today?

The Hebrew word for prayer is "tefillah." This phrase literally means to "judge yourself." Prayer is more than just a shopping list of wants or a time of praise. Prayer is supposed to be a time to dwell in YHWH's presence and hear from His Spirit. In Jeremiah 33:3 YHWH says, "call to me and I will answer you and tell you great things you do not know." From this simple verse we can see that prayer is calling, listening, and receiving. It's not just pleading, complaining, or thanking. Prayer should be a time to build our relationship with YHWH through daily conversation. A conversation is two way communications and prayer should be the same. The Priests in the tabernacle understood prayer's importance.

It was the duty of the priesthood to offer incense offerings throughout the day to YHWH. These sweet aromas are a picture of prayer for us today. Of course the priests didn't just foreshadow prayer, they themselves prayed. As ministers of the Most High, the kohanim / priests had to serve physically and spiritually. Today, we do not have a Temple in Jerusalem because WE are the Temple of YHWH. 1 Corinthians 6:19 explains that our bodies are now the tabernacle or temple of YHWH. The Almighty doesn't just dwell in heaven somewhere, YHWH is right here with you now, dwelling in the holy of holies of your heart/spirit.

The most basic priestly duty during Older Testament times was to ensure that YHWH's "tent of meeting" was just that – a "tent of meeting between YHWH and mankind." The temple was to be a "house of prayer." Prayer is supposed to be a time to dwell in His presence and experience YHWH. Do you use your Temple for prayer and worship or something else?

May 23

The Savior willingly gave his existence as an offering to YHWH for all mankind. The Romans didn't take his life. The Jewish leaders didn't really kill him. Sadly though, for many years anti-Semitism has been taught in the church by suggesting that the Jewish people killed the savior. This idea breeds dislike and disgust of the Hebrew people.

The Jews did not kill Y'shua. Nor did the Romans. No one took Y'shua's life from Him. He gave up His life freely for all mankind. "I lay down My life that I may take it again. No one has taken it away from Me, but I lay it down on My own initiative. I have authority to lay it down, and I have authority to take it up again," John 10:17-18.

By offering Himself as a terumah /offering gift to mankind, Y'shua gave up His life. No one person is responsible for killing him because each and every person who has ever lived is guilty of murdered the Man of Sorrows. Without us, He would have not died. By this, YHWH showed His great love for us as while we were sinners, Messiah died for us. Our response to his gift should be to offer our lives back to Him. We must give terumah to YHWH once we accept His terumah for us! "Present yourselves to YHWH as a living sacrifice (terumah) and be not conformed to the pattern of this world but be transformed by the renewing of your minds," says Romans 12. One translation says, "in view of YHWH's mercies, offer yourselves as a sacrifice, living and set apart for YHWH. This will please him; it is the logical 'Temple worship' for you."

In view of Y'shua's gift we are to respond and release all of who we are and everything we have to YHWH. Allow your mind to be renewed by His eternal word. Worship Y'shua for His sacrifice. "YHWH said unto me, Son of man, know and behold with thine eyes, and hear with thine ears all that I say unto thee concerning all the ordinances of the house of YHWH, and all the laws thereof; and know well the entering in of the house, with every going forth of the sanctuary," Ezekiel 44:5.

May 24

Churches have "altar calls" every Sunday. This is a time for believers to come forward with their sins and problems to find solace through prayer. Sadly though, most "altar calls" do not involve death or sacrifice but people falling in the floor. True "altar calls" should involve sacrifice of self upon the altar of YHWH.

When one gives Himself to YHWH, he opens himself up to receive from YHWH. "Whoever finds his life will lose it, and whoever loses his life for my sake will find it," Matthew 10:39.

Even if sacrifice looks like losing, it is actually about receiving. When a person gives an offering, they are empting their hands to be filled again. It is better to give than receive. Just picture a person clenching a lamb that is to be offered, and then releasing that lamb to be killed. Only after the animal is sacrificed can the blood be applied.

To give up something, to sacrifice a desire or habit, is to release control and accept liberation. It is only when a person gives; that they can accept back a blessing. Sacrifice is surrender.

To surrender is to give up, loose, and be conquered in battle. This is a great picture of the struggle waging inside every man. For before an army surrenders, there is usually a great battle. Combat is fierce during the fight. But, when one side surrenders, things change. Those who were once fighting against the enemy are now ruled. We don't need to fight YHWH! We just have to surrender! Waive the white flag, and be ruled by the Man of War. Receive mercy from the Great King. Surrender and receive.

It is odd, that the majority of the Mitzvoth in the Torah deal with the issue of temple worship and sacrifices. These commands are highly structured and controlled. Yet, even the rabbis have been perplexed that more of Torah is about sacrificing than any other subject. Why would Elohim use exact details to describe the sacrificial system, yet be silent in regards to the specifics of so many other issues? Why would the Bible speak about the correct way to kill animals and be silent on stem-cell research, global warming, and such?

The detailed commands surrounding the temple and tabernacle show us how meticulous we should be when coming before YHWH. Each of the sacrifices commanded in the Scriptures, from the red heifer to the Passover lamb, points to the Messiah's sacrifice.

When Y'shua surrendered His life, He set the prime example for us to follow. May we pray, "not my will, but thine will be done." The sacrifices were a way to draw near to YHWH and connect with Him. This is of course prophetic of Y'shua. He is spoken of in every single offering and every single sacrifice.

Truth For Today

May 25

What do you do when you have a message that you want to send to someone? Well, you might write the message, fold it, place it in an envelope, seal it up, write the name and address of the person you want to send it to, and drop it in the mail box. Of course you can't forget the most important step...there is no way a message is going to be delivered if you don't put a stamp on it. Most of us give very little thought to how important stamps are until we have an important message to deliver.

Y'shua had a very important message to deliver. In the time that Y'shua lived, they didn't have a Post Office where you could go and send a message. They didn't even have email! In ancient times, if you had a message, it was usually delivered in person. That's what Y'shua did. The Bible says that Y'shua traveled all around Galilee, delivering the good news of YHWH. "The time has come," Y'shua said. "The kingdom of YHWH is near. Repent and believe the good news!"

The message that Y'shua was delivering 2,000 years ago is just important today as it was then. There are still many people who need to hear the good news of YHWH's love for them. Sin separates people from YHWH but Y'shua has provided a way that people can come to the Father. Every 24 hours over 150,000 people die and meet their maker. How many of these know Messiah? How many of them have heard the good news of Y'shua? If we are waiting on missionaries or evangelists to spread the good news of Y'shua then we are waiting on someone else to do our job. The "Great Commission" was given to all believers.

How is the message going to be delivered? Y'shua has called his disciples to deliver the good news. As believers and followers of Messiah, we are YHWH's postage stamps. Some may be called to take the message to people in a land far, far away. Others may be called to take the message to a neighbor just down the street. The important thing is to carry the message. If a little postage stamp can take a message to someone on the other side of the world, can't we take the message of YHWH's love to our friends and neighbors who live nearby?

We have all been called to be YHWH's "witnesses." Do you witness for or against the living Messiah? Who can you purposefully witness to today?

Truth For Today

May 26

Each and every classroom has a few basic rules. Teachers may forbid talking, chewing gum, or listening to an iPod during class time. The people in Y'shua' day had to follow rules too. One day a lawyer asked Y'shua, "Teacher, which is the greatest commandment?" This question was a puzzling query. Would the Messiah choose one of the Ten Commandments or single out one of the 613 laws?

Y'shua answered him, "'Love YHWH with all your heart and with all your soul and with all your mind,' this is the greatest commandment. And the second is like it: 'Love your neighbor as yourself.' On these two commandments hang all the law and the prophets." In other words, Y'shua was saying that if we could keep these two commandments, we would not have any trouble keeping the others. These two commandments are what is most important. But, here is a question for you – "How do we love YHWH and love our neighbor?"

Our "neighbor" is whoever is near us. Right now your neighbor may be a friend, spouse, or coworker. Later today, your neighbor may be the waitress that serves you or the cashier at the local gas station. Your neighbor is whoever is near you at any time during the day.

The way we love YHWH and love our neighbor is to follow the other commandments in the Bible. Treat your neighbor as you would want to be treated. Share the love of the Messiah and fulfill the royal law.

The commandments cover many areas of life. The Torah tells us how to dress, what to wear, when to worship, how to get along with people, and even what to do when people bully or mistreat you. The commandments in the Bible are like a pair of shoes. How? Well, a pair of shoes is good for you! Shoes keep your feet protected and they help you walk on the earth. The commandments are good for us, protect us, and help us walk during our lives. The Hebrew word for commandment is "mitzvot." The mitzvoth are not to punish or stop us from living a fun life. The mitzvoth were given to bless us and allow us to enjoy life. It's because we love YHWH that we obey His mitzvoth. It's because we love YHWH that we observe Shabbat, celebrate Passover, eat clean foods, and treat other people with respect and love.

It is important that you begin to learn the commandments and allow the love of YHWH to flow through you so that you obey the mitzvoth. Love YHWH first. Then love your neighbor through your obedience to the Torah.

May 27

For many years Bible commentators have somehow blamed Father YHWH for Pharaoh's obstinate heart and actions. They teach that YHWH had violated Pharaoh's free will and made him treat Israel and Moshe with contempt. This is simply not the case. What happens to Pharaoh and Egypt is Pharaoh's fault. Don't blame YHWH. And don't blame YHWH for what happens in your Pharaoh-like life. If a person sets himself against the Mighty One of Israel there will be consequences. "Do not be deceived: Elohim cannot be mocked. A man reaps what he sows," Galatians 6:7.

Any action performed sets off an undeniable chain of events that will result in that action being responded to. Scientists will tell you that for "every action there is an equal and opposite reaction." It seems that for His own purposes YHWH allows people to wallow in their sins for a season. "The one who sows to please his sinful nature, from that nature will reap destruction; the one who sows to please the Spirit, from the Spirit will reap eternal life," Galatians 6:8.

Pharaoh simply would not yield to YHWH. It did not take a divine action on behalf of YHWH to cause Pharaoh to be disobedient to the words "let my people go." Pharaoh had no one to blame for his cruel attitude and behavior but himself. Five times his heart was set itself against the will of YHWH. As a direct result, Pharaoh's heart continued to grow cold five times more. Five times Pharaoh sowed a "steadfast" heart and five times he received a "hardened" heart. Five plus five equals ten, right? There were ten plagues right? It seems to all add up.

The plagues were proving Beresheet / Genesis 12:3, "I will bless those who bless you, and whoever curses you I will curse." Pharaoh had at least ten opportunities to heed YHWH's commands but did not. During each act of rebellion his heart moved farther away from YHWH's will and grew colder in the process. Each of the plagues occurred to teach Pharaoh, the entire world, and even Israel about YHWH. We should learn from Pharaoh and guard our heart so it does not become hardened.

Be careful today because you will reap what you sow.

Truth For Today

May 28

Hebrews / Ivrim 11:1, "Now faith is the assurance of things hoped for, the conviction of things not seen."

Do you believe that Australia exists? Have you ever been there? How can you be sure Australia is real if you have never been there or seen the continent with your own eyes?

You can certainly see pictures of the land of Australia and talk to people who have been there. Many reputable people agree that it is there. Based on these evidences, you have no reason to doubt that there is a continent named Australia on the other side of the world. We may not see YHWH himself in this life, but there is evidence all around that he exists, and that he keeps his promises. This is not to say that we will always understand everything about YHWH. We can't.

The apostles said to YHWH, "Increase our faith!" Y'shua replied, "If you had faith the size of a mustard seed, you could say to this mulberry tree, 'Be uprooted and planted in the sea,' and it would obey you," Luke 17:5-6.

The story is told of a man who read this verse in the Bible and decided to put it to the test. There was a large tree in his front yard, so he went out to that tree and said, "In the morning when I wake up from my sleep, I want you to be gone." That night the man went to bed. When he woke up the next morning, he went to front door, opened it, and looked out into his front yard. "Just as I thought!" the man said. "It's still there."

Well, first of all, the man didn't have mustard seed sized faith, did he? In fact, he didn't have any faith at all. When he told the tree to be moved, he never expected it to happen. In the second place, the man misunderstood what Y'shua was trying to teach his disciples.

Y'shua was not suggesting that we go around trying to move trees just to prove that we have faith. What Y'shua was trying to teach his disciples -- and what he wants us to learn -- is that it doesn't take a great faith to produce great results. Why? Because the results don't depend on us, they depend on YHWH. If the results depended on the size of our faith then we would all be in trouble.

True faith is trusting YHWH for the results and being faith-full in all that we have been called to do. Follow the Ruach today and put your mustard seed faith to work. YHWH will bring the rain, sunshine, and fertilizer. YHWH will take care of the results.

TRUTH FOR TODAY

May 29

Romans 3 says that we “all have sinned and fallen short of the glory of Elohim.” Sin is a "self-centered" act. It is a state of rebellion against YYHWH. It is the exact opposite of love. The scriptures state in Romans “where sin increased, grace increased all the more, so that, just as sin reigned in death, so also grace might reign through righteousness to bring eternal life through Y’shua our Messiah.” Through these verses a person can understand the effects of sin. Sin has affected everyone that has lived since the beginning of time. Sin separates man from the Heavenly Father. Sin makes mankind in need of forgiveness. Without forgiveness there is no eternal life, no grace, and no righteousness. This is all because of sin. To remedy sin is one of the reasons why the Messiah came.

Y’shua actually walked fully in the Torah commands and never broke the law or sinned. Or to put it plainly Y’shua kept the Torah in its entirety. And therefore to follow Y’shua man must follow the Old Testament Law. A life patterned after Y'shua, or after the Torah, will be a life absent of sin! For Y’shua never broke the law. The Bible says in 1 John 3:4 that “sin is lawlessness.” Therefore, if Y'shua kept the law or obeyed the law He never sinned.

Sin or torah-less-ness separates man from YHWH. Sin also hardens a person’s heart to the things of YHWH. When a person sins, that person is putting a layer between their heart and YHWH. The more a person sins, the greater the layers become. Unless dealt with through the blood of Y’shua, sin will bring condemnation and death. The Old Testament has a rich vocabulary for sin. The Hebrew word Chata means, “to miss the mark.” The word could be used to describe a person shooting a bow and arrow and missing the target with the arrow. When it is used to describe sin, it means that the person has missed the mark that Elohim has established for the person’s life. The Hebrew word Aven describes the crooked or perverse spirit associated with sin. Sinful persons have perverted their spirits and become crooked rather than straight.

There are four main ways that people treat their sins. Think on these today and ask the Spirit of YHWH to deliver you from sin’s power. First, we pretend we don't see it. This is true for almost everyone as no one wants to amidst they did something wrong. Next, we argue what we did was right. This is a type of excuse driven reasoning. Thirdly, we often decide we don't care what the rules say; we're going to do it our way anyway. This is rebellion at its worst. And then finally, we might agree it’s wrong, but just try to cover it up.

YHWH, however, wants to erase our mistakes for us. First we must see that sin is wrong, agree with YHWH that it's wrong, turn away from it to make it right, and ask YHWH to forgive us or erase it. Sin does not have to beat us! “Sin shall not be your master, because you are not under the law of sin, but under grace,” Romans 6:14.

May 30

One of the fruit of the Spirit of YHWH is kindness. To be kind to someone is to show hospitality, love, and concern. Take a few minutes today to review a few examples of kindness. Then, decide to show extra kindness to someone today.

- Laban was kind in Genesis 24:31, "And he said, Come in, thou blessed of YHWH; wherefore standest thou without? for I have prepared the house, and room for the camels."
- Jethro was hospitable in Exodus 2:20. "And he said unto his daughters, And where is he? why is it that ye have left the man? call him, that he may eat bread."
- Manoah loved others in Judges 13:15, "And Manoah said unto the angel of YHWH, I pray thee, let us detain thee, until we shall have made ready a kid for thee. "
- Samuel was generous, "1 Samuel 9:22 And Samuel took Saul and his servant, and brought them into the parlour, and made them sit in the chiefest place among them that were bidden, which were about thirty persons."
- David shared in 2 Samuel 6:19, "And he dealt among all the people, even among the whole multitude of Israel, as well to the women as men, to everyone a cake of bread, and a good piece of flesh, and a flagon of wine. So all the people departed everyone to his house."
- Barzillai was old in age but kind in heart, 2 Samuel 19:32, "Now Barzillai was a very aged man, even fourscore years old: and he had provided the king of sustenance while he lay at Mahanaim; for he was a very great man."
- Job did well in 31:32, "The stranger did not lodge in the street: but I opened my doors to the traveler."
- The story of Zaccheus's kindness is known throughout the world and is found in Luke 19:6, "And he made haste, and came down, and received him joyfully."
- Lydia showed the fruit of the Spirit in Acts 16:15, "And when she was baptized, and her household, she besought us, saying, If ye have judged me to be faithful to YHWH, come into my house, and abide there. And she constrained us."

Will you be numbered among these kind people?

Truth For Today

May 31

Sin is following the temptation to disobey YHWH, to act wickedly, or to break YHWH's law.

Temptation can be broken down into three categories from 1 John 2:16. This passage explains how temptation is activated in our lives. This passage also correlates exactly with the original sin of Adam and Eve / Chawa. "For all that is in the world, the lust of the flesh, and the lust of the eyes, and the pride of life, is not of the Father, but is of the world."

The lust of the flesh refers to the cravings of sinful man. It describes those sinful things that make us feel good. Eve saw that the fruit was good for food. The lust of the eyes describes our sinful desire for material possessions. Finally, the pride of life describes the notion that we are better than the next person. Eve saw the fruit could make her wise and a YHWH.

We need to recognize the role of Scripture in overcoming temptation. The Psalmist stated, "Thy Word have I hidden in my heart, that I might not sin against Thee," Psalms 119:11. When YHWH's Word becomes an integral part of the believer's life, it fortifies that person against temptation's power. The Messiah Himself demonstrated the Word's power when He resisted Ha Satan's temptations with a quote from the Old Testament / Tanakh (Matthew 4:7). A prayerful study of Scripture is an absolute prerequisite to defeating temptation. The Word not only warns of the enemy's methods, but it empowers against attacks as seen in Ephesians 6:11-17).

Another essential to victory is to avoid temptation. On several occasions, the Moshiach told His disciples to pray that they might not fall into temptation (Matthew 6:13; Luke 22:40). Some believers understand that temptation is not the same as sin, so then feel that they can enjoy the enticements of temptation without any harm. This behavior becomes a type of game—seeing how much titillation one can "enjoy" without falling into overt sin. Such an attitude is sinful in itself, for it fails to take seriously YHWH's commands for holiness in attitude as well as in action.

A third way to overcome temptation is to combine these aforementioned aspects and to simply "pray the Scriptures." Take time each day to declare the Scriptures over your life. As you guard the commandments in prayer the commandments will guard you from sin. Don't let the pride of life, the lust of the flesh, or the lust of the eyes to overcome you today.

June

June 1

Do you ever just struggle with life?

We must recognize that we are indeed in a war and the battlefield is our mind. We are constantly faced with decisions to think right. If we think wrong we will get wrong results but if we think righteous then we will get righteous results.

Now, the concept of war in Biblical terms is very different than our idea of war today. We envision nuclear bombs, drone missiles, submarines, and fighter jets when we think about war. In Biblical days war was much more combative and personal. Armies would march right up into each other's face on a battlefield and hand to hand combat.

"For though we walk in the flesh, we are not waging war according to the flesh. For the weapons of our warfare are not of the flesh but have divine power to destroy strongholds. We destroy arguments and every lofty opinion raised against the knowledge of YHWH, and take every thought captive to obey Messiah," 1 Corinthians 10:3-5. Here we can see that this is not a carnal natural battle with living breathing demons but it is indeed patterned after earthly war. The Scriptures describe the enemy's tactics as "ploys, schemes, and wiles." The dark side comes against us in our thought process because ha satan knows that if we think a certain way then we will behave a certain way. The goal of the enemy is to "steal, kill, and destroy," as seen in John 10:10. By planting thoughts and temptations in our way we can easily slip into destruction.

One of the main ways the enemy attacks us is through something called a "stronghold." This is a military term that perfectly describes how satan seeks to control and dominate our lives. Through a stronghold the enemy can gain entrance and power over us and therefore disable our faith from being active and effective.

Pray to YHWH today and ask if there are any strong holds in your life that need to be overcome. Read more about this subject in tomorrow's reading.

June 2

What exactly is a "stronghold?" Well, before suburbs and metropolitans, people gathered in herds and tents. Finally, when tribes decided to settle on a land they built homes or huts. To protect their community from dangerous people or animals, a wall was built around their city. The thicker and larger the wall, the more protection it offered. (Think about the Great Wall of China or the walls around Jericho.) As time progressed a tower or lookout was eventually erected as part of the city. This was a place of refuge, strength, security, power and vision. From a strong tower the townspeople could hide during a siege, watch for opposing forces, or launch attacks. A strong tower became a stronghold for the people to place their trust in for protection and care.

An evil strong hold is anything that "exalts itself over the knowledge of YHWH" in our lives. Anything that steps between you and your relationship with Y'shua is indeed a stronghold. Through the establishment of a strong tower in our lives the adversary can turn our worship and adoration away from YHWH. You see, all strongholds aren't inherently evil. YHWH Himself is supposed to be our strong tower. We should be running to YHWH for protection, meaning, power, and strength. Proverbs 18:10, "The name of YHWH is a strong tower, the righteous run into it and are safe." YHWH is to be force of vision and meaning in our lives. We should run to him when we are in fear, frustration or fault.

Sadly though we often run to other things. We binge on ice cream when we are sad, we gossip when we are mad, we yell when we are angry, and we cry when we are afraid. Our minds are so used to just allowing our emotions to run rampant until some level of security is found. This is why people fall into alcohol and substance abuse. Something in the bong or the bottle brings comfort and relief. Instead of going to YHWH people turn to whatever will dull the pain. We often run right into and up the stairs of the enemy's strong tower in our lives.

Strongholds are everywhere. Before a person comes to have faith in Messiah there are already strongholds present in their thinking. Even while a person is faithful in their walk with YHWH there can be strongholds present. A stronghold of satan is just that – it's anything and any area that the kingdom of darkness has a "strong hold" on your life. It's an area that you have somehow and in some way given over control to the enemy. A stronghold isn't an occasional sin or slip up. We all fall and do the wrong thing sometimes. Instead, a stronghold is an area of thought that is directly opposed to the Scriptures. Do you have any strongholds in your life?

June 3

Strongholds are anything you run to for comfort, love, protection, joy, or vision other than your relationship with YHWH.

Probably the most debilitating strongholds are those of idolatry, unforgiveness, bitterness, guilt, addiction, unloving spirit, depression, and deception.

Strongholds are far reaching and must be absolutely conquered before they absolutely conquer us. How do you know if you have a stronghold? Well, you can judge a tree by its fruit. If any of the behaviors in Galatians 5:19-21 are prevalent in your life or happen more than once a week then you may indeed have a stronghold. Allow the Ruach HaKodesh to speak to you regarding these thoughts or behaviors. Remember that you might not be acting these out yet but if the thoughts are there then a stronghold may be there as well. Colossians 3:5-8 also lists a few strongholds that hold us back from all that YHWH has. "Therefore put to death your members which are on the earth: fornication, uncleanness, passion, evil desire, and covetousness, which is idolatry. Because of these things the wrath of God is coming upon the sons of disobedience, in which you yourselves once walked when you lived in them. But now you yourselves are to put off all these: anger, wrath, malice, blasphemy, filthy language out of your mouth," Colossians 3:5-8.

A strong hold is anything that exalts itself over the knowledge of YHWH. Satan uses strongholds to make us think that we have no hope and that he is powerful. The truth is that satan is a defeated foe and his one and only power is deception. If the enemy can deceive us to pretending or thinking incorrectly then the enemy can defeat us.

Colossians 2:15 explains that the enemy has already been defeated. Therefore we are simply enforcing what Y'shua has already done. We are not trying to get victory so that we can reign in life. We are to be reigning in life through the victory of Y'shua!

Now you know what a stronghold is and how the enemy uses them to battle your soul. Now you can deal with this fortress. You can allow the Spirit and the Word to lead you to demolish the works of darkness. We've already learned that our warfare is not carnal, fleshly, or in the natural realm. You may think it's your spouse, your boss, your minister, or your friends that are the problems you face but that's not true. There is something in you and in other people that is fighting against you. You are in a war and it's time to get serious about winning the battle in our minds and lives.

June 4

"Once when Ya'acov / Jacob was cooking some stew, Esau came in from the open country, famished. He said to Ya'acov, "Quick, let me have some of that red stew! I'm famished!" Ya'acov replied, "First sell me your birthright." Esau said, "Look, I am about to die. What good is the birthright to me?" But Ya'acov said, "Swear to me first." So he swore an oath to him, selling his birthright to Ya'acov. Then Ya'acov gave Esav some bread and some lentil stew. He ate and drank, and then got up and left. Esav despised his birthright," Beresheet / Genesis 25:29-34. Why did Esav do this? Why was this exchange so important and tragic? Did Esav trade his preeminence just because he was hungry or was there a deeper issue? What is so bad about this event that because of this the scriptures say that Esau was "godless" and not worthy of following?

The birthright of the firstborn is a central theme and part of the Israelite lifestyle and lifecycle. The firstborn son of a Hebrew father is given special rights and is highly valued. He is the heir to the family and head of the household when the father is absent. The firstborn or "bachor" in Hebrew would receive double the inheritance of the other sons when the father passed. "The father must acknowledge the firstborn by giving him a double share of all he has. That son is the first sign of his father's strength. The right of the firstborn belongs to him," Deuteronomy 21:17.

One might casually look at the story of Ya'acov and Esav trading the birthright and think that Ya'acov / Jacob was being overly deceptive and took advantage of a famished man. But this is simply not the case. Esav did not sell his birthright simply because he was hungry. Esav sold his birthright, his mishpat bachor, because he had not concept of its meaning. Again, Esav despised his position and inheritance. This word for "despised" is "bazah." The Strong's Exhaustive Concordance and Dictionary states that this word literally means, "to disesteem:-despise, disdain, contemn (-ptible), + think to scorn, vile person." Believers are to not be like Esav. We must not despise our birthright, our destiny and inheritance as Israel. The temptation is present and the trade looks pleasing but we must be careful not to follow Esau's example.

Consider these verses...

"YHWH says, 'Israel is my firstborn,'" Shemot / Exodus 4:22.

"If you belong to Messiah you are a seed of Avraham and heirs according to the promise," Galatians 3:29.

"I am Israel's father, and Ephraim is my firstborn son," Yermi'yahu / Jeremiah 31:9

June 5

There are six commandments found in the Scriptures that you can do at any time and at any place. By keeping these simple mitzvot you can create divine space around you and impact your world. It has been said that, "the surest method to develop and maintain a deep and everlasting relationship with YHWH is by learning and internalizing the profound message contained in the Six Constant mitzvoth, as they are the basic components of a person's sense of attachment and connection to YHWH."

These 6 commands are the fabric of our relationship and the energy that infuses our actions. As we absorb their ideas and internalize their message we will began to slowly experience a deeper connection with YHWH. Notice the word "internalize" has been used." These are not outward commands that draw attention of those around us. Instead, the constant mitzvoth are internal intentions of our mind, hear, and soul. As we focus our thoughts on Him then our entire outlook on life changes and we can become a true vessel in which His spirit can flow. While the 613 commands are requirements for us, the 6 constant commands are the essence of our relationship. You could call these the "cocoa beans" of deep dark chocolate love of YHWH.

These commands can be considered six walls that surround a person, reminding us to always focus on YHWH. This is how we can be in the world but not of the world.

The first command which is considered above us is also the first of the 10 Commandments. We are to know YHWH. "I am YHWH your Elohim who brought you out of Egypt."

The next mitzvoth is below us and should be below us. We are to not to recognize or worship any other gods. We are not to sink to the level of those in this world but remain focused on YHWH. We stomp upon the enemy and his ways when we walk with YHWH. "May the YHWH of peace crush satan under your feet," says Hebrews.

The third of the six constant mitzvoth is to recognize that YHWH is Echad - YHWH is One. This realization is to stay in front of us at all times. This of course is found in the great "shema" of Deuteronomy 6. To our left and to our right are the balancing mitzvoth of gevurah / judgment and chesed / mercy. YHWH's right hand embraces us in love teaching us to love YHWH. This is the 4thconstant commandment. To our left is the fear of YHWH. The fear of YHWH should always be before us. Finally, the sixth command is behind us and tells us to not trust our heart or eyes.

When we keep these mitzvoth in mind and walk in them, we are in essence living in divine space. We are actually creating a cube of space around us - above, below, to the front, behind, left and right. This cube is symbolic of the tents or tabernacles that YHWH commanded Israel to dwell. As you keep these commandments today you are building a sukkah for YHWH to inhabit.

June 6

Throughout the Older Testament, the people of Israel built more and more high places of rebellion. "And the children of Israel did secretly those things that were not right against the YHWH their Elohim, and they built them high places in all their cities, from the tower of the watchmen to the fenced city," 2 Kings 17:9.

It is from a high place in Numbers 22:41 that Balak took Balaam to curse Israel. The same happens today. The enemy seeks to enthrone himself upon the high places of the world. The Hebrew word that is often used to describe a false place of worship and honor is very interesting. It is the same Hebrew term used in Isaiah to describe the heights from which Satan fell. This is the Hebrew term "bama." A bama is anything that exalts itself over the wisdom, power, or knowledge of YHWH.

Now, you might think that the high pagan places today do not apply to you. Well, think again. There are high places that work in each of our lives every day in the way we think. A high place is anywhere that a thought or emotion exalts itself over the knowledge of YHWH. The spirit of Balak and Bilaam is alive today and operating behind the thoughts of the mind.

2 Corinthians 10:3-6, "For though we live in the world, we do not wage war as the world does. The weapons we fight with are worldly. On the contrary, they have divine power to demolish strongholds. We demolish arguments and every pretension that sets itself up against the knowledge of Elohim, and we take captive every thought to make it obedient to Messiah. And we will be ready to punish every act of disobedience, once your obedience is complete.

This section of Scripture from 2 Corinthians is key to understanding high places. These aren't just places of pagan idolatry worship BUT strongholds in our very thought patterns. There are high places everywhere! Ezekiel 16:24, "That thou hast also built unto thee an eminent place, and hast made thee a high place in every street."

Our thought life is the battle ground of worship and the place of high places. We must go up to the high places and tear down the devil's kingdom. The enemy is enthroned upon the feelings and emotions. High places include thoughts of selfishness, unloving spirits, ridicule, unforgiveness, impatience, jealousy, anger, doubt, and fear. These are high places in each of our lives that must be recognized, removed, repented for, and replaced with YHWH's truth. Ha Satan is enthroned upon high places of thought that exalt themselves over the knowledge of YHWH. The solution to such evil is recognizing that YHWH is enthroned upon the praises of his people. Strongholds may abound – high places are all around – yet they can be defeated!

June 7

High place worship feels real, looks real, and tastes real but it is not the Biblical worship experience that is based on spirit and in truth. On a high place is where asherah poles were erected and where Molech offered human sacrifices. High places originate with the original rebellion of the satan and are still play today.

Isaiah 14:12-17, "How you are fallen from heaven, O Day Star, son of Dawn! How you are cut down to the ground, you who laid the nations low! You said in your heart, I will ascend to heaven; above the stars of Elohim I will set my throne on high; I will sit on the mount of assembly in the far north; I will ascend above the heights of the clouds, I will make myself like the Most High.' But you are brought down to Sheol, to the depths of the Pit. Those who see you will stare at you, and ponder over you: Is this the man who made the earth tremble, who shook kingdoms, who made the world like a desert and overthrew its cities, who did not let his prisoners go home?' This passage shows how the enemy tried to exalt himself into a high place. In the King James translation, verse 12 reads: "How art thou fallen from heaven, O Lucifer, son of the morning! How art thou cut down to the ground, which didst weaken the nations!"

The enemy wanted to go up. He wanted the attention, the praise, the power and the place of the exalted one. This is the pattern the enemy started and millions follow every day.

One prime example of high place worship occurred in 1 Kings 12 when the kingdom of Israel was torn in two. The wicked king Jeroboam encouraged the nation of Israel to ascend the high places of false worship. 1 Kings 12:27-33 relates how Jeroboam set up high places with false worship heights, including false days, false places, and false ways. High place worship is a false system that rebels against the Almighty's call to go up to Jerusalem.

Ask the Holy Spirit to reveal any high places in your life today. Will you tear them down and allow YHWH to build Himself up in your life?

June 8

We must tear down the devil's high places. We do this by going up to be with YHWH. Leviticus 26:30, "YHWH said, I will destroy your high places, and cast down your images, and cast your carcasses upon the carcasses of your idols and my soul shall abhor you."

To defeat the high places, the strongholds that the enemy has in our lives, we must change the way we worship. We need to be like the angels in their worship of YHWH that circle the throne of YHWH twenty four hours a day and seven days a week proclaiming "holy, holy, holy." They don't worship YHWH because of what he has done. Instead, they worship YHWH for WHO he is! There is a difference in worship and praise when it comes to reflecting on just who YHWH is. Praise is thanking YHWH for what He has done in our lives and in the Scriptures. We should enter His gates with thanksgiving and His courts with praise. Then as we ascend we are to begin changing our words and our thoughts to be totally directed to HIM. We need a few minutes each day to just reflect on YHWH's nature and character. This time of true worship can change the rest of our day and week as it empowers us to rely upon YHWH greater. "I will bless YHWH at all times, His praise will continually be on my mouth," Psalm 34:1.

Think about the plague of snakes and the pole that was lifted up in the desert to save the people from the sickness. This stake was to represent Y'shua as He was lifted up but it came to be a high place. 2 Kings 18:4 explains, "He removed the high places, and broke the images, and cut down the groves, and broke in pieces the brazen serpent that Moses had made: for unto those days the children of Israel did burn incense to it: and he called it Nehushtan." The past moves of YHWH don't matter if YHWH isn't moving in your life today!

When was the last time you prayed and got an answer, or saw miracles, or witnessed and had someone accept the Messiah before your very eyes? So what if YHWH saved you when you were 12 – what are you doing now? So what if the red sea parted if you don't have victory in your life today? So what if there are 613 commandments if you can't get the unforgiveness and bitterness out of your life? So what if an image of a snake saved people if it was later going to be worshipped?

We must learn to go up to Jerusalem through praise and through prayer if we will overcome the strongholds in our lives and in the lives of others. The thought patterns of the world, of the satan, of evil, need to be torn down through the spiritual weapons of warfare. Our weapons are mighty in Y'shua for the pulling down of high places as we go up to Jerusalem with YHWH.

June 9

The sword of the Spirit is part of our armor as seen in Ephesians 6. Do you know what the sword was for a Temple priest? It was their blade that they used to sacrifice animals with.

For the priest, this sword of the Spirit was a double-edged sword they used to kill the animals for sacrifice. The Word of YHWH is used to kill the animal flesh. We all have an animalistic nature. It is called the flesh or "the nefesh" and our animal desire or drives will lead us against what YHWH wants. It leads us to be prideful. It leads us to be selfish. Yet, the Scriptures tell us in Hebrews 4 that the "Word of YHWH is like a sharp double-edged sword that is able to pierce even to the dividing parts, the being and the Ruach...between the joints and the marrow and bone and is a discerner of the thoughts and the intents of the heart."

So what does the Word of YHWH, the sword of sacrifice, do? When you sacrifice, it divides between the joints and the marrow and the bone. It cuts off the flesh. Don't let people tell you that sacrifices have been done away with. It's absolutely not true. Do we have a temple building where we sacrifice? No. But do we have a temple body where we sacrifice? Yes. Our body is the temple of the Ruach HaKodesh, right? So where do the sacrifices occur? They occur right there inside of you. Every day, you are going to be given opportunities to decide whether you are going to sacrifice what your flesh wants, what you want to say, what you want to do, what you want to think. Will you allow the Word of YHWH to put it to death?

Here's a great thing about the sacrifices in the temple. They were humane. They were quick. They were done so the animal would feel no pain. That's the way the Word of YHWH should act to us. In Hebrews it says that the "word of YHWH is quick and powerful." That is how the sacrifices were to be done in the temple. Quick and powerful. One cut, it's done. Kill the animal. That's how it should be for us. Quick and powerful. Our defense and our offense is the Word of YHWH. We are to be swift and quick to say, "Ha'Satan...it is written."

The Word isn't just to be studied or memorized. We are to use the Scriptures as a sword to fight our flesh and our enemy. Take up the sword of the Spirit and cut loose from all that holds you back.

June 10

The Jewish Sages have divided the Torah commands into two basic categories. The first, called "mishpatim" are considered to be rulings that are basically rational. These are often translated as "judgments." Statements like "do not murder" and "do not steal" are easy to reason out and therefore fit without difficulty into this area of interpretation. The second category of Mitzvot is called "chok." These are directions given to man as decrees and are usually translated as such. Chok are found in verses that deal with seemingly irrational concepts like inflicting yourself on Yom Kippur or wearing tassels.

Mishpatim conform to a sense of just living. Chukim can only be understood as a decree from YHWH the King. There are many chukim / rulings and mishpatim found throughout the Bible. For example, Leviticus 16-21, begins with instructions on how to properly observe the Day of Atonement and continues with specific thoughts on animal or meal offerings and laws prohibiting sexual relations within certain relationships. The second section stresses the set apartness of the Israelite through the mitzvoth. Verses in this area deal with everything from honesty to charity to idolatry. Some of these concepts are easy to fathom while others are seemingly unfathomable.

Chasidic thought teaches that "chok" emphasizes the supra-rationality of our commitment to Elohim, while Mishpat stresses the function of the mitzvoth as educators and enlighteners of human life. Y'shua said in Mattitiyahu / Matthew 18:3 that we must come to him with the faith of little children. Western or Greek thinking instinctively says that before you do something you should understand the purpose and reason why. Biblically mandated obedience says to just do it. Western or Greek thinking teaches to reason and then obey while many of the mitzvoth in the Torah can only be understood after they have been experienced. This faith is truly experiential. This means that to grasp the importance and meaning of Torah one must first experience the power and obedience of Torah. It is difficult to delight in the Sabbath until the first time you experience Sabbath rest. It is hard to comprehend why a person should eat kosher until you eat kosher foods. Surely you don't have to know exactly how the microscopic electrical parts of your computer work but you still use your computer, right? It is the same with the chok of the Torah. In fact it is the same with the whole of Torah. All of Torah is indeed chok.

To us it makes sense not to kill or steal. It doesn't make sense to refrain from marring the edges of our beards. Yet to YHWH it is the same. A mitzvot is a mitzvot. A decree is a decree. Obedience is obedience. You don't have to fully understand why you are following Torah to follow Torah. Just understand that you are obeying the will of Almighty YHWH.

June 11

Y'shua our Messiah said that, "You shall be my witnesses in Jerusalem, and in all Judea, and Samaria and to the ends of the earth," Acts 1:8. When Y'shua said this He did not say whether our witness would be for or against Him. He just said that we would be His witnesses! Our actions prove who we really are and who we really worship...YHWH or self.

Man is responsible for YHWH's honor in the eyes of the world. When man follows the precepts of the Torah then YHWH is revered. In Hebrew the phrase "Kiddush Hashem" denotes more than just respecting the Eternal, it is also the term applied to believers who are martyred for their faith. The Rabbis have taught that an Israelite faced with the strictest of persecutions should sacrifice his life to honor YHWH, to Kiddush Hashem. "The idea of "Kiddush Hashem" was declared obligatory in the case of three commandments and a person had to suffer death rather than violate them: idolatry, fornication including incest, adultery, and, under certain circumstances, any infraction of the moral code, and murder. One should violate all other commandments rather than suffer death," says the Encyclopedia Judaica. This of course is the most extreme way to honor YHWH. Not surprisingly though, this is the way the Son of Man honored YHWH. "For YHWH demonstrated his own love for us (glorified His own Name) in this: While we were still sinners, Moshiach died for us," Romans 5:8.

On the other side of this coin is the concept of chillul Hashem or profaning the name of YHWH. "You shall faithfully observe my commandments: I am YHWH. You shall not profane My holy name, that I may be sanctified in the midst of the Israelite people – I YHWH who sanctifies you, who brought you out of the land of Mitzrayim / Egypt to be your Elohim, I am YHWH," Leviticus/Vayikra 22:31-33. When a person does not faithfully obey the devar YHWH / word of YHWH then YHWH's name is profaned or blasphemed.

In the Tanakh, Jeremiah the prophet spoke to the nation about profaning the name of YHWH when they broke the Torah to fulfill their own selfish desires. Also in Amos 2:7 another Prophet condemned sinful actions and immorality as chillul Hashem. These examples prove that what you do either praises the Name of YHWH or profanes the Name of YHWH.

There are so many believers who say they follow the Bible yet their actions prove them to be hypocrites. Too many people say one thing and do another. This type of religion is void of any spiritual power and has become sour to the world. Yes, talk is cheap but what really makes a difference in people's lives is when YHWH's name is praised through faithful trusting obedience. Benjamin Franklin said, "a good example is the best sermon." Who can disagree with that?

TRUTH FOR TODAY

June 12

The word baptism comes to the English language from the Greek word "baptizos," which means to "wash or immerse." This Greek concept is derived from the Hebrew term "t'vilah." Does this mean that baptism is really a Hebrew concept?

Yes, before John the Baptist came preaching "repent and be baptized," immersion was already an accepted practice in the life of the Hebrew people. As John the Baptist stood in the Jordan River, he wasn't doing anything radical or new. T'vilah / immersion was part of the Biblical faith before Messiah came. Judaism today continues to use immersion. This proves that baptism is not just as a sacrament ordained by the Roman church, but an action commanded by the Scriptures. T'vilah is in essence a gateway into being kedusha or set apart.

T'vilah is the physical act of immersing into a body of moving water, called a "mikvah" in Hebrew. The Encyclopedia Judaica says that a mikvah is a, "a collection of water, a pool or bath of clear water, immersion in which renders ritually clean a person who has become ritually unclean through contact with the dead (Num. 19) or any other defiling object, or through an unclean flux from the body (Lev. 15) and especially a menstruant. It is similarly used for vessels (Num. 31:22–23)."

Immersion is found all throughout the Older Testament and John the Baptizer came the multitudes accepted his call as common. It wasn't unusual for a person to be proclaiming holiness through immersion in water and it shouldn't be uncommon today. Part of our message should be immersion. Y'shua sent us into the world with the commission to t'vilah new believers into His name and ways.

When was the last time you were immersed in water? What is holding you back from being mikvahed again?

June 13

Ever feel abandoned, forgotten, or kicked to the curb? If so then you're not alone. In fact, you are just like the Bible character named Mephibosheth. Mephibosheth? The name doesn't ring a bell, does it? That's too bad because his story is inspiring. It's also an all too familiar story that seems to repeat itself in our modern world.

Mephibosheth could have been great but tragedy struck and his life was forever changed. His father died. His grandfather died. And he was crippled in both feet. As a child he was dropped on accident and never recovered. Ever felt dropped by loved ones, supposed friends, or other believers?

For years, Mephibosheth was left for dead and pretty much forgotten by the entire world. Unimportant and unloved, he settled in the land of Lo-Debar Israel. Even his hometown described his horrible state. "Lo" is the Hebrew word for "no" and "debar" is Hebrew for "words." Mephibosheth lived in a state of "no words" and revelation from YHWH. (Ever been in a spiritual state of longing like that?) Desperation was the norm for Meph until one day when everything changed.

Like the story of Cinderella, Mephibosheth is rescued from the muck and mire and given a place in the king's palace. You see, Meph was the son of Jonathan and the grandson of King Saul. King David had been searching for the cripple for many years as he had promised Jonathan that he would always care for his family. King David's men found Mephibosheth wallowing in the pig pen of Lo-Debar. They rescued him from shame and brought him to the King. For the rest of Meph's life he would live like a prince and be treated with the respect and blessing of royalty.

What David did for Mephibosheth is a picture of what Messiah did for you. Ephesians 2:4 says that you are now "seated with Messiah in heavenly places." Though you were once dropped and forgotten by others you now have a place at the King's table.

Rejoice in this truth today.

June 14

The armor of YHWH, found in Ephesians 6, includes two weapons that we should take up in our battle against the enemy and his strongholds. First, we have the "sword of the Spirit which is the word of YHWH." Second, we have "prayer." The weapons of our warfare (prayer and Scripture) are mighty for the pulling down of strongholds. Notice that our sword is attached to the rifle of prayer to give us a Spiritual bayonet of power. A sword by itself can do some damage and a gun by itself can wound, but together as "the believer's bayonet" we can have the victory.

The Word of YHWH is to be a sword. In fact you can't spell the word "sword" without the term "word." The Scriptures are "sharper than any two edged sword" and deliver a cutting blow. The Word is to be used offensively. We aren't just to read, study, obey, and know the Scriptures. We are to battle with the Bible! The Word of YHWH empowers our soul to overcome the lusts of the flesh, the pride of life, and the lusts of the eyes. Remember that even the Messiah defeated satan with the sword of the word. Y'shua said, "it is written... it is written... it is written..." How often do you say this same phrase? Once a day? Once a week?

The Bible is to be a sword to fight off the enemy. To use it correctly we need to pull the word out of its sheaf and put it in our hearts through memorization and prayer. We need to recognize the role of Scripture in overcoming temptation. The Psalmist stated, "Thy Word have I hidden in my heart, that I might not sin against Thee," Psalms 119:11. When YHWH's Word becomes a central part of the believer's life, it empowers that person against temptation's power. The Messiah Himself demonstrated the Word's power when He resisted Ha Satan's temptations with a quote from the Old Testament / Tanakh (Matthew 4:7).

Our second weapon is prayer. Prayer is most effective when it is in line with YHWH's will. When you pray the Scriptures you are perfectly praying YHWH's will. Take up the Word as a weapon and say it out loud as a prayer. Make Scriptural declarations against hell's stronghold. Build yourself up when you say the Scriptures aloud because faith comes by hearing the Word. Praying the Scriptures brings out the Mind of Messiah. When you declare the Word you heart it and Satan hears it!

How can you pray the Scriptures today?

June 15

Strongholds are anything you run to for comfort, love, protection, joy, or vision other than your relationship with YHWH. Probably the most debilitating strongholds are those of idolatry, unforgiveness, bitterness, guilt, addiction, unloving spirit, depression, and deception.

Strongholds are far reaching and must be absolutely conquered before they absolutely conquer us. How do you know if you have a stronghold? Well, you can judge a tree by its fruit. If any of the following behaviors are prevalent in your life or happen more than once a week then you may indeed have a stronghold. Allow the Ruach HaKodesh to speak to you regarding these thoughts or behaviors. Remember that you might not be acting these out yet but if the thoughts are there then a stronghold may be there as well.

"Now the works of the flesh are evident, which are: adultery, fornication, uncleanness, lewdness, idolatry, sorcery, hatred, contentions, jealousies, outbursts of wrath, selfish ambitions, dissensions, heresies, envy, murders, drunkenness, revelries, and the like; of which I tell you beforehand, just as I also told you in time past, that those who practice such things will not inherit the kingdom of YHWH," Galatians 5:19-21.

"For I fear lest, when I come, I shall not find you such as I wish, and that I shall be found by you such as you do not wish; lest there be contentions, jealousies, outbursts of wrath, selfish ambitions, backbitings, whisperings, conceits, tumults; lest, when I come again, my YHWH will humble me among you, and I shall mourn for many who have sinned before and have not repented of the uncleanness, fornication, and lewdness which they have practiced," 2 Corinthians 12:20-21.

Remember that a strong hold is anything that exalts itself over the knowledge of YHWH. Satan uses strongholds to make us think that we have no hope and that he is powerful. The truth is that satan is a defeated foe and his one and only power is deception. If the enemy can deceive us to pretending or thinking incorrectly then the enemy can defeat us.

Now you know what a stronghold is and how the enemy uses them to battle your soul you can deal with this fortress. You may think it's your spouse, your boss, your minister, or your friends that are the problems you face but that's not true. There is something in you and in other people that is fighting against you. You are in a war and it's time to get serious about winning the battle in our minds and lives.

June 16

The Scriptures were never meant to only be read during Sunday school or studied like a history text for a college class. The Bible contains the power to "demolish" strongholds. The word "power" in 2 Corinthians 10:3-5 is from the Greek term "dunamai," which is where we get the phrase "dynamite" from today. Strongholds are to be demolished and can be demolished through two sticks of dynamite. The word is one stick and prayer is another stick. Now, one stick of dynamite is powerful but two sticks together can blow up a huge building. Praying the Word or declaring the Word will tear down any stronghold of satan.

The words we save have such power and authority. Remember that YHWH spoke and the entire universe came into existence. The Tower of Babel was created when people agreed together as seen in Genesis 11:6. When you speak and believe the Word you can experience all that YHWH has for you. Job 22:28, "you shall declare a thing and it shall be established." There are several places in the Scriptures that explain how the words we say are seeds that will either produce a bountiful or scare crop. See Luke 8:11 and 2 Corinthians 9:6 for more on this. Finally, the book of Revelation says that we overcome by "blood of the lamb and the word of our testimony." Through the words of faith we proclaim we can defeat the strongholds and attacks of the enemy. Y'shua said "it is written" and the enemy was defeated. We must learn to say the same and then we will experience the same victory Y'shua did.

Will you take a stand against the enemy today?

June 17

The same power that brought Y'shua out of the tomb is in you today and tomorrow and with you at all times. If we pray or sing and ask YHWH to bless us then we are ignoring what the Bible already says. If we pray or sing and ask YHWH to fill us or "come" then we are being ignorant of what the Bible already says. YHWH has already filled us. The scriptures state that if two or three are gathered together then he is with us already.

The presence of YHWH is in us which means Satan can't win. 1 John 4:4 "greater is her that is in us than he that is in the word." The disciples had power. The first believers had power. We have power if we just acknowledge it and use it. Philemon 1:9 tells us to think on meditate and acknowledge YHWH's presence and YHWH's power. That's when our faith becomes effective for US and not for YHWH. We need to get serious about all that YHWH is doing in us and through us.

The ark of the covenant was in the midst of the mishkan which was in the midst of the camp of Israel. All Israel camped around the tabernacle. Exodus 25:8 tells us the meaning of the mishkan / tabernacle, the purpose of the tents, and even why we are to remember the wilderness journey from Egypt to the Promised Land during the festival of Sukkot.

The presence of YHWH was meant to be in the midst of the people Israel. This can again be seen in Joel 2:2, "And ye shall know that I am in the midst of Israel, and that I am YHWH your Elohim, and none else: and my people shall never be ashamed." This verse from Joel has special Sukkot meaning. YHWH wants to be in the midst of Israel in the midst of our camp. YHWH was never meant to be separate or separated.

When Adam and Eve were created in the Garden of Eden they had a perfect relationship with YHWH. Then after the fall, that relationship was hindered and YHWH was no longer in the midst of their lives. "Then the man and his wife heard the sound of YHWH Elohim as he was walking in the garden in the cool of the day, and they hid from the YHWH Elohim among the trees of the garden," Genesis 3:8. One reason that Adam and Eve hid from YHWH is because they realized a difference in the voice of YHWH. Before sin, His voice was inside of them and they were united with YHWH in perfection. Now, the voice was on the OUTSIDE. The loss of the voice scared them so much that the first couple hid among the trees (perhaps behind the tree of knowledge.) The voice was separated because Adam and Eve had chosen to eat from the wrong tree and seek after the knowledge of good and evil. We too are tempted with the same tree – the tree of knowledge. Will you win over temptation today?

June 18

Adam and Eve should have been listening to the voice and eating from the tree of life! This fall teaches us a very good and timely lesson. Until we have eaten from the tree of life we shouldn't worry about knowledge of the other spiritual issues. The tree of life or "eytz chayim" is the Torah of YHWH as revealed in the first five books of the Bible. To eat from the tree of life is to take the Torah and digest it until the Torah becomes part of our very inner being. This digestion of the Torah tree of life will produce the fruit of the spirit like love, joy, peace, patience, kindness, goodness, gentleness, faithfulness and self-control. Sadly, we spend so much time worrying about the minutia of the Torah. Countless hours are devoted to the little things, like the latest revelation from some Internet teacher. Now is the time to get serious about the Tree of Life and the holiness of YHWH. Too many believers squabble over calendars or outward observances like diet or homeschooling. Too much time is wasted learning about the newest conspiracy theory. Sadly, there are many people who choose to eat from the tree of knowledge with many hours of studying and yet these same people spend very little time listening to the Ruach in prayer. Knowledge is not the answer. Adam and Eve had knowledge. Having a relationship with Y'shua and His people is what we should be focusing upon. We must take the knowledge that we have learned and apply it through listening to the voice of YHWH and seeking the greater commandments of love, mercy, and justice.

Rabbi Sha'ul / the Apostle Paul makes his case for such seriousness when he states that knowledge is nothing but dung. We should not choose the tree of knowledge over the tree of life. What matters is walking in His Word and gaining the power of the anointing. Philippians 3:8, "Yes doubtless, and I count all things but loss for the excellency of the knowledge of Messiah Y'shua my Master for whom I have suffered the loss of all things, and do count them but dung, that I may win Christ." Paul makes it very clear that "all things" are "but loss" compared to knowing Y'shua. Indeed, he goes as far to use the word "dung." This shows us that whatever we do that doesn't directly help our relationship with YHWH and other people is waste. Many good deeds, many good ideas, and many good books are nothing but waste. What dung is there in your life? What is wasting your time from prayer and fellowship with YHWH? What we know; what we think we know; our obedience; our Torah observance; is nothing BUT dung compared to winning Messiah. Rest in Y'shua today!

TRUTH FOR TODAY

June 19

The following verse can transform your life...."therefore, since we have these promises, dear friends, let us purify ourselves from everything that contaminates body and soul, perfecting holiness out of reverence for YHWH," 2 Corinthians 7:1.

Wow. What an amazing concept is presented here in 2 Corinthians. Our body and spirit can be contaminated by sin and sinfulness. Of course our spirit is made one with YHWH's Holy Spirit at salvation so it is safe, but our mind (soul) and our body can be held hostage. Your mind or emotions and your body can absolutely be made unclean and therefore are in need for purification by the Word. Read 2 Corinthians 7:1 again and again until you understand that YHWH's holiness will cause us to purify ourselves.

It is YOUR personal job and responsibility to purify yourself from whatever can make your tamei. It's not the preacher's job, nor is it your spouse's responsibility. Each of us must apply the Promise of the Spirit and keep ourselves clean from sinful actions and sinful thoughts. As we seek YHWH and hunger and thirst for His righteousness, we will be filled and YHWH will do his part to sanctify us through his word. 1 Thessalonians 5:23, "Now may the Elohim of peace make you holy in every way, and may your whole spirit and soul and body be kept blameless until our Master Y'shua comes again." Notice in this verse that YHWH is called the "elohim of peace" or the "Elohim of shalom."

We often and easily lose sight of the amazing changes that took place in us during salvation. This is because the change of salvation was in the invisible hidden realm. We live in the visible realm and too often place our focus on the physical. If we debate and discuss outward observance to the Bible without first dealing with the heart then we are in dangerous waters. It is through the Spirit in us that the observance to the commandments and our outward holiness finds true meaning. By having the right motives, of allowing the Spirit to flow through us, we can change acts of obedience into holy motions. Y'shua came to make peace between us on the outside and the inside! Memorize 2 Corinthians 7:1 today and allow the Scriptures to change your life!

June 20

"And we have known and believed the ahava / love that YHWH has for us. YHWH is ahava / love, and he who stays in ahava, stays in YHWH, and YHWH in him," 1 John 4:16.

YHWH loves us too much to allow us to wallow in sin or walk in the flesh. When we have a problem, when we fall, when we sin, and even we face pain or sickness we should ask YHWH to reveal His ahava / love to us in a greater way. EVERYDAY we should beseech YHWH for a greater revelation of His ahava / love. Have you done this today? The next time you are stressed or have an issue of prayer, you should FIRST ask YHWH to reveal His love to you in that situation. Before you reach for that prescription medication simply call upon YHWH to give you a greater understanding of His ahava. People see YHWH through our ahava / love: "Beloved, if YHWH so loved us; we also should love one another," 1 John 4:11.

We are to know and experience the ahava of YHWH and keep His love before us at all times. Once our mind is conformed to YHWH's ahava / love THEN we will be able to show YHWH's love to others. "Beloved, let us love one another, for ahava is from YHWH; and everyone who has ahava is born from YHWH and knows YHWH. He who does not have ahava does not know YHWH for YHWH is Ahava," 1 John 4:7-8,

Our love towards each other and towards the world is evidence of our faith. Our ahava / love witnesses for our faith. People see the love of YHWH through our love. To be effective, each act of faith, each prayer, and each good deed must be from the motivation of love. We can keep the whole Torah and yet not act in love. Such actions are vain. 1 Corinthians says that you can speak in the tongues of angels but if you have not love then you are clanging cymbal. The language of angels is the Hebrew language! You can speak perfect Hebrew BUT if you do not love then you sound like a loud gong.

How can you show real love today? Who can you reach out to in love?

June 21

Did you know the Jews do not call their Bible the "Old Testament? You're not going to find a Jew carrying around an Old Testament, and for good reason. When we say that there's the Old Testament and there's the New Testament, did you know that we're actually creating a dividing line? In your very own Bible is a dividing page that separates the "Old Testament" from the "New Testament." Have you ever thought about ripping that page out of your Scriptures? Maybe you should.

Many times, people have a dividing line in their mind about how YHWH. Religious people reason that "YHWH related to man with the Law then but now He uses grace." Imagine you want to dress up a little nicer to go to work. You go to the closet, pull out an old plaid sports coat. The jacket was tucked way back in the closet and you just know wearing this will make a statement for you today. After some eye brows are raised a few laughs are had you realize the jacket is 30 years out of style and your statement of fashion is not a good one at all. We often view "old" as bad and "new" as better. The old has been done away with. You could take that over to what we call the Old Testament and the New Testament as many people believe that YHWH chose the Jewish people in the Old Testament but because they rejected the Savior, then He chose the Gentiles in the New Testament. The word "old" means that something replaced. Is this true in your life?

Why not call the "Old Testament" the "Older Testament?" Or better yet, use the same phrase that Y'shua used by calling it the "Tanakh." The Tanakh or TNK stands for the "Torah, Nevi'im, Ketuvim."

The Torah is the first five books of the Bible and includes loving instructions on how to treat each other and YHWH. Then, in the Hebrew Bible, we have the Nevi'im, or the prophets. Finally, we have the Ketuvim. The other writings like the Proverbs, the Psalms, and such make up the Ketuvim

In the Beatitudes of Matthew 5 Y'shua about the writings and the prophets, and in Luke 24:44, "Y'shua said to them, 'These are My words that I spoke to you while I was still with you, that everything written about Me in the Torah, the prophets, Nevi'im, and the Psalms, that's part of the writings, Ketuvim, must be fulfilled. Every Jew that heard Him when He said that, "Oh, He talking about the Tanakh." The Torah, the Nevi'im, the Ketuvim. The Tanakh. Will you allow a division to grow in your mind about the Bible?

June 22

Many teachers in Christianity subscribe to the theology of "dispensationalism." This dangerous idea says that the Church and Israel are two different groups and that God deals with the Church one way and He deals with Israel another way. Dispensationalism says that God has a plan for the Church and one plan for Israel, and there was the age of law, and now we're in the age of grace. Dispensational theology teaches that salvation has always been by faith in YHWH but that faith has been placed on different things at different times.

Dispensationalism teaches that God relates to man differently at differently times in history. We are told that there was the age of innocence, Genesis 1-3, age of consciousness, the age of human government, the age of promise (that was Genesis 12 thru Exodus 19), the age of the law from Exodus 20 to Acts 2, and then in Acts 2, with Pentecost, with the birth of the Church, began the age of grace. Then finally there is that 7th dispensation, which is the millennial kingdom. Supposedly we are in the "church age" and are awaiting the "millennial kingdom." Confused? You're not alone.

Dispensationalists teach that the Old Testament applies mainly to the Jews while the New Testament is for the Christians. The Old Testament is good for bedtime stories, or sermon illustrations, but we don't have to really do what it says or so they think. Most dispensational churches teach new believers to start their walk of faith by reading the Gospel of John. Starting in the middle of a book is never a good idea. If you were reading an 800 page Stephen King novel and started on page 400 then you would be totally lost. Well, most dispensationalists assert that since the Torah, the writings of the prophets are not specifically directed to the Church, then they do not have to be followed (unless you're talking about tithing.) Confused more? You're not alone.

Basically, dispensationalists believe that since the Torah was given only to Israel, it doesn't apply today. The big problem with this type of teaching is called antinomianism. What is antinomianism? "Nomia" is the Greek word for law. Antinomianism is the teaching that the Law of Moses has been abolished and done away with and is no longer necessary or even practical for today. Of course, that is contrary to Matthew 5 which says that until heaven and earth pass away the Torah of YHWH remains.

Dispensationalism is a dangerous and confusing manmade idea that separates YHWH into different boxes of time. The Almighty says, "I am YHWH and I change not." We need to rid ourselves of antinomianism and this preposterous idea of dispensations. Study the scriptures for the truth and learn that YHWH relates to all mankind through His word and His son.

TRUTH FOR TODAY

June 23

Ephesians 2:11-15, "Therefore, remember that you formerly were the Gentiles, in the flesh, who were called uncircumcision by the so-called circumcision, which is performed by the flesh of human hands. Remember that you were at that time separated from Messiah, excluded from the Commonwealth of Israel, strangers to the covenant of promise, having no hope and without YHWH in the world. But now in Y'shua, you who were formerly far off have been brought near by the blood of Y'shua. For He Himself is our peace who made both groups into one and broke down the barrier of the dividing wall by abolishing in His flesh enmity, which is the law of commandments contained in ordinances, so that in Himself He might make the two into one new man thus establishing peace and might reconcile them both in one body to YHWH through the cross or execution stake, by it, having put to death the enmity, and He came and preached peace to you who were far away and peace to those who were near. For through Him, we both have access in one spirit to the Father. So you are no longer strangers and aliens, but you are fellow citizens with the saints and are of YHWH's household, having been built upon the foundation of the apostle's and prophets, Y'shua Himself being the chief cornerstone in whom the whole building being fitted together is growing into a holy temple in YHWH, in whom we are also being built together into a dwelling of YHWH in the spirit."

This passage of scripture clears up a few things. It says first of all, in verse 11, "Remember that you were formerly Gentiles." You can't be a Christian Gentile. It's an oxymoron. The word Gentile in Greek is "ethnos." It is from this word that we get the term "ethnicity" from in English. Ethnic means "nationality." According to Ephesians 2, believers are "former" gentiles or nations. When a person is born again he is grafted into the commonwealth of Israel. Ephesians 2:12, "remember that you at that time were separate from Messiah and you were excluded from the Commonwealth of Israel and strangers to the covenant of promise, having no hope and without YHWH." When we have Y'shua, what happens? We are included in the Commonwealth of Israel. We have the covenants. We have the promises.

Romans 10:12 says, "There is no difference between the Jew and the Greek (Gentile), for the same master over all is rich unto all that call upon Him." Galatians 3, "There is neither Jew nor Greek, there is neither bond nor free, there is neither male nor female, for we are all one in Y'shua." If you are born again, you are one in Y'shua with YHWH and Israel. Paul spoke about this many times stating that YHWH doesn't have two groups of elect people. Exodus 12:49. It says, "There shall be one law for the citizen of Israel and for the Gentile who dwells among you." Do you see yourself as a gentile or an Israelite? Why?

TRUTH FOR TODAY

June 24

The following is a statement that is found in both the book of Exodus and the New Testament. This passage describes the nation of Israel at Mount Sinai and the believing assembly after the resurrection. Could it be that the two are the same? Both the Old and the New Testament say, "you are a chosen generation, a royal priesthood, a holy nation."

Have you ever wondered why YHWH revealed his plan and purpose of Israel to you and not someone else? Why wasn't Billy Graham given a revelation of the name of YHWH Y'shua or the nation of Israel? Why did YHWH choose you and not Joyce Myer or T.D. Jakes?

Well, YHWH chooses the unlikely. He chose David. He chose the virgin and Moses the murderer. He could have chosen a famous TV preacher, and you know what? Torah would have all been about them. If a popular teacher would have started teaching the Hebrew Roots first then the movement would have been about them and nothing else. Instead of revealing the Torah to the popular, YHWH has chosen a small band, a remnant of believers all over the world who are opening up their eyes to turn the world upside down. That's us. We are a chosen generation. Our message is the return of Y'shua and our identity as Israel.

People say, "Oh, I cannot wait for the imminent return of Jesus." Well, the book of Acts in chapter 3 explains when the Messiah will return. Acts 3:19-20 says, "Therefore, repent and return so that your sins may be wiped away in order that the times of refreshing may come from YHWH that He may send Y'shua, the Messiah appointed for you, whom Heaven must receive until the period of restoration of all things which YHWH spoke about by the mouth of His holy prophets in the ancient times." It tells us here that Heaven must receive Y'shua until the restoration of all things spoken about by the prophets. Y'shua just can't come back tomorrow. He is being held in Heaven until certain things are restored on Earth. These things are what the prophets talked about.

What did the prophets talk about? The restoration of Israel. They kept calling the nation back to YHWH. They said, "Repent! Return to YHWH!" The prophets in the Scriptures spoke to the people about returning to YHWH and His service.

The purpose of the nation of Israel was to be a nation of priests, a royal priesthood who served YHWH. Priests served YHWH in the Temple. They used their gifts and abilities to bless YHWH and other people. You are a priest and you have certain talents as well.

What are your abilities? Where has He gifted you? What can you do? Now, do it for Him. You have been called from the world to be a "chosen generation." Choose to serve YHWH today and be part of the restoration of Israel.

Truth For Today

June 25

We are to have a renewed mind and a sacrificed body. "In view of YHWH's mercy you re to present yourselves to YHWH as a living sacrifice. Do not conform to the pattern of this world but be transformed by the renewing of your mind," Romans 12:1-2.

In the Temple, the outer court is where all sacrifices would take place. This is a perfect picture of the flesh where we must choose to use the body for the right reasons. The body is not evil or sinful. YHWH made mankind and said "it is very good." He blessed our bodies and created us to represent Him to creation. The body is 100% under the control of the mind. When you think about something you do it. If you think about skipping rope you are not going to throw a football. If you are thinking about taking a shower, then your body is not going to drive over a cliff. You do whatever you think about. However, the body can be a place of problems.

Through the portals of the body our soul/mind is fed information. The five senses of sight, taste, sound, touch, and smell provide data for your mind to process twenty four hours a day, seven days a week. The details of life flow to the filter of the mind and either stops there or flows to the Spirit for consideration. For example, when your senses tell you that it's Friday your mind can find solace in the fact that the work week is almost done. Your mind can dwell on all the fun things waiting for you to do on Friday night and Saturday. Or, if you allow this through of TGIF to filter into your soulish holy realm then the Holy Spirit can quicken you to prepare for the seventh day Sabbath. Instead of planning to be busy, busy, busy on Saturday your Spirit will cause you to rethink your Sabbath day plans and rest. If a thought doesn't make its way to the Spirit (if you don't take it captive to the obedience of Y'shua) then you can be fooled.

Haven't you tasted a piece of gum and thought you were eating a real grape? Even our noses can be tricked by scented candles and our hands fooled by a counterfeit dollar. The enemy constantly blasts us in these 5 areas in order to dominate our faith and destroy our life. For example, we hear the prognosis and we automatically think the worse. We see the bank balance and know that we will run out of money before we run out of month. The five senses will lead us to live in a world of doubt and unbelief. This is why we must learn to develop and depend upon a sixth sense. A sixth sense? That's the sense of faith.

The sixth sense of faith is a force that can overcome the false forces all around us. Faith is how we go on even though our five senses tell us to stop. The sixth sense of faith objects to the negativity of the world all around us. Faith or "emunah" in Hebrew believes the Word of YHWH over the words of despair. Emunah is victorious over fear and doubt brought about the five senses. Emunah / faith is also how we reach out into the Spiritual realm and experience all that YHWH has for us. Walk by faith and not by sight today through prayer and the Scriptures.

June 26

Ephesians 2 says we are "saved by grace through faith, it is not of yourselves for it is a gift of YHWH." Here from this popular passage we can learn many things. First, we can see that we are saved by grace through faith. Salvation is not just about our eternal destination (that's redemption.) Salvation is about wholeness or shalom. Salvation is the whole package of redemption, sanctification, mercy, favor, and healing. When Y'shua died for us he shed his blood for our sins and gave his body for our bodies. At salvation all of YHWH's love and favor is available to us in the Spiritual realm. We are endued with power and even given the very Spirit of YHWH. 1 Corinthians 6:17, "he who is joined to the Master is one spirit with YHWH." At salvation we are given many gifts. Faith or "emunah" is a gift of YHWH that he has given each and every believer. When you are born again you are given the very faith of YHWH as a gift in your spirit. Ephesians chapter two states that "faith" is a "gift of YHWH."

Our evil sinfulness even stops us from coming to YHWH. That's why we need the gift of faith to believe His Word. The faith and faithfulness of YHWH is already inside of you. This means that you don't need more faith. You have all of the faith of YHWH in you right now because He gave you his faith. Paul said this in Galatians, "I am crucified with Messiah, and nevertheless I live. This life I live in the flesh I live by the faith of the son of YHWH." We don't live by faith "in" Y'shua. We live by the faith "of" Y'shua. It is through His faith that we live and move and have our being.

Galatians 5 lists the fruit of the Holy Spirit and faith is part of the list. "The fruit of the Spirit is love, joy, peace, patience, kindness, FAITHfulness..." Notice that the fruit of the Spirit is a life full of faith. We have the same faith of Peter, James, John and the Messiah. When Peter / Kefa was writing to in the saints in 2 Peter 1:1 he spoke to those "with the same faith." The same faith / emunah Peter had is in each and every believer. Now, remember that Kefa prayed and saw miracles. Peter preached and saw three thousand converted. Peter was a courageous leader. All of this happened through faith; the same faith that is in you right now through the Spirit of YHWH.

Today, don't allow your senses to fool you. Reach into the sixth sense of faith and allow the Spirit of YHWH to manifest in your life.

June 27

The design that Moses was given by YHWH for the tabernacle / mishkan was very specific. The entire tent had to be built "according to the pattern" and with very distinct materials and utensils. Each item was planned out and each area was designated for certain reasons. The end purpose was to glorify YHWH and His glory comes on His terms. You are exactly the same way.

YHWH has a plan and pattern for your life. Like the mishkan / tabernacle you are to bring Him glory by following His distinct ways. If you allow His "rivers of living water" to flow out of you then your life will manifest the shekinah glory and his purposes will come to fruition.

From creation, mankind was made three parts just like the Tent of Meeting. When the Bible said "you are the Temple of the Holy Spirit" it wasn't kidding. You were designed just like the mishkan. How?

Well first, the Mishkan had an "Outer Court" that surrounded the entire Tent of Meeting. In the Outer Court was the brazen altar and the place of animal sacrifices. This was called the "court of the gentiles" because both clean and unclean / Jew and gentile were allowed to freely roam in the outer court. Your outer court is your body.

Next, the Mishkan had a place called the "Inner Court" that encompassed several important elements of worship like the table of showbread and the Menorah. This was also called the "Holy Place" because only Priests who had been made holy through purification could enter in. Your inner court is your soul, mind, or emotional realm

A thick veil separated the holy place from the innermost part of the mishkan. This centralized section is called the "holy of holies." Here in the "kadosh ha kedoshim" was the glorious ark of the covenant, which was made of pure gold. The ark featured the "mercy seat" where the presence of YHWH would fill the temple with glory. Your holy of holies is your spirit.

You aren't just a believer in Y'shua; you are the temple of YHWH. The Holy Spirit of YHWH dwells in you and fills your spirit. Study 1 Thessalonians 5:23 today to learn more about your spirit, soul, and body.

TRUTH FOR TODAY

June 28

The presence of YHWH was meant to be in the midst of the people Israel. This can be seen in Joel 2:2, "And ye shall know that I am in the midst of Israel, and that I am YHWH your Elohim, and none else: and my people shall never be ashamed." YHWH wants to be in the midst of Israel in the midst of our camp. YHWH was never meant to be separate or separated.

When Adam and Eve were created in the Garden of Eden they had a perfect relationship with YHWH. Then after the fall, that relationship was hindered and YHWH was no longer in the midst of their lives. "Then the man and his wife heard the sound of YHWH Elohim as he was walking in the garden in the cool of the day, and they hid from the YHWH Elohim among the trees of the garden," Genesis 3:8. One reason that Adam and Eve hid from YHWH is because they realized a difference in the voice of YHWH. Before sin, His voice was inside of them and they were united with YHWH in perfection. Now, the voice was on the OUTSIDE. The loss of the voice scared them so much that the first couple hid among the trees (perhaps behind the tree of knowledge.) The voice was separated because Adam and Eve had chosen to eat from the wrong tree and seek after the knowledge of good and evil. We too are tempted with the same tree – the tree of knowledge. The desire to know more tempts us today.

Adam and Eve should have been listening to the voice and eating from the tree of life! This fall teaches us a very good and timely lesson. Until we have eaten from the tree of life then we shouldn't worry about knowledge of the other spiritual issues. The tree of life or "eytz chayim" is the Torah of YHWH as revealed in the first five books of the Bible. To eat from the tree of life is to take the Torah and digest it until the Torah becomes part of our very inner being. This digestion of the Torah tree of life will produce the fruit of the spirit like love, joy, peace, patience, kindness, goodness, gentleness, faithfulness and self-control. Are these fruit prevalent in your life or do you need to work on your garden?

YHWH wants us to listen to His voice. Y'shua said "my sheep hear my voice." We should be able to listen to the Spirit of YHWH and follow his directions on a daily basis. It's only when we are hearing the voice of the Good Shepherd that we can experience the abundant life promised in John 10. In fact, to learn more about the connection between the abundant life and the voice of YHWH take a few minutes today to read and review John 10.

June 29

In Biblical times, as it should be today, names carry great significance and importance. Naming a child was and should be something done with much thought and consideration as a name is reflective upon a person's behavior and character. Just think about what comes to mind when you hear the name "Michael Jackson" and you will get the point. "The ancient Israelites believed that names had mystical powers and that in many ways they reflected the character of a person," says one source. Unfortunately though, if you pick up your King James Version or NIV and read through the scriptures the English names you find aren't really the correct names of the individuals. What you do find are poor substitutes and charades. The words and names found in your Bible were not the words and names used thousands of years ago.

The Bible was originally written in Hebrew. When Hebrew is changed or translated into any other language MUCH is lost in the process. No other language can adequately convey the message and inspiration of the set apart Hebrew tongue. Even English in all of its grandeur is a poor alternate for Hebrew. That is why it is so important to learn to pray, read, and talk in Hebrew. It is a great mitzvah / commandment to use the holy language in study and worship. The restoration of the Hebrew language and the abandonment of gentile dialects are just part of the restoration of all things as spoken of in Acts 3 and Zephaniah 3:9, "For then will I return to the people a pure language, that they may all call upon the name of YHWH, to serve him with one consent."

Did you know that Joshua was never called Joshua? And Moses was never called Moses? While the Hebrew words of the Scriptures were translated into (poor) English equivalents the original names of the Biblical characters were transliterated or changed to something similar. The Hebrew family of Abraham, Isaac, and Jacob never heard the English names of Abraham, Isaac, and Jacob. This name changing that has taken place removes the Israelite identity of the people and creates a story of English speaking people with English sounding names.

When the name of a person is changed so is there character and what you think about a person. For example the Hebrew parents of the Messiah were not the very English couple of Mary and Joseph. Their names were very Hebrew – Miriam and Yosef. Do you study or use the Hebrew names originally found in the Bible? Why or why not?

June 30

Y'shua is the Messiah that walked in the midst of the sinners of the world. The real Messiah didn't stay away from the dirty of the world. He stayed with sinners, talked to prostitutes, and befriended lepers. We do not worship a Savior is too high above us to recognize our concerns. Y'shua can relate to every facet of our lives because of a prophecy in Leviticus chapters 26. Here in verses 11 and 12 we see the promise of the indwelling power of YHWH Y'shua - "Moreover, I will make My dwelling among you, and My soul will not reject you. I will also walk among you and be your Elohim and you shall be my people." These promises are for the Messianic kingdom, for the time when Y'shua was on the earth, and today.

Just a few verses from the above referenced passage is the discussion of the "yovel" or the jubilee year. Every 50 years, debts are forgiven and land is restored. YHWH is an Elohim of restoration. Yovel is proclaimed with a sounding of the shofar, much like the return of Y'shua will be heralded with a shofar blast. "You shall then sound a ram's horn abroad on the tenth day of the seventh month; on the day of atonement you shall sound a horn all through your land," Leviticus 25:9. Every 50 years is a time of freedom and consecration. It is like the time when Y'shua said, "The Spirit of the YHWH is upon me because he has anointed me to bring the good news to the afflicted; he has sent me to bind up the brokenhearted, to proclaim liberty to captives and freedom to the captives and the favorable year of YHWH," Luke 4:18-19. These verses show us that the time of yovel / jubilee is a reminder of how it was when Y'shua was with man – the blind could see, the dead lived, and what was lost was restored. Every year can be a type of yovel for those that understand that Y'shua —came to set the captives free.

Y'shua is not a god that is separated from the pain of life. He is with you no matter what you face today and he wants to set you free from the pain of anything you may face. Praise YHWH today for His love towards you.

July

TRUTH FOR TODAY

July 1

"I am leaving you with a gift - peace of mind and heart. And this peace isn't peace like the world gives. So don't be troubled or afraid," John 14:27.

The word "stress" is an architectural term that measures the pressure a building can withstand. Too much stress and a sky scraper can easily fall. Of course, there are more people falling from stress today than buildings. Stress is a killer that ruins families and the faith. The enemy knows that if we are stressed and focused on our problems or issues then we can't be focused on YHWH and His word. YHWH's word speaks of this issue time and time again.

We are told in James / Ya'acov 3:16 that "where there is envy or strife, there is confusion and every evil work." The verse word for "strife" can also mean "stress." YHWH is telling us that if we have strife or stress then we are opening a huge door to the enemy. Giving in to stress is putting a spiritual bull's eye for every demon of hell to attack and test us. We must do everything we can do stop and limit the stress we each face.

Stress affects our emotions and our health. It causes people to overeat, overreact, and over exaggerate problems. This is why we must guard our hearts verses anything that would steal our peace. Y'shua told us in John 14:1 to "let not your heart be troubled, trust in YHWH and trust in me." This may seem like an impossible command but it is a passage that should emanate from our life each day. Read in context, John 14:1 is even more compelling.

First, Y'shua tells his disciples (and us) to not be troubled through trusting Him. Then Y'shua tells them about all the bad things that are going to happen. Is this crazy or what? Get this - Y'shua says "trust me" and then he says "hang tight with me through the tough times." What we can learn from this is that if Y'shua expected his disciples to not let their heart be troubled through the death and crucifixion of their Messiah then we certainly shouldn't get stressed out over our daily issues of life. Compared to what the disciples experienced our stress is definitely minimal. Also in context we can see why we are not to let our heart's be troubled.

In the entire chapter of John 14 Y'shua describes the glory of heaven and life after death. If we keep our focus on our future destiny with YHWH then our mind shouldn't be controlled by stress. Even if we face harsh tragedies, we can trust Y'shua that heaven awaits and His goodness will one day be revealed. Life may be hard but we are to remember that we have a home waiting for us. When stress tries to overtake you today, simply say "I will not be troubled because I know my home is with YHWH in heaven." The troubles we face today are nothing compared to the glory we will experience says Romans 8:18. Our life doesn't have to collapse under stress and pressure if we focus on promises of YHWH. We really are too blessed to be stressed!

TRUTH FOR TODAY

July 2

Life is full of choices. We choose what side of the bed to wake up on, what flavor toothpaste to use, and what color socks to wear. Some decisions are minimal while others are major. To experience the renewed mind on a higher level we must daily decipher and decide upon the Hebrew way.

Unfortunately, the way of life that has emerged in the world today is staunchly opposite to the mitzvot of Torah. Like a computer, we have been programmed to operate within the world's parameters. All we know is how the world acts. Much of the religious church mirrors the current culture, yet we must mirror the ancient paths. We now have to be re-programmed or renewed towards Yah's ways. The Hebrew road is our pathway towards YHWH's "good, pleasing, and perfect will."

The Hebrew approach is a Torah-based method for life's decisions. This worldview covers everything from faith to family to finances. It will cause us to think and therefore, to act more like the Ivrim of the Scriptures. Life, every thought, word, and action will be YHWH-oriented.

One fundamental difference between the Hebrew way and the worldly or Greek mindset is between knowing and doing. While the ancient Greeks and the modern person is concerned with knowledge and belief, the Hebrew wants to do right. Society's accommodation of differences says we can separate what we believe from what we actually do. President Clinton's Lewinsky affair is a prime example of how our culture allows the notion of separating actions and devotion. The President said he was devoted to his wife, yet his actions proved the opposite. While the church teaches that faith is all about belief, the Hebrew way, according to Ya'acov 2:14, faith is all about action and doing. "What good is it, my brothers, if a man claims to have faith but has no deeds? Can such faith save him?" (For more examples of the differences between the Hebrew and the Greek/Western types of thinking, we have prepared a short graph at the bottom of this teaching.)

The world separates the religious from the secular. For most in this world, there is recreation time, work shifts, and the worship hour on Sunday. For the Hebrew, everything is spiritual. The lines are blurred between the religious and, pretty much everything else. The hand of the Creator can be seen behind the events of the day; the 7pm news broadcast is an expose of the signs of the times. As a believer you must acknowledge that you are not just an American or an African – you are a Hebrew who is on a quest to reclaim your culture and heritage.

TRUTH FOR TODAY

July 3

When you live according to the soulish realm your life will result in chaos. Emotions and feelings come and go. This is why YHWH tells us in Deuteronomy 6 to "love YHWH with all your heart (spirit) and all your soul (emotions) and all your strength (body.)" To love YHWH with all of your soul is to reflect His fruit in your soul and allow the Spiritual realm to cross over into your thoughts and emotions. This is why meditating on the Word is so important.

When your natural mind dwells on the Spiritual mind of Messiah you can release the power of the Holy Spirit and overcome the emotions of the moment. Read that sentence again and let it sink into your spirit... "When your natural mind dwells on the Spiritual mind of Messiah you can release the power of the Holy Spirit and overcome the emotions of the moment."

YHWH has given us emotions and feelings to indicate how you think. Our mind and our body respond to the circumstances around us and give loud warning sounds to us. For example, if your emotions are tense then you are probably frustrated or stressed. If you are feeling sad then you might have just watched a sad movie. If you are happy then something good probably just happened to you.

Remember that the mind/soul is like a computer that has been programmed to function in a specific way. Single thoughts become code of habit and eventually establish programs of behavior. For the mind computer to function properly there must be a "reset" and a reprogramming of the Word of YHWH as the central thoughts code. "To be carnally minded is death, to be spiritually minded is life and peace," Romans 8:6. Being carnally minded is not sinful. Carnal thoughts are simply natural thoughts; a way of thinking not focused on the Spirit. It's not wrong to think about work, family, or entertainment. There is a problem when carnal thoughts dominate life. "Don't think about what you eat," Matthew 6:31. This verse could also say, "doesn't think about the latest news, TV show, town gossip, conspiracy, or viral video."

"Set your mind on things above," Colossians 3:2. Do this today and allow your life to be changed by the Word of YHWH.

TRUTH FOR TODAY

July 4

On July 4, 1884 the people of France presented to the United States an amazing gift. This award would come to symbolize freedom and democracy to the all the world. In the waters of the New York Harbor, the Statue of Liberty stands tall, shining its light as a beacon of hope for those in search of independence. The statue was originally named, "Liberty Enlightening the World." This name accurately describes America's purpose as 'the land of the free and the home of the brave', where opportunity is given freely to everyone who comes to the land.

In a similar fashion, the Creator has given to us His own symbol of freedom – His Word and His Will, as revealed in the first five books of the Bible. These writings are called the "Torah" in the ancient Hebrew language. However, Torah is often mistakenly referred to as "the Law" in English Bibles. The Torah is not some legalistic list of observances that should be followed to 'earn' salvation. On the contrary, the Torah is the Almighty's instructions for living. The Torah describes how man should raise a family, approach the Holy One, and live a life that has meaning and abundance. In fact, it is the Torah that is quoted over 110 times in the New Testament. The truth is that the Torah is the Bible the Savior used, and the foundation of our faith. The Torah is YHWH's "Statutes of Liberty."

Like the torch held by Lady Liberty, we were created to shine the Light of Torah in the darkness. And, the Torah, similar to the gift from France, expresses our purpose and guides us to our divine destiny of shining the Light of freedom to the world. "I YHWH have called you in righteousness; I will take hold of your hand. I will keep you and will make you to be a covenant for the people and a light for the Nations, to open eyes that are blind, to free captives from prison and to release from the dungeon those who sit in darkness. "I am YHWH; that is my name! I will not give my glory to another or my praise to idols. See, the former things have taken place, and new things I declare; before they spring into being I announce them to you," Isaiah 42:6-9.

As with any gift, the Torah was given freely. The Sages of Judaism teach that "the living oracles of the Torah would be given in many tongues or languages, and that all 70 known nations at the time of the exodus would and could receive the grace that Israel was receiving at Sinai. It was YHWH's purpose to deliver His Word in tongues, so that all known nations could and should walk in the light of Torah, as 'a lamp to their feet, and a light to their path' (Psalms 119: 105).

It was the nation, the people of Israel that accepted the gift of the Torah. This newborn nation received their national constitution on a special day at Mount Sinai. From that moment on, we who associate with the faith of the Bible have bound ourselves to that gift. Let your light, your Torah observance, shine today. Praise YHWH for the freedom found in the Torah!

TRUTH FOR TODAY

July 5

Immersion is one way YHWH has prescribed us to come near to Him. "O Yerushalyim / Jerusalem wash your lev / heart from wickedness, that you may be saved. How long shall your worthless thoughts stay in you" Yermi'yahu / Jeremiah 4: 14.

Immersion into water is an integral part of our drawing near to YHWH. Like a wedding ring shows the promise of marriage, mikvah is symbolic of our marriage to YHWH. After the wedding band the bride and groom may enjoy the honeymoon, and after our mikvah / immersion into Y'shua can we enjoy the fruit of abundant and eternal life. Talk about drawing near! Going to a mikvah is also like going to a funeral. Our own. Our dipping into the waters is symbolic of our dying to self and being resurrected a new creation in Messiah. "And this water symbolizes baptism that now saves you also--not the removal of dirt from the body but the pledge of a good conscience toward Elohim. It saves you by the resurrection of Y'shua Ha Moshiach, who has gone into heaven and is at YHWH's right hand--with angels, authorities and powers in submission to him," 1 Kefa – 1 Peter 3:21,22.

When we immerse ourselves we are following the example of Y'shua. We are also clinging to our hope that His blood will remove all sin and uncleanliness from Him. Without Him we have no hope. With Him, we can trust that "he is faithful and just and will forgive us our sins and purify us from all unrighteousness," Yochannan Alef / First John 1: 19. To see how vivid this idea is within the Scriptures, let's first turn to the book of Yermi'yahu / Jeremiah, for an amazing look at our hope. "Although our sins testify against us, O YHWH, do something for the sake of your name. For our backsliding is great; we have sinned against you. O Hope of Israel, its Savior in times of distress, why are you like a stranger in the land, like a traveler who stays only a night?" Yermi'yahu / Jeremiah 14:7, 8. Our sins give evidence against us that we are in desperate need of salvation. We cannot work ourselves to Heaven or solve our own Spiritual problems. We need a Redeemer. We need our Savior Y'shua. Well, the words translated "O Hope of Israel" in the above verse points to our salvation. The normal Hebrew word of "hope," which is "tikvah" is not used here. Instead a different word is found within the ancient Hebrew text, which alters the meaning and the translation greatly. The Hebrew reads, "Mikvah Israel Yahshua!" The literal, correct, translation for this verse would read, "O the Immersion of Israel is Salvation / Y'shua." Our mikvah into Y'shua's blood and water is our salvation.

What did you learn in this reading today?

Truth For Today

July 6

The purpose of the spoken word is to express the emotions of the heart, to build up or tear down. The scriptures say in Mishlei / Proverbs 18:21, "The power of life and death is in the tongue." This is illustrated first in the sefer Beresheet (Book of Genesis). Creation (life) and the fall (death) both manifested because of the power of the tongue. Through the spoken word all things came into being. The earth was formed, the ocean was given its' salty taste, the zebra was painted with stripes, and the crown of creation, man himself, was made by the mouth of YHWH. The sages say that, "YHWH breathed upon Adam and Adam became a speaking spirit." We know that the adversary spoke through the serpent "did Elohim really say?" From Adam to the tower at Bavel all people spoke the sacred language of Hebrew. Because of the misuse of the mouth, YHWH then scattered the tower builders and gave the different languages to mankind.

The power of words is seen in the story of Yitzchak (Isaac) giving his blessing in Beresheet 27:35. Yitzchak's blessing was pronounced over the wrong son but the deed was done. Once the blessing was spoken it could not be retracted because words are eternal. Yes, once you say something you can never take it back. Words are indeed like toothpaste. Once it's out it's not going back in! The expressions your vocal chords make continue as sound waves forever. "The grass withers, and the flowers fade, but the words of YHWH remains forever," Yesha'yahu / Isaiah 40:8.

In Hebrew the word for mouth is "peh." Peh literally means "talk, wish, word, two edged, saying, sentence, and sound." A lip in Hebrew is "sawfaw" which is defined as "natural boundary of the mouth, speech, beard, upper lip, and language."

James / Ya'acov says in chapter 1 verse 26, "If anyone considers himself to be religious and yet does not keep a tight rein on his tongue, he deceives himself and his religion is worthless."

The power of life and death is in your very mouth. You can build up or you can tear down. Will you allow your words today to bring life or death?

July 7

Rosh Chodesh is the Hebrew term for "renewed moon." The Biblical month begins with the crescent New Moon, also called first visible sliver. The root of the term Rosh Chodesh is "chadash," which means to repair or renew. Each month the darkness of the night is illuminated by the moon's light. Judaism recognizes that when the slightest "fingertip" or sliver of the moon is visible then it is the first of the month. Rosh Chodesh is a time to come together with other likeminded believers and "sound the shofar on the new moon" as the word says in Tehillim (Psalms) 81:3. This is a time to look to YHWH in worship and prayer.

Honestly, is there a better way to remind Israel of its high calling than to view the crescent moon that marks the start of each month? On Rosh Chodesh the moon's light breaks forth from the darkness and brings Light to the world as a reminder to Israel about its calling and purpose.

Looking to the moon we realize the seasons. Tehillim 104:19 says, "The moon marks off the seasons, and the sun knows when to go down."

Also, the Talmud states "anyone who blesses the New Moon is like one who receives the Shekinah / manifest glory of YHWH." Did you get that?

Anyone who blesses the New Moon is like one who receives the Shekinah."

You see, there is a direct connection between YHWH's calendar and the Shekinah – the glorious presence of YHWH. One rabbi has written that the, "concept of the New Moon represents the goal of the Torah." Why is this? How does the Rosh Chodesh bring the presence of YHWH?

July 8

Israel left bondage in Egypt with a two-fold mission:

1) To be a nation set apart to YHWH through His Torah. Shemot / Exodus 19:5-6, "Now if you obey me fully and keep my covenant, then out of all nations you will be my treasured possession. Although the whole earth is mine, you will be for me a kingdom of priests and a holy nation.' These are the words you are to speak to the Israelites."

2) To take the Torah to the world and thus be the "light to the nations," Isaiah 42:5, "This is what YHWH Elohim says— he who created the heavens and stretched them out, who spread out the earth and all that comes out of it, who gives breath to its people, and life to those who walk on it: "I, YHWH, have called you in righteousness; I will take hold of your hand. I will keep you and will make you to be a covenant for the people and a light for the Gentiles, to open eyes that are blind, to free captives from prison and to release from the dungeon those who sit in darkness. I am YHWH; that is my name! I will not give my glory to another or my praise to idols. See, the former things have taken place, and new things I declare; before they spring into being I announce them to you."

What does this two-fold mission have to do with the New Moon, with Rosh Chodesh?

Well, the main property and purpose of the moon is that it does not reflect its own light; rather it reflects the light of the sun. Even at the darkest point of the night, when the sun is hidden by darkness, the moon can be seen.

Tehillim (Psalm) 89:35-37 teaches that the people of Israel are like the moon! The mission of the moon and the mission of Israel is the same – it is to reflect Light. As the moon shatters the black of night, we too as Israel are to shine the Light of Torah into the darkness of this world. The moon and in fact Israel do not exist for their own sake but for that of the whole world. "The Light of the righteous shines brightly," Mishlei / Proverbs 13. We have been called out of bondage to receive the Light, share the Light, and be the Light. Our purpose is to bring salvation to the world.

"And now YHWH says— he who formed me in the womb to be his servant to bring Ya'acov back to him and gather Israel to himself, for I am honored in the eyes of YHWH and my Elohim has been my strength—he says: "It is too small a thing for you to be my servant to restore the tribes of Ya'acov and bring back those of Israel I have kept. I will also make you a light for the Gentiles, that you may bring my salvation to the ends of the earth," Yesha'yahu / Isaiah 49:5-6.

July 9

Worse than a Friday the 13th, the 9th of Av commemorates some of the most horrible events in Biblical history. The ninth day of the fifth Hebrew month of Av is one of the saddest days on the calendar for many reasons. According to historical documents it was on this date that the first Temple was destroyed. And the second temple was destroyed. It was also on this day that King Ferdinand in 1492 set this date as the final day a Jewish person was allowed to be in the entire country of Spain. Years later, World War One, which began the downward spiral towards the Holocaust, began on the ninth of Av. In 1999 Muslim terrorists bombed a Jewish community center in Buenos Aires, Argentina, killing 86 people and wounding some 300 others. "...Should I weep in the fifth month [Av], separating myself, as I have done these so many years?" Zachariah 7:3.

Today, Tish B'Av "primarily commemorates the destruction of the first and second Temples. The first was destroyed by the Babylonians in 586 B.C.E. while the second by the Romans in 70 C.E. This date is the ending of a three-week period of increased bereavement that normally starts on the 17th of Tammuz. During these three weeks all joy is suspended. Jews may not visit cinemas, purchase new clothing, get their haircut, alter their home, eat or drink joyously, swim, knit, or bath for pleasure," says ou.org.

For us Tish B'Av is a reminder of the sadness of life. We are told in Romans 12:15 to "rejoice with those who rejoice and mourn with those who mourn." This verse shows us the power of empathy. Instead of mourning in sympathy for someone we are to show empathy and mourn with others. Tish B'Av is a day to show empathy and remember the events of the past. Perhaps spending this day in fasting and prayer to seek YHWH is another way we can relate to the Jewish people and show our love and concern.

Truth For Today

July 10

Do you ever wonder why a lion tamer would enter the circus ring with bar stool? Sure, the whip and the pistol make excellent tools to ward off dangerous lions, but why a bar stool? Well, lion tamers use the stool to confuse the lion. They hold the stool out by its seat and push the ferocious animal away with the legs. The lion actually tries to watch all three legs at one time and gets dizzily confused. The stool is the most important item used in the ring because it messes up the focus of the beast. The king of the jungle is nothing but a baby kitten when its focus is off. We, too, are easily off guard when our concentration is broken and we don't control our thoughts.

In life, we get out whatever we focus on. The person at the summit of a mountain did not fall there. Likewise, it takes effort to reach the pinnacle in our spiritual life. If we are negative, if we complain a lot, if we just can't seem to have any joy, then, we probably need to really engage our focus. There is a Biblical principle that states that we reap what we sow. When we plant positive, Torah-based thoughts, our life will then reap positive, Torah-based outcomes. This doesn't mean that things will be easy or everything will go our way. What engaging our focus does though, is preparing our soul to look to YHWH in the good times and in the bad. If we are focused, then we are determined, we are alert, and we are unwavering. The key here is found in Tehillim / Psalm 16:8. "I have set YHWH always before me. Because of his right hand, I will not be shaken." We need to memorize this pasuk. Write this verse down on a note card and keep it before you. "I have set YHWH always before me. Because of his right hand, I will not be shaken," Psalm 16:8.

Looking to YHWH, really seeing His hand throughout the events of our day will lead to a great transformation. The seemingly bad things that happen will turn into learning events. The good things will bring about praise the Almighty. The humdrum stuff will provide even more opportunities to learn and rejoice. "Remember the YHWH in a distant land, and think on Yerushalyim / Jerusalem," says Jeremiah / Yermi'yahu 51:50. Even Rabbi Sha'ul wrote that, "whatever is true, whatever is noble, whatever is right, whatever is pure, whatever is lovely, whatever is admirable-if anything is excellent or praiseworthy-think about such things," Philippians 4:8. We can't let our mind wander, or wonder, when things go crazy or bad. We look to YHWH. We pray. We control our thoughts. We can ask, "How would Y'shua handle this situation?" Reading the Torah daily strengthens our renewal. What we put in is what we get out. Now is the time to start putting Torah into our mind. Have you read the Torah today?

July 11

"If ye love me, keep my commandments. And I will pray the Father, and he shall give you another Comforter, that he may abide with you forever; even the Spirit of truth; whom the world cannot receive, because it seeth him not, neither knoweth him: but ye know him; for he dwelleth with you, and shall be in you," John 14:15-17. Read this passage. And read it again.

"The grass withereth, the flower fadeth: but the word of our Elohim shall stand forever," Isaiah 40:8.

Understand that when Isaiah said this the only scriptures the believers had was the Torah of Moses. So, if you believe that this verse is true then you must believe that all the teachings, commandments, and principles in the scriptures are for you. They haven't passed away. In fact, this verse says that they shall "stand forever."

Man has created the doctrine of the dispensationalism. Dispensationalists teach that part of the Bible was for yesterday while part of it is for today. This is totally opposite of what the scriptures themselves teach in 1 Peter 1:25, "but the word (torah) of the YHWH/ the Lord endureth forever," and in Psalm 119:142, "Thy righteousness is an everlasting righteousness, and thy law is the truth."

If the word is eternal (which it is) that means it was to be followed yesterday, is to be obeyed today, and should be kept tomorrow. According to Ezekiel 36:26 this obedience to the Torah is to flow from a heart of love and not obligation. Our Savior based His complete life and ministry on the Torah given by the Almighty Father. He did not negate it nor abolish it. "Do not think that I have come to abolish the Law or the Prophets; I have not come to abolish them but to fulfill them. I tell you the truth, until heaven and earth disappear, not the smallest letter, not the least stroke of a pen, will by any means disappear from the Law until everything is accomplished," Matthew 5:17 & 18. Heaven and earth have not disappeared so then the Torah should still be followed.

July 12

If you don't guard our heart, you will soon begin to doubt your actions and become trapped by doing only what is required of you. Don't let this excuse of only "blind obedience" to take you captive.

YHWH doesn't want just our actions. He wants our life. He wants us. The Scriptures have an answer for those who would question what is required of believers. "Israel what does YHWH your Elohim require of you, but to fear YHWH your Elohim, to walk in all his ways, and to love him, and to serve YHWH your Elohim with all your heart and with all your soul," - Devarim / Deuteronomy 10:12. Notice that walking in his way, observing the mitzvoth, and loving YHWH with all of the heart are equal. What does YHWH require? He requires all that we are.

"What does YHWH require of you, but to do justly, and to love mercy, and to walk humbly with your Elohim," Mica'yah / Micah 6:8. If our heart's condition is right before YHWH, it is as if we are obeying all of the mitzvot, because we will be obeying the mitzvoth. Y'shua said, "'You shall love the YHWH your Elohim with all your heart, with all your soul, and with all your mind. This is the first and greatest commandment. And the second is like it: 'You shall love your neighbor as yourself. On these two commandments hang all the Law and the Prophets," Mattitiyahu / Matthew 22:38-40. This verse corresponds with the previous pasuk (passage) in Micah.

When we love YHWH with all our heart, we will do justly. When we love Him with all of our soul, we will view others in compassion and so we will love mercy. And when we love Him with all of our mind, we will keep our mind upon Him and walk humbly in His Spirit. One ancient Jewish writing says, "when a man's love to the Holy One is roused, the "right hand" is moved only by a threefold impulse, by "heart", "soul", and "might", for it does not say, "with all thy heart or with all thy soul", etc., but "and with all thy soul", etc.: all three are essential and necessary. Then does the Holy One respond and stir up His Right Hand towards that man."

YHWH wants your heart. He wants all of you. His desire is for His people to submit to His will for their lives. This will is revealed throughout the Torah. To obey the Torah without giving our heart to YHWH is great loss. To submit to the Almighty and seek to walk in obedience to the Torah is great gain. Ask the Holy Spirit / Ruach HaKodesh to reveal places in your heart that need to be submitted to YHWH and His reign.

July 13

"But you are not to be called 'Rabbi,' for you have only one Master and you are all brothers. And do not call anyone on earth 'father,' for you have one Father, and he is in heaven. Nor are you to be called 'teacher,' for you have one teacher, the Moshiach," Matthew 23:8-10.

In this verse, Y'shua was not banning people from being called 'dad,' or 'rabbi.' Understand that the terms "rabbi" and "father" are perfectly acceptable for a believer to use in designation of relationship and authority. Y'shua was saying that the rabbi-talmid system culminated with Himself.

No longer were the disciples to make other disciples in their own names. The disciples were to proclaim the name and the teachings of Y'shua above their own. They were not to look to other Rabbis as the final source because Y'shua is our Rebbe! "You have one teacher, the Moshiach," He said. We are not to make talmidim of ourselves but talmidim of Y'shua. His halakha, or way to walk out the Torah, is what we are to proclaim - not our own personal interpretations in our own name. (Rabbi Sha'ul supported this when he talked about some believers being of Paul or Apollos in said in 1 Corinthians 1:12.)

"Provide yourself with a Teacher (of the Torah) and get yourself a companion, and judge all men in the scale of merit," says the Pirkei Avot 1:6. Today, believers are to submit to and ordain a leader to speak the Word into their lives. This leader should be submitted to in all areas and followed as the leader follows Messiah. "Remember those who led you, who spoke the word of YHWH to you; and considering the result of their conduct, imitate their faith," Hebrews / Ivrim 13:7. You shouldn't consider yourself a student of Rabbi Daniel or Rabbi Johnny-Come-Lately. As a follower of Y'shua, you are a talmid of Y'shua submitted to a local leader. The local leader provides accountability, teaching, fellowship, encouragement, and training. Have you submitted to someone for accountability? If not, is pride holding you back?

July 14

TRUTH FOR TODAY

As we return to true worship and as we learn about our Hebrew roots of the Scriptures we begin to see the impact and importance of the commandments. These aren't just rules to learn and then file away in our brain's halls of knowledge. You don't just learn Hebrew roots; you do them! The commandments are not followed for salvation. We gain eternal life only by grace through faith in Y'shua and Y'shua only. The commandments teach us how to live once we have been born again. They keep us on the straight and narrow and define sin for us.

He didn't just save us so we could go to heaven on a rapture bus. If that was the case, then the moment we were born again then we would have been whisked away to the stars. Instead, we were born again to shine HIS light to this world and show others His glory. The commandments He has given teach us how to enjoy this life and live it to the fullest. He didn't give us chocolate, or nice clothing, or beautiful music, or dance, or a sense of humor, or love, or sex, or money, or long life to take them away from us. He gave us all of this to show us how to enjoy them! Through every minute of our day and every second of our life we can glorify YHWH and experience His presence. We do this through His commandments.

The commandments of the Bible connect us to YHWH and allow us to walk in His perfect will. Y'shua prayed, "Thy kingdom come, thy will be done in earth as it is in heaven." We bring His kingdom to earth when we do His will on Earth.

The Hebrew word translated for commandments is "mitzvoth." This term literally means to “command, combine, or connect.” Through obedience to the commands of YHWH we combine our life to His and connect to His will. The root word for mitzvah is "tzavta", which literally means "to join" and "Tzevet" which means "team". “It is through the "Mitzvot" – commandments of the Torah, that the Jew is able to fuse divinity into his life, draw himself closer to the divine, and personally fulfill his biblical commitment partaking in the everlasting covenant between the G-d of Israel and the Jewish people that was established on Mount Sinai.

The mitzvoth connect us to YHWH. These actions empower our world and allow our ordinary actions to become supernatural actions of divine will. Our mundane world can be transformed into divine space by knowing, fulfilling, and focusing on the mitzvoth.

This is the reason why the commandments were given to us. They were not given to punish or restrict us. But they WERE given to show us the proper path for a relationship with YHWH and with man. The Torah is for our benefit and not our punishment! Y'shua made this clear when He said, "the Sabbath was made for man and not man for the Sabbath." Keeping Shabbat, like any other mitzvoth, creates a divine space so that we can connect to YHWH. How can you connect to YHWH today?

July 15

The Scriptures state, "if you belong to Christ, then you are Abraham's seed, and heirs according to the promise," Galatians 3:29. The original word for "seed" in this verse is "sperma," which means a "physical seed or descendant." Christians are not just spiritual heirs of salvation but direct physical descendants of Abraham, Isaac, and Jacob.

Jacob, whose name was changed to Israel, fathered twelve sons. These twelve sons and their families became known as the twelve tribes of Israel. Israel isn't just a small sliver of land in the Middle East. And Israel isn't just the Jewish people! Israel is the family of Abraham. This family's bloodline has been scattered all over the world. As Romans 2:29 states, the identity of all disciples is Israel.

History proves that shortly after the rule of King David, the nation of Israel was tragically split in two. In 586BCE the two tribes that made up the Southern Kingdom were taken captive by the Babylonians. 70 years later many of these people returned to the Southern Kingdom, known as Judah, and rebuilt the Temple. They kept the Law and sought to worship as prescribed in the Scriptures. Today, the descendants from Judea are known as the "Jews."

In 722BCE the Northern Kingdom, comprised of 10 tribes from Ephraim, were scattered by the Assyrians. These Israelites mixed into the nations. Thus they lost their identity and forgot their Hebrew heritage. They continued to grow and multiply, spreading their bloodline all over the world. A recent NBC News article estimates over a tenth of today's population is directly descended from this group. Today they are known as the "lost 10 tribes of Israel."

The Jewish people began their return to the Land in 1948. As fulfillment to Biblical prophecy in Ezekiel 37 and elsewhere, the lost tribes are slowly returning to their identity as people recognize they are Israel.

The Savior said in John 4:22, "Salvation is of the Jews." This doesn't mean that a person must convert to Judaism. This means the true pathway of faith can be found within the lineage and lifestyle of the Hebrews. All of the promises in the Bible made to Israel are for today. All of the commandments in the Bible that were given to Israel are also for today. Being Israel isn't about being Jewish, but recognizing the identity theft of the world and the Almighty's true plan for man. How can you live out your Israelite identity today?

July 16

Have you read verses like Psalm 7:17, "I will sing praise to the name of the Lord most high" and questioned to yourself who you are supposed to be praising. Sure, you know it's the Lord, but does he have a name. Does the Father have a name?

In Exodus 3 Moses is attracted to the mountain by a bush that burns, yet is not consumed. Here he comes face to face with the creator of the universe. The Almighty wants Moses to deliver His people Israel from the bondage of Egypt's Pharaoh. The only problem is Moses is a novice when it comes to leading people. It's been many years since he left Egypt and he's doubtful the people will even accept this worn out old man as a legitimate deliverer sent from above. For the people to accept him, Moses needs a miracle. He needs a higher authority to vouch for him.

This is Moses' first encounter with the mighty one of Abraham, Isaac, and Jacob and it is certainly a memorable one. Here on Mt. Horeb the Lord passes before Moses and "the Lord said moreover unto Moses, Thus shalt thou say unto the children of Israel, The Lord God of your fathers, the God of Abraham, the God of Isaac, and the God of Jacob, hath sent me unto you: this is my name for ever, and this is my memorial unto all generations." Here in Exodus 3:15 the Lord reveals His eternal name as "Yahweh." This is His memorial name forever. Wow! The Lord does have a name and it's not Billy or Bob - it's Yahweh. From here on throughout the Bible, Yahweh is used over 6,000 times exclusively as the name of the Father. According to most scholars Yahweh or YHWH is the personal name of the Lord!

In the King James Version whenever you see the words "Lord" or "GOD" in all capital letters the translators are alerting you that Yahweh is the Hebrew word behind the English. Whenever you find the English word "Lord" in capital letters the translators are letting you know that the sacred name of YHWH is being used. But, YHWH says emphatically in Exodus 3 that YHWH "is my name forever, and this is my memorial unto all generations."

This name was not intended to be hidden by scribes and translators; rather Yahweh Himself gave it to man as a sign of His existence and as a means of personal relationship. This is similar to how you introduce yourself on a first name basis when you want to get to know someone - YHWH gave us His personal name so we could approach Him with intimacy. Other titles such as Adonai and El Shaddai are just that - they are titles that describe His attributes and actions. These titles have reference to qualities and are derived from actions. But "YHWH" indicates nothing but His existence. Moses needed a miracle to give him favor before Pharaoh and the leaders of Israel. That miracle was found in the power of a name. Here YHWH reveals Himself to Moses as the great I AM, the One who Was and who Is, and who Is to come.

July 17

"For since by man came death, by Man came also the resurrection of the dead. For as in Adam all die, even so in Moshiach shall all be made alive," 1 Corinthians 15:21, 22.

To be led by the Spirit is to be led by the Word. One cannot separate the two. "The Torah is spiritual and to be spiritually minded is life and peace," says Romans / Romiyah 7:14, 8:6. Torah was given by the Ruach. Therefore when we are exhorted to "walk in the Spirit," Scripture is telling us to conform our lives to the Torah. This is illustrated vividly with the creation account.

In the beginning, YHWH told Adam to "be fruitful and multiply." He allowed Adam to eat from the Eytz Chayim, the Tree of Life. But, Adam sinned by eating from the WRONG tree. Instead of following the instructions (Torah) of YHWH, Adam ate from the tree of the knowledge of good and evil. Because of the fall, he harvested the fruit of the flesh. "Now the works of the flesh are well known, among which are these; adultery, fornication, uncleanness, indecency idolatry, witchcraft, hatred, quarrels, jealousies, rage, strife, selfish ambition, stubbornness, heresies, envy, murder, drunkenness, wild indecent parties, and all such things," Galatians / Galutyah 5:1-21.

Adam failed to eat from the Eytz Chayim and was cast from the Gan Eden. As a result of the fall, man is born with a fleshly Adamic nature –the desire to produce the fruit of the flesh and NOT the fruit of the Spirit. Those who walk according to the desires and lusts of the animal flesh produce the fruit of the flesh. Natural desires lead to a natural crop. We've all heard horror stories of people who hired a religious contractor to do repairs or remolding in their homes and were taken advantage of. Or we have seen the news of individuals who go on a shooting spree and kill people. These are just a few examples of what happens if you walk in the flesh. We are no different when we act upon our desire to receive for self alone. We must deny the flesh and eat from the Eytz Chayim – the tree of Life.

Flesh and blood cannot inherit the Kingdom of YHWH. Our souls need to be delivered from the aftertaste of the forbidden fruit. The first Adam failed to tend and keep the Garden. He chose knowledge of evil over the tree of Life. The second Adam, Y'shua, gave his life upon a tree to give us access once more to the Eytz Chayim. "For since by man came death, by Man came also the resurrection of the dead. For as in Adam all die, even so in Moshiach shall all be made alive," 1 Corinthians 15:21, 22.

Today, rely upon the Word and the Spirit to help you deny the flesh and walk in the Spirit.

July 18

Noah is a shadow of the Messiah. Genesis says that Noah was "righteous in his generation." This doesn't mean that he was perfect but that his heart was pointed towards the Almighty. It is said in Genesis 7:5 that "Noah did all that YHWH commanded him." Noah understood the importance of obedience. He was given specific measurements to follow and he obeyed in all ways. This is similar to Y'shua the Messiah who came in the Father's image. Y'shua said, "I tell you the truth, the Son can do nothing by himself; he can do only what he sees his Father doing, because whatever the Father does the Son also does," John 5:19.

What separates Noah and Y'shua is that though Noah's actions were admirable, he still wasn't perfect. The drunkenness of Noah and the events that ensued show a distinct difference between the patriarchs of our faith and Messiah. Noah, Abraham, Moses, David and others were people of faith and we can learn from their lives. But, our true example should not be these sinful humans. Only the Messiah Y'shua is to be our role model and source of inspiration. We should always look for Y'shua in the lives of the Patriarchs. The lives of people like Noah simply point to the greatness of Y'shua.

Noah saved the world through his boat made of wood. The ark would be covered inside and out with pitch. The Hebrew word for "pitch" is "kaphar." This Hebrew term is usually translated "atonement" and "ransom" in the rest of the Old Testament. This coating is a picture of the atoning power of Messiah's blood, which atones for our sins. The one door on the side of the ark is a picture of the pierced side of Y'shua from which water and blood flowed. YHWH used wood to save the world with Noah. The Messiah used wood to save the world through Y'shua. May we never forget what our Master Y'shua did when he paid the death penalty for sin as he died upon the wooden execution beam. "YHWH showed His great love for us like this: while we were still sinners, Messiah died for us," Romans 5:8.

July 19

Y'shua quoted a Hebrew idiom when He said He came "not to destroy the Law or the prophets." He was using a familiar phrase easily understood during Biblical times. If someone heard a Torah teaching and didn't agree, they would say that the Teacher was "destroying the law." If they heard a heard a teaching they thought was the right interpretation they would then say, "yes, this is fulfilling the law." Y'shua had been accused of misinterpreting the Torah, yet He said that He was actually rightly and correctly teaching it. Traditional Jewish writings support this idiom, "Should all the nations of the world unite to uproot one word of the Law, they would be unable to do it," Leviticus Rabbah 19:2. To understand the meaning of this verse, everything hinges on the meaning of the words "destroy" and "fulfill" in verse 17. What does Y'shua mean by "destroy the Law" and "fulfill the Law"? "Destroy" and "fulfill" are technical terms used in rabbinic argumentation. When a sage felt that a colleague had misinterpreted a passage of Scripture, he would say, "You are destroying the Law!" Needless to say, in most cases, his colleagues strongly disagreed. What was "destroying the Law" for one sage was "fulfilling the Law" (correctly interpreting Scripture) for another," wrote Bivin and Bizzard in their book Understanding the Difficult Words of Jesus.

In plain English, Y'shua is saying, "Never imagine for a moment that I intend to abrogate the Law by misinterpreting it. My intent is not to weaken or negate the Law, but by properly interpreting Elohim's written Word, I aim to establish it, that is, make it even more lasting. I would never invalidate the Law by effectively removing something from it through misinterpretation. Heaven and earth would sooner disappear than something from the Law. Not the smallest letter in the alphabet, the jot or yod, nor even its decorative spur, the tittle, will ever disappear from the Law," wrote Bivin and Blizzard on page 155.

What we can learn from this can impact our life. There are many statements in the Scriptures that meant one thing when they were originally written or said, but because of religion mean something totally different today. As students of the Scriptures, it is important that we return to a Biblical understanding where the Bible is free to affect us as it did the people who first heard its words.

Do you read the Scriptures from a modern mindset or do you search for the truth and desire to return to the ancient paths?

July 20

Whenever you read the term "salvation" in an English Bible, it is almost certainly the name of the Messiah translated from the Hebrew. His name is actually found all throughout the Older Testament. When the Patriarch Jacob (Ya'acov in Hebrew) prayed in Genesis 49:18, he actually used the name of the coming Savior. He said, "I have waited for thy salvation / Y'shua." Jacob trusted in Y'shua even before Y'shua was born into this world! In Psalm 62:6, David too proclaims his faith in Y'shua, "He alone is my rock and my Y'shua / salvation, I will not be moved." People living during Older Testament times were redeemed by putting their faith in Y'shua. The sacrificial system did not save anyone. In Hebrews 10:4 we read, "for it is not possible that the blood of bulls and goats could take away sins."

Salvation has always been by grace through faith in the salvation of the Almighty. His very name doesn't just mean salvation, it is salvation! "Neither is there salvation / Y'shua in any other: for there is none other name under heaven given among men, whereby we must be saved," Act 4:12. Y'shua came to save us from our sins and to redeem man from the curse of the law.

Have you trusted Y'shua for your salvation? Obedience to the Torah does not save you. Good works do not save you. Jewish lineage does not save you. Church membership does not save you. We are saved by the person and the name of Y'shua! Blessed be His wonderful name!

TRUTH FOR TODAY

July 21

"I can do everything through Messiah who gives me strength. Yet it was good of you to share in my troubles," Philippians 4:13, 14. Astonishingly, before the fall is when YHWH fixes man's first and primary dilemma. Six times in the first chapter of Genesis YHWH creates something and then the scriptures declare, it was "good" or "tov." But, in Beresheet / Genesis 2:18 the first problem, the first predicament in the entire Bible is revealed. The "it was tov" statements now change. And the first "it was not tov" statement is made. Up to this point everything in creation was perfect, that is until YHWH Himself said, "It is not tov that the man should be alone; I will make him a help mate for him" Beresheet / Genesis 2:18. YHWH had created the heavens and the earth and had formed man from the ground. YHWH had then brought to man every living animal to find a suitable companion. In the greatness and glory of creation though, something was wrong. It was not good for man to be alone.

Alone? How could man be alone? Well the emet, the truth is that Adam had a perfect relationship with the creator and Adam had all of his spiritual needs met. He lived in a perfect world and had all of his physical needs met. How could he be alone?

Adam's physical and spiritual needs were fully met, yet Adam's need for human relationships was void – not tov. This first human crisis left Adam with the need of other people. This need YHWH could not meet nor fulfill directly – yet YHWH did it indirectly – by providing for Adam a suitable helper. In the same way that YHWH does not supernaturally zap man with nutrients every day, YHWH has provided a way for man to receive the vitamins and minerals he needs through solid food and liquids.

Adam was created with relational needs and YHWH has provided for Adam's needs by creating other people, namely Chava.

A person cannot correctly say that all that they need is YHWH, just as a person cannot fairly say that all that they need is other people. YHWH created Adam (man) with the need for both spiritual and human relationships. Philippians 4:13 must be read in context of verse 14. "I can do everything through Messiah who gives me strength. Yet it was good of you to share in my troubles," Philippians 4:13, 14. We need other people. How can you reach out to someone to share the love of YHWH today?

July 22

"Behold, I set before you this day a blessing and a curse; a blessing, if ye obey the commandments of the YHWH you Elohim, which I command you this day: and a curse, if ye will not obey the commandments of YHWH your Elohim/God, but turn aside out of the way which I command you this day, to go after other gods, which ye have not known," Deuteronomy 11:26-28. These verses don't guarantee us physical prosperity or blessing in the way that we might think. This section of scripture indicates that obedience to YHWH creates the environment for blessing. All blessings are potential as we obey.

What bring major confusion is that we have our own unique definition of blessing. We picture a blessed person as someone with good health, lots of money, a house with a white picket fence, a nice family of 2.4 children, and a new car. Just because someone is materially wealthy doesn't mean they are obedient to Torah!

What needs adjusting is our recognition of YHWH's blessings and YHWH's curses. Here is a truth -YHWH's blessings and YHWH's judgment are USUALLY NOT discernible or understandable. We should leave such judgment to YHWH. For example, was Bill Gates blessed with money and fortune because he obeyed Torah? Was it really YHWH's judgment that brought about the holocaust?

Being rich doesn't mean you have kept the mitzvot. Having a bad day doesn't mean you are a heathen.

The Jewish rabbis have taught us that the mitzvoth's reward is the mitzvot itself. This means that we should obey the commandments regardless of reward. The reward of obedience is obedience. That's worth repeating - "the reward of obedience is obedience."

Remember this point - We don't HAVE to keep the Torah. We GET the PRIVLEDGE to keep the Torah! Some call hurricane Katrina judgment on New Orleans but couldn't Katrina have been YHWH's mercy? If Katrina would have hit Mexico City certainly millions would have died! Is it really our place to determine blessing or cursing? Galatians 6:7, "Do not be deceived: YHWH cannot be mocked. A man reaps what he sows."

We need to mature as believers and STOP this constant focus on blessings and curses. A mature person obeys YHWH because it is the right thing to do. YHWH is our blessing - not new house, good job, or whatever. "O YHWH; early will I seek You; my soul thirsts for You; my flesh longs for You. In a dry and thirsty land where there is no water. So I have looked for You in the sanctuary, to see Your power and Your glory," Psalm / Tehillim 63:1-2.

July 23

"If I forget you, O Jerusalem, let my right hand forget what it's supposed to do," Psalm 137:5. In Isaiah 60:12 the Bible warns us: "For the nation that will not serve you (Israel) will perish; it will be utterly ruined." The restoration of the nation of Israel in 1948 was a miraculous event and fulfillment to prophetic scripture. Isaiah 66:7-8, "Before she goes into labor, she gives birth; before the pains come upon her, she delivers a son. Who has ever heard of such a thing? Who has ever seen such things? Can a country be born in a day or a nation be brought forth in a moment? Yet no sooner is Zion in labor than she gives birth to her children."

As prophesied in Scripture, the enemies of Israel have constantly surrounded the nation with threats, war, and terrorism. Within hours of Israel's declaration of independence the Muslim countries of Egypt, Syria, Jordan, Iraq, and Lebanon invaded Israel in 1948. The Jewish nation swiftly defeated these enemies. Then in 1967 Israel defended itself during the six day war and regained control of Jerusalem. In 1973 Israel was once again attacked by Egypt and Syria but the Hebrew people won that battle and even extended their borders further. To these victories Leviticus 26:3, 7-8 says, "If you follow my decrees and are careful to obey my commands... You will pursue your enemies, and they will fall by the sword before you. Five of you will chase a hundred, and a hundred of you will chase ten thousand, and your enemies will fall by the sword before you."

The Scripture commands Bible believers to "Pray for the peace of Jerusalem: they shall prosper that love thee," Psalm 122:6. We are to speak out for Zion's sake (Isaiah 62:1), to be watchmen on the walls of Jerusalem (Isaiah 62:6) and to bless the Hebrew people (Genesis 12:3). The Biblical obligation to defend Israel in their time of need should not be ignored by our nation. The Holy Land matters in Scripture and it should matter to our nation today. Have you prayed for the peace of Jerusalem? How can you take a stand for Israel?

July 24

"Pray for the peace of Jerusalem: "May those who love you be secure," Psalm 22:6. Through YHWH's "shalom" or "peace," we can make it through a bad day or a string of terrible events. The book of Ephesians proves how this is possible. "He is our Shalom, Who hath made both one, and hath broken down the middle wall of partition between us." -- Ephesians 2: 14. Our shalom is the presence of Master Y'shua. It is Him. Nothing more and nothing less. He is our peace. The Prince of Peace is our wholeness. He is the one that completes us.

To illustrate this, a Jew who accepts Y'shua as Messiah is often called "completed Jew." Rav Sha'ul wrote, "For YHWH was pleased to have all the fullness dwell in Him, and through Him to reconcile to Himself all things, all things, whether things on earth or things in heaven, by making shalom though His blood, shed on the execution stake," -- Colossians 1:19, 20.

Every time we use the word "shalom," we should be reminded that we are speaking about Y'shua. He is our peace. Now, apply this idea to Tehillim / Psalms 122:6 where we are told to "pray for the peace of Jerusalem." When we do this, we are actually praying for the salvation of Jerusalem. As we pray for the peace of Jerusalem, we are praying that all Israel comes to know Y'shua as their Master and Savior! The Talmud confirms this in Megillah E: 33-35, "And where is the horn of the righteous exalted? In Jerusalem, as it says, Pray for the peace of Jerusalem, may they prosper that love thee. And when Jerusalem is built, David will come, as it says." The Jews have this truth, yet many are so blind that they don't see it and accept Y'shua as their Messiah!

As we walk in Shalom we are walking as Y'shua walked and thus replicating His life. "My covenant was with him of life and shalom; and I gave them to him for the fear wherewith he feared me, and was afraid before my name. The law of truth was in his mouth, and iniquity was not found in his lips: he walked with me in shalom and equity, and did turn many away from iniquity," -- Malachi 2. Y'shua was never in a hurry nor did he ever worry about life. He lived in total shalom. Y'shua focused on YHWH, brought forth the Kingdom of Heaven. Having Y'shua's focus is what enables us to have the Shalom promised in the Scriptures. "He wilt keep him in perfect peace, whose minds is stayed on Thee," Isaiah 26:3. Pray for the peace of Jerusalem today - pray for the lost souls to come to know Y'shua as their messiah.

July 25

"I believe, help thou my unbelief," Mark 9:24. In Mark 9 a man comes to the Savior and says that the disciples could not help his son. The boy is vexed by demons. He foams at the mouth, gnashes his teeth, and becomes rigid. Y'shua's response is interesting:

"O unbelieving generation, how long shall I stay with you? How long shall I put up with you? Bring the boy to me."

Notice in this verse that Y'shua didn't ask the talmidim if they had been fasting. Instead he confronted their unbelief. Y'shua asked the boy's father, "How long has he been like this?" "From childhood," he answered. "It has often thrown him into fire or water to kill him. But if you can do anything, take pity on us and help us." Y'shua replied 'If you can'? Everything is possible for him who believes." Immediately the boy's father exclaimed, "I do believe; help me overcome my unbelief!" Y'shua rebuked the shadim / demons and the boy was healed. Later, the talmidim came to Y'shua and asked "why couldn't we cast it out?" He replied, "This kind can come out only by prayer."

Read this passage again in context and see what "only comes out by prayer and fasting." In context, what comes out is NOT demons BUT unbelief!

It was unbelief that held back the disciples from casting out the shadim. The scriptures are clear that demons must flee at the faith-filled command of the believer. It tells us in the book of Ya'acov / James that the demons know that YHWH is one and shudder. The shadim / demons are scared of the truth! Unbelief is what was keeping the boy bound by the adversary. We must learn to pray like his father - "I believe BUT help my unbelief!"

Deliverance from ha satan (the adversary) is not about holy water, catholic rites. It's all about the balance of emunah / faith and works that declares to the captives. Yesha'yahu / Isaiah 61:1, "The Ruach of the Master YHWH is upon Me; because YHWH has anointed Me to preach the Besorah to the meek; He has sent Me to bind up the brokenhearted, to proclaim liberty to the exiles, recovery of sight to the blind and the opening of the prison to them that are bound." This was Y'shua's ministry and this is our ministry today! Biblical deliverance ministry is about recognizing open doors to the enemy, declaring the truth of the scriptures, and living in freedom. The Gospels show us the correct pattern of deliverance ministry. To the reader of the Newer Testament it seems that Y'shua was really into deliverance ministry. He is seen casting out demons everywhere he goes. We should be doing the same by using the truth of the Scriptures and our authority as born again saints to proclaim freedom to the captives. How can you apply this truth to your day?

July 26

"For if you forgive men when they sin against you, your heavenly Father will also forgive you. But if you do not forgive men their sins, your Father will not forgive your sins," Matthew 6:14-15.

There are several words in the Hebrew language for forgiveness. The one most often used in modern Hebrew today is "slichot." If you were on the streets of Israel today and bumped into someone you would simply say "slichot" for "forgive me" or "pardon/excuse me." This word means a total absolution and pardoning of the offense. Slichot is also the name of a section of prayers spoken during times of repentance and on Yom Kippur. Because a person either sins against the Almighty YHWH or against another person, slichot is a two dimensional action. Slichot is given either from man to man or from the Creator to man. In Hebrew the sins against another person are called "bein adam le-havero." These sins against other people must be forgiven before forgiveness from YHWH is granted.

The Messiah's comment on this subject in the book of Mattitiyahu / Matthew reflects the rabbinical teachings of his time. "For if you forgive men when they sin against you, your heavenly Father will also forgive you. But if you do not forgive men their sins, your Father will not forgive your sins," Mattitiyahu / Matthew 6:14-15. The Talmud has several sayings that read almost identical to this verse. Both the person who has sinned and the person who has been sinned against have an obligation to accept and give. "All who act mercifully (forgivingly) toward their fellow creatures will be treated mercifully by Heaven, and all who do not act mercifully toward their fellow creatures will not be treated mercifully by Heaven," says one Jewish writing.

To get forgiveness you must grant forgiveness. Forgive when asked. That's pretty basic isn't it? Well, it is also pretty hard. When you've been hurt, when your integrity has been questioned, or when people are untrustworthy it is very difficult to put the past behind you. Yet you must. Messiah Y'shua taught this when he told his talmidim to pray, "Forgive us our sins, for we also forgive everyone who sins against us."

Messiah Y'shua taught that to get forgiveness you must give it. Who do you need to forgive? How can you release the pain you have suffered and get to a place of loving the person who offended you?

July 27

Bear with each other and forgive whatever grievances you may have against one another. Forgive as YHWH forgave you. And over all these virtues put on love, which binds them all together in perfect unity," Colossians 3:13-14.

Forgiveness brings harmony and wipes the slate clean. It fixes the broken and reaches out in love. In Beresheet / Genesis 37:26-27 the very same brother, brother Y'hudah, who sold Joseph into slavery offers himself as a slave to Yoseph in order to spare Binyamin. Through this selfless act of substitution Judah / Y'hudah was actually seeking slichot /forgiveness and righting the wrongs of the past. Messiah Y'shua acknowledges this when He said "greater love hath no man than he who lay down his life for his friends."

The Jewish Talmud says, "if you have done your fellow a little wrong, let it be in your eyes great; if you have done him much good, let it be your eyes a little; if he has done you a little good, let it be in your eyes great; if he has done you a great wrong, let it be in your eyes little." True forgiveness does this for you. It breaks down the walls that have been built over the years. It reveals what is hidden beneath angry faces and harsh words. Forgiveness brings to surface the pains of the past and acknowledges that wrong is wrong.

Slichot realizes that to "err is human," people will be offended and therefore we must be quick to start over with love and forgiveness. "Bear with each other and forgive whatever grievances you may have against one another. Forgive as YHWH forgave you. And over all these virtues put on love, which binds them all together in perfect unity," Colossians 3:13-14. Slichot should put an end to bitterness and strife and help bring healing to the family of Messiah.

Chances are that you will be hurt by your family or friends today. Are you ready to forgive?

July 28

"What advantage then is there in being a Jew? Much in every way for they have been trusted with the very words of YHWH," Romans 3:1-3.

All traditions are not bad! The Hebrew word for tradition is "masoret." The Encyclopedia Judaica says, "Masoret is the general name for tradition. It is found in Ezekiel 20:37 and means originally "bond" or "fetter." Tradition is the discipline which establishes the correct practice and interpretation of the Torah and was therefore regarded as a hedge or fetter about the Law. Since this knowledge was handed down by successive generations, it was also associated with the Hebrew word masor, denoting "to give over." The term masoret is used to include all forms of tradition, both those which relate to the Bible and those which concern custom, law, historical events, folkways, and other subjects." Masoret / traditions remain virtually unchanged over long periods of time to provide examples, uniformity, and help with belief.

Jewish people's obedience to the Torah is not just mindless or faithless work. No, their practice of Torah has over time developed into a culture of events that express a lifestyle. Judaism is not just a religion but a lifestyle. "Tradition has given Judaism a continuity with its past and preserved its character as a unique faith with a distinct way of life," says one source.

To find the answer on "how" to keep certain commandments in the Bible we can look to the Jewish people. The Jewish people's faithful obedience to the Torah over the years serves as an example on how to fulfill the commandments. The Jewish people have kept the Torah for thousands of years. They have hashed out the difficult verses and set standards on the way to live. The majority of Jewish observances concerning the Torah are of benefit. By following the traditional adherence to the Torah your actions can model that of the first believers in Messiah. The early Believers were "just like the Torah keeping Jews" and their accepted practices differed in no way, teaches the church historian Eusebius. When you keep the Torah you will "look" Jewish because the Jewish people are the only group that actually observes the commandments in the Torah. Is this really a bad thing?

TRUTH FOR TODAY

July 29

"And it shall come to pass, that from one new moon to another, and from one Sabbath to another, shall all flesh come to worship before me, saith YHWH," Isaiah 66:23. Rosh Chodesh or the "New Moon" is very important as it is the exact time that YHWH called Israel as a nation out of darkness. The very first commandment given to the nation of Israel was to honor the New Moon. Rosh Chodesh is also when YHWH's presence originally filled the mishkan, the tabernacle.

"So the tabernacle was set up on the first day of the first month...Then the cloud covered the Tent of Meeting, and the Shekinah of YHWH filled the tabernacle. Moshe could not enter the Tent of Meeting because the cloud had settled upon it, and the glory of YHWH had filled the tabernacle," Shemot / Exodus 40:17, 34, 35.

Every Rosh Chodesh is a special time to stop and reflect, to stop and think about our calling. As we glimpse into the sky and see the small sliver of a moon illuminate the darkness we can be reminded of our purpose: to shine forth the Light! The moon creates no light itself but reflects the light of the sun. We are to do the same. YHWH is the light and we are to reflect His power and plan for the world.

We should not strive to bring attention to ourselves and we should do away with selfish ambitions. Religiosity clouds the light. Selfishness hinders the Light from shining. Doing "our thing" stops us from doing YHWH's will. If you are fulfilling your own desires for ministry then perhaps you are creating your own light. Through any way possible are you drawing attention to nice things and people more than YHWH?

We should not compromise the truth of our faith. Today's culture says to blend in and be a part while YHWH says "to come out and be separate." If you get along well with people of the world then maybe you are hiding the Light.

Just as the moon reflects the light of the sun, we as Israel are to reflect the Light of YHWH.

July 30

"For we wrestle not against flesh and blood, but against the rulers, against the powers, against the world forces of this darkness, against the spiritual forces of wickedness in the heavenly places," Ephesians 6:12. Wrestling is an amazing sport. You know, the fierce face off on the mat to pin the opponent through precise moves. The best of colleges and even the Olympics feature this high contact sport. The fake wrestling found on the television is a very poor reflection of this intense battle of the body and the will.

Real wrestling is all about wearing down the opponent. Wrestlers grapple, twist, maneuver, and press to win. They don't knock out or paralyze. They wrestle and wear out to win. "For we wrestle not against flesh and blood, but against the rulers, against the powers, against the world forces of this darkness, against the spiritual forces of wickedness in the heavenly places," Ephesians 6:12.

It's no surprise that this is how our enemy fights. We wrestle not against flesh and blood but against powers and principalities. The dark forces want to wear us out so we give in or give up. As long as we are in the ring or squared up on the mat we can win. But once our will is surrendered we are toast. The opponent wants us to waive the white flag yet it's by pressing in that we achieve the victory. We are told in James / Ya'acov to "submit to YHWH, resist ha satan and he will flee from you." Resisting isn't easy. It is an active persistence to not be swayed. Every day is a wrestling match against our souls and for our joy.

Yes. It's our joy that the adversary wants. He knows the joy of YHWH is our strength so if he can get us to relinquish our joy then he can win.

We lose our joy, or "simcha" in Hebrew, when we are tired, weary, sick, stressed, or busy. Without simcha we quickly go down for the count. With joy we can win.

Simcha is a fruit of the Holy Spirit and is found inside the born again spirit of every believer. You have the joy of YHWH within you. Joy isn't something you need to pray and ask YHWH for - you just need to believe you already have it and act upon it. Draw out the joy of YHWH from the Ruach Ha Kadosh inside of you. As you guard and walk in that simcha you will automatically defeat the enemy because he will not be able to tire and frustrate you.

Choose today to live in the joy of YHWH. Choose the same tomorrow. And the next day. And the one after that. Soon you will be wrestling and wearing down the dark forces instead of them defeating you.

July 31

"Give attendance to the reading of Torah, to exhortation, to teaching," says First Timothy 4:13. The Torah has been divided into weekly reading portions or "parashot" to help us dig into the first five books of the Bible each year. Reading this small section of the Scriptures each week is a great way to build your faith and understanding of YHWH.

In the book of Deuteronomy / Devarim, Moshe spoke the Torah aloud as an example. He told Yisra'el that they should read the Torah aloud on Rosh Chodesh, and Feast days. Later Ezra the Scribe would institute reading the Torah aloud on Mondays, Thursdays, and Shabbat Afternoons (Nehemiah 8:1). The Brit Chadasha continues this theme when it teaches that "Faith cometh by hearing and hearing by the word of Elohim." Without the Torah being read aloud it is difficult for faith to truly set in. "Give attendance to the reading of Torah, to exhortation, to teaching," says First Timothy 4:13.

Y'shua the Moshiach set an example for all believers when he attended the synagogue for Torah reading on many occasions. (Surprisingly he never went to church to hear a sermon!) "And He came to Nazareth, where He had been brought up: and, according to his practice, He went into the synagogue on Shabbat, and stood up to read," Luke 4:16. Y'shua never stopped the Torah reading in the synagogue to do miracles or teach. He read from the Torah and things just started to happen!

Some may say that the "Spirit should lead" what is done during worship services and that is perfectly fine. The Spirit of Truth or "Ruach V'Emet" will certainly lead as the Devar YHWH / word of YHWH is presented. "All writing are given by the inspiration of YHWH, and are profitable for teaching, for reproof, for correction, as Torah in righteousness: that the man of YHWH may be perfect, fully equipped to all good deeds / tov mitzvot," 2 Timothy 3:16,17. We are to "worship in Spirit and in Truth" says the Messiah. This must include openness to the Torah of YHWH. "Elohim is Ruach: and they that worship Him must worship Him in Ruach and Emet," John / Yochannan 4:24. The Ruach HaKodesh will minister and move as we first delve into the Emet or Truth of YHWH.

Have you read the Torah portion for this week? Take some time today to catch up on the weekly reading. Ask the Holy Spirit to lead you into all truth as you open the Torah.

August

TRUTH FOR TODAY

August 1

"YHWH showed his great love for us that while we were still sinners Messiah died for us," Romans 5:8. When Y'shua offered Himself as a sacrifice Y'shua took upon the Torah violations of the whole world.

"He is despised and rejected of men; a man of sorrows, and acquainted with grief: and we hid as it were our faces from him; he was despised, and we esteemed him not. Surely he hath borne our grief, and carried our sorrows: yet we did esteem him stricken, smitten of Elohim, and afflicted. But he was wounded for our transgressions; he was bruised for our iniquities: the chastisement of our peace was upon him; and with his stripes we are healed. All we like sheep have gone astray; we have turned everyone to his own way; and YHWH hath laid on him the iniquity of us all. He was oppressed, and he was afflicted, yet he opened not his mouth: he is brought as a lamb to the slaughter, and as a sheep before her shearers is dumb, so he openeth not his mouth. He was taken from prison and from judgment: and who shall declare his generation? for he was cut off out of the land of the living: for the transgression of my people was he stricken. And he made his grave with the wicked, and with the rich in his death; because he had done no violence, neither was any deceit in his mouth. Yet it pleased YHWH to bruise him; he hath put him to grief: when thou shalt make his soul an offering for sin, he shall see his seed, he shall prolong his days, and the pleasure of YHWH shall prosper in his hand. He shall see of the travail of his soul, and shall be satisfied: by his knowledge shall my righteous servant justify many; for he shall bear their iniquities," Isaiah / Yesha'yahu 53:3-11.

The Torah refers to the punishment of flogging for various serious offenses. The Sages limited this harsh punishment to only 39 lashes, that is, one minus the total of 40 allowed by Devarim 25:3. It is no secret that Y'shua was flogged by part of the vicious torture he endured as part of His crucifixion. Historically, flogging or "scourging" involved whipping with thirteen strikes on the chest and twenty-six on the back. Often the victim died from the beating that was done to tear open the skin with metal-laced whips.

"Then Pilate took Y'shua and had him flogged. The soldiers twisted together a crown of thorns and put it on his head. They clothed him in a purple robe and went up to him again and again, saying, "Hail, king of the Jews!" And they struck him in the face," John / Yochannan 19:1-4.

May we never forget what Y'shua did for us when he offered his life as a sacrifice. Praise YHWH for His Son Y'shua who bore our shame and took our pain!

August 2

"And YHWH spake unto Moshe, saying, speak unto the children of Israel, and say unto them, concerning the feasts of YHWH, which ye shall proclaim to be holy convocations, even these are my feasts," Leviticus 23:1-2. The events in Leviticus 23 are not Jewish feasts; these are feasts of YHWH. Most of us did not grow up in synagogues where the holy days of YHWH, like the Feast of Trumpets, is celebrated, so learning how to celebrate and keep these days can be a challenge. Yet, we are called to study, search, and then act upon what we have learned. The seven feasts of YHWH are set apart times of worship, rest, and fellowship.

Leviticus 23:2, "And YHWH spoke to Moshe, saying, speak to the children of Israel, saying, in the seventh month, in the first day of the month, ye shall have a Sabbath, a memorial of blowing of trumpets, a holy convocation." This is "Yom Teruah," the first of the fall festivals.

Yom Teruah is the "Feast of Trumpets." We can see its significance in Leviticus 23 and throughout the scriptures. Yom Teruah is given to us as a "miqra kodesh" or a "holy convocation." It, like the other feast days, is a rehearsal and a reminder. We are to be reminded of what took place in the past and we are rehearsing something for the future. We are to remember YHWH by blowing a trumpet or "shofar." The sound of the trumpet is to remind us to gather for worship and warfare.

Numbers 10:3, 10, "And when you shall blow with them, all the assembly shall assemble themselves to thee at the door of the tabernacle. Also in the day of your gladness, on your solemn days, in the beginnings of your months, you shall blow with the trumpets over your burnt offerings, over the sacrifices of your peace offerings; that they may be to you a memorial before YHWH: I am YHWH your Elohim."

We can also rehearse the coming fulfillment of this holy day with the shofar of YHWH will sound and the day of YHWH will commence. "The great day of YHWH is near; it is near and hastens quickly...a day of the shofar and alarm against the fortified cities and the high towers..." Zephaniah 1:14

Yom Teruah is considered the first the day of the "Yamim Noraim" or the "Ten Days of Awe." Beginning with Yom Teruah there are ten days until Yom Kippur. This is a time to seek YHWH and dwell in His presence. These are 10 days of soul searching, repentance and making amends with other people. The sounding of the shofar on Yom Teruah reminds us to take time to ask forgiveness from those we might have offended. We need to hear the call, get right with other people and seek YHWH's face. How can you spend time today getting ready for the shofar call of Yom Teruah?

August 3

"Let no man therefore judge you in meat, or in drink, or in respect of an holy day, or of the new moon, or of the Sabbath: which are a shadow of things to come; but the body is of Messiah," Colossians 2:16-17.

This passage is often misunderstood and made a mess. Colossians first says to let no man judge you regarding feast days. Your feast keeping is between you and YHWH. You should be judging yourself in regards to HOW you keep the feast days of YHWH - not "if" you keep them.

This verse is clearly spoken to believers who are already keeping the feasts days. What Paul or Rabbi Sha'ul was saying is that people may keep the feast days differently but we are not judge them in "how" the feast day is observed. What is primarily important is that the Holy Days of Leviticus 23 are kept.

Colossians 2:17 also calls these days of worship "shadows of things to come." Eating kosher food or clean food, keeping the holy days or the new moon or the Sabbath days and observing other commands are shadows of things to come. These things haven't passed away! No, Colossians says that they are "shadows of something greater that is coming in the future."

A shadow is a resemblance of something bigger. A shadow is not intricately detailed. It is only an outline. This is exactly how we keep the clean laws or the feast days. We are to try and our efforts may be "like" the real thing but our efforts are only a shadow of what we will be doing in the future. In the coming Messianic Kingdom we will keep the commandments and celebrate the feast days properly.

Take the holy days serious and make your worship sincere but remember that we are just in the shadow. There is coming a day when we will rule and reign with Y'shua and celebrate His moadim / feasts in fullness. Yes, we are in the shadow of something greater that is soon to come!

During the millennial kingdom we will all be keeping the feast days and celebrating in the glory of our Father. "From one New Moon to another and from one Sabbath to another, all mankind will come and bow down before me," says YHWH in Isaiah 66:23.

August 4

How easily we accept less than the perfect love / ahava of YHWH and then wonder why we are left empty and unfulfilled. We think we need other things like a good relationship, a tasty meal, or some hidden knowledge. What really need is a greater revelation of the Almighty's love to us and in us. Don't settle for less. Open up your heart, the inner you, and let his love ripple over you today.

"I have loved you with an everlasting love; I have drawn you with loving-kindness. I will build you up again and you will be rebuilt...and you will go out to dance with joy," Jeremiah / Yermi'yahu 31:3, 4.

The ahava / love of YHWH is everlasting. This means it doesn't leave. It is always with you and for you. YHWH loves you no matter what you do or what you have done. The love of YHWH is filling. When we desire to sense his love we must allow the truth in His word to destroy the feelings and emotions of our mind. We may not feel loved. We may not feel loveable. But, regardless of how you feel today know that YHWH loves you. He cares for you. He is for you and wants the best for you. When your feelings don't align with what the Bible says about YHWH's love then it's time to change your feelings. "YHWH has poured out his love into our hearts by the Holy Spirit, whom He has given us," Romans 5:5.

YHWH wants to "bind up the broken hearted" and heal the pains of your past. Those regrets that nag you every now and then don't have to sting so badly. The scriptures offer healing and hope. Think on those words... healing and hope. Today you can let Y'shua bind up your heart like a doctor in the hospital. Allow Him to dress your wound with his love. Agree with His ahava / love and invite his healing to come.

August 5

The sixth month after Passover is the Hebrew month of "Elul." This name originates from the time the Hebrew people were in Exile in Babylon. Before the Babylonian exile the only month that was named was the month of "Aviv."

Today, the month of Elul is a time of prayer and preparation of the Holy Days of the Fall. The Hebrew word "Elul" is related to verb meaning "to search." This month is a time to search.

Jewish tradition is to spend the month of Elul in repentance and searching out the sin in your life. However, in your searching be careful that you aren't looking for the wrong things. It is not your job to search your own heart for sin or error. It is also not your job to search someone else's life for problems. When we begin digging up issues we often bring condemnation on ourselves and others. It is the Holy Spirit that should be doing the searching. We are to yield to the Ruach's power and conviction. Deciding to search out your own life or to turn over a new leaf are admirable actions. You can even be sincere in your desire to be a better person during this holy time. Yet you can be sincere and be sincerely wrong at the same time. "YHWH hear my voice when I all and be gracious to me and answer. My heart says this, 'Master, I will seek your face,'" Psalm 27:7-8.

Instead of searching for sin, we are to search for the Spirit. Instead of introspection we need to do have some Ruach expectation. YHWH says to "call upon me while I am near." He also says that he rewards those who diligently seek Him. Psalm 27:7-8, "YHWH hear my voice when I all and be gracious to me and answer. My heart says this, 'Master, I will seek your face.'"

Here's the awesome point - because you are a born again believer, the Ruach HaKodesh - the Holy Spirit of YHWH dwells in you. This means that YHWH is never far away. He isn't hidden by problems or even sin. The Spirit will never leave you nor forsake you. Now is the time to release you heart and soul and ask the Spirit to search you. Yield to the power of the Ruach to test your motives and your missions. The sixth month is indeed a special time of drawing near but this drawing near should not come from our flesh. Romans 7 states that "no flesh can please YHWH." It is faith that pleases Him. This is a time to activate our faith and trust the Ruach to do His job. The Spirit will lead us into all truth and change us as YHWH sees fit. Make the presence of YHWH your desire and not change, repentance, or even holiness. As you seek Him, then YHWH will lead you into these things.

Finally, it is tradition to recite Psalm / Tehillim 27 during this month. Take the words of this Psalm today and speak them over your life. Pray this Psalm and ask the Ruach of YHWH to search and lead you.

August 6

When we gather to worship on the appointed times of YHWH we are to look back and learn from the historical events of our past. Every Shabbat we can remember creation, and the redemption out of Egypt. During Passover we recall the blood covering of the Passover Lamb. Shavuot, commonly called Pentecost, is when the Torah was given and the Ruach HaKodesh / Holy Spirit was poured out. And the Feast of Tabernacles, Sukkot, reminds us of the 40-year wilderness journey to the Promised Land. "In the seventh month, on the first day of the month, you shall observe a day of solemn rest [shabbaton], a memorial proclamation with a blast of trumpets / teruah, a holy convocation," Leviticus 23:24

What about Yom Teruah, the Feast of Trumpets? What is so special about this day? Interestingly, the Bible refers to this holy day as Yom Zikaron Teruah, the "the day of remembering the sounding of the Shofar." The Rabbis explain to us that during the Feast of Trumpets, or Yom Teruah, many wonderful things are to be remembered. They teach that during this time: Adam was created, the flood waters dried up, Enoch was taken up (Genesis 5:24), Sarah, Rachel, Samuel all were conceived (1 Samuel 1), Egyptian slavery of the Hebrews ended, Job contracted leprosy, and the sacrifices built on the altar by Ezra started to be offered.

The Feasts illustrate events that have already occurred. They are also spiritual blueprints for things to come. "Let no individual man therefore judge you in meat, or in drink, or in respect of a feast day, or in the Rosh Chodesh, or in the Shabbat days: which are shadows of things to come," Colossians 216,17a. This verse clearly teaches that the moadim / feast days of YHWH are shadows of the future. Some preachers and teachers say that some of these holy days have been "fulfilled" by Messiah. However, the Scriptures say that they are "shadows" of what is ahead. The shadow is seen and experienced before subject is seen. Paul wrote these words after the Messiah had resurrected and ascended, so he was not speaking of the Savior's first coming. The feast days are shadows - pictures of things to come!

The feasts are not the substance but shadows. They haven't been totally fulfilled - they are pictures of what is coming. With Yom Teruah we can see a glimpse of the future and the past. For Messiah "shall descend from the Shamayim / heavens with a shout, with the voice of the chief heavenly Malach / messenger, and with the shofar and the shout of YHWH: and the dead in Moshiach shall rise first: Then we who are alive and remain at His return shall be caught up together with them onto the clouds, to meet the Master in the air: and so shall we ever be with the Master," First Thessalonians 4:16 & 17.

August 7

The first two words in the Torah (Genesis 1:1) are "Beresheet Aleph," translated "in the beginning." By turning this Hebrew phrase around, to read "aleph b tishrei," we see that on the on the First of Tishrei, or Yom Teruah, man was created. This is how people can reference Yom Teruah as Rosh Hashanah or "Rosh Hashanah."

Beresheet / Genesis 1:1-2:3 describes the creation account in generic terms. Then in amazing repetition, the entire creation account is repeated in Genesis 2:3 onward. Why would the Bible be so redundant? Why is the creation story repeated and expanded?

An answer to these questions can be found by reading between the lines. In the first creation account of Genesis 1:1-2:3 everything is great! The world, the animals, and man are created. YHWH calls his work "tov" or good. Amazingly, there is no fall in the first chapter of Genesis.

However, there is some major drama in the second telling of intelligent design. Go ahead, read these verses and be amazed. The temptation and the fall occur only in the second edition of creation. Perhaps the riddle of the fall of man is to show us the potential of Yom Teruah, the day of creation.

Man was created for the purpose of the Divine. We were made in His image for His purpose. "Thou art worthy, O Master, to receive glory and honor and power: for thou hast created all things, and for thy pleasure they are and were created," Revelation 4:11.

Every year at Yom Teruah we are to be reminded of how creation should have been. We can also perceive the promise of tomorrow. YHWH made us for His tov pleasure. When sin entered the world during the second creation story, man was cut off from fellowship with YHWH. "Your sins have separated you from your Elohim; your sins have hidden His face from you," Yesha'yahu / Isaiah 59:2. Yom Teruah gives us the opportunity to go back in time to the Garden of Eden. Through our actions during these holy days we can rewrite our future. We can change our habits and change our future. Now is the time to give direction to your life. For the way you begin the new year, will determine the remaining year.

Intimacy with the Creator is the promise of Yom Teruah. For on this day and the days that follow, including Yom Kippur and Sukkot, we can experience the closeness of the Garden of Eden. Through prayer, judging ourselves, teshuvah, and trusting in the atoning work of Messiah, our fellowship is restored as we re-create creation.

August 8

"Concerning the feasts of YHWH, which ye shall proclaim to be holy convocations, even these are MY feasts," Leviticus 23:2. A 2008 Time magazine cover story listed the "Re-Judaizing of Jesus" as one of the "Ten Ideas That Are Changing the World." According the editors of Time, the Hebrew roots movement will have more impact on the future than money and politics. The article explains that to properly understand the Savior of the New Testament one must accept the precepts and customs of the Old Testament. Such a return to the Rabbi Y'shua leads many people to begin celebrating what are mistakenly called the "Jewish Festivals."

These are days of worship that were not given only to the Jewish people but for all who call upon the Elohim of Abraham, Isaac, and Jacob. Leviticus 23:2 explains, "Concerning the feasts of YHWH, which ye shall proclaim to be holy convocations, even these are MY feasts." The Biblical festivals are holy days that the Almighty has chosen. They are HIS feasts, which include Passover and Pentecost in the Spring and several festivals that usually occur in September or October.

One of the fall holy days is Yom Kippur, or the Day of Atonement. It was on this day, during Temple times, that the High Priest would enter into the Holy of Holies and present a special once a year sacrifice. Atonement was granted if the people were truly repentant of their sins and the priest was obedient in his actions. Today, Yom Kippur is observed by fasting for a period of 25 hours. "It shall be a holy convocation unto you; and ye shall afflict your souls. And ye shall do no work in that same day: for it is a day of atonement, to make atonement for you before YHWH your Elohim," Leviticus23:27-28. Yom Kippur is prophetic of the great white throne judgment of Revelation 20.

Yom Kippur, like the other fall festivals of YHWH are opportunities to experience true Biblical worship as the Creator intended. When a person begins to keep the Festivals of Elohim their eyes are often opened to a greater understanding of the Scriptures and end times prophetic events. How can you prepare for Yom Kippur today? How can you include others in your observance of these worship times?

August 9

The Bible has affected mankind in countless ways. It is the best-selling book of all time. Harvard, Yale, and Princeton once based their curriculum upon the Scriptures. For many years Webster's Dictionary predominately defined words from their usage in the King James Version. The message of the Bible has sparked wars like the Crusades, changed lives of horrible sinners like Jeffrey Dahmer, and become part of everyday speech. Phrases like "cleanliness is next to godliness" are repeated over and over as coming from the good book. But, do many of the popular sayings we attribute to the Bible actually originate from the Scriptures?

Surprisingly, phrases like "this too shall pass" or "once saved, always saved" are not in the Bible. "A bird in the hand is worth two in the bush" is a phrase from a newspaper in 1833. And "beggars can't be choosers" was first used in a 1546 book of proverbs.

Perhaps the most used unbiblical statement derives from a hymn written by William Cowper. He wrote that "God moves in a mysterious ways." Today, this statement is repeated over and over by believers and unbelievers alike. The truth is that the Almighty is not mysterious whatsoever. The Creator can be known and understood through His word. We are the ones with a problem of understanding the infinite. For a Bible believer, nothing about the Creator should be mysterious as EVERYTHING can be for the good. Everything that occurs is not good but can work for our benefit. Romans 8:28, "And we know that all thing work together for the good to those who love Him and are called according to His purpose."

Error brings more error. We delude ourselves when we erroneously attribute man's ideas for Biblical wisdom. The only way to know if what we think is in the Scriptures is to study and know the Bible. The truth of the Bible will set us free from error and misunderstandings.

"All Scripture is inspired by YHWH and is useful to teach us what is true and to make us realize what is wrong in our lives. It corrects us when we are wrong and teaches us to do what is right," 2 Timothy 3:16.

August 10

The following statement is alarming but true..."sin isn't a problem for YHWH anymore." Our sins cannot separate us from YHWH. All of our sins have been charged to Y'shua's account. Hebrews 9:11 - 12, "Now the Messiah has appeared, high priest of the good things that have come. In the greater and more perfect tabernacle not made with hands (that is, not of this creation), He entered the holy of holies once for all, not by the blood of goats and calves, but by His own blood, having obtained eternal redemption."

When Y'shua was on the tree he paid the price for all sin. Hebrews 9:26, "But now he has appeared once for all at the end of the ages to do away with sin by the sacrifice of himself."

Yes, Isaiah says in chapter 59 that "your sins have separated you from YHWH." And that is true for an unbeliever. As a born again believer in Y'shua, the blood of Y'shua separates you from your sins.

When YHWH looks upon us he doesn't see sin. He only sees Y'shua. 1 Corinthians 6:17 says that "he that is joined to YHWH is one spirit with YHWH." This is a life changing revelation because it frees us from a "works" based salvation. This doesn't give us a license to sin, to do so would just be stupid. Sin opens the door to the adversary. Romans 6:16, "Don't you know that when you offer yourselves to someone to obey him as slaves, you are slaves to the one whom you obey-whether you are slaves to sin, which leads to death, or to obedience, which leads to righteousness?" Sin brings curses upon us. These curses are NOT sent by YHWH but by ourselves.

The Emet / truth is that if we've been born again and follow Y'shua then His blood has been applied to ALL our sins - past, present, and future. We don't need to do good works, fast on Yom Kippur, or give millions of dollars to be forgiven. We simply need to accept REALLY accept what Y'shua has done. His blood has been applied to the Mercy seat ONCE and FOR ALL. His Mercy has been extended. No longer does a high priest or even Y'shua have to enter into the holy of holies each year to atone for our sins. IT IS FINISHED. No longer do we have to afflict ourselves, kill a chicken, or beg forgiveness in prayer to hope that YHWH is in a good mood and is willing to pardon us. Y'shua is the lamb, whose blood is worthy. He is our High Priest and our mediator. "But now he has appeared once for all at the end of the ages to do away with sin by the sacrifice of himself," Hebrews 9:26. Take a few minutes today and praise Him for his love!

August 11

"Do not let any unwholesome talk come out of your mouths, but only what is helpful for building others up according to their needs, that it may benefit those who listen. And do not grieve the Ruach HaKodesh, with whom you were sealed for the day of redemption," Ephesians 4:29 & 30. These verses undoubtedly show that unwholesome speech is so evil that it grieves the Holy Spirit. The Greek word for "unwholesome" is "sapros" it literally is defined as "rotten." Lashon hara or "negative speech" is like nasty, stinking rotten meat. That's pretty rough.

And just how exactly do you keep meat from going bad? You season it with salt. Meat is preserved through salt. "Let your conversation be always full of grace, seasoned with salt, so that you may know how to answer everyone," Colossians 4:6. Salt is also used in scripture as a word picture for the Torah. According to this verse our conversations should be full of everlasting mercy and seasoned with the Torah!

If you desire to tame your tongue and win this constant battle over the habit of speaking lashon then you must let the Word be upon your heart and lips.

The book of Ephesians says, "Let the word of Messiah dwell in you richly as you teach and admonish one another with all wisdom, and as you sing psalms, hymns and spiritual songs with gratitude in your hearts to Elohim. And whatever you do, whether in word or deed, do it all in the name of the Adon Y'shua, giving thanks to YHWH the Father through him."

His word should dwell in us, in our heart and then will overflow out of us into our speech. What is the word of Messiah? The scriptures are clear about this, "The word (Torah) became flesh." The Torah is the word of Messiah and the Torah is to dwell in us richly. The Torah is the written instruction of the Almighty found in the first five books of the Bible. "Do not let the Book of the Torah depart from your mouth; meditate on it day and night, so that you may be careful to do everything written in it. Then you will be prosperous and successful," Joshua / Y'hoshua 1:8.

When we speak the words of the Scriptures we will stay away from evil negative speech. Psalm 19 makes this clear, "let the words of my mouth and the meditations of my heart be acceptable to you YHWH." When we think on the Word throughout our day we will speak the Word throughout our day. Let your talk be seasoned with salt today.

August 12

Torah teaches in Beresheet / Genesis 6:9, that "Noach was a righteous man, perfect in his generation." This isn't a compliment. It is actually a condemnation. One Jewish rabbi said that “had Noach lived in Avraham's generation, he wouldn't be regarded as anything special. Indeed, there is a big difference between the righteousness of Noach and the righteousness of Avraham.” For when Avraham was warned of the destruction of Sodom and Gomorrah, he didn't build a car and drive away from town. Instead, he interceded for the wicked. He said to YHWH, "Will you sweep away the innocent along with the guilty," Genesis / Beresheet 18:23. Avraham pleaded for the town, until he finally implored YHWH to forgive them if only ten innocent people could be found.

The Torah shows that Moshe too shielded his entire generation. When Israel sinned, Moshe said "And now if You would only forgive their sin! If not, erase me from the book that You have written," Shemot / Exodus 32:32. YHWH "would have destroyed them had not Moshe, His chosen, confronted Him in the breach," Tehillim / Psalms 106:23. Noach did nothing, Avraham pleaded, and Moshe offered. Yet it was who Y'shua who gave his own life for the wicked and the sinful. And Y'shua prayed. He "began to be sore amazed, and to be very heavy; and said to his talmidim / disciples, My soul is exceeding sorrowful ... And He went forward a little, and fell on the ground, and prayed," Mark 14:33-35. Y'shua prayed and acted. He coupled his cries to Abba YHWH with actions of selflessness. On the execution stake, He said, "Father forgive them for they know not what they do." Noach used wood to build an ark; Moshe walked with a cane of wood; Y'shua gave his life upon the wooden tree.

Those being overtaken by the flood of evil need the prayers of Israel. "Let the priests, the ministers of YHWH, weep between the porch and the altar, and let them say, Spare Thy people, O YHWH, and give not Thine heritage to reproach," Yo'el / Joel 2:17. The concept is pretty simple. One is to pray to the Master of the Harvest for the harvest. The intercessor should pray continually, "keep not silent, and give Him no rest...day and night," Lamentations 2:18, 19. We are to "stand in the gap" for the world around us. This calling to tefillah / prayer isn't for a select few, but all believers. Will our generation be guilty of the sin of Noach? Y'shua said, "As in the days of Noach, so it will be when the son of Man returns," Mattitiyahu / Matthew 24:37. How sad. However, our actions can make a difference. Our prayers and petitions can change the future. Let us pray that the Father would draw our generation unto Himself. Will Y’shua find faith on the earth or will he find us building our boat? "Oh, that one might plead for a man with Elohim, as a man pleads for his neighbor," Iyov / Job 16:21.

What did you learn today?

Truth For Today

August 13

The physical world is just an illusion. The truth is hidden in the olam. When Y'shua walked the face of the earth, He raised the dead and healed the sick. According to tradition, He did one miracle that had never been performed before - he gave sight to the blind. Y'shua was just peeling the mask of the world away and revealing YHWH's reality. "Y'shua went teaching in their synagogues and proclaiming the gospel of the kingdom and healing every disease and every affliction among the people," Matthew 4:23.

In Hebrew, the word for world is "olam." According to Strong's Exhaustive Concordance and dictionary 'olam' literally means, "concealed." It comes from a root Hebrew word 'alma' meaning "to veil or hide." This world is like a mask upon Elohim's face. We see the creation, but we don't always see the Creator. We don't see that YHWH and His creation are one. So, we must peel back the olam and reveal "Melek Ha Olam" - the king of the world of hidden things. Each time we repeat a blessing with this phrase, we can be reminded of our need to search and study, to reveal the world's lies and the Creator's hidden truths. We can be reminded that YHWH is king of the hidden things. "From now on I will tell you of new things, of hidden things unknown to you. They are created now, and not long ago; you have not heard of them before today. So you cannot say, 'Yes, I knew of them.' You have neither heard nor understood; from of old your ear has not been open," Yesha'yahu / Isaiah 48: 6, 7, 8.

In YHWH's reality, a burning bush doesn't burn, the humble are exalted, truth is hidden in parables, and man can walk on water.

In YHWH's reality, fishing nets are full, bread appears from the heavens, and people escape fiery furnaces without a hint of smoke.

In YHWH's reality "the will the eyes of the blind be opened and the ears of the deaf unstopped. The lame will the lame leap like a deer, and the mute tongue shout for joy. Water will gush forth in the wilderness and streams in the desert. The burning sand will become a pool, the thirsty ground bubbling springs. In the haunts where jackals once lay, grass and reeds and papyrus will grow. And a highway will be there; it will be called the Way of Holiness," Yesha'yahu / Isaiah 35:6-18.

YHWH's reality, His kingdom, His will, is for us to break free from this world and be renewed by this emet / truth. "Therefore, I urge you, brothers, in view of Elohim's mercy, to offer your bodies as living sacrifices, holy and pleasing to Elohim--this is your spiritual act of worship. Do not conform any longer to the pattern of this world, but be transformed by the renewing of your minds so that you may test and approve what Elohim's will is--his good, pleasing and perfect will," Romans 12:1-2.

August 14

It was on Yom Kippur that a special service took place in the Temple / Tabernacle involving the Cohen HaGadol / High Priest. The HaCohen HaGadol would enter the Most Holy Place and make blood atonement for himself, the priesthood, temple, and all of Israel. "The High Priest shall bring a bull and two goats as a special offering. The high priest sacrificed a bullock as a sin offering for himself and for his house," Leviticus 16:6.

After filling his censer with live coals from the altar, he entered the holy of holies where he placed incense on the coals. Next, he took some of the blood which was taken from the slain bullock and sprinkled it on the mercy seat of the Ark of the Covenant (Leviticus 16:13) and also on the ground in front of the mercy seat, providing atonement for the priesthood (Leviticus 16:14-15). Then he sacrificed a male goat as a sin offering for the people. Some of this blood was then also taken into the holy of holies and sprinkled there on behalf of the people (Leviticus 16:11-15). Next, the high priest took another goat (called the "scapegoat"), laid his hands on its head, confessed over it the sins of Israel, and then released it into the desert where it symbolically carried away the sins of the people (Leviticus 16:8,10). The remains of the sacrificial bullock and male goat were taken outside of the city and subsequently burned; the day finally concluded with some additional sacrifices.

All of this was necessary because according to the Bible, the penalty for men's sins is the sacrifice of another life. The shedding of blood was required to atone for the sin. "The wages of sin is death, but the gift of YHWH is eternal life," Romans / Romiyah 3:23.

Torah remains forever therefore; there is still the need for blood atonement. Sin always requires a sacrifice.

The Bible says the wages of sin is death - blood must be shed. Through the shedding of blood, man is brought near to YHWH. When Y'shua died he paid the ultimate price and accomplished what the blood of bulls and goats could not. "In burnt offerings and sacrifices for sin thou hast had no pleasure. Then said I, Lo, I come (in the volume of the book it is written of me,) to do thy will, O YHWH. Above when he said, Sacrifice and offering and burnt offerings and offering for sin thou wouldest not, neither hadst pleasure therein; which are offered by the law; Then said he, Lo, I come to do thy will, O YHWH. He taketh away the first, that he may establish the second. By which will we are sanctified through the offering of the body of Y'shua Ha Moshiach once for all," Hebrews 10:6-9. Y'shua is our High Priest. Take some time today to praise Him for His sacrifice and ministry.

August 15

"As it was in the days of Noah, so it will be at the coming of the Son of Man," Matthew 2:37.

The 24th Chapter of Matthew provides many insights into the end of days. "Take heed that no man deceive you. For many shall come in my name, saying, I am Christ; and shall deceive many. And ye shall hear of wars and rumors of wars: see that ye be not troubled: for all these things must come to pass, but the end is not yet. For nation shall rise against nation, and kingdom against kingdom: and there shall be famines, and pestilences, and earthquakes, in divers places. All these are the beginning of sorrows. Then shall they deliver you up to be afflicted, and shall kill you: and ye shall be hated of all nations for my name's sake. And then shall many be offended, and shall betray one another, and shall hate one another. And many false prophets shall rise, and shall deceive many. And because iniquity shall abound, the love of many shall wax cold. But he that shall endure unto the end, the same shall be saved," Matthew 24:4-13. Notice that the Messiah doesn't mention a 'rapture" but insists that "he that endures until the end shall be saved."

In this same chapter the Savior compared the wickedness of the last generation to the days of Noah. "As it was in the days of Noah, so it will be at the coming of the Son of Man," Matthew 2:37. Here, the Savior was giving mankind a hint regarding the timing of His return. To understand this prophecy we must look to the original Hebrew used in the account of Noah in Genesis 6.

"The wickedness of man was great in the earth, and every imagination of the thoughts of man's hear was only evil continually," Genesis 6:5. "The earth was corrupt and filled with violence," Genesis 6:12. "The end of all flesh is come before me; for the earth is filled with violence through them; and I will destroy them," Genesis 6:13.

The increase of wickedness prompted the great flood cleansing. In these verses, the Hebrew word translated as "violence" and "wickedness" is a message from beyond. The actual word in the Hebrew is "hamas." The world was destroyed because sin/violence/hamas increased. The Savior was speaking of the growth of "hamas" when He said, "as it was in the days of Noah so it will be when the Son of Man returns."

Today, "Hamas" is the name of the Islamic terrorist organization that uses negative propaganda and military might to wage war against Israel. The Savior prophesied the exact name of the group that would oppose Israel and bring forth the time of tribulation. Perhaps, we indeed are living in the time that will see the hamas / violence increase until the return of Messiah.

August 16

We must keep the message the message. With the various issues of the Scriptures and wonderful instructions on righteous living, it's easy to get sidetracked and lose focus of what's most important. Often times all religious groups are guilty when it comes to losing sight of the life and resurrection of Y'shua. "Paul was preaching the good news about Y'shua and the resurrection," Acts 17:18.

Christianity, as a whole, uses the cross as its central theme and focus. The death of the Messiah on the execution beam is surely significant, but the Savior's death is not to be the center spotlight. Neither should we make the nuances of the nation of Israel or even the Torah our focal point. Throughout the book of Acts we can clearly see and understand what our message should be and must be.

Acts 4:1-2, "And as they spake unto the people, the priests and the captain of the temple and the Sadducees came upon them, being sore troubled because they taught the people, and proclaimed in Y'shua the resurrection from the dead."

"With great power the apostles continued to testify to the resurrection of Y'shua and much grace was upon them all," Acts 4:33.

"Paul was preaching the good news about Y'shua and the resurrection," Acts 17:18.

How far we have fallen from the truth of our gospel and the hope of our resurrection. Our message should be the same as that of the Apostles of the first century. They didn't teach only about the restoration of Israel or the cross of Christ. The Apostles shared Y'shua and his resurrection. We must return to sharing and centering our attention on the person of Y'shua. Yes, His death was a powerful event and yes, his teachings are life changing. But a dead god doesn't do much good for people. Nor does a list of "do's" and "don'ts." It is the power of the resurrection of Y'shua that we need to walk in and share with others.

August 17

There are lots of people that believe that the Torah is just too difficult to follow. They say that since you can't keep it perfectly then you shouldn't even try. They bicker that the Savior has 'done away' with the ceremonies of the 'Old Testament.' "Who wants to live like a Jew anyway" they question. Sadly, these people have a point.

They are right when they taunt that the Torah is not easy to follow. They are wrong when they preach that the Messiah did away with the teachings of Moses. Here's the point - if you are totally honest, you will agree that obeying the words of the Torah is not necessarily easy. Yet the Torah is beneficial.

Haven't you struggled with certain commandments? Haven't you wondered 'exactly' how you should keep the mitzvot? Doesn't the Torah go against every part of your surrounding family life, workplace, and world? Has your obedience to YHWH's will separated you from friends and loved ones? Does confusion or frustration ever make you want to give up and walk away? Have you ever felt alone in your life of Torah? If so, then good! Your frustrations just mean that the Torah is working! The word of YHWH is separating you from this world and its comforts. "For the word of YHWH (the Torah) is living and active. Sharper than any double-edged sword, it penetrates even to dividing soul and spirit, joints and marrow; it judges the thoughts and attitudes of the heart," Ivrim (Hebrews) 4:12.

It is perfectly normal to struggle in Torah observance. Don't let anyone beat you down because you are trying. The Divine Will is directly opposite to every part of our society. The Torah is opposed to every bit of the fleshly nature. Yet, this is how your life was destined to be lived. The Torah lifestyle is how the Almighty purposed His people to exist. "When a person knows and grasps in his mind a Torah law... he thereby grasps and holds and encompasses with his mind the divine wisdom and will... while his mind is simultaneously enveloped within them. This makes for a wonderful union, like which there is none other and which has no parallel anywhere in the terrestrial world, whereby complete oneness and unity, from every side and angle, is attained," says one ancient Jewish writing. Romans 2:13 says, "it is those who obey the law who will be declared righteous."

You must understand that YHWH is actually growing you when your faith is frustrated or when you doubt. When your ego is experiencing pain, you are very pregnant and about to give birth. Don't give up. Living Torah is a struggle, but it is worth it. The Torah itself declares some wise words on this subject. Write these words down. Memorize them and reflect upon them often.

August 18

The seven Biblical Holy Days can be found in Leviticus 23 and throughout the rest of the Scriptures including the Newer Testament. The Gospels record the Savior celebrating these days. And we, as his disciples, should follow his example. These festivals have literal, spiritual, messianic, and prophetic applications that can enhance a person's spiritual walk with YHWH.

The Festival of Sukkot or Tabernacles usually occurs in the months of September or October. This seven-day celebration commemorates the exodus from Egypt in a unique way. YHWH has commanded us to build a sukkah (booth or tent) and dwell in it for seven days. This camping out is done to help us remember the wilderness journey of the Israelites. "Celebrate the Feast of Ingathering at the end of the year, when you gather in your crops from the field," Exodus 23:16.

"On the fifteenth day of the seventh month, when you have gathered in the fruit of the land, you shall celebrate a chag / feast to YHWH seven days: on the first day shall be a Shabbaton / day of rest and on the eighth day shall be a Shabbaton. You shall dwell in Sukkot (booths or tents) seven days; all that are native Israelites shall dwell in Sukkot. That your generations may know that I made the children of Israel to dwell in Sukkot, when I brought them out of the land of Egypt: I am YHWH," Leviticus / Vayikra 23:39, 42, and 43.

Leviticus 23 teaches us to remember the tests and trials of the nation of Israel. Instead of being an audience to paid professional preachers we should actively participate in all elements of worship. Each of us has been called to build a booth and dwell in it for several days. Bible-based worship connects the body and soul through actions and thought. When we keep Sukkot by dwelling in the sukkah we step into the shoes of nation of Israel. This role-playing is a powerful tool for teaching. For, what happened to them happened for us. "You should not be ignorant of how your ahvot / fathers were under the cloud and all passed through the sea; and were immersed into Moses in the cloud and in the sea; and all did eat the same spiritual food. Now all these things happened to them for EXAMPLES: and they are written for our warning, upon whom the ends of the olam hazeh / world have come," 1 Corinthians 10:1-3, 11.

In this verse from Corinthians the word translated "example" is the Greek term "tupos." It is from "tupos" that we get the English word "type" or "model." The events in the desert wilderness were types and models for us today. Everything that happened to Israel, from the brazen serpent to the water from a rock, is a type and pattern for future generations. Through these marvels YHWH was teaching His people to trust Him. At Sukkot we are to spend extra time considering these types and apply the truth we learn. Now is the time to prepare your heart (and your tent) for the festival of Sukkot and all that YHWH has for us during this season.

August 19

Many years ago, Moshe (Moses) became the deliverer with the message, "Let my people go." It took ten terrible plagues to soften the resistance and will of Pharaoh. Yet even after the first-born was struck down, the Egyptian ruler pursued his slaves. And again, YHWH saved His people. Pharaoh and his army were cast into the sea. A cloud of smoke and a pillar of fire protected Israel as they began their journey towards the Promised Land. The people were out of Egypt and on their way to a place flowing with milk and honey. Bnai Israel / the children of Israel were on the path to claim their inheritance that was first promised to Father Abraham. They left Egypt for the land of Eden. But because of the sin and disbelief the Hebrews found themselves in a place unfamiliar and undesired. The nation was destined to wander the wilderness for forty years.

Do you see yourself in a similar situation? Is your life different than you had once desired? Do you find yourself in an unfamiliar place with problems galore? What happened to Israel happened for you. Learn from their example this powerful point - the wilderness was not their destination, it was only part of the journey. The Israelites didn't set out to wander around for forty long years. The nation of slaves didn't leave Egypt to get lost in the sand. No! They were set free to claim their inheritance in the Promised Land. It could be said, "a funny thing happened on the way to the Promised Land!" That funny thing is called life.

It is the same for us today. Many times in our life we can be found doing things and experiencing factors that we never dreamed. Remember that the hard times you face are just part of the journey. What you are going through now - the life you have now - is not the Promised Land but part of the journey.

A believer can mature to great spiritual levels by grasping this simple message. What happened to the people of Israel in Biblical times is a picture of what happens to people today. History repeats itself. The times may have changed but the scenarios are still the same. Everything - everything - that occurs in your life is a message from the supernatural side. YHWH is speaking behind the details of the day. In every way the Creator is calling us closer. How can you be closer to Y'shua today?

August 20

The Fall Festivals of YHWH give us a time to recall the power of YHWH to protect and redeem His children. We also remember the work of the High Priest in the Temple and the seriousness of our sin.

The Moadim / feastivals of YHWH are like a cycle that continues each year. We start with Passover and end with Sukkot exactly six months later. The Torah says that after Shavuot we wait until Yom Teruah or the "Feast of Trumpets." This is a day of shouting and excitement. Yom Teruah is on the first day of the seventh month, called "Tishrei" in Hebrew. Yom Teruah is a day of sounding shofars and calling us out of spiritual slumber. We are to seek YHWH and repent of our evil ways. The sounds of the shofar should alert us that the serious Fall holy days are here!

After the Feast of Trumpets is Yom Kippur or Yom Kippurim – the Day of Atonements. There are ten days from the "Feast of Trumpets" until Yom Kippur. These are called the "ten days of awe." During these ten days we are to seek YHWH and prepare ourselves for the Day of Atonement. The Day of Atonement is a solemn day that marks the time when the High Priest would make special sacrifices and go behind the veil in the Temple to enter into the Holy of Holies. We read about this and learn all about the High Priest in Leviticus 16. The High Priest would make special sacrifices because the nation of Israel sinned or "missed the mark." Y'shua is our High Priest that gave Himself so that we could be born again.

Five days after Yom Kippur is "Chag Sukkot" or the "Feast of Tabernacles." It is during Sukkot that we are commanded to dwell in a "sukkah" or "tent." When we spend time in a sukkah we remember many things. First, we can remember how the Israelites spent 40 years in the wilderness as they were on their way to the Promised Land. This is very important. We can also remember how life is like a tent – it is temporary only for a short time. Finally, we can remember that Y'shua came to the earth to "tabernacle" with mankind. It is believed that Y'shua was even born during the Festival of Tabernacles or Sukkot. If you have ever celebrated Sukkot then you know how exciting this time of worship and fellowship can be.

These Holy Days give us time to spend with each other and to learn from YHWH. They start in the Spring and finish in the Fall and then start over in the Spring! YHWH has given us these special days to be a like an ongoing party that we could enjoy His commandments and learn what it means to be Israel. Start thinking today about the Fall holy days and begin preparing to celebrate the Messiah.

August 21

The Spirit of YHWH doesn't just wait until church on Sunday morning or Shabbat to speak. The message of YHWH's will is constantly going forth proclaiming His holiness.

Revelation 4:8, "Each of the four living creatures had six wings and was covered with eyes all around, even under his wings. Day and night they never stop saying: "Holy, holy, holy is the YHWH Elohim Almighty, who was, and is, and is to come."

YHWH is constantly speaking to us and we must condition our ears to listen to Him. YHWH is saying "can you hear me now? Luke 8:18 says to "consider carefully how you listen."

Now, if we can readily admit that we hear from the voice of YHWH – what about the opposite? How often do you think that hear from the enemy of YHWH – the adversary ha satan?

We are in a spiritual war and the enemy is speaking to us so much that most of us don't even recognize that he is talking. We have agreed with the enemy for so long on so many subjects that we think it's our thoughts or our feelings when actually we are listening to the enemy.

2 Corinthians 10:4, "The weapons we fight with are not the weapons of the world. On the contrary, they have divine power to demolish strongholds. We demolish arguments and every pretension that sets itself up against the knowledge of YHWH, and we take captive every thought to make it obedient to Messiah."

Ephesians 6:12, "For our struggle is not against flesh and blood, but against the rulers, against the authorities, against the powers of this dark world and against the spiritual forces of evil in the heavenly realms."

These verses show us that there are spiritual powers that berate with the sole purpose to destroy our faith and our families. There is a spiritual battle being fought in the spiritual and physical realms. The enemy is planting thoughts and attitudes into our lives and we usually don't even recognize that such is coming from him. Our actions, attitude, obedience, motivations, and thoughts dramatically affect our spirit. Did you know that evil spirit can give you evil thoughts? The enemy, the accuser of the brethren, is also constantly speaking against us and to us in direct opposition to the word of YHWH. The enemy speaks mostly through the power of sin and the power of thought. This is why we must take every thought that comes into our mind captive and compare it to the Scriptures. Ask yourself, "is this a thought Y'shua would have?" If not get rid of it. If so, then act on it! Do this today.

August 22

Rejoicing at the sight of the small silver crescent in the sky is a practice spoken of often in the Bible, yet forgotten by most Bible believers. To return to the Creator's reckoning of time is like setting a divine appointment for spiritual enlightenment and peace.

At creation, the moon and sun were given to establish "signs, seasons, days, and years," Genesis 1:14. The Biblical month begins after the moon has waned into darkness and first begins to reflect the slightest bit of light. The first day of the biblical month is called "Rosh Chodesh" in Hebrew. This term literally means, "new head." Rosh Chodesh is a special time each 29 or 30 days to gather with other believers for prayer and celebration.

Traditionally a ram's horn or "shofar" is used to announce the new month. Psalms 81:3-4. "Blow up the trumpet in the new moon, in the time appointed, on our solemn feast day. For this is a law of God." During Biblical times, the New Moon would accompany special Temple offerings. Numbers 10:10, "Also in the day of your gladness, and in solemn days, and in the beginnings of your months, ye shall blow trumpets over your burnt offerings."

To celebrate the first glimpse of the crescent is not to worship the moon, but to recognize it as the anchor to the Creator's calendar system. The Biblical day begins as the sun sets and the moon is first visible. This is understood from the book of Genesis when YHWH declares after each day of creation "and there was evening, and there was morning." The day starts at evening. The seventh day from the start of creation was set aside as "Sabbath" time of rest. The Saturday Sabbath was commanded before the giving of the Law of Moses and was never changed to Sunday in the New Testament. The Sabbath is not counted from the sighting of the moon but from the initial act of creation. As the moon cycles through darkness, it begins to grow in visibility. The full moon is the mid point of the month. The astronomical new moon is completely dark and is not the same lunar phase spoken of in the Bible.

The observance of New Moon is spoken of in the Law of Moses, reinforced throughout the Prophets and referenced in the New Testament. Colossians 2:16 clearly states that no individual is to judge another person on HOW to keep the Sabbath or the New Moon. What is important is that the Sabbath and New Moon are observed. The body of Messiah, or the local assembly, can provide guidelines for "how" the day is to be kept. This subject is important, for without true New Moon mania it's impossible to recognize other days on the YHWH's calendar. As the moon pulls the oceanic tide, so too New Moon is pulling people back to worship on the correct days and in the correct ways. This restoration will continue until the end of time, when the entire world will keep the correct Sabbath and New Moon. "From one New Moon to another and from one Sabbath to another, all mankind will come and bow down before me," says YHWH," Isaiah 66:23.

August 23

Galatians 5:6, "For in Y'shua faith works through love." Here we see that Love is what empowers our faith to move mountains, to move people. If you truly love somebody then you can extend faith to bring them out of a horrible situation. A friend or family member that is living in sin or rebellion against YHWH can be reached through prayers of thankfulness to YHWH. Instead of telling YHWH how awful and terrible the person is and how their sin is ruining their life, try praying from the position of victory and gratitude. Make your prayers positive and speak faith through your love. Try praying, "YHWH I love this person and I know you love them more than I do. I know that what they are doing is not the best for them so I pray blessing into their life. I ask you to reveal your full potential to their spirit and I thank you that they are seeking you. I thank you that this person has a hunger and a thirst for your righteousness. I praise you that things are better for my loved one and hear my prayers." Love shown through prayers of thanksgiving can empower your faith to break through boundaries and have influence.

Gratitude as well shows that you are not a victim. You may have had some bad things that happened to your life, but you are not a victim. You are the master of your own destiny. You choose tomorrow, you choose today. When you say, "thank you YHWH," you are expressing that you are not a victim. Being thankful declares that no matter what has occurred in our lives, no matter what has happened, YHWH wants the best for us and we trust Him.

In the Book of Acts, we can read a story about some guys that had an excuse to be negative and have a victim mentality. If anyone deserved to have a pity party, it was Paul in Silas. Acts 16 tells of how Paul and Silas were moving in the spirit, praying for people and ministering the gospel. Do you know what happened to them? They were put in jail. Their clothes were ripped from their bodies and they were beaten.

Can you put yourself in their shoes for a minute? (Technically, they did not have any shoes, because they were naked!) Put yourself with them for a moment. You are sharing Y'shua with people. You are walking in the ministry that YHWH called you to do. All of a sudden a group of people get upset with how or what you are saying. They grab you in violence. They humiliate and shame you by ripping your garments from your body and then they tie your hands behind your back. A whip is used to rip the skin off. Your head is throbbing. Your body aches. Suddenly you are thrown into the bottom of the jail and chains are placed in your arms and legs. How would you feel at that moment? Would you honestly feel like being grateful to YHWH or would you want to curse the cause of Messiah? Would you want to rejoice in praise or would you wish things had gone differently? Take time today to rejoice in the good or the bad.

August 24

"YHWH said to Moses, 'The tenth day of this seventh month is the Day of Atonement. Hold a sacred assembly and deny yourselves,'" Leviticus 23:26

Ten days after the "Festival of Trumpets" is the solemn holy day of "Yom Kippur." This is the day of atonement that remembers the work of the High Priest, as seen in Leviticus 16.

During temple times, it was on this day and this day alone that the High Priest would go beyond the veil and enter the holy of holies. While the Kohen Hagadol (High Priest) was doing this offering, the entire nation of Israel would pray and seek YHWH.

"The tenth day of this seventh month is the Day of Atonement. Hold a sacred assembly and deny yourselves,'" Leviticus 23:26. The phrase "deny yourselves" in Hebrew is "inul nefesh." From these two words we can discern much about YHWH and His plan for man. First, "nefesh" is the "appetite" of man. The nefesh is where the fleshly desires live.

Ancient Jewish writings describe the nefesh as the "animal soul." Nefesh is the animalistic desires inside man. These desires are influenced by the five senses. What you taste, see, touch, hear, and smell feed your animal soul / flesh. In the Bible, "nefesh" is most often translated "soul, life, creature, appetite, will, desire."

The nefesh is also the ego. In the Newer Testament it is called "the flesh." Left uncontrolled, the nefesh will lead man to break YHWH's commands and abandon His instructions. This is yet another reason that the holy days of YHWH are to be honored. On Yom Kippur we are told to "inul nefesh" or to "afflict our flesh." This is traditionally done by fasting for the entire day of Yom Kippur. Yet, for a believer in Y'shua we are to "inul nefesh" every day of our lives. We aren't to live without food but we are to live a fasted lifestyle. Like the animals that were laid upon the altar, we are to kill the desires within us. Otherwise, these desires will kill us! The wages of sin is death.

How do we "inul nefesh" today? Y'shua said to take up his cross/execution stake and follow Him. That's it. We simply follow Him and allow His Spirit to do the affliction. YHWH will lead us into all truth, change us into His glory, and show us what to change in our lives. We are to "submit to YHWH" and by doing so we naturally "resist the devil" and "inul nefesh." We are to experience a type of Yom Kippur every single day when we allow the High Priest Y'shua to work in our lives.

August 25

The Apostle Paul wrote of our battle with sin when he said, "We know that the law is spiritual; but I am unspiritual, sold as a slave to sin. I do not understand what I do. For what I want to do I do not do, but what I hate I do and if I do what I do not want to do, I agree that the law is good. As it is, it is no longer I myself who do it, but it is sin living in me," Romans 7:14-17. Sin is more than just an act. It is a living spiritual power that can actually overcome individuals.

Consider that our bodies are the temple of the Holy Spirit. "Do you not know that your body is a temple of the Holy Spirit, who is in you, whom you have received from YHWH? You are not your own; 20 you were bought at a price. Therefore honor YHWH with your body," (1 Cor. 6:19-20).

We have an outer court – the flesh and the body. We have an inner court – the mind. And we have the holy of holies – our soul. YHWH resides in our soul. Our mind is the area that we must act as priests over and make priestly decisions to follow YHWH. The flesh is the outer court. In temple times the outer court was called the "court of the gentiles" because uncleanliness was allowed in the outer court. When Y'shua rebuked demons and cast them out of people He often called them "unclean spirits." The enemy of sin lives in our flesh and often speaks to our mind. We have been taught that a believer can't possess a demon BUT the real question is "can a demon possess a believer?" The flesh is the realm of fallen man. It is the realm of sin and the demonic.

Paul said that "in my flesh dwells no good thing," Romans 7:18. We have often thought that our enemy was three fold – the FLESH, the WORLD, and the DEVIL. What if we truly only have ONE enemy? What if the FLESH is actually the enemy at work in us? What if the world is the enemy at work outside of us? Satan is the god of this world and the prince of the power of the air.

Genesis 4:7, "If you do what is right, will you not be accepted? But if you do not do what is right, sin is crouching at your door; it desires to have you, but you must master it."

The flesh is the playground and Satan is the bully that gets stronger and stronger every time we sin. The demonic are always sending message to us to continue our evil habits. We think it's the flesh or we think its US but it is not! It is SIN! We think it is our urge or desire or want or addiction or need but it is not! Think of it this way – there is no difference between YHWH and his words and His commands. There is also no difference between Satan and his words and his commands. We must submit to YHWH and resist the adversary and his voice.

Ask the Holy Spirit for wisdom on this teaching today.

August 26

How do you find relief from all the stress of life? The help of booze, drugs, sex, money, or fun is only temporary. Do you really want lasting help from above? The story is told of three guys who were fishing on a lake one day, when the Messiah walked across the water and joined them in the boat. When the three astonished men had settled down enough to speak, the first guy asked humbly, "Messiah, I've suffered from back pain ever since I took shrapnel in the Vietnam war... could you help me?"

"Of course, my son," the Savior said, and when he touched the man's back, he felt relief for the first time in years. The second man, who wore very thick glasses and had a hard time reading and driving, asked if Messiah could do anything about his eyesight. The Savior smiled, removed the man's glasses and tossed them in the lake. When they hit the water, the man's eyes cleared and he could see everything distinctly.

When Y'shua turned to heal the third man, the guy put his hands up and cried defensively, "Don't touch me! I'm on long-term disability!"

This guy didn't want to be different. He was actually happy with his problems. Are you like these guys or do you long to be better? We each face all types of trouble: homes are foreclosed, sickness comes, jobs are lost, families fight, and cancer tests come back positive. These events tell us to give up, worry, and be stressed. These are lying signs and wonders. The voices from our pain and problems are sent directly from the enemy to discourage and defeat you. If you have heard these voices then it was not YHWH talking. "For at the coming of the Savior there will be great activity on the part of Satan, in the form of all kinds of deceptive miracles, signs, and marvels, as well as of wicked attempts to delude," 2 Thessalonians 2:9.

Satan wants us to focus our attention on the pain and problems because he knows that misery loves company. The more we begin to think about how bad things are or how bad things could be, then the worse it gets. Have you ever heard someone say that when it rains it pours? The more negative we are the more negativity we attract. When you think about your sickness, problem, or pain then you are FEEDING the evil and giving it power over you. We have agreed with the enemy for so long on so many subjects that we think it's our thoughts or our feelings when actually we are listening to the enemy. "The enemy comes to steal, kill, and destroy," John 10:10. If something is destroying your life then it's not from YHWH. Instead of succumbing to stress and the way things have been, resist the enemy and seek the goodness of YHWH today. Spend a few extra minutes in prayer before you do anything else today.

TRUTH FOR TODAY

August 27

"My Yah shall supply all of my needs according to his riches in glory," Philippians 4:19. This verse teaches us that all of our needs are met in glory. But, where is glory? Glory is where YHWH is. Glory is YHWH. YHWH is your source for all that you need. Our responsibility is to respond to His ability. YHWH is all we need because YHWH is our source. YHWH delights in giving us Himself and when we have Him we have everything His grace provides for us emotionally and spiritually.

When we need love we really need Y'shua. When we have a question and seek wisdom we can received the spirit of Wisdom. As life deals us defeat the divine Comforter quiets our soul. He is our peace. He is our strength. YHWH is our source and the culmination of all of our needs.

Let's see this more clearly in Luke 11:11-13, "Which of you fathers, if your son asks for a fish, will give him a snake instead? Or if he asks for an egg, will give him a scorpion? If you then, though you are evil, know how to give good gifts to your children, how much more will your Father in heaven give the Holy Spirit to those who ask him?"

Fathers know how to give gifts. We buy presents for holidays, anniversaries, and birthdays. And if we know how to give gifts then think of how YHWH can give us of Himself. The gift we need is more of Him. The gift we need is His Spirit / Ruach.

Today, you may have other needs. You may be hungry, cold, frustrated, or tired. You may need a house, a car, a friend, or job. We can't deny that these are real issues but these needs are secondary. Our greatest need is for YHWH and His Messiah. We need Him more than we need anything else or anyone else.

John chapter 4 speaks of a woman who sought meaning in the natural realm. She was often let down. The woman met the Messiah at a well because she had the need of water. She was physically needy. The woman had a tattered past of many husbands and was living with a man that wasn't her husband. She was emotionally needy. The woman knew of the prophecies of Messiah and the rift between Jews and Samaritans. She was spiritually needy. All of her needs were met in Y'shua. She came face to face with the reality of a loving Savior when she approached the well that day. She left satisfied and touched by the presence of Y'shua. Her needs are like ours today and her solution is the same as ours today. We need more of Him and less of us. We need YHWH's presence and a revelation of Y'shua in our lives. Seek this today and finally be fulfilled.

TRUTH FOR TODAY

August 28

It takes a mature believer to show love or "ahava." We must choose to put our personal differences or personal convictions aside and love others, even if they are in sin. Y'shua fellowshipped with the outcasts and ate with the sinner. Have you done this or do you constantly dwell on differences with other believers?

You are to love your neighbor as yourself. What exactly does this mean?

- Show forgiveness when offended. If you have any interaction with people then you will be offended. Be ready to be hurt. Be ready to forgive.

- Offer acceptance to others who are different. We must love those who do not keep Torah. You must also love others who may keep commandments differently than you. Your walk of faith will be VERY lonely if you only accept and fellowship with those who you agree with 100% of time. Don't allow personal convictions to separate you from others. In reality there are very few issues that should be "fellowship breakers."

- Model compassion as you "put yourself in their shoes." Y'shua raised Lazarus from the dead and performed many miracles as He had compassion upon the people. True ahava / love is full of compassion and acceptance.

- Act in patience with people. Realize that you aren't perfect either! YHWH has not perfected you or your neighbor. Give people time to grow in the faith. Don't be so judgmental to those who are keeping Torah. Love and support the growth of others.

- Speak in kindness and make a choice to serve others. Stop the talk about others and serve them! This is a simple but hard choice.

- Make unconditional love your goal. Unconditional love means there are no expectations. When you love in this manner you are most like Y'shua.

When we express ahava / love we make a connection with a person or with YHWH. The true relationships that have meaning in our lives are full of mutual giving. So, what have you done for your friends, spouse, rabbi, children, or your co-workers lately? How much giving have you done over the past 24 hours or week? Our love to each other our biggest witness to lost world.

The ahava / love of YHWH should compel us to reach others with the same love that He has extended to us. What can you do today to reach out to others in ahava / love? Decide on something and then do it.

August 29

Do you ever wonder if YHWH has favorite children? Does heaven favor those folks with all the money or the churches with the biggest buildings? How is it that some believers can go through horrendous emotional stress while others are hardly ever bothered by even a hangnail?

The Bible specifically states that YHWH does favor certain people. It has been said that "God doesn't play favorites" and that "he loves everyone the same." This idea seems nice but is it Biblical? Romans 9:13 states that YHWH "hates Esau but loves Jacob."

The scriptures indicate a disdain for Esav because of the heart of Esav. Esau's mind and emotions were set against the things of YHWH. Esau was a rebellious son who did not inherit the promises of YHWH. Jacob wasn't perfect either, as he had his own set of problems, but Jacob's heart was set on knowing the Mighty One of Israel and walking in His ways.

It is indeed the heart that makes the difference in life. And it's the heart that led YHWH to make the statement that Esau was hated while Jacob was loved. YHWH offers His love and His favor for everyone in the world. People choose to walk in his favor or to walk away from his favor. Jacob walked in YHWH's favor while Esau walked out of His favor.

Those who seek after the Almighty are blessed with his presence and His favor. We each have a choice to walk in YHWH's favor or to walk OUT of YHWH's favor. The Bible indicates that we each were each created for a purpose and a great plan. You were made in His image and YHWH doesn't make junk! As the crown of His creation you were given a choice to follow His ways or to go your own separate way. Those who seek after Him can walk in his favor and even ask favors of Him!

Strangers ignore the cries of children at the toy isle in Wal-Mart but parents respond differently. Because of relationship, a mother may do her son a favor and buy him a new toy. Well, YHWH's favor is great for everything we need in life – not just the toys. It is His provision, His love, His power, His protection – it is HIM! As children of the Most High we are to recognize the importance of favor and seek His face. For those who don't seek first His kingdom the reward is doom. In fact, the scriptures tell the story of how Israel suffered defeat because they did not seek His favor in 1 Samuel 13:12.

There are countless verses throughout the Bible that speak of YHWH's favor. In English Bibles it is referenced as "grace" or "favor" or "love" or "mercy." It is all the same. "Now is the time of YHWH's favor," according to 2 Corinthians 6:2. You can experience his love! Do you want his favor? Are you asking for it? Are you expecting it?

TRUTH FOR TODAY

August 30

When someone says, “can you do me a favor?” they are asking for an act of kindness. If Bob says that the Green bay Packers are his favorite football team he is saying that he likes, honors, and exalts them above all other football teams.

When YHWH’s favor is upon you then you will experience his kindness over and over again. When you are YHWH’s favorite then you are the apple of His eye and the chosen son. YHWH’s favor can be understood as his provision, preparation, and presence.

The Almighty takes care of us. Mary was favored with a child, Ruth was shown favor and her needs were met, and Joseph was shown favor by the prison warden. The New Testament believers in Acts experienced YHWH’s favor through miracles, signs, wonders, and multiplication. The Psalmist said, “I have never seen the righteous forsaken nor his see begging for bread, “Psalm 37:25.

When we have his favor we have his preparation. YHWH guides you and goes before you to make a way. YHWH will set things in motion for you. He will guard your future. “All things work together for the good of those that love YHWH and are called according to His good favor,” Romans 8:28. Noah found “favor” in the eyes of YHWH, Israel left Egypt as favored by YHWH, Ruth was favored by Boaz, Esther was favored by the King and was spared, and Mordechai was favored through righteousness. The Scriptures say, “surely, YHWH blesses the righteous and surrounds them with favor as a shield.”

Finally, YHWH’s favor is also his presence. He is with you in the midst of every trial. Though he may not always remove the problem, he will always reveal himself in the solution. He loves you and longs to bless you. Devarim 31:8, “YHWH himself goes before you and will be with you; he will never leave you nor forsake you. Do not be afraid; do not be discouraged." YHWH was with Joseph through his trials, YHWH was with Daniel in the lions’ den & other tests, and Moses was given a revelation of YHWH’s name through divine favor in Exodus 33:3.

Do you want His presence? Do you need his preparation? His provision? What would you do to get His favor? Would you sell your house or your car? Would you trade your most prized possession for the presence of YHWH?

The level in which you search for YHWH and expect Him to move is equal to how YHWH reveals Himself. His favor is available! All you have to do is ask for it and receive it! You can’t earn it or buy it. You can search for it, pray for it, and walk in it. Do this today.

August 31

Mankind is sin sick. "All have sinned and fallen short of the glory of YHWH," Romans / Romiyah 3:23. So what is sin? Well, the book of 1 John speaks vividly on this subject and answers this question with a profoundly simple response. The definition and the remedy for sin are both discussed in 1 John 3:4-7, "Everyone who sins breaks the law; in fact, sin is lawlessness. But you know that he appeared so that he might take away our sins. And in him is no sin. No one who lives in him keeps on sinning. No one who continues to sin has either seen him or known him. Dear children, do not let anyone lead you astray. He who does what is right is righteous, just as he is righteous."

Every man, woman, and child on the earth has been infected by sin. From birth, we enter into the Adam's family and suffer the consequences of the Fall. No one is good enough, holy enough, or wealthy enough to stop the effects of sin. Like dying people in a sick ward, sin causes man to be separated from YHWH and His holiness. "See, YHWH's hand is not shortened, that it cannot save; neither His ear heavy, that it cannot hear: But your iniquities have brought separation between you and YHWH, and your sins have hid His face from you, that He will not hear," Isaiah 59:1,2.

Sin sickness, like many major illnesses leads to death. "The wages of sin is death, but the gift of YHWH is eternal chayim / life," Romans 6:23. To those who trust the Great Physician there is healing and life. BUT, death must come first. Sin always produces death. The old self, the old man, must die in order for the eternal life of YHWH to come inside a person. Physical death is just the result of spiritual death that already exists within man. Y'shua said, "I am the resurrection and the life, he that believes in me, though he were dead, yet shall live," John 11:25. Trusting Y'shua is the only way to eternal life.

John 3:16 is the most well-known verse from the entire Bible. And for good reason. This verse explains the Besorah / gospel in a nutshell. "For YHWH so loved the world, that He gave His only brought forth Son, that whoever believes on Him should not perish, but have everlasting life," John 3:16. What is interesting is that these very words were spoken to a Jewish leader named Nickdimon / Nicodemus. Y'shua was making it crystal clear that the only way a person can experience the resurrection life is to trust in Moshiach. Judaism won't do it. Torah obedience doesn't save. Man's ways, religion, good deeds, or church membership is not the answer. To be delivered or saved from eternal death a person must put their trust in Y'shua. The name Y'shua means "YHWH is salvation." When a person says, "I am saved," they are actually saying "I am trusting in Y'shua – YHWH's salvation." We are delivered from eternal death through the sacrifice of Y'shua. Who can you share salvation with today?

September

September 1

The two most powerful words in the entire universe are something that you might not ever consider as meaningful. But, you can harness the power of YHWH by using these simple two words properly. In Exodus 3, YHWH Almighty reveals his name to Moses. He says "I am YHWH." His name is a sign of his existence. It is a picture of his power. It is an announcement of His authority. Just think of the name Beethoven and what comes to mind when that name is mentioned? What about the name of Pharaoh? To Moses YHWH says, "I am that which I am."

We call Him YHWH but his name is "I Am." What kind of a name is this? In Hebrew the phrase "I am that which I am" is the phrase "eyeh hasher eyeh." This literally means "I will be that which I will be." YHWH's name is an action – it means "to be." His name is NOT the phrase "I was." He says I will be! What will He be? YHWH is anything you need today. To your every need, YHWH says "I am." He is what you need – your answer, treasure, solution.

In John 6 the Master Y'shua uses the phrase "I am" to describe himself with miracles and might. You can use the same phrase to release spiritual power. Whatever your desire, the outcome of I AM will always come to pass. If you say "I am tired, I am sick, I am frustrated, not happy, sad, stressed, drowsy, dumb, unlovely, not good, defeated, wore out, unloving, not patient. I am drowning in debt. I am a failure. I am no good at relationships," then you will get those results. When you say "I am blessed, I am chosen, I am anointed" then you will get those results.

Here is the truth, every time we use words like "I am, my, and mine" then we are actually using the great gift of "I am." When you choose to focus on how YHWH sees you then you can overcome the world. When you line up your "I ams" with the Scriptures then you can "reframe" your world. We are to use His name just like he did to create miracles in our lives.

In the 10 Commandments, found in Exodus 19, we read of the command to "not take the name of YHWH in vain." What is the name of YHWH? His name is a verb. His name is an action. His name is "I AM." There are many ways that we can take it in vain or bring it to nothingness. One way to take his name in vain is not to use his name properly. How do you use the phrase "I am?"

If you don't use His name "I am" then other people will do it against you. They will fill in your blanks and say things about you. They will describe you and try to describe your world for you. Use His name properly and don't allow others to push their ideas upon your life. What you say you will see. You could say "I am blessed... I am happy... I am cared for, having needs met, abundant, fruitful, lovely, loved, full of spiritual power, overcoming, gentle, confident, and compassionate." YHWH's name "I am" can change your life today. Will you let it change you?

September 2

Is Allah god?

A careful reading of Exodus 3 reveals more than just the story of a burning bush. Here on Mt. Horeb the Almighty passes before Moses and "the LORD said moreover unto Moses, Thus shalt thou say unto the children of Israel, The LORD God of your fathers, the God of Abraham, the God of Isaac, and the God of Jacob, hath sent me unto you: this is my name for ever, and this is my memorial unto all generations." Here in Exodus 3:15 the LORD reveals His name as the four lettered Hebrew tetragramatron yod-hey-vav-hey or "YHWH."

Throughout the Bible, "YHWH" is used over 6,000 times exclusively as the name of the Father. The King James Version capitalizes the words "LORD" or "GOD" in an effort to alert the reader that "YHWH" is the Hebrew word behind the English. YHWH says emphatically in Exodus 3 that "this is my name forever, and this is my memorial unto all generations." This name was not intended to be hidden by scribes and translators; rather YHWH Himself gave it to man as a sign of His existence and as a means of personal relationship. This is the Father's name.

Christianity as well has ignored the name of YHWH by substituting generic terms like "God" in English or "Dios" in Spanish. These words are not specific to the deity of the Bible and can easily reference Allah or Buddha. "God" or "Gad" in Hebrew is the false Babylonian deity of good fortune or luck and not of the Bible. This is according to Strong's Concordance #H1407-1411. This can also be referenced to Genesis 30:11. The Oxford Etymological Dictionary of the English Language agrees. It teaches that 'god' comes to our English language from the ancient Sanskrit language meaning - to invoke by incantation, sorcery, magic. The Encyclopedia Americana says under this topic that "god is a common Teutonic word for personal object of religious worship, formerly applicable to super-human beings of heathen myth." While further research reveals that the Druids called the sun 'Gud, Gudh, Goth, or Gott' which were later translated into English as "gawd" or "god." In most English Bibles, the term "god" is a poor translation from the Hebrew term "elohim." The word "elohim" literally means "mighty one, judge, or deity."

Using such replacement terms is in direct opposition to Isaiah 42:8 which states, ""I am YHWH, that is My name; I will not give My glory to another." One can say the true name of YHWH in prayer, praise, study, and witnessing. By using the Sacred Name a believer can experience the power of spiritual intimacy. The Father's name is not God or Billy Bob; it is "YHWH." YHWH has given us His personal name so we could approach Him with intimacy. When Muslims, Mormons, and Messianics use the word "god" it can very confusing. Today use the name YHWH and let people know who you worship!

September 3

Y'shua never told anyone to "accept him into your heart and you will be born again." When asked about eternal life, the Savior once replied, "If you want to enter into life, keep the commandments," Matthew 19:17.

The Messiah taught that true spiritual conversion begins with a proper use of the Law of Moses to point out the errors of sin. The wages of sin is death unless people repent of their law-breaking sins, trust the Almighty for forgiveness, and turn from their wicked ways. The Law of Moses, or Torah, is the instruction book for mankind that is found in the first five books of the Bible. These pages describe the righteous straight and narrow path a person should walk once they accept the Savior. The Torah also acts as a mirror to reflect mankind's sinfulness as compared to YHWH's high standards. The Torah defines sin but it itself is not sinful. A single violation of just one of the Old Testament commandments rendered a person sinful and deserving of eternal death. This strict death penalty was placed upon the Savior when he died at Golgotha. Those that confess their sins, change their behaviors, and submit to the Bible are born again through the Holy Spirit. Luke 24:46-47 states, "It is written, and thus it was necessary for the Christ to suffer and to rise from the dead the third day, and that repentance and remission of sins should be preached in His name to all nations, beginning at Jerusalem."

A person who has accepted the true gospel will bear the spiritual fruits of love, joy, peace, patience, kindness, goodness, faithfulness, gentleness, and self-control. A lack of this good spiritual fruit is a telltale sign that a person has accepted a false gospel and is perhaps a false convert. "Examine yourselves to see whether you are in the faith; test yourselves. Do you not realize that Christ Y'shua is in you—unless, of course, you fail the test?" 2 Corinthians 13:5. The full gospel of Y'shua is a message of repentance that produces real change.

September 4

In Luke 13 Rabbi Y'shua tells a short parable about a fig tree that didn't produce much fruit. "He spoke also this parable; a certain man had a fig eytz / tree planted in his vineyard; and he came and sought fruit on it, and found none. Then he said to the dresser of his vineyard, See, these three years I came seeking fruit on this fig eytz / tree, and found none: cut it down; why should the ground be wasted? And he answering said to him, Master, leave it alone this year again, until I shall dig around it, and cast manure on it: And if it bears fruit, well: and if not, then after that You shall cut it down," Luke 13:6-9.

In this story, the tree is given ample time to mature and produce fruit. Yet, the tree remains barren. The Master gives the plant one more year to prove itself. For this tree and for us, time is of essence. Time is never recovered, so we should stay busy producing fruit or else face the judgment. Notice too, that this parable is unfinished. We don't know from the text what happened after one more year? Did the tree flourish and become fruitful? Did the fig tree reward the caretaker's investment in it? Or was it still barren and ordered to be removed?

The call of responsibility commands today's believer to finish the story. Will we be fruitful? Will we satisfy the Savior? Will we walk in the Ruach or will we waste time?

As a person walks is submission to the Torah, the fruit of the Spirit is able to develop. "I am the Emet Vine, and My Abba is the Gardener. Every branch in Me that bears not fruit He takes away and every branch that bears fruit, He purges it, that it may bring forth more fruit. Now you are clean through the word that I have spoken to you. Remain in Me, and I in you. As the branch cannot bear fruit by itself, except it stays in the Vine; neither can you, except you remain in Me. I am the Vine, you are the netsarim / branches: He that stays in Me, and I in him, the same brings forth much fruit: for without Me you can do nothing," John 15:1-5. Here, Y'shua identifies Himself as the Vine. In Yochannan / John chapter one, the Messiah is called the "Torah made flesh." So, if Y'shua is the Torah made flesh and Y'shua is the Vine, then... the Vine is the Torah!

The Torah is "a tree of life / eytz chayim to them that take hold of her: and happy is everyone that takes hold of her," Proverbs 3:18. To walk in the Spirit is to eat from the Tree of life and produce much fruit. Torah explains how we abide in Y'shua and produce the fruit of the Spirit. This takes time as we abide in YHWH. We must be careful that we produce fruit in season and that our leaves do not wither.

September 5

The scriptures tell us to “study to show ourselves approved” in 1 Timothy 2:15. We are told to “remember the days of old; consider the generations long past. Ask your father and he will tell you, your elders, and they will explain to you,” Deuteronomy 32:7.

The truth is that the first believers were very “Jewish” in their worship and lifestyle. In fact, historical writings prove that the early followers of Messiah were so Jewish that most people could not tell them apart from the majority of the Jews. “The Nazarenes do not differ in any essential thing from [the Orthodox Jews], since they practice the customs and doctrines prescribed by Jewish Law; except that they believe in Messiah. They believe in the resurrection of the dead, and that the universe was created by the Almighty. They preach that The YHWH is One is One, and that Messiah is his Son... They are very learned in the Hebrew language. They read the Law,” wrote the early Church Father Epiphanius in his doctrinal book: Adversus Haereses, (Against Heresies) Panarion 29.

The Savior Himself said, “Salvation is of the Jews,” in John 4:22. This doesn’t mean that one must convert to Judaism to be saved. What Messiah was teaching is that the true pathway of faith can be found within the lineage and lifestyle of the Hebrews. The Jewish people make up just a small portion of the greater Israel family that has been scattered all over the world. This nation of Israel is being regathered as millions of people around the world are recognizing their Hebrew roots. This isn’t about being Jewish. It is all about recognizing that “if you belong to Messiah, then you are Abraham’s seed, and heirs according to the promise,” Galatians 3:29. Multitudes are rejecting false worship and returning to the ancient path set by the Savior. He came teaching, healing, and proclaiming a message of repentance. Y’shua’s message was that “the kingdom of heaven is here.” As we are returning to the truth of the Scriptures and the Hebrew language we are establishing the kingdom of YHWH on earth and allowing his will to be done.

Make a list of five people to share this truth with today and call or write them.

TRUTH FOR TODAY

September 6

The Torah has predominately two ways of teaching – direct commands and indirect principles. First is the direct commandment. This is the "thou shalt" and the "thou shalt not" statements found throughout the scriptures. Direct commandments are mostly from the Almighty to His people Israel. They are specific in context – meaning these commands either point a person to a correct action or they point a person away from an incorrect action. These instructions leave little room for discussion and are either followed or dismissed by the believer. Sometimes these are guidelines that simply don't make any sense, while some direct commands make perfect sense.

While most of the direct commandments in the scriptures are for all believers, some are given specifically to certain people at certain times. For example YHWH specifically told Noach to build the ark – he did not tell you to do so. But, a person can learn many lessons from studying the account of Noach and the ark. This is the second way the Torah teaches through – indirect principles. Indirect principles are often subtle messages that always support direct commandments. Indirect principles are just as important as the direct commandments, yet they are implied through examples and accounts instead of given through straight statements. These principles usually stress the heart of the issue. They are typically communicated through Biblical stories of real people, living their real lives, in this real world.

Furthermore, the Messiah used indirect principle teaching through His parables. Indirect principles and the Messiah's parables will always point to a direct commandment and therefore will NEVER lead a person to disobey a direct commandment of the Bible. Indirect principles are taught throughout the pages of the scriptures, teaching man how to correctly follow many of the direct statements. Many times these principles fill in the blanks left by generations of time that has passed since the Torah was given until today.

Whether directly through commandments or indirectly through parables or true stories, the Scriptures teach us how to live so that we can fulfill the greatest commandment to love YHWH and love our neighbor.

How much time will you use to read the Scriptures today?

September 7

"For by grace ye are saved through faith and not of yourselves: it is the gift of YHWH," Ephesians 2:8, 9.

First, notice that we are saved by "grace through faith." Grace alone does not save. Nor does faith alone. Together the two provide the path of salvation. Separate they provide very little. Grace by itself or faith, by itself, brings death. Consider salvation to be like H20. Hydrogen, like grace, is a powerful element. But hydrogen can be manipulated and used to cause death. (Consider the hydrogen bomb!) Oxygen, like faith, is important. But too much oxygen produces a toxicity syndrome and sudden damage to the central nervous system. Together though, hydrogen and oxygen combine to make up something mankind cannot live without – water! Let's examine these concepts from a Biblical / Hebraic perspective to gain a better understanding of what happens when a person is born again.

Grace in the set apart Hebrew language is the word "chesed" or "chen." These terms describe unearned favor. Chesed / grace is the undeserved, unmerited advantages and privileges YHWH gives His children. The Greek word translated "grace" is "charis." It is from this word that we say that someone is "charismatic" or had "charisma." Every good and perfect gift is provided by His chesed. Through YHWH's chesed, He has provided salvation for everyone on Earth. "For the favor of YHWH that brings salvation has appeared to all men," Titus 2:11. But not everyone is saved.

Each person much personally accept, through faith, the Messiah Y'shua. Chesed is how we are saved and how we are to live. When we have his Chesed we have his favor, power, and blessings. The door of salvation is the entry point to chesed. Once you have received salvation by grace you should act "gracious" and "grace-full" to other people. As you do this you are showing the light of YHWH to all.

Learn more about "grace" in tomorrow's reading.

September 8

Salvation is not just about escaping hell. Deliverance from wrath is just the first outpouring of YHWH's grace / chesed upon His children. When a person accepts Moshiach Y'shua that person enters into the fullness of chesed offered by YHWH. There is so much more to the faith than just eternal life in heaven.

YHWH's chesed or “grace” is YHWH giving us all that we will ever need. By His chesed, we have everything necessary. What do you need today? It has already been provided by chesed. Through His chesed, YHWH has met our physical, spiritual, emotional, relational, and financial needs. We read in Ephesians 1:3 that YHWH has "blessed us with every spiritual blessing in heavenly places." We have accepted the gift of salvation that was provided by the work of Y'shua over two thousand years ago. In a similar manner, we should openly recognize that ALL of our needs have already been met by His chesed. When Y'shua said, "it is finished," He was describing the total outpouring of YHWH's chesed. Though we deserve judgment, we have been given favor. It’s already a done deal. YHWH's favor is upon us totally and fully. YHWH can't love you more than He does right now. All of your needs have already been met by His chesed. The favor of YHWH has provided everything that you will ever need, starting with eternal life.

Through faith a person brings into the physical realm what has already been provided in the spiritual realm. Faith is the currency mankind uses to relate to YHWH. "Without emunah / faith it is impossible to please YHWH," says Hebrews 11:6. Consider chesed to be like a huge "all you can eat" buffet. Everything in the Father's will that you can imagine is on the table. Faith pulls a chair right up to the buffet and begins to feast!

Faith, or "emunah" in Hebrew, is simply our positive response to what YHWH has already done. What is interesting about emunah is that it does NOT move YHWH. Faith does not make YHWH do anything. By chesed or mercy, YHWH has already done it all. Like forgiveness, healing and blessing is already a done deal. We must step out in emunah / faith to get it. We are told to "walk by emunah / faith and not by sight." This means our day to day life should be focused on the "substance of things hoped for and the evidence of things not yet seen." Faith is not just a statement of belief BUT the effects of belief. Through emunah, we disperse YHWH's favor to the world.

When a person is born again, he reaches out and accepts what Y'shua did thousands of years ago. This is a pattern that is to be repeated after salvation as well. Each day, for every need, we are to look to YHWH as our provider. The scriptures tell us to "seek ye first the kingdom of YHWH and ALL these things will be added unto you." How can you seek His kingdom today?

September 9

To walk in the Holy Spirit is to walk in the Word of YHWH. Life in the Word is the same as life in the Spirit. Compare these two passages of Scripture:

Colossians 3:16-20, "Let the word of the Moshiach dwell in you richly in all chochmah / wisdom; teaching and admonishing one another in the Tehillim and with Ruach-filled songs, singing with unmerited yourselves to your own husbands, as it is fit in the Master. Husbands, love your wives, and be not bitter against them. Children, obey your parents in all things: for this is well pleasing to YHWH."

Ephesians 5:18-22, "And be not drunk with wine, in which there is excess; but be filled with the Ruach; Speaking to yourselves with the Tehillim and songs of praise and spiritual songs, singing and making melody in your lev / heart to the Master YHWH; Giving hodu / thanks always for all things to Abba YHWH in the Name of our Master Y'shua ha Moshiach; Submit yourselves one to another in the fear of YHWH. Wives, submit yourselves to your own husbands, as you would to YHWH."

To be led by the Spirit is to be led by the Word. One cannot separate the two. "The Torah is spiritual and to be spiritually minded is life and peace," says Romans / Romiyah 7:14, 8:6. Torah was given by the Ruach. Therefore when we are exhorted to "walk in the Spirit," Scripture is telling is to conform our lives to the Torah.

Study these simple verses and stand firm in your faith. Don't allow others to persuade you that the Spirit and the Torah are in opposition.

September 10

In the Hebrew language a righteous person is called a "tzadik." A tzadik is a person totally rooted and grounded in YHWH and the Torah. The Encyclopedia Judaica clearly and impressively defines exactly what a tzadik is. The encyclopedia says that a genuine tzadik is one who, "carries out his obligation to Elohim and to man by obeying the precepts of the Torah."

Proverbs 21:15 teaches that acting justly is a tzadik's greatest reward. This does not mean that a tzadik is perfect or sinless. To the contrary, perhaps the greatest difference between the tzadik and the evildoer is that when the righteous fall down, they get back up again, Proverbs 24:16. Other tzadikkim mentioned in the Bible are Avel, Lot, Yochannan / John the Immerser, Yoseph the earthly father of Y'shua and of course Y'shua Ha Moshiach. "Y'shua grew in wisdom and stature, and in favor with Elohim and men," Luke 2:52. Y'shua's righteousness was in the sight of "Elohim and men." Of Yochannan / John the Immerser's parents it is said in Luke 1:6, "And they were both righteous before Elohim, walking in all the commandments and ordinances of YHWH blameless."

Titus 1:8 says all followers of the Scriptures are to be a "lover of hospitality, a lover of good men, sober, righteous, holy, and temperate." Don't be mistaken; the life of a righteous person is not some mystical existence full of only heavenly highs. As Y'shua said, "our Father which is in heaven: for he maketh his sun to rise on the evil and on the good, and sendeth rain on the just and on the unjust," Mattityahu / Matthew 5:45. The way of life and routine of the tzadik is special because the tzadik functions as the mirror between man and YHWH, reflecting YHWH's character to mankind.

The restoration of righteousness is prophesied in the scriptures as one of the ways that YHWH is reuniting His kingdom of Israel and spreading the good news of Y'shua. ""The days are coming," declares the YHWH, "when I will raise up to David a righteous Branch, a King who will reign wisely and do what is just and right in the land. In his days Judah will be saved and Israel will live in safety. This is the name by which he will be called: YHWH Tzdakenu. "So then, the days are coming," declares YHWH, "when people will no longer say, 'As surely as the YHWH lives, who brought the Israelites up out of Egypt,' but they will say, 'As surely as YHWH lives, who brought the descendants of Israel up out of the land of the north and out of all the countries where he had banished them.' Then they will live in their own land," Yermi'yahu / Jeremiah 23:5-8. In Yesha'yahu / Isaiah 60:21 & 22 it is said, "Then will all your people be righteous and they will possess the land forever. They are the shoots I have planted, the work of my hands, for the display of my splendor." YHWH is reuniting His people by restoring true tzedekah / righteousness to Israel.

September 11

"Likewise the Spirit also helpeth our infirmities: for we know not what we should pray for as we ought: but the Spirit itself maketh intercession for us with groanings which cannot be uttered," Romans 8:26. The Bible, with sixty-six books from Genesis to Revelation, uses the term "allah" on 32 occasions. Hidden behind the English in Daniel 9:11 and other verses are actual references to the god of Islam. Yes, Daniel chapter 9 verse 11 references Allah and perhaps prophetically speaks of the terrorist events of 9/11/2001 when commercial airliners were used as suicide bombs. This verse states that because of disobedience to the Bible, the "curse is poured upon us." Isaiah 24:5 and 6 uses the word "allah" as well. These verses read, "The earth also is defiled under the inhabitants thereof; because they have transgressed the laws, changed the ordinance, broken the everlasting covenant. Therefore hath the curse devoured the earth, and they that dwell therein are desolate: therefore the inhabitants of the earth are burned, and few men left." In these verses, the Hebrew word for "curse" is spelled with the Hebrew letters aleph- lamed-hey and is pronounced "allah." According to the Bible, the Muslim deity "allah" is a "curse" to the world.

These facts are not to suggest that every Muslim is a terrorist or an evil person. Islam is full of good hearted people who are sincere in their faith. Yet, a person can certainly be sincere and be sincerely wrong at the same time. Don't be misled by those who seek to be politically correct by calling Islam a religion of "peace." From the very words used in the Islamic faith, it is easy to discern that Muslims and Bible believers do not worship the same god. Islam leads people away from the Mighty One of Abraham, Isaac, and Jacob and the Almighty's only begotten son who once said, "I am the way, the truth and the life, no man comes to the father except through me." Take time today and pray for the Muslim people. Then, when you come across an Islamic person share the truth of the Bible. Don't hate the Muslims. Speak to them in love. Pray for them often. "Likewise the Spirit also helpeth our infirmities: for we know not what we should pray for as we ought: but the Spirit itself maketh intercession for us with groanings which cannot be uttered," Romans 8:26.

Take a few minutes today and pray for the millions of Muslims around the world.

September 12

In Exodus / Shemot 25:1-2, the tabernacle was constructed totally of free-will offerings. Most English Bibles state that this terumah / offering was "given" but the Hebrew literally reads that the offering was "taken." This fact of mistranslation illustrates the difference between the Biblical mindset of charitable donations and the Western or Greek mindset of giving. Just read the Jewish Stone's Tanakh translation, "YHWH spoke to Moshe, saying, "Speak to the children of Israel and let them take for Me a terumah / offering, from every man whose heart motivates him you shall take My terumah / offering," Exodus / Shemot 25:1 & 2. The word that is often mistranslated "as give" is the Hebrew term "laqach" which literally means to "take, accept, bring, carry away, fetch, seize, and take away." What's the difference between giving and taking?

One well-learned Jewish sage has taught that the obvious implication of this verse, that Israel was to "take" some of their possessions and "give" them to the collection. Yet a person can only give what is truly theirs in the first place. To the Hebrew, it should be understood that man actually has nothing. Whatever we do have – money, talents, children, belongings - is actually YHWH's. "The earth is YHWH's and everything in it," Tehillim (Psalm) 24:1. You can't give to a ministry or to the poor because nothing is really yours to give in the first place. YHWH graciously gives man stewardship and dominion over the earth. In reality we are just custodians, all we do is shuffle His world around.

To make this point, just read the items that Israelite ex-slaves were to give for the building of the mishkan: "These are the terumah / offering you are to receive from them: gold, silver and bronze; blue, purple and scarlet yarn and fine linen; goat hair; ram skins dyed red and hides of sea cows; acacia wood; olive oil for the light; spices for the anointing oil and for the fragrant incense; and onyx stones and other gems to be mounted on the ephod and breast piece," Exodus / Shemot 25:3-7. How many ex-slaves do you know of that have these kinds of possessions? Well, the grand resources used for the mishkan were the plunder Israel received as they left Mitzrayim / Egypt! "And the children of Israel did according to the word of Moshe; and they borrowed of the Egyptians jewels of silver, and jewels of gold, and raiment," Exodus / Shemot 12:35. The Israelites "borrowed" from the Egyptians the majestic possessions that YHWH "lent" Egypt.

Notice that YHWH did not make Israel give the terumah. No, YHWH commanded that each person should give generously as their heart led them. Desire led Israel into establishing the tabernacle. True terumah / offerings are taken from a grateful heart, responding to the need. Terumah starts with a heartfelt and sincere desire to take back to YHWH what He has given man. What is YHWH asking you to give others today? How will you respond?

September 13

"I will rebuild the fallen tabernacle of David," Acts 15:16. A popular phrase among believers today is that the Father is rebuilding the temple of David. This expression can be found in some of the latest best-selling books and is sung in several popular messianic praise and worship songs. Let's find out what Acts 15:16 really means when it says, "I will rebuild the fallen tent/house/temple/tabernacle of David."

The phrase "house of David" is found 25 times in the King James Version and is used predominantly in regards to David's family or lineage and NOT to a physical building or temple. You've heard the saying that it's the people that make the difference between a house and a home, well in David's case his house is the Israelite people. We must understand that when the scriptures talk about Israel, that the Bible is not just referring to a small nation in the Middle East but to ALL Israel scattered amongst the nations – all followers of Messiah are Israel!

At times David's house consisted of just the tribe of Judah (1 Kings 12:20), at other moments David's house was a few mighty men (1 Chronicles 11:10), while at David's death his house was the entire Hebrew people united in peace (Zechariah 12:10). The true Tabernacle of David is a people united in peace and not a building made by man. The physical building comes after the nation experiences YHWH's shalom as an outward sign of His approval and power(this will even take place during the end times and reign of Moshiach Y'shua upon this earth).

In Acts 15:16 the King James Version translates the Greek word "skene" as "tabernacle" but this is not the best rendering of the meaning. The Greek word "skene" is from the root word "skeuos," which specifically means "a wife as contributing to the usefulness of the husband." The KJV also mistranslates the word "fallen" which should read "flown away." And the KJV word "build" could better be interpreted as "raise up." Let's substitute those meanings into the verse: "After this I will return, and will raise up again my bride that has left me." Now a crystal clear picture is given as to what the Father's will is for these last days. He is preparing His bride. He is bringing His people together and building them "to make in himself of twain one new man, so making peace," Ephesians 2:15.

So, when the scriptures speak of the "house of David" it means the "family or children of David." This family of David includes not only those who followed in his lineage but also those before it. The twelve tribes of Israel comprise the house of David that YHWH is rebuilding in our day! The people of Israel are called the "house of David" because from His kingly lineage the Moshiach would come and because of the peace that was established while David and his son reigned. We are the tabernacle/house of David and our house is being rebuilt! Who can you share this with today?

September 14

For some strange reason most believers have a dangerous disease called "Bible dyslexia." Dyslexia is when you read something correctly but your mind mixes up the words. A simple sentence is gibberish to a person with dyslexia. A person with Bible dyslexia reads a passage from the Scriptures and gets it all mixed up as well. Don't think you have this problem? Think again.

The Messiah said "if you love me, keep my commandments" in John 14:15. The order of this sentence is important! First we make a mental and spiritual decision to love Him. Then we keep the commandments. First we are born again into his family. Then we obey out of the love for him. It's very dangerous to read the scripture verse backwards. When we have "Bible dyslexia" this verse says something totally different. The incorrect reading says obey him then love him. That's not what the Bible says. Obedience brings our body and emotions under the authority of YHWH. It must start and flow from a heart of love or it is simply legalistic observance. We must love YHWH and then obey Him.

Here's another verse we get backwards. Y'shua said, "He who loves me will be loved by my Father, and I too will love him and show myself to him," John 14:21. Love me, he says, and I'll show myself to you. It makes sense but we jumble it up.

We think we have to "see YHWH move" or "feel his presence" and then we can love him. We think that our heart will be quickened to love him AFTER He comes through for us in some area in life. That's not how the spiritual realm works. First we are to love him and then we see him! Simply put, first we love and seek him and then we find him. The more we love YHWH the more we can see YHWH! Understanding this simple principle will stop you from getting mixed up with Bible dyslexia.

Together these two verses teach a powerful lesson. Together we read "when you love me you will keep my commandments THEN I will show myself to you. You will really see and experience me when you love me and obey out of that love." Love and admiration for the Messiah must be our priority and then we can obey. As we obey we will see YHWH greater and greater. John 3:30 puts it this way, "He must increase, and I must decrease." That's something to think about today!

September 15

Another example of "Bible dyslexia" is Galatians 5:16. Bible Dyslexia? That's when you read something in the Scriptures correctly but your mind mixes up the words. The enemy wants to steal the true meaning of the Scriptures from us and will do anything he can to stop us from walking in abundance. When we have "Bible dyslexia" we fall prey to the enemy's ploys by misapplying what the Scriptures say.

Galatians 5:16 is supposed to be a verse that sets us free and teaches us how to live in the peace and blessing of the Holy Spirit. "Walk in the Spirit and you will not gratify the lusts of the flesh," says the passage in Galatians. The order of this sentence is important! This one verse can have a huge impact on our life IF we don't flip flop it. But, most people read this verse and read it in reverse. We mistakenly read it to say, "do not gratify or fulfill the lusts of the flesh and you will walk in the Spirit."

If we read Galatians 5:16 incorrectly then we will think that denying our flesh, cleaning up our act, or "acting" righteous equals walking in the Holy Spirit / Ruach Ha Kodesh. By misreading this verse we think that the true faith is nothing but giving up the things in life you enjoy. That's not what the Bible is teaching!

Order is important for Galatians 5:16. First we "walk in the Spirit of YHWH" and THEN we "deny the lusts of the fleshly sinful nature." First we seek YHWH and submit to Him and THEN the devil must flee, says James / Ya'acov 4:7.

If all we focus on is "denying the flesh" then all we will walk in will be bitterness and frustration. By focusing on the life in and of the Spirit of YHWH we will deny the flesh naturally. Walking in the Spirit is akin to walking with YHWH. When our relationship with Y'shua grows we will not want to walk away from Him through selfish actions. We can be like Enoch, who "walked with YHWH and was no more" if we stop Bible dyslexia. Focus on your relationship with Y'shua in you and the flesh will take care of itself. That's something else to think about today!

September 16

A remnant is a 'small piece of an original that has not been mixed.' A remnant is like the beginning, yet remains through the end. It was a remnant of the original oil that was used by the priests during the Chanukah story. And even the priests themselves were a remnant of the original bloodline that served at the tabernacle in the wilderness. Like their ancestors the priests had to stand up and defy the world of compromise. They also had to 'tikkun' or fix/rectify the errors of their past.

During Israel's journey from Egypt the priests gave in to the people and compromised true worship. "And when the people say that Moshe delayed to come down out of the Mount, the people gathered themselves together to Aharon, and said to him, Get up, make us elohim, that shall go before us; for as this Moshe, the man that brought us up out of the land of Mitzrayim / Egypt, we do not know what has become of him. And Aharon said to them, Break off the golden earrings, which are in the ears of your wives, and of your sons, and of your daughters, and bring them to me. And all the people broke off the golden earrings that were in their ears, and brought them to Aharon. And he received them at their hand, and fashioned it with a graving tool, after he had made it a golden calf: and they said, these be your elohim, O Israel. Which brought you up out of the land of Mitzrayim / Egypt," Shemot / Exodus 32:1-4.

Aharon gave in to the nation's request and gave them the idol of the golden cow. Remember, if you don't learn from the past then you are doomed to repeat it. If we don't tikkun the errors of our ancestors then we may replicate them. Compromise cannot be tolerated within the family of Israel. It not only has to be stopped, it also has to be fixed. Because of the sin of the golden cow, the nation was in need of tikkun / restoration.

Perhaps part of Israel's tikkun / restoration was the actions of Pinchas. "And when Pinchas, the son of El-Azar, the son of Aharon the kohen, saw it, he rose up from among the congregation, and took a javelin in his hand; and he went after the man of Israel into the tent, and thrust both of them through, the man of Israel, and the woman through her belly. So the plague was stopped from the children of Israel," Bamidbar / Numbers 25:7-15. Tikkun / restoratin of Aharon's sin took place as Pinchas the priest killed a public sinner.

The remnant continues now as you face the monster of compromise. Everyday you have an opportunity to learn from the past and change the future. Will you compromise or will you stand true to your faith?

September 17

Did YHWH just save us so we could have eternal life? Are we learning about our Hebrew roots just so we can make Jewish people jealous of our Torah keeping? What is the real reason we believe?

We were created by YHWH to live in His presence and experience his favor. It was only mankind that was made in His image and only mankind can have an intimate relationship with him. YHWH created the world and said "it is good" and when he created man and woman YHWH said "it is very good." As the crown of his creation mankind was given the task to represent YHWH to the entire world. We were told to have dominion, power, and multiplicity. We are supposed to enjoy our relationship with Him and share His goodness with all of creation. This is a pretty simple concept. Enjoy his favor and extend his greatness.

Abraham was set apart and called out of his home and family to have relationship with YHWH. From Abraham every nation in the entire world would be blessed. It is in Genesis 12 that we see YHWH blessing Avraham saying, "I will make you into a great nation and I will bless you; I will make your name great, and you will be a blessing. All peoples on earth will be blessed by you." This amazing promise finds its fulfillment NOT in the Jewish people but in the Jewish Messiah Y'shua. From Y'shua every nation is blessed because every tribe and tongue can join covenant relationship with the Almighty. Abraham was to be a blessing to the world through his faith and righteousness. We are Abraham's children and "heirs according to the promise" according to Galatians. Like the prophets, priests, and kings of Israel of old we are to extend the kingdom of YHWH throughout every kingdom in this world.

We can read of the culmination of Abraham's blessing in Revelation 7:9-10 and 19:10. This quote from Revelation is about the end of days after the battle of Armageddon and the rise of the Anti-christ. All of the eschatological events end with every knee bowing and every tongue confessing that Y'shua is master.

If this is Abraham's calling and if this is what really matters in the end, then shouldn't we be about the same? Is our faith to be focused on Israel, kabbalah, gematria, the nuances of the Hebrew language, calendars, or the greatness of our Messiah? We need to focus on the end time action of Matthew 24:14. This verse gives us a promise – not a theory – about when Y'shua will return. "This gospel of the kingdom will be preached in the whole world as a testimony to all nations and then the end will come," Matthew 24:14. The end of the world will come when the message of our magnificent Messiah goes to the ends of the earth. Consider that in the country of Afghanistan there are 26 million Muslims and 14,000 Christians. Should we try to convert these 14,000 born again Christians to the Hebrew roots or should we be praying for and reaching out to the 26 million unbelievers who will spend eternity separated from YHWH?

September 18

A ba'al teshuvah, or master of teshuvah, is compared in rabbinical writings as totally being born anew or "born again." The Messiah spoke of this when he said, "In reply Y'shua declared, "I tell you the truth, no one can see the kingdom of YHWH unless he is born again" Yochannan / John 3:3. And Peter also wrote of this, "For you have been born again, not of perishable seed, but of imperishable, through the living and enduring word of YHWH."

Through trusting belief, the ba'al teshuvah has died to his sins and torah breaking and is born anew into the kingdom of light through totally rejecting a life of rebellion and accepting Torah obedience in return. "What is a ba'al teshuvah," Rabbi Y'hudah said, "a ba'al teshuvah is one who has the opportunity to do the same sin and this time he does not do it. This is a true ba'al teshuvah."

This born again person is brought near to YHWH, under the wings of the Almighty. "Repentance brings man under the wings of YHWH, the words of Ezekiel, 'They had the hands of Elohim which extended beneath the wings of the cherubim to receive the penitents from the power of judgment," says the Talmud. This rabbinical reference clearly points to how Teshuvah brings man near to YHWH as found in Psalm 91:1, "He who dwells in the shelter of the Most High will rest in the wings of the Almighty." The person doing teshuvah submits himself to King YHWH.

You see, this closeness is only possible by a person being truly sorry for their sin and changing their behavior. It's the sin that prevents this closeness from occurring. This born anew turns from the sinful act and returns to a new life with YHWH, reminiscent of that in the Garden.

"Submit yourselves, then, to Elohim. Resist the devil, and he will flee from you," James 4:7-8. Before a person can resist the devil, or resist the yetzer hara or fleshly inclination, a person MUST submit to YHWH through teshuvah. Too many people try to ride the fence between submitting to YHWH and resisting the Adversary, never really doing teshuvah but thinking their sins are forgiven. These are people who continue their transgression yet, seemingly and constantly ask forgiveness for the problem area. This is because they are not fully submitting to YHWH, or they have sin strongholds that need to be dealt with.

One example of a real ba'al teshuvah is the prostitute woman Ra'hab who helped protect the Israelite spies as they reconnoitered the land. Because of Ra'hab's teshuvah she and her family were spared from death as the Israelites conquered the city. Ra'hab is remembered in the scriptures a person who came near to YHWH and His people through turning from sin and returning to YHWH through words and actions. Ra'hab is even one of the women in the direct lineage of the Messiah Y'shua. What sins do you need to confess and turn from today?

September 19

"You shall dwell in tents seven days, that your generations may know that I made the children of Israel to dwell in booths, when I brought them out of the land of Egypt," Leviticus 23:42-43.

The Scriptures and historical records indicate that the Savior was most likely born during the Festival of Tabernacles, which occurs in September or October. The Festival of Tabernacles, called "Sukkot" in Hebrew, recalls the wilderness voyage of the Israelites towards the Promised Land. For forty years the Hebrew people dwelt in tents and were fed heavenly manna. To remember the exodus journey, the Israelites were instructed in Leviticus 23 to hold an annual seven day celebration.

The story of John the Baptist proves that the birth of Messiah took place at Sukkot. Elizabeth (John's mother) was in her sixth month of pregnancy when Y'shua was conceived (Luke 1:24-36). John's father was a priest serving in the Jerusalem temple during the course of Abijah (Luke 1:5). Nine months from the temple service would have been about the month of March for the most likely time for John's birth. Adding another six months (the difference in ages) brings us to the end of September as the most likely time of Messiah's birth.

Y'shua was born in the town of Bethlehem, in order to fulfill a prophecy found in Micah 5:1-2. This Bethlehem birth occurred because of a Roman census that was taking place. For tax purposes, King Herod and the Romans were known to take their censuses according to the prevailing customs of the occupied territories. Each Hebrew male journeyed to Jerusalem three times a year, at Passover, Pentecost, and the Feast of Tabernacles. The towns around Jerusalem (like Bethlehem) would fill to capacity as the observant Hebrews made their pilgrimage to Jerusalem. There was no room at the inn because the vacancies were filled by the travelers.

John the Baptist was born at Passover and Y'shua was born 6 months later during Sukkot. The puzzle of the Messiah's birth date comes together with the knowledge of this festival. The birth of the Savior was not an independent event that could have occurred on any date. The Sukkot birth was a prophetic picture of "Emmanu-el" or "god with us." John 1:14 says that the "word became flesh and dwelt among us." The Greek term for "dwelt" in the oldest manuscripts is the exact same Greek word used to reference the Old Testament tabernacle." So, this verse could actually read - "the word became flesh and tabernacle among us." The manifest presence of the Creator was the message of Sukkot during the times of Moses, the birth of Y'shua, and today. Sukkot is not a "Jewish holiday," but rather a Biblical festival given to all believers for joy and spiritual growth. Sukkot is the time to say, “Happy birthday Y'shua.”

September 20

TRUTH FOR TODAY

Every Saturday millions of people around the world participate in a one year reading cycle of the Bible. While most modern people read a verse or two every week, there is a long-standing tradition to weekly read aloud and study various chapters of the Bible. People everywhere will examine the same portion of Scripture. This tradition comes to us from Judaism and was kept by the Savior and the early believers. Call it the original water-cooler conversation. This isn't a vain tradition of man that makes void the word BUT an inspired tradition that was handed down from Moses and supported by Paul. Who are we to argue with them?

"What special privilege, then, has a Jew? The privilege is great from every point of view. First of all, because the Jews were entrusted with the word of YHWH," Romans 3:1, 2. Clearly the Jewish tradition of reading the Bible through the year is a good one to follow. Is there more proof that we should be reading the Word aloud and discussing it? In the book of Deuteronomy, Moses spoke the commandments aloud as an example. He told the new nation of redeemed slaves to read the Word aloud. Later Ezra the Scribe instituted reading the Scriptures aloud.

The Newer Testament continues this theme when it teaches that "Faith cometh by hearing and hearing by the word." Without the Bible being read aloud and discussed it is difficult for faith to truly set in. "Give attendance to the reading of Torah, to exhortation, to teaching," says First Timothy 4:13. Here we are commanded to gather with others to HEAR the Torah read. This doesn't just mean to get your family together and preach to them. Instead, if you have a group nearby, then you are to give attendance to the Torah reading. "Torah" is the Hebrew word for teaching and instruction. Torah is often mistranslated "law" in most English Bibles. The Torah is YHWH's instructions for mankind found in Genesis to Revelation. To the Jews, the Torah is specifically the first five books of the Bible.

The Torah has been divided into 54 readings that correspond to the calendar year. These portions contain various nuggets of truth that deal with every issue in life. The sections are usually named after the first important Hebrew word or phrase used in that section. For example, the section on the evil king Balak and the evil prophet Bilaam is titled "Balak." And the first portion in the Torah is called "Beresheet" after the first Hebrew word found in the Bible, which means "beginning."

While most new believers start their Bible reading with the Gospels, it is the first five books that set a foundation for the rest of the word. You can't pick up a Stephen King novel and turn to the middle to begin reading. And you certainly shouldn't do that with the Bible. Start your reading cycle this week with the Torah. If you can, join with others to read and discuss the word.

September 21

TRUTH FOR TODAY

"The eighth day, there shall be a holy convocation for you," Leviticus 23:34. Though we like to camp during Sukkot and hope that it doesn't rain, Sukkot is about water. As Sukkot ends another celebration is held. This holy day is often considered the 8th day of Sukkot but it is actually an altogether different holiday. "On the fifteenth day of this seventh month is the Festival of Sukkot, seven days for YHWH... on the eighth day, there shall be a holy convocation for you," Leviticus 23:34. The connection between rain and Shemini Atzeret will teach us much if we will allow our minds to be opened to YHWH's Torah. May the Ruach Ha Kodesh reveal Y'shua to us in Shemini Atzeret as seen in Luke 24:45.

In Israel there is an early rain season and a time for the latter rains. It doesn't rain every other day in the Holy Land. The "Early Rains" were the heaviest rains and they came during the months of September and October. The rivers would swell from the rains and it was these rains that would soften the parched, dry land from the hot summer months. The first rains are and were for the fruit crops. The latter rains would be in the spring for the harvest of grain.

The early rains are mentioned in Deuteronomy 11:14. To read this verse in context is to unlock treasures from YHWH's word. Deuteronomy 11:8, "Observe therefore all the commands I am giving you today, so that you may have the strength to go in and take over the land that you are crossing the Jordan to possess." Verses 12-22 urge Elohim's people to be faithful to Him, to keep His commandments. This passage reminds the Israelites that they have seen the signs of YHWH's glory and now they must trust Him for the future. The rain will come as the people are obedient to YHWH and show mercy to people. The persistence of the rain is linked directly to the faithful obedience of the people. Rain in the Holy Land is conditional to the mercy and love of YHWH's people. Deuteronomy 11:16, "Take heed to yourselves, that your heart be not deceived, and ye turn aside, and serve other Elohim, and worship them; And then YHWH's wrath be kindled against you, and He shut up the heaven, that there be no rain, and that the land yield not her fruit; and lest ye perish quickly from off the good land which YHWH giveth you."

In the Scriptures, rain is symbolic of a new way of life. Rain is necessary for crops to produce, farmers to harvest, and life to continue. Rain is dew from heaven. It is substance from the Almighty. It occurs as a result of Israel's obedience and faith. Praying for rain was a central act of worship for those living in Israel during ancient times as drought meant hunger. It is the same for us today. Praying for rain is actually praying that people accept Y'shua and follow His plan for their lives. May we pray for the rain/reign of the Spirit in our lives as we trust YHWH and for rain for the Land of Promise.

TRUTH FOR TODAY

September 22

Have you ever wondered what the hardest commandment to follow in the Bible is? Is it the prohibition against telling lies or observing a Sabbath rest that is most challenging? What about the laws of clean and unclean? There are literally thousands of commands in the holy book; we each have our own personal struggles with the ordinances. What burns you the worst? Is there something you find difficult to obey?

The Messiah explained that the greatest commandment was to love YHWH and then love your neighbor as yourself. For most of us the greatest commandment is the hardest commandment. It's not easy to love others. Do unto others as you want them to do want to you is a nice Sunday school lesson, but is hard to apply in everyday life. Of course this was not called the "easiest commandment" it was called the "greatest commandment." So how do you do it? How do you love others who mistreat you, abuse you, misuse you, or neglect you? "Love hopes all things, bears all things, and believes all things," 1 Corinthians 13:7.

First Corinthians 13:7 gives us some insight into this subject. This passage says "love hopes all things, bears all things, and believes all things."

Ah ha! That's how we do it. There is no deep esoteric knowledge needed and no Hebrew word study required to love. To love your neighbor is to believe for the best. Plain and simple. Just believe for the best. Isn't that what you want from other people? Don't you want to be given the benefit of the doubt?

Y'shua asked us, "How can you love YHWH whom you don't see if you can't love man that you do see?" Loving your neighbor is how you love YHWH. Being kind or generous to people around you is how you are kind and generous back to YHWH.

We must choose to love which means to believe the best for and of people. Instead of jumping to conclusions or instantly fighting back when offended we need to stop and give the benefit of the doubt. The Messiah never struck back or retaliated when he was offended and he calls us to show the same pity and compassion for others he displayed.

When you are offended today remember this message. Reach out in love to your neighbor. Give the benefit of the doubt.

September 23

Sin is any act, thought, or word of rebellion that violates the will of YHWH as revealed in the Torah (Bible). The Messianic writings explain it this way "Anyone who commits sin violates Torah, for sin is the transgression of the Torah," Yochannan Aleph / First John 3:4. To sin is to transgress or disobey the Torah. When we break a Torah commandment we also break our connection with YHWH. As we rebel we are unplugged from our power source. Through choosing our ways over His Words, we separate ourselves from close fellowship with Him.

After Adam originally sinned in the Gan Eden, Adam does something really strange. He hides. Here is a man now hiding in the bushes that had "walked with YHWH in the cool of the day." Why would he be hiding? Adam sensed that he did something wrong and this disobedience brought about the emotion of fear. Now get this, Adam wasn't afraid of snakes. He wasn't even scared of a talking snake that had tempted him to sin. But, Adam was terrified of the consequences of his actions. Adam was hiding because he was scared to death, and of death! He was terrified!

Adam, who once had a perfect, unhindered, relationship with YHWH, was now hiding because of his sin. The Rabbis teach that it was on Yom Kippur that Adam fell. Also, on that first Yom Kippur, animals were sacrificed as blood atonement for the remission of Adam and Chawa's sins. The skin from these animals clothed Adam and Chawa's nakedness and covered their sinfulness. Each time they looked upon their "clothing" they were reminded of their fall and the consequences of sin.

Through the Ruach HaKodesh we can then live in constant awareness of the effects of our Torah keeping and our Torah breaking. This awareness doesn't cause us to walk around legalistically obeying commandments. Nor does it cause us to be neurotic about our actions. Rather, this constant awareness actually blesses us, as we stay tapped in to YHWH and His will. "Blessed is the man that fears YHWH, who delights greatly in His mitzvoth," Tehillim / Psalm 112:1. As we delight in His Torah we fear breaking our connection by violating His word. "Every branch in Me that bears not fruit He takes away: and every branch that bears fruit, He purges it, that it may bring forth more fruit," said Y'shua in the book of Yochannan / John. In all honesty, it is because of a lack of fear that we sin. Sin is rampant within churches, synagogues, and homes because we do not fear its consequences.

The fear of sin will cause us to be concerned about outcome. As we truly learn to fear / yirah YHWH we will become afraid of going astray. Will you have the fear of YHWH today?

September 24

Is fear a factor in your relationship with YHWH? "Fear YHWH and turn from evil," says a wise man in Proverb 13. The fear of YHWH is the means by which we turn away from evil. As we turn to YHWH and from evil we are made wise and we in essence fear sin. As we have the fear of sin we have the fear of YHWH. Should you walk around in dread of sin and its consequences? Should you always be thinking of sin? NO! This isn't the fear of sin. The fear of sin will cause you to think about sin as YHWH does.

Think of it this way, perhaps the fear of YHWH is, in fact, the things He is afraid of. Perhaps the fear of YHWH is having His fears in mind all of the time. Just imagine YHWH being scared!

If YHWH could be afraid of anything, what would it be?

What would cause the Creator of the universe to shrink back and shiver?

What makes Elohim scared? What are YHWH's fears?

If YHWH could be afraid of anything, it would be separation caused by sin. The one thing that could make YHWH recoil in shock is the idea of the Creator being separated from the creation. With this in mind, let's understand that to have the fear of YHWH is to actually have His fears and to personally fear what He fears. It is to fear the consequences of sin.

Yes, to have the fear of YHWH is to actually be concerned about what concerns Him. It is to dread what He dreads and run from what He runs from. It is to be upset over the same things that He gets mad at. Friend, to have the fear of YHWH is actually to have the fear of sin. YHWH is scared of the only power in the universe that separates Him from His creation, the power of sin, and He wants us to have that same fear.

In Proverbs / Mishlei we are told that, "The fear of YHWH is to hate evil: pride, and arrogance, and the evil halakha / way to walk, and the perverted mouth," Mishlei / Proverbs 8: 13. To yisar / fear YHWH is to fear sin, because it separates us from Elohim. What does it mean to fear sin? What does it mean, Hebraically, to sin? To fear sin we must first understand exactly what sin is and how it affects mankind. "But your iniquities have separated between you and your Elohim, and your sins have hid his face from you, that he will not hear," Yesha'yahu / Isaiah 59:2.

September 25

"If anyone thirsts, let him come to Me and drink. He who believes in Me, as the Scripture has said, out of his heart will flow rivers of living water," John 7:37-38.

Numbers 29:35, "On the eighth day you shall hold a solemn gathering; you shall not work at your occupations." This eighth day of Sukkot is called in Hebrew "Shemini Atzeret." This term literally means "the eighth day of holding" or the "eighth day of assembly." On this day, we are commanded to gather together for worship and prayer. "Rabbinic literature explains the holiday this way: Elohim is like a host, who invites us as visitors for a limited time, but when the time comes for us to leave, He has enjoyed himself so much that He asks us to stay another day," says the Jewish Virtual Library. There are not many specific commands for this day of worship. In fact, this day is usually forgotten by many observant Jewish and Christian people.

Christianity insists that the Law of Moses has been superseded by the New Testament; therefore the festivals should not be celebrated. In Judaism, Shemini Atzeret has sadly been replaced by modern holiday of Israel called "Simchat Torah." This holiday occurs on the 9th day of Sukkot. Simchat Torah is a day for rejoicing in the Torah and marks the end of yearly Torah reading and the beginning of the new cycle. Judaism, for the most part, has replaced the reverence of Shemini Atzeret for "Simchat Torah." The Jewish tradition of Simchat Torah is a good time to rejoice for the Word of YHWH, yet the Biblical festival of Shemini Atzeret is a great time to hear from YHWH about His presence and power. Traditionally in the synagogue, Shemini Atzeret is commemorated only by adding a specific prayer to the daily petitions. This prayer is a request for rain.

A prayer for rain is important as in ancient Israel; Shemini Atzeret coincided with the beginning of the rainy season. Accordingly, prayers for rain or "tefillat geshem" and good crops were recited. Many Orthodox Jews still recite the ancient prayers at this time. The connection between rain and Shemini Atzeret will teach us much if we will allow our minds to be opened to YHWH's Torah. May the Ruach Ha Kodesh reveal Y'shua to us in Shemini Atzeret. Luke 24:45, "Then he opened their minds so they could understand the Scriptures." This must be our prayer on about holy day of Shemini Atzeret.

On the last and seventh day of Sukkot the priest would circle the altar seven times and then pour the water on the altar to wash away the blood of the morning's sacrifices. This ritual is known as "Simchat Bet Ha-sho-evah" or "the Rejoicing of the House of Drawing Water." It was during this festival, during this time that Y'shua said, "If anyone thirsts, let him come to me and drink. He who believes in Me, as the Scripture has said, out of his heart will flow rivers of living water," Yochannan / John 7:37-38.

September 26

"But you, Bethlehem Ephrath, who are little to be among the thousands of Judah, out of you shall come forth to me that is to be ruler in Israel; whose goings forth are from of old, from ancient days." Micah 5:1

The major events in the life of our Messiah correspond directly with the festivals of YHWH given in Leviticus 23. Y'shua was offered as the Passover Lamb. He is the first born from the dead and the first fruits of the resurrection. Y'shua gave us his Spirit at Shavuot/Pentecost. We can also discern that Y'shua will return at the Feast of Trumpets and judge the world during Yom Kippur. Where does this leave the final feast of Sukkot?

Well, Chag HaSukkot - the "Feast of Tabernacles" is the time of tabernacling or dwelling with YHWH. John 1 says that Y'shua became flesh and "dwelt" among us. The Messiah came to live with mankind during this time. Most theologians believe that Y'shua's ministry lasted 3 and one half years. Being that Y'shua died on Passover, if you backtrack the time you will see that He was born during Sukkot. Christmas isn't the birthday of Messiah. Sukkot is Messiah's birthday.

Remember that there was no room in the inn for Joseph and Mary (Miriam) to stay in Bethlehem. The book of Luke states a census was being taken of all Hebrews. Surely the Romans would count and tax the Hebrews when more Hebrews were in Israel.

During this festival of Sukkot all Hebrew males were commanded to come to Jerusalem. Bethlehem is only a few short miles away from Jerusalem, so evidently the inn was full with Sukkot travelers. Or perhaps the inn was a place to pay to put up your own sukkah and not a "hotel" as has always been thought. There was no room for the couple so Y'shua was born in a Sukkah - not a manger.

The sukkah is a temporary dwelling, like a tent, that reminds us of the wilderness journey the Israelites camped in for forty years. The physical body of Y'shua was a temporary dwelling for the Messiah. Matthew 2:1 teaches that the "wise men" or "rabbis" that came from the east to Y'shua and saw the star - oddly it is tradition that you should be able to see the stars through the roof of your sukkah. Also the shepherds were out at night and saw the star of Y'shua. They traditionally would have been out during this time of Sukkot and the weather in Israel is permitting for this type of activities. The Mishnah states that the shepherds in Bethlehem would normally bring in their flocks to a "protective corral" during the months of November through February. So the idea that shepherds were in the fields at night during this time is very possible. (They certainly were not in the fields at night in December!) The Festival of Tabernacles is a special time to celebrate the birth of Y'shua.

TRUTH FOR TODAY

September 27

It's one thing to study what other people say about the Feast of Tabernacles. It's something totally different to only read and meditate on what the Scripture says about the holy day. Read these verses and learn more:

- "Celebrate the Feast of Harvest with the first fruits of the crops you sow in your field," Exodus 23:16.
- "YHWH said to Moses, "Say to the Israelites: 'On the fifteenth day of the seventh month YHWH's Feast of Tabernacles begins, and it lasts for seven days. The first day is a sacred assembly; do no regular work. For seven days present offerings made to YHWH by fire, and on the eighth day hold a sacred assembly and present an offering made to YHWH by fire. It is the closing assembly; do no regular work."
- "'These are YHWH's appointed feasts, which you are to proclaim as sacred assemblies for bringing offerings made to YHWH by fire-the burnt offerings and grain offerings, sacrifices and drink offerings required for each day. These offerings are in addition to those for YHWH's Sabbaths and in addition to your gifts and whatever you have vowed and all the freewill offerings you give to YHWH," Deuteronomy 7:6-8.
- "'So beginning with the fifteenth day of the seventh month, after you have gathered the crops of the land, celebrate the festival to YHWH for seven days; the first day is a day of rest, and the eighth day also is a day of rest. On the first day you are to take choice fruit from the trees, and palm fronds, leafy branches and poplars, and rejoice before YHWH your Elohim for seven days. Celebrate this as a festival to YHWH for seven days each year. This is to be a lasting ordinance for the generations to come; celebrate it in the seventh month. Live in booths for seven days: All native-born Israelites are to live in booths so your descendants will know that I had the Israelites live in booths when I brought them out of Egypt. I am YHWH your Elohim.'" So Moses announced to the Israelites the appointed feasts of YHWH," Leviticus 23:35:-44.
- "Then have them make a sanctuary for me, and I will dwell among them. Make this tabernacle and all its furnishings exactly like the pattern I will show you," Exodus 25:8.
- "And the Word became flesh and dwelt among us and we beheld His glory, the glory as of the only begotten of the Father, full of grace and truth," John 1:14.

Truth For Today

September 28

It's best to let the Bible interpret the Bible. Here are a few more verses about Sukkot. Study and meditate on these today:

- "YHWH will wash away the filth of the women of Zion; he will cleanse the bloodstains from Jerusalem by a spirit of judgment and a spirit of fire. Then YHWH will create over all of Mount Zion and over those who assemble there a cloud of smoke by day and a glow of flaming fire by night; over all the glory will be a canopy. It will be a shelter and shade from the heat of the day, and a refuge and hiding place from the storm and rain," Isaiah 4:4-6.

- "When the seventh month came and the Israelites had settled in their towns, the people assembled as one man in Jerusalem. Then Jeshua son of Jozadak and his fellow priests and Zerubbabel son of Shealtiel and his associates began to build the altar of the God of Israel to sacrifice burnt offerings on it, in accordance with what is written in the Law of Moses the man of Elohim. Despite their fear of the peoples around them, they built the altar on its foundation and sacrificed burnt offerings on it to YHWH, both the morning and evening sacrifices. Then in accordance with what is written, they celebrated the Feast of Tabernacles with the required number of burnt offerings prescribed for each day," Ezra 3:-4.

- "In the last days the mountain of YHWH's temple will be established as chief among the mountains; it will be raised above the hills, and peoples will stream to it. Many nations will come and say, "Come, let us go up to the mountain of YHWH, to the house of the Elohim of Jacob. He will teach us his ways, so that we may walk in his paths." The law will go out from Zion, the word of YHWH from Jerusalem. He will judge between many peoples and will settle disputes for strong nations far and wide. They will beat their swords into plowshares and their spears into pruning hooks. Nation will not take up sword against nation, nor will they train for war anymore. Every man will sit under his own vine and under his own fig tree, and no one will make them afraid, for YHWH Almighty has spoken. All the nations may walk in the name of their gods; we will walk in the name of YHWH our Elohim for ever and ever," Micah 4:1-5.

- "If anyone thirsts, let him come to Me and drink. He who believes in Me, as the Scripture has said, out of his heart will flow rivers of living water," Yochannan / John 7:37-38

September 29

Dance is a forgotten element of Biblical worship that is slowly being restored to the true faith today. The sister of Moses, named Miriam, danced as she crossed the Red Sea after the exodus. King David danced as the Ark of the Covenant was moved to Jerusalem. Even Y'shua spoke of how dance accompanied the return of the prodigal son in Luke 15:25. The book of Psalms is full of references to dance and highly active movement. Psalm 149 says to praise the Almighty with "dancing and making melody."

So, should we do the hokey pokey during worship services? History indicates that dance was once practiced by New Testament believers. In the book, Dance in Christian Worship, the author suggests that in the first five centuries of the faith, "dance was still acceptable because it was planted deep in the soil of the Judeo-Christian tradition." After the rise of the Catholic Church through Roman Emperor Constantine, the dance as a type of worship was performed only by the priests. During the Dark Ages the priestly theatrical dance morphed into liturgical processionals. And by the time of the reformation, Martin Luther and others had totally removed dance from the order of service. The statues of the synod of Lyons prohibited dancing in 1566 and imposed the punishment of excommunication upon those who led dances in church.

For over 1500 years, religious consensus seemed to indicate that dance belongs to the heathen nations or bars, and not to those who seek to follow the Messiah. Such continued to be the prevailing thought until recently when modern media instigated the popularity of dance through radio, television, dance clubs, reality competitions, and even worship centers.

Nowhere in the Bible is worship dance considered to be sin. It was practiced during Biblical times and definitely has a place in scripturally accurate worship settings. Congregations should allow interpretive dance, waving of hands, and congregational dance or "Davidic dance" that takes place in circles.

According to Matthew 11:17 and Luke 7:32, dancing represents one's joyful response to the good news of salvation. Because you have been saved you can dance unto YHWH and cut loose in the Spirit! The next time you are in a worship service why not dance like David?

September 30

In 2008, the famed Time Magazine ran a cover story that listed the Top Ten Ideas that are changing the world. For the category of Religion, the magazine's editors chose the "Re-Judaizing of Y'shua" as the most life changing spiritual movement on the face of the earth. The article spoke of the Hebrew Roots movement as a growing force of Christians that forsake common Christian practices in search of the Bible based faith that is rooted in the Hebrew lifestyle and scriptures. Thus, we are called the "Jewish Roots" movement or the "Hebrew Roots" movement. These terms fit nicely. As we learn the customs, language, and lifestyle of the Biblical times we can more truthfully know our Messiah. Our movement is in search of the Hebrew Roots – a worship experience in spirit and in truth.

The word "root" has special meaning. A root is a deep foundation of a plant. Roots are hidden down below the surface are often hard to discover. Roots must be dug out and this takes effort. Our Hebrew roots are the same. We must look past the surface of the accepted ways of Christian and Jewish worship and dig into our Bibles to really get to the root of the issues. As we go deeper into the Scriptures we do indeed find that we are part of the Olive tree of Israel. This doesn't mean that we are Jewish! Remember that Israel is comprised of twelve tribes. The identity of the two tribes of Judah and Levi is known today as the Jewish people. This leaves 10 tribes that remain to be discovered and recovered. That's us! We can understand this clearly in Romans 11. The hidden root is an Israeli olive tree. This olive tree has vast importance and we must learn all about it! Understand this – if you are born again – if you have accepted the Messiah as your master and savior, then you are NOT just a New Testament Christian. You are not just a Baptist or Methodist or Pentecostal. No! All who call upon the Savior in true repentance and faith ARE ISRAELITES! Your identity is so important.

It is in Jeremiah 11:16, that YHWH identifies the Olive Tree as the symbol of Israel. "YHWH called your name Green Olive Tree, lovely and of good fruit."

Hosea prophesies that in the end-time Israel shall once again be restored and its "branches shall spread; his beauty shall be like an olive tree" (Hosea 14:6)

Paul also in the new covenant uses this same analogy for Israel in Romans 11:16-21. Paul is explaining that because of their sin the ENTIRE nation of Israel were separated from YHWH. By faith we can ALL be grafted back into the common wealth of Israel. Praise YHWH today for His plan for your life!

October

TRUTH FOR TODAY

October 1

From the 10 Commandments we learn "Remember the Sabbath day, to keep it holy. Six days shalt thou labor, and do all thy work: But the seventh day is the Sabbath of the YHWH thy God: in it thou shalt not do any work, thou, nor thy son, nor thy daughter, thy manservant, nor thy maidservant, nor thy cattle, nor thy stranger that is within thy gates. For in six days the YHWH made heaven and earth, the sea, and all that in them is, and rested the seventh day: wherefore the YHWH blessed the Sabbath day, and hallowed it," Exodus, chapter 20

Now, compare this verse to a calendar. What day is the seventh?

Sunday is clearly the first day of the week and therefore cannot be the Biblical Sabbath! The Savior kept the seventh day Sabbath and so did the apostles, including Paul. "And because he was of the same craft, he abode with them, and wrought: for by their occupation they were tentmakers. And he reasoned in the synagogue every Sabbath, and persuaded the Jews and the Greeks. And he continued there a year and six months, teaching the word of Elohim among them,"- Acts, chapter 18:3, 4, 11. Paul's actions were the same as the Savior's. They were both in the synagogue on the Sabbath. "Now when they had passed through Amphipolis and Apollonia, they came to Thessalonica, where was a synagogue of the Jews: And Paul, as his manner was, went in unto them, and three Sabbath days reasoned with them out of the scriptures," Acts 17:1,2.

"And he came to Nazareth, where he had been brought up: and, as his custom was, he went into the synagogue on the Sabbath day, and stood up for to read," Luke 4:16.

From creation, the Seventh day has been Saturday. Mankind has not lost track of time, nor confused which day is which. Nowhere in the Bible is the day of worship changed from Saturday to Sunday. Take the words of Exodus 20 to heart and remember the true Sabbath day and keep it set apart.

October 2

The Hebrew word for Heaven is "shamayim." Judaism refers to Heaven as the "Olam Haba" or the "world to come" and even the Garden of Eden in the same way. Biblically, shamayim is where the soul experiences the greatest possible pleasure - the feeling of closeness to YHWH. It's a place of peace and rest. The Olam Haba is a time that we will be reunited with loved ones. We shall meet our Savior face to face and know him without limits. In the Shamayim we shall lay aside the cares of this world and bask in YHWH's presence. We should look forward to skipping on streets of gold and experiencing the place and peace of the Almighty. The book of Revelation describes Shamayim as a time when YHWH will wipe every tear from our eyes. There will be no more death, mourning, sickness, crying or pain. Heaven is a place without deadlines, mood swings, labor pains, dirty houses, flat tires, sadness, or sin. It's a time and place of perfect perfection. Think about those words for a minute. The Olam Haba is a time and place of perfect perfection. I can't even fold a paper airplane perfectly, so it's tremendously difficult for me to really imagine place of perfection and peace. Yet the Bible describes our future home as such.

Heaven is high above our problems in this world. "For as the Heaven is high above the Earth, so great is His mercy toward them that fear Him," Psalm 103:11.

Heaven is YHWH's dwelling-place. "And hearken Thou to the supplication of Thy servant, and of Thy people Israel, when they shall pray toward this place: and hear Thou in Heaven Thy dwelling place: and when Thou hearest, forgive," 1Kings 8:30.

YHWH fills Heaven. "Can any hide himself in secret places that I shall not see him? saith YHWH. Do not I fill heaven and earth? saith the YHWH," Jeremiah 23:24.

The Saints are rewarded in Heaven. "Rejoice, and be exceeding glad: for great is your reward in Heaven: for so persecuted they the prophets which were before you," Matthew 5:12.

Take your wildest idea of what heaven is like; think of how wonderful and awesome eternity shall be and multiply it by one million. Now multiply that idea by 10 billion. That's nowhere close to how great the Olam Haba is. 1 Corinthians 2:9, "No eye has seen, no ear has heard, no mind has conceived what YHWH has prepared for those who love him." Heaven will be what we have always longed for. It is the presence of YHWH unfettered and unabated.

YHWH knew that we would long for such place. Each person on earth has an internal eternal need for the soul's satisfaction found only in Shamayim While on our journey of life, it is just natural to long for home.

October 3

If the people will just follow the instructions of YHWH then they will be the envy of the whole world. But, if we are stubborn and rebellious then we will face the consequences of our sin. Exile is foretold for rebellious people.

The Hebrew word for 'curse' found all over the Bible is "awrar." This word means to "execrate or bitterly curse, to declare to be hateful or abhorrent; denounce, to denounce evil against, or to imprecate evil upon; to curse; to protest against as unholy or detestable; hence, to detest utterly; to abominate." This is not a pretty sight! The Israelites received awrar upon themselves for disobeying YHWH.

The opposite of "awrar" is "baracha," which means to be "blessed." This ancient Hebrew word means to "to kneel, by implication to bless YHWH (as an act of adoration), and (vice-versa) man (as a benefit); also bless, congratulate, greatly, indeed, kneel (down), praise, salute, thank." As you can see these terms are complete opposites.

"And it shall come to pass, if you shall listen diligently to the voice of YHWH Your Elohim, to shomer / guard and do all His mitzvot which I command you this day, that YHWH Your Elohim will set you on high above all nations of the earth: And all these blessings shall come on you, and overtake you, if you shall listen to the voice of YHWH Your Elohim. Blessed shall you be in the city, and blessed shall you be in the field. Blessed shall be the fruit of your body, and the fruit of your ground, and the fruit of your cattle, the increase of your cattle, and the flocks of your sheep. Blessed shall be your basket and your bowl. Blessed shall you be when you come in, and blessed shall you be when you go out," Deuteronomy 28:1-6. The blessings continue and the curses are presented all throughout the Bible. There are in fact twelve curses within Devarim 27:15-26 – one curse for each tribe.

The theme of all of this is that the nation of Israel, each individual in Israel, had the choice of life or death. We too must choose our future. What has happened in our past doesn't really matter. How we were raised, what faith we grew up with, our thoughts, our feelings, our doctrines, our desires, and our problems don't mean much. Now that we have been presented the choice we must decide to either follow YHWH or not.

Are you willing to follow YHWH in order to receive blessings and life? Or would you rather have things your way and inherit curses and death? Is there an area in your life that you just won't surrender to the Almighty? Do you follow vain traditions just because they are comfortable? Are you living obedience or acting in disobedience? Your actions prove your answer, and right now is the perfect time to consider your devotion.

October 4

"YHWH spoke to Moshe saying: Speak to the children of Israel and you shall say to them, When you arrive in the Land to which I am bringing you, and you eat from the bread of the Land, you shall set aside a gift for YHWH. The first portion of your dough, you shall separate a loaf for a gift; as in the case of the gift of the threshing floor, so shall you separate it. From the first portion of your dough you shall give a gift to YHWH in all your generations," Bamidbar / Numbers 15:17-21.

In the Hebrew language the term for "bread" is "lechem." While "lechem" is the usual bread eaten daily, there is a special bread saved for the holy days called "challah." There are traditionally two loaves of Challah served at the Shabbat dinner table. The two baked loaves are symbolic of many things including the showbread of the temple and the double portion of the manna received in the Wilderness before Shabbat. They can also represent the two tablets of Torah, the two witnesses, the two people – Ephraim and Judah, the two commands to "remember" and "keep" the Shabbat.

The dough of Challah is normally twisted with three braids and these braids are even meaningful of the mitzvot. The Rabbis teach that the "three braids are symbolic of the commands to observe Shabbat that appear in the Ten Commandments. One braid represents the word 'zachor' or 'remember' in Hebrew. A second braid represents the word 'shamor' or 'guard' in Hebrew. The third braid is for 'b'Dibbur Echad' - that these commands of 'Remember' and 'Guard' were said by Elohim simultaneously and as one unit," says one source. The three rows can also point to the Creation, the Exodus, and the Messianic Era.

Even the way Challah is cut is a visible teacher for the Israelite. Most people serve Challah with a knife present but never use the knife at all, just as the Torah recounts that the patriarch Avraham, was tested by YHWH, and did not use the knife on his son Yitzchak. The bread is to be torn from the loaf, first by the priest or head of the household and then by everyone else.

Eating challah on the eve of Shabbat is a worthwhile tradition that teaches many lessons. Plus, it tastes good too! The next time you have a taste of challah or any lechem say this blessing: "Baruch atah YHWH eloheynu melech ha olam ha motzi lechem min ha'aretz" or "Blessed are You YHWH our Elohim, king of the universe, who brings forth bread from the earth."

TRUTH FOR TODAY

October 5

Ever think about life and death or heaven? Well, when we die our body goes to the ground. Genesis 3:19 shows that we are dust and to the dirt we must return. However, we aren't just mud pies! We are spiritual beings and at death our spirit returns to be with YHWH and goes directly to heaven. Immediately when you die you go to heaven. We can learn from 2 Corinthians 5:8 that there is no soul sleep or waiting to get into the Pearly Gates. "To be absent from body is present with YHWH," 2 Corinthians 5:8.

The Hebrew word for heaven is "shamayim." Heaven is a glorious place that Y'shua has been preparing for us since His ascension. John 14:2, "In my Father's house are many mansions: if it were not so, I would have told you. I go to prepare a place for you."

The Apostle Paul / Rabbi Sha'ul; said in 1 Corinthians 2:9, "Eye hath not seen, nor ear heard, neither have entered into the heart of man, the things which YHWH hath prepared for them that love him." According to this,

Heaven is better than your wildest dreams! In Shamayim we will be occupied with living and enjoying life without sin. We will be with loved ones, study Torah, and have fun.

Judaism speaks of 7 Heavens and we know the Bible speaks of at least 3. Shamayim of the air and atmosphere around the earth as in Genesis 1:20. Shamayim of the universe and the realm of the sun and moon as in Genesis 1:14 and shamayim that is YHWH's home and abode as in Isaiah 63:15.

Heaven is a place of:

- Beauty, Revelation 21:10-11
- Immortality, Revelation 21:4
- Light, Revelation 21:23
- Perfection, 1 John 3:2
- Joy, Revelation 19:6-8

The Rabbis have said, "This world is like a lobby before Heaven. Prepare yourself in the lobby so you may enter the banquet hall." The world is how we prepare for the Shamayim. How often do you think of you eternal home? "Set your mind on things above, not on things that are of the earth," Colossians 3:2.

October 6

Colossians 1:27 identifies the anointing as, "Christ in you, the hope of glory." The word translated "Christ" in English Bibles is the Greek word "Christos" which means the "anointed or Messiah." This Greek phrase is similar to the Hebrew word "Moshiach" which is translated into English as "Messiah." The meaning of Moshiach is the same as the meaning of Christos. Accordingly, Colossians 1:27 now reads, "The Messiah, the Moshiach, the Anointed One - the Anointing in you is the hope of kavod." Messiah, the anointing, lives in the believer to bring forth kavod / glory.

In ancient times, YHWH would anoint an individual to function effectively in a particular office. For example, certain people were chosen as prophet, priests, or kings. Y'shua, the Anointed One said, "The Ruach of the Master YHWH is upon Me, because He has anointed Me to proclaim the Besorah / gospel to the poor; He has sent Me to heal the brokenhearted, to proclaim deliverance to the captives, and recovering of sight to the blind, to set at liberty those that are bruised, to proclaim the acceptable year of the Master YHWH," Luke 4:18, 19. Y'shua manifest the kavod of YHWH on this earth and therefore He was anointed. Y'shua was anointed – He was covered with the kavod for a specific purpose and mission. He has passed His anointing on to us as we walk in His kavod. "But you have an anointing from the Kadosh-One," 1 John 2:20. The anointing disables the flesh, allowing the believer to accomplish the full will of YHWH.

"YHWH is my Shepherd; I shall not want. He makes me to lie down in green pastures: He leads me beside the still mayim. He restores my being: He leads me in the paths of tzedekah / righteousness for His Name's sake. Yes, though I walk through the valley of the shadow of death, I will fear no evil: for You are with me; Your rod and Your staff they comfort me. You prepare a shulchan / table before me in the presence of my enemies: You anoint my head with oil; my cup runs over. Surely tov and rachamim shall follow me all the days of my chayim / life: and I will dwell in the house of YHWH le-olam-va-ed," Psalm / Tehillim 23.

It is in the shadow of death that there is uncertainty, pain, and suffering. Yet, it is in death's presence that the anointing increases. The kavod of YHWH is made manifest through trials and testing. YHWH uses the hard times to bring about a greater revelation of His significance. He does NOT punish us with problems and pain but allows believers to experience sorrow to bring about a greater revelation of His glory. YHWH is glorified in the life of the believer amidst sickness, suffering, tyrant bosses, crazy teenagers, and the stresses of life. "For our light and tiny afflictions, which is just for a moment, prepares for us a far greater and limitless glory, le-olam-va-ed," 2 Corinthians 4:17.

October 7

Like a friendly, next-door neighbor, we have grown up with our theologies and have trusted them to be the answers to some of our deepest questions. The problem is that most of man's theologies are just that – man's theologies ...or man's theories. According to the Online Etymological Dictionary the word 'theology' is from the Greek language and literally means the "account or treating of the gods." The Baptists, Catholics, and Lutherans all have their theology figured out and have placed their 'god' in a tightly made box of ideals. The dilemma is that YHWH is 'Ayn Sof" or 'incomprehensible and beyond knowledge'. YHWH is so great we really cannot understand Him.

Halakha leaves room for differences as long as the Torah is upheld. What is "halakha?" One teacher has said, "Torah is the doctrine and halakha is the way to walk. There is much freedom in halakha." Theology leads to walls of separation that shout, "If you don't believe exactly as I do, then, you are not welcome or you are not going to heaven." Halakha provides freedom and room for growth. Halakha says, "We do it this way, yet you may do it another way. The important thing is that we are doing YHWH's Will of the Torah." The Scriptures allow congregations, Rabbis, and families to fulfill the mitzvot in different yet meaningful ways.

To have our mind renewed we must accept halakha and reject man's ways. "Halakha" is a Hebrew word that literally means 'a way to walk or act' or the way 'to go' in obeying the commands. It is found throughout the scriptures and is based on a verse from Shemot / Exodus. "And thou shalt show them the way wherein they are to go and the work that they must do," Shemot / Exodus 18:20. When a teacher/Rabbi sets halakha that teacher is saying, "we're going to obey this command in this manner." The root word of "halakha" is the word 'yaw-lak,' which is defined as to 'walk, prosper, grow, and carry.' Halakha is interpretation of scripture with ideas and descriptions on how to live out the commandments. It is a way of applying Torah to everyday life. Halakha may differ from teacher to teacher and from family to family. Some halakha / walk is strict, with boundaries of protection fenced around the Torah. Some halakha is loose and liberal. Even other groups have 'minhag' or local customs on halakha of certain issues. It can be wide, but it must not break Torah and Torah's literal interpretation. Just like walking, halakha takes effort. It is easy to receive theological rhetoric from a priest or professor. It is hard to "study to show thyself approved unto Elohim, a workman that needeth not to be ashamed, rightly dividing the word of truth," but this is what we must do.

October 8

Shalom is a well-known Hebrew phrase that is also used as a greeting. On the surface, shalom means "peace, hello, and goodbye." Because of its popularity, the true meaning of this term has been obscured. Shalom is greater than just the absence of war and it better than a fleeting feeling of happiness. Strong's Exhaustive Concordance defines "shalom" as, "to be well, happy, complete, in good health, prosperous, to be whole, and wholly." When the fruit of the spirit is listed, shalom is directly connected to love and joy. The walk in the spirit is a walk in shalom. It is a walk in peace and a walk in wholeness. The events of Luke, chapter 8 shed some interesting light on this.

"But as He went the people thronged Him. And a woman having an issue of blood twelve years, which had spent all her living upon physicians, neither could be healed of any, came behind Him, and touched the border of His garment; and immediately her issue of blood stanched. And the Savior said, 'Who touched Me?' When all denied, Peter and they that were with Him said, 'Master, the multitude throng Thee and press Thee, and sayest thou, Who touched Me?' And Messiah said, 'Somebody hath touched me; for I perceive that virtue has gone out of me.' And when the woman saw that she was not hid, she came trembling and falling down before Him, she declared unto Him before all the people for what cause she had touched Him, and how she was healed immediately. And He said unto her, 'Daughter, be of good comfort; thy faith hath made the whole; go in Shalom,'" – verses 42-48.

In this story, the woman with the issue of blood received her healing as she touched the tzittzit / fringes upon the garment of the Messiah. Her faith led her to reach out for the Savior, and the end result was her healing. Not only did the flow of blood stop; she was also completely made whole. Don't miss this. She was healed and made whole. She had found the Messiah. The void in her soul was now overflowing with shalom. Her life was now filled with Him. The woman had come face to face with the Prince of Peace and she would never be the same.

This fruit of safety and wholeness comes as we do the same. We can be whole as we seek to reach out to the Messiah and accept His plan for our lives.

Truth For Today

October 9

Y'shua told an interesting story in Luke 10. "A certain man went down from Yerushalyim / Jerusalem to Jericho, and fell among thieves, who stripped him of his garment, and wounded him, and departed, leaving him half dead. And by chance there came down a certain kohen that way: and when he saw him, he passed by on the other side. And likewise a Levi, when he was at the place, came and looked at him, and passed by on the other side. But a certain Shomronite, as he journeyed, came to where he was: and when he saw him, he had compassion on him, And went to him, and bound up his wounds, pouring in oil and wine, and set him on his own beast, and brought him to an inn, and took care of him. And in the morning when he departed, he took out two pieces of silver, and gave them to the innkeeper, and said to him, Take care of him; and whatever more you spend, when I come again, I will repay you. Which of these three, do you think, was a neighbor to him that fell victim among the thieves? And he said, He that showed rachamim to him. Then said Y'shua to him, Go, and do likewise," Luke 10:30-37.

Here, the Good Samaritan loved his neighbor. How did he love his neighbor? By showing mercy! Notice who passed by – a kohen / priest and a Levite. These dedicated servants of YHWH were no doubt busy doing the exact letter of the Law BUT they passed by an opportunity to show the love of the Law. This is a danger that we must conquer as well. As we seek to obey YHWH and walk according to His word, we must not forget The Spirit of the Torah. All of our actions should be towards the goal of loving YHWH and loving those that are near us. To show mercy is to love our neighbor.

This message of mercy is difficult because we like the idea of a "god in a box." It's much easier to kick the sin out of the camp and cast the sinner to hell than it is to love someone and meet their needs. Remember that Y'shua ate and fellowshipped with sinners, tax collectors, lepers and liars. He discipled prostitutes. Y'shua didn't just tell His followers to learn Torah – He admonished them to live the Torah. If Y'shua was with us today, He would no doubt have lunch with the homosexuals, unwed mothers, and welfare recipients at the local housing project. How can you show mercy and love to someone today? Don't just read about the Good Samaritan – be a Good Samaritan!

October 10

"Teshuvah" is the Hebrew term for "repentance." It literally means to "turn from and return to." Believers are to turn from their sinful life and return to the reign of YHWH and His ways. This is the message of the Gospel and the message of the kingdom: "In those days Yochannan / John the Immerser came, preaching in the Desert of Judea and saying, "Repent, for the kingdom of heaven is near," Mattitiyahu / Matthew 3:2.

True teshuvah is a total abandonment of an evil act and a direct effort to correct the wrong and do the right. It includes regret and sorrow but does not stop there. Teshuvah is characterized by joy – joy found in the renewal to connection with YHWH. It doesn't just promise to do better next time; it rights the wrong and really does do better next time. It's a direct command for every follower of the Bible, "Repent! Turn from your idols and renounce all your detestable practices," Ezekiel 14:6. Notice this verse includes repenting and turning from sin.

This was John / Yochannan's message and it became Y'shua's message. "From that time on Y'shua began to preach, "Repent, for the kingdom of heaven is near," Mattitiyahu / Matthew 4:17.

When a person repents, truthfully and selflessly repents the action of teshuvah returns the person to the kingdom rule of the Garden of Eden. When you walk in the Kingdom you take your rightful place as one who is "seated in high heavenly places and rules and reigns with Messiah"

Teshuvah, or turning from selfish sinful ways, should be our call to each other and to the lost world. As we make the call to "repent" we walk in the shadow of the prophets and priests of old that encouraged people to return to the rule and reign of heaven in their lives.

TRUTH FOR TODAY

October 11

"And YHWH Elohim called to Adam, and said to him, where are you? And he said, I heard Your voice in the garden, and I was afraid, because I was naked; and I hid myself. And He said, Who told you that you were naked? Have you eaten of the eytz / tree that I commanded you that you should not eat?" Beresheet / Genesis 3: 10, 11.

Just think about what happened to Adam for a minute. Here is a man, now hiding in the bushes that had "walked with YHWH in the cool of the day." Why would he be hiding? Adam recognized that he did something wrong and that this, most-certainly-known disobedience brought about the emotion of fear. As a child who had been caught red-handed, Adam hides from His Father.

Now get this, Adam wasn't afraid of snakes. He wasn't even scared of a talking snake that had tempted him to sin. But, Adam was terrified of the consequences of his actions. Adam hid because he recognized his fall from his exalted state and knew that a holy and awesome Mighty One would most-certainly know about the situation. Additionally, he recognized that YHWH would be displeased, for he and the woman had done precisely what they'd been forbidden! To Adam, fear was more than just reverence and awe; Adam was hiding because he had a reason to be scared to death! He was terrified! Adam, who had a perfect, unhindered, relationship with YHWH, was now hiding because of his sin! Likewise, even as children of our earthly parents, we know that doing what our earthly Dad says pleases him and does not warrant his wrath! Like Adam, we, as children of Abba YHWH, know that we are caught. We ought to fear our heavenly Father! Perhaps there is more to this issue than we have been taught. Perhaps we should do a little more hiding.

Friend, to fear YHWH is to possess an emotional trait equal to a leash on a dog. The fear of YHWH allows us to go and do as our Master allows. Then, our leash will be tugged if we go a little too far on our own. Our leash is pulled back when we don't see the impending danger of our actions or if we cross a dangerous line. It's the idea of "yirah YHWH." Scary Hebrew terminology? Not really. The phrase "yirah YHWH" is pretty simple to grasp. It literally means to be, "terrified, exceedingly dreadful, morally reverent, terribly frightened." We need the restraint that the yirah YHWH provides.

How can you show the fear of YHWH in your life today? What does the fear of YHWH mean to you? Study this subject further and allow your life to be changed by the fear of YHWH.

Truth For Today

October 12

"Every talmid / disciple fully trained will be like his teacher," Luke 6:40. This one verse encompasses this entire subject. Memorize and meditate on this verse. "Every talmid fully trained will be like his teacher," Luke 6:40! The purpose of discipleship is to exactly mirror your Master Y'shua.

First Fruits of Zion Ministry has written "in the first century the disciples of the Sages had four major tasks to perform. These tasks describe the cultural context of the institution of discipleship in the Gospels. It was the job of the disciple to memorize his teacher's words. It was a disciple's job to learn the tradition of how his teacher kept the commands of Elohim and interpreted the Scriptures. Every detail about the teacher was important to the disciple. A disciple's highest calling was to be a reflection of his teacher. A disciple studied to do the things his Master did. It was the job of the disciple, when fully trained, to raise up his own disciples. The goal was to pass the torch of discipleship from generation to generation."

Throughout the gospels the Savior made several distinct comments about discipleship, which express the marks, the goals, and the costs of being a talmidim of the Savior.

The Master Y'shua first made it clear that the goal of being a talmid / disciple was to be a living reflection of the Rabbi. "Every disciple will be like his teacher," says Luke 6:40. This following of the Master Y'shua consumes every part of life. Bible believers are called to eat the kosher foods He ate, wear the tzittzit / tassles He wore, have the beard that He had, and teach the message He gave. When it comes to being a talmid / disciple even the 'little' things matter.

The proof of being a talmid / disciple is given when we choose to follow Him wholeheartedly. This takes time. Discipleship is a marathon not a sprint! Discipleship is for those who follow the Moshiach for the long haul. "Y'shua said, "If you hold to my teaching, you are really my disciples. Then you will know the truth, and the truth will set you free," John 8:31. Being a disciple requires discipline! Can't you see the similarities between the words "disciple" and "discipline"? A talmid / disciple of Y'shua will reflect Y'shua to the world.

Truth For Today

October 13

"Mishpachah" is the Hebrew term for family. It literally means a 'circle of relatives, family, tribe or people." This term is used throughout the Scriptures in reference to the people YHWH chose to bring about His will in the earth. In the Tanakh, the word "mishpachah" was used to describe the larger patriarchal clan which included those persons related by blood, marriage, slaveship, and even strangers or sojourners.

"Bayit" is the Hebrew term for house. This word speaks of the physical place where the family, the mishpachah resides. It also literally means the 'household' or clan of people, temple, or residence. "Central to this household was the oldest male relative who was viewed as the 'father, master, and ultimate authority, thus signifying the family as the father's house. All who belonged to him were similar in beliefs and values. In Genesis 7:1 Noach and his household were directed to enter the ark. Beyond the household was the larger clan, the tribe, and the nation which were descendants of Abraham, the origin of the people of Israel," says the Holman Bible Dictionary.

YHWH is the Elohim of the family of Avraham, his children, and his grandchildren. Avraham was indeed fruitful when it came to imparting belief to his children! "For now YHWH hath made room for us, and we shall be fruitful in the land. And he went up from thence to Beersheba. And YHWH appeared unto him the same night, and said, I am the Elohim of Avraham thy father: fear not, for I am with thee, and will bless thee, and multiply thy seed for my servant Avraham's sake," Beresheet / Genesis 26:22-25. The same family mission given to Adam was passed to Noach and to Avraham, Yitzchak, Ya'acov and to us. We are to "be fruitful and multiply" in our families.

First we are to be fruitful by bearing love, joy, and peace in our mishpachah. Then as we show the fruit of the Spirit it will multiply automatically. Plants multiply through their seeds found in their fruit. Abraham passed down his faith by living it out before his mishpachah. We are to do the same.

October 14

"And she shall bring forth a son, and thou shalt call his name "JESUS" for he shall save his people from their sins," Matthew 1:21 (KJV). Here in Matthew chapter 1 the angel is giving to Mary the name of the Messiah. His name is defined for the reader as "he shall save his people from their sins." The Hebrew speaking, King of the Jews was given a Hebrew name – Y'shua. His name "Y'shua" is the actual Hebrew word for "salvation" or "deliverance." The Holman Bible Dictionary, a Baptist publication says "Jesus is the Greek form of Joshua, meaning "YHWH is salvation."

Most people will tell you that the name of the "Son of God" is Jesus. But, that's really not His name. Jesus is an English transliteration of a Greek substitute for the real name of the Savior. When the Messiah walked the face of the earth He was not called Jesus, He was called Y'shua.

A short study into how English Bibles were translated will lead you to understand that while scholars and scribes translated the texts of the Bible from the original Hebrew scrolls, they transliterated the names of Bible characters. A translation is transference of direct information from one language to another. While a transliteration is a changing of the original word to "make it fit" another language. Because of this "Moshe" in Hebrew became "Moses" in English. "Yermi'yahu" became "Jeremiah" and "Y'shua" became "Jesus." The problem with this type of conversion is that Jeremiah may be easier to read in English than "Yermi'yahu" BUT the true meaning, purpose, and identification with the original name is lost. Just think about this example; let's say your name is Robert. If you were to travel to Mexico, Russia, or China your name would still be "Robert." Though the people in these countries might speak "Robert" with their accent they wouldn't change your name to fit their language. Doing so would offend you. In this example, your name is Robert no matter where you go and no matter what other people call you. And the Savior's name is Y'shua regardless of what we have been taught in the past.

Changing Y'shua's name also changes our perception of Him and can easily lead to misunderstanding His words and His actions. Call Him by His true name and receive the blessings of speaking the emet / the truth. Y'shua is His name!

October 15

It is odd, but the majority of the mitzvot / commandments in the Torah, deal with the issue of temple worship and sacrifices. These commands are highly structured and controlled. Yet, even the rabbis have been perplexed that more of Torah is about sacrificing than any other subject. Why would Elohim use exact details to describe the sacrificial system, yet be silent in regards to the specifics of so many other issues? Why would the Bible speak about the correct way to kill animals and be silent on stem-cell research, global warming, and such?

The detailed commands surrounding the temple and tabernacle show us how meticulous we should be when coming before YHWH. Each of the sacrifices commanded in the Scriptures, from the red heifer to the Passover lamb, points to the Moshiach's true sacrifice.

The sacrifices can be confusing. The truth is that since the temple is not standing, one actually obeys the Torah by not offering animal sacrifices. However, none of the Torah has passed away. The mitzvot concerning the sacrifices remains. "The grass withers and the flowers fade, but the word of our YHWH remains forever," Yesha'yahu / Isaiah 40:8. The sacrifices before Y'shua pointed to His coming. However, they did NOT stop when He came. Y'shua went to the Temple and so did Paul. The book of Acts shows that the early believers continued to make sacrifices at the Temple. Rabbi Sha'ul (Paul) also made sacrifices and took vows at the Temple AFTER Y'shua's death. The sacrifices continued being made until the Temple was destroyed in 70AD. Just as the sacrifices before His coming pointed to Him, the sacrifices AFTER His coming pointed BACK to Him.

When Y'shua surrendered His life, He set the prime example for us to follow. May we pray, " ...not my will, but thine will be done." This is the whole issue of the sacrifices. Y'shua gave up his very life and has called us to do the same. We are to climb upon the altar and offer ourselves to Him. We are also to study the sacrificial system and apply what we learn. Praise YHWH for Y'shua's ultimate sacrifice!

October 16

Teshuvah / repentance is essential for a believer to have a relationship with YHWH, for it encompasses the broken and contrite heart the Almighty seeks in His people. During these end times, it will be the restoration of teshuvah in the lives of Bible believers that reaches the heart of Elohim and the hearts of man. To prove this point, the word "repent" can be found more times in the Book of Revelation than in any other book in the Bible. Teshuvah will play a huge part as the events of the end times unfold in the coming future.

"Great is Teshuvah for it makes the redemption of the Messiah come near," says the Talmud. Teshuvah will also usher in the coming full restoration of the nation of Israel, "and if they have a change of heart in the land where they are held captive, and repent and plead with you in the land of their captivity and say, 'We have sinned, we have done wrong and acted wickedly'; and if they turn back to you with all their heart and soul in the land of their captivity where they were taken, and pray toward the land you gave their fathers, toward the city you have chosen and toward the temple I have built for your Name; then from heaven, your dwelling place, hear their prayer and their pleas, and uphold their cause. And forgive your people, who have sinned against you," 2 Chronicles 6:37-39. Israel will be redeemed only through teshuvah. The Torah has promised that ultimately Israel will return towards the end of her exile.

Teshuvah is happening everyday as people believe the words of the Bible and return to YHWH, the Sacred Name, the Torah and the Biblical festivals.

Even the book of Acts speaks of this when it says to Israel, "Repent, then, and turn to Elohim, so that your sins may be wiped out, that times of refreshing may come from YHWH, and that he may send the Messiah, who has been appointed for you—even Y'shua. He must remain in heaven until the time comes for Elohim to restore everything, as he promised long ago through his holy prophets," Acts 3:19-21. This popular Messianic verse about the "restoration of all things" is based upon Israel doing teshuvah! Simply put, the motivating and benefiting factor of the restoration of all things is that teshuvah must come. Teshuvah will bring about, and usher in the restoration of all things!

October 17

Obedience is so important to relationship with YHWH and other people. Study, meditate and share these verses today:

- James 4:7, "Submit yourselves therefore to YHWH. Resist the devil, and he will flee from you."
- Isaiah 1:18-20, "Come now, and let us reason together, saith YHWH: through your sins be as scarlet, they shall be as white as snow; though they be red like crimson, they shall be as wool. If ye be willing and obedient, ye shall eat the good of the land: But if ye refuse and rebel, ye shall be devoured with the sword: for the mouth of YHWH hath spoken it. "
- Proverbs 22:4, "By humility and the fear of YHWH are riches, and honor, and life."
- Romans 6:17, "But YHWH be thanked, that ye were the servants of sin, but ye have obeyed from the heart that form of doctrine which was delivered you."
- Proverbs 19:16, "He that keepeth the commandment keepeth his own soul; but he that despiseth his ways shall die. He who obeys instructions guards his life, but he who is contemptuous of [YHWH's] ways will die."
- Hebrews 3:15, "While it is said, Today if ye hear his voice, harden not your hearts, as in the provocation. "If you hear YHWH's voice today, do not be stubborn..."
- Hebrews 4:11, "Let us labor therefore to enter into that rest, lest any man fall after the same example of unbelief."
- Romans 6:12, "Let not sin therefore reign in your mortal body, that ye should obey it in the lusts thereof. That is why you must not let sin reign in your mortal bodies or command your obedience to bodily passions."
- Luke 6:46, "And why call ye me, Master, Master, and do not the things which I say?"
- Matthew 7:21, "Not every one that saith unto me, Master, Master, shall enter into the kingdom of heaven; but he that doeth the will of my Father which is in heaven."
- 1 John 3:18, "My little children, let us not love in word, neither in tongue; but in deed and in truth.

October 18

Matthew 22: 34-40, "Hearing that Y'shua had silenced the Sadducees, the Pharisees got together. One of them, an expert in the law, tested him with this question: "Teacher, which is the greatest commandment in the Law?" Y'shua replied: "'Love the YHWH your Elohim with all your heart and with all your soul and with all your mind.' This is the first and greatest commandment. And the second is like it: 'Love your neighbor as yourself.' All the Law and the Prophets hang on these two commandments."

When Y'shua issued the great commandment he wasn't telling the people not to follow the other aspects of the Law. Just as if the government issued a new law concerning driving, people would still have to obey stop signs and the other safe driving rules. Love is to be the foundation of all Torah obedience. Here Y'shua insisted that the "Law and the Prophets" hang on man's relationship with YHWH and people. Yes, Israel is to love YHWH and love people...but how does a person do that? Easy! By following the Torah!

Our Heavenly Father wants us to be a people "set apart." This is accomplished through obeying the mitzvot and learning the principles behind the mitzvoth. We can't achieve full union with our Father through the mitzvot alone. We must totally give our life to Him and intensify our efforts toward His glorious end result of being like Him. King David understood this as he wrote, "I will delight in your mitzvot," -- Tehillim / Psalm 119: 24.

The truth is that YHWH is not satisfied with the deeds alone. He looks to the condition of the heart behind the deeds. He doesn't want us to worship our actions. He wants us to worship Him. He wants us to love him with all that we are. Before we obey, He wants us to question our actions. What is the reason behind our actions? How healthy is our heart? When we preach obedience to the Torah we fall short of the full and true message of the Torah. YHWH wants Torah-submission not Torah-observance. "This people draweth nigh unto me with their mouth, and honoureth me with their lips; but their heart is far from me," Mattitiyahu / Matthew 15:8 "He answered and said unto them, Well hath Esaias prophesied of you hypocrites, as it is written, This people honoureth me with their lips, but their heart is far from me," Markus / Mark 7:6.

Watch your obedience today. Do you obey out of love or out of selfish ambition? Are you trying to please YHWH through obedience or are showing Him your love when you keep the mitzvoth?

October 19

James 1:16 commands believers to be careful when laying a foundation of beliefs. It says plainly "Don't be deceived, my dear brothers." Deception is a dangerous tool used by the enemy to block a believer from fully understanding the scope of the word.

Deception will separate the Bible into two books: the Old Testament and the New Testament. Deception will present the "God" of the "Old Testament" as a mean old gray-haired being ready to punish sinners and the "God" of the "New Testament" as a kind, compassionate man. Deception will lead people down the path of manipulation, condemnation, and intimidation disguised as "grace." And deception will cause a well-built building to fall.

For the believer it is more important to do things right than it is to do the right things. This means that you should search out your own beliefs and prove them according to the Torah. If what you believe doesn't line up with the teachings of Moses then your foundation has some major faults. 1 Timothy 4:16, "Watch your life and doctrine closely." Persevere in them, because if you do, you will save both yourself and your hearers." Make sure how you are living is based upon the Word and not man's teachings or doctrine.

Not knowing the Torah leads to a spiritual life void of meaning and power. Y'shua said, "You are in error because you do not know the Scriptures or the power of YHWH."

Teachers and historians agree that the Bible is divided into seven segments:

1) The Torah, which includes Genesis – Deuteronomy 2) The Prophets, which includes Joshua, Judges, Samuel, Kings, Isaiah, Jeremiah, Ezekiel, and the Twelve Minor Prophets 3) The Writings, which is all the other books 4) The Gospels, Matthew through John 5) The Acts of the Apostles 6) The Letters, Romans through Jude 7) The Apocalypse, the book of Revelation

Notice that this list begins with the Torah, so obviously the Torah should be the starting place for all believers. Also notice that the Torah lays the blueprint for obedience and worship while all the other portions of the scripture simply magnify, elaborate on, and explain the Torah. The Bible is all about the Torah; the rest is just commentary.

TRUTH FOR TODAY

October 20

In the spiritual realm is the Creator and His angelic messengers. There are also fallen angels or demons. The word devil comes to the English language from the Greek "diabolos," which means "liar, thief, accuser, and enemy." The devil sure is real but he isn't some little red guy with a pointy tale and pitch fork. This idea and, indeed, much religious doctrine regarding the devil and hell is derived from Mesopotamian folklore and the classic book, "Dante's Inferno." The Bible never says that satan rebelled with a third of the angels or that satan is omnipotent or omnipresent. Satan exists but he's not what most people think.

The word "satan" is an ancient Hebrew word that is now used in the English language. The adversary's name was NOT changed from the Hebrew. Normally in English Bibles, the names for people and places were transliterated and transformed into a new term. For example, the Hebrew "Moshe" is rendered "Moses" and the name "Y'shua" is "Jesus" in English. Though every other name from the Hebrew scrolls was changed for English Bibles, the translators kept the hideous name of the adversary the same. In Hebrew, he is called "ha satan" which literally means "the accuser" or "the adversary." Ha satan is like a prosecuting attorney that confronts and accuses believers in an effort to belittle them and render them powerless.

The enemy comes against the saints daily to wear them down. He accuses and he lies. He is active in every type of rebellion yet he is NOT responsible for sin. Flip Wilson was wrong when he said, "the devil made me do it." Satan's part is to simply tempt, pry, and appeal to man's fleshly desires. He knows that most people are not going to murder, rob banks, and commit heinous sins. So, he comes as an angel of light and then attacks people at their points of weakness.

Though Hollywood portrays the enemy with unlimited power and strength, the Bible shows that deception is ha satan's ONLY power. This is how he attacks. He comes as a harmless idea or action and then misleads the masses. He deceived Adam and Eve in the garden and hasn't stopped since. Deception is tricky because a person doesn't know that he is being deceived. The Scriptures declare that ha satan has deceived the entire world – including ALL Christians. 1 John 5:19 says that the "whole world is under the influence of the evil one." This deception reaches the Baptists, Lutherans, and Pentecostals. Masons and Muslims are deceived as well. The enemy has deceived the entire world regarding his power and faith in general.

Pray today and ask YHWH to reveal to you any deception in your life.

TRUTH FOR TODAY

October 21

The Pew Research Center found that 79% of American Christians believe in the Second Coming of Christ. Today the doomsday prophet is not some bearded man with a placard proclaiming "the end is near." Instead, gloom and doom seems to be the message of newspapers, the Internet, and television. News headlines read like Bible prophecy. "And great earthquakes shall be in divers places, and famines, and pestilences; and fearful sights and great signs shall there be from heaven," Luke 21:11. Does this mean the Savior can come back any time soon or do certain things have to occur first?

Perhaps the surest sign that time is short is the return of the nation of Israel to the Middle East. To Israel the Almighty said, "I will take you from among the heathen, and gather you out of all countries, and will bring you into your own land," Ezekiel 36:24. Many prophecy teachers consider the reestablishment of Jerusalem as the capital city as THE sign of an impending apocalypse. "And they shall fall by the edge of the sword, and shall be led away captive into all nations: and Jerusalem shall be trodden down by the Gentiles, until the times of the Gentiles are fulfilled," Luke 21:24. The Messiah promised that the generation that saw such a miracle would certainly behold His return. (Matthew 24:34)

Does this mean that the return of Y'shua is imminent? Well, many sorrows have begun, but there is still more that must occur before the eastern sky splits. To state that "Jesus could return at any time" is to ignore numerous statements in the Scripture about the rise of an anti-Christ leader and a huge world war against the tiny nation of Israel. Yes, things are bad in various parts of the world but that doesn't mean the four horsemen of Revelation are riding.

How can a person prepare for the coming of Revelation? What should someone do about the mark of the beast? Some believers are storing food while others are learning survival skills. Many are buying gold in anticipation of the collapse of the dollar. The Savior addresses such a dilemma when He said, "Watch and pray always that you may be accounted worthy to escape all these things and stand before the Son of Man," Luke 21:36. The world will come to an end one day. Between now and then, it's important to focus on Spiritual growth. The pursuit of holiness will guide the believer through whatever the future holds. Listen to the voice of the Spirit. If you are led to take certain precautions then do so. But, don't allow fear of Armageddon stop you from living an abundant life. Who can you share this message with today?

October 22

The story is told of a student named Yahuda who traveled a great distance to see a famous Rabbi. When he arrived on Friday morning he immediately went to see the rabbi. As soon as Yahuda walked into the room, the Rabbi asked him not to stay for Shabbat. Yahuda was shocked. "But, rebbe, I have come so far. Is there any way I can spend Shabbat with you? The rebbe looked at him with sad eyes. "The truth is, my young friend, I see death surrounding you, and it seems that you are destined to die this Shabbat. It would be better for you to go to a small village and die there." The man was heartbroken. He had one more day to live. He took up his bags and dragged himself out of town.

While on the road, Yahuda encountered a wagon loaded with students of the Torah. They were singing loudly and having a wonderful time. The wagon stopped when they saw him going away from the city. "Friend," they yelled out, "you are walking the wrong way. The Rabbi is this way. Come with us." Yahuda turned slowly, and sadly said," I cannot go. The Rebbe has turned me away." The students surrounded him, "But why?" This was astonishing. The rabbi had never sent anyone away. Yahuda told them that he was going to die and that the rabbi had told him to find a small village. The students at once said, "Nonsense. You do not have to leave. Why should you die all by yourself, where you don't know anybody? Maybe the rebbe was worried that it would ruin our Shabbat. But it won't. Come. If you have to die, do it at the rebbe's table. This way, if you get sick, and need help, we will be there to hold you up. Come, friend, do not worry about a thing."

So Yahuda joined this singing group and climbed into the wagon. They started toward the town, and one of the students said to Yahuda," Friend, as long as you are going to die, if you have any money, we could use something to drink to keep us all warm." Indeed, he did have money. They stopped at the first store and bought a great deal of wine. Each time someone lifted his cup, he turned to the benefactor, Yahuda, and cried, "L'chaim, l'chaim, may you live a healthy, long life. " One after another of these blessings rang out. Yahuda actually began to get rosy in the cheeks. He forgot what the Rabbi had said. Actually, everyone was having too much fun to be thinking about death. And so, round after round, the blessings poured in for him.

They arrived at the Rabbi's home in a very happy state. When Yahuda once again went to greet the rebbe, the great Rabbi looked at him with amazement. The rebbe's large eyebrows arched, and he said, "It is wonderful, my young friend. The Angel of Death is gone. What a rabbi cannot do for his students, his students can do for one another with their blessings of l'chaim." What does this story teach you today?

TRUTH FOR TODAY

October 23

During prayer, when one says "baruch atah YHWH" or "baruch Hashem YHWH," one is expressing how praised and exalted YHWH is. The Talmud teaches that this proclamation of Yah's greatness is to be uttered regardless of hearing good news or bad news. We are to bless YHWH always. Speaking blessings helps the believer view all of life's events as neither good nor bad. Everything that happens is an opportunity for the Light of YHWH to shine and man to learn from YHWH. The Creator is blessed and exalted, regardless of the circumstances of man. The more one repeats this truth, the more one believes it.

"Rejoice always, pray without ceasing, in everything give thanks; for this is the will of Elohim," 1Thessalonians 5:16-18. This Newer Testament quote is in agreement with the Talmud in Menacoth E:18 that says "man is bound to say one hundred blessings daily." How is this so? In Devarim 10:12 it is written, "and now Israel, what does YHWH your Elohim require of you?" The word for "what" can also be interpreted to mean "one hundred." From here, the Rabbis have declared that man is to speak at least 100 blessings a day. This might at first sound crazy or legalistic. But, just imagine how a person's outlook on life would change if one would be in prayer all day, praising YHWH for the good, the bad, the mundane, and the extraordinary

Praying like this or blessing YHWH so many times isn't necessary for salvation but it sure doesn't hurt! Well, do you only do what is mandatory to live? Do we only eat, sleep, and breathe all the days of our lives? Certainly not. We fill our days with events, actions, and much more than just what is mandatory to continue life. We do things that bring benefit to our happiness and pleasure to our soul. These "fillers" are what brings meaning to existence. These blessings are what bring meaning to our faith.

How can you bless YHWH today?

October 24

The Torah is the story of the family of Israel. How the family began with just one righteous person named Avraham, its years in slavery, the exodus, the claiming of the Promised Land, and how it set up the theocratic government is all discussed in Genesis, Exodus, Leviticus, Numbers, and Deuteronomy. The Rabbis of Judaism have studied the Torah for thousands of years and have comprised a list of commandments found in the Torah. There is a total of 613 mitzvot that were given to the children of Israel as they began to set up their nation. It is important to understand that these mitzvoth, or commandments, were lovingly established for the nation of Israel for instructions on how to be the set apart nation that worships YHWH. All of these commands are eternal and all of these commands are for all of Israel. "The grass withers and the flowers fade, but the word of YHWH remains forever," says the Psalmist.

Never in the whole scriptures is the Law spoken against as bad or contrary to YHWH's will. In fact, in several places, especially in the Psalms, you can find peace, joy, and blessing come from keeping the Torah and meditating on it. Read Psalm 1 and Psalm 119 for a great example of how believers are to approach the Torah.

The Torah does not include the Oral Law or Talmud, the traditional Jewish teachings / interpretation of the Torah. For believers in Y'shua the Talmudic writings are available for reference but are not considered totally inspired by the Spirit. Nor should followers of the faith bank on the traditions of church fathers as doctrine. The Bible is the only word of YHWH.

The Torah explains exactly how a believer should eat, live, worship, treat other people, and marry. Almost all of life's experiences are discussed in the first five books of Moshe. And according to the Bible itself, not following these commands is sinning. According to the Holman Bible Dictionary, "sin is transgression of the law. Elohim established the law as a standard of righteousness; any violation of this standard is defined as sin. Deuteronomy 6:24-25 is a statement of this principle from the perspective that a person who keeps the law is righteous. The implication is that the person who does not keep the law is not righteous, that is, sinful."

The Hebrew word "aven" describes the crooked or perverse spirit associated with sin. Sinful persons have perverted their spirits and become crooked rather than straight. It also has the connotation of the breaking out of evil. Sin is simply the opposite of righteousness or moral straightness in the Torah. The most notable advancement in the New Testament view of sin is the fact that sin is defined against the backdrop of Y'shua, the living Torah, as the standard for righteousness. His life exemplifies perfection. The exalted purity of His life creates the norm for judging what is sinful." Do you allow the Torah to speak to your life regarding sin and righteousness?

October 25

"Lashon hara" is the Hebrew term the sages of our faith have named wicked words. Lashon hara literally translates "evil tongue" or "evil speech" or even "negative communication." It includes defamation, slander, slur, lying, harmful information, and perverse speech. We all know people who claim to be super-spiritual believers yet their witness is destroyed by a tongue full of gossip. Well, the Talmud says that lashon hara hurts three people: "he who relates it, he who accepts it, and of whom it is said."

The basis against speaking lashon hara is found in Vayikra / Leviticus 19:16 & 17, "Do not go about spreading slander among your people. Do not do anything that endangers your neighbor's life." Sefer / book of Shemot says, "do not spread false reports," and in sefer Titus 3:2 the word tells us to "speak evil of no man." Truly, these verses are speaking against more than just lying. Lashon hara is negative or perverse speech – even if it is true. A biblical example of lashon hara is the twelve spies who were sent to inspect the Promised Land. The ten fearful spies who brought a negative report were spreading lashon hara while the two spies whose report was made in faith spoke words that glorified YHWH. Either our words are full of faith or fear, life or death, blessing or cures.

Lashon hara also includes curses, either against another person or self-imposed. These statements can incorporate wishes of evil, negative confessions, and "you never" or "you always" statements. These declarations must be dealt with or they will bring negative penalties. Just as the ten spies who spoke lashon hara caused Israel to wander in the wilderness for 40 years, the lashon hara we speak will also bring harmful consequences. Yes, life and death is in the tongue and we, as believers must make a choice to either yield our tongue to the Spirit or suffer the effects of the sin of lashon hara.

Will you speak lashon hara today? How can you be careful to avoid this evil talk?

TRUTH FOR TODAY

October 26

As we are attached to the vine we will have good fruit. "If ye abide in me, and my words abide in you, ye shall ask what ye will, and it shall be done unto you," John 15:7. At the time of Y'shua, a golden grapevine was draped across the four columns at the entrance to the Temple. Josephus records that its beauty was such that it was known as a marvel of size and artistry. He said that all who saw it "admired with what costliness of material it had been constructed."

The Mishnah (an ancient Jewish writing) says that people would sometimes make a freewill offering at the Temple by purchasing a golden leaf, berry, or cluster which the priests would then attach to this huge vine. Often those who gave generously to the Temple had their names inscribed on the golden leaves. This was a custom that all were familiar with in Jerusalem. Can you imagine having your name written on a vine that hung at the ancient Israeli gate to the Temple?

When Y'shua depicted Himself as the True Vine, He was undoubtedly contrasting Himself with this artificial vine, suggesting that if the disciples would offer themselves to Him to the degree that people offered their substance to this golden symbol, the result would be abundant spiritual fruit.

As modern believers, we can sometimes focus on the religious symbol represented by the golden vine and miss the true vine of Messiah's life. May we always seek the YHWH Himself rather than religious activities that might make us feel good but do not help us walk with YHWH. Prayer and spiritual action (flowing in the gifts of the Ruach HaKodesh) must accompany our actions.

Y'shua called himself the vine in John 15. Read this chapter today for some amazing insights...

- John 15:2, "Every branch in me that beareth not fruit he taketh away: and every branch that beareth fruit, he purgeth it, that it may bring forth more fruit."
- John 15:6, "Y'shua said, "If a man abides not in me, he is cast forth as a branch, and is withered; and men gather them, and cast them into the fire, and they are burned."
- John 15:4, "Abide in me, and I in you. As the branch cannot bear fruit of itself, except it abide in the vine; no more can ye, except ye abide in me."

What did you learn from today's reading?

October 27

The Scriptures state, "if you belong to Christ, then you are Abraham's seed, and heirs according to the promise," Galatians 3:29. The original word for "seed" in this verse is "sperma," which means a "physical seed or descendant." Christians are not just spiritual heirs of salvation but direct physical descendants of Abraham, Isaac, and Jacob.

Jacob, whose name was changed to Israel, fathered twelve sons. These twelve sons and their families became known as the twelve tribes of Israel. Israel isn't just a small sliver of land in the Middle East. And Israel isn't just the Jewish people! Israel is the family of Abraham. This family's bloodline has been scattered all over the world. As Romans 2:29 states, the identity of all disciples is Israel.

History proves that shortly after the rule of King David, the nation of Israel was tragically split in two. In 586BC the two tribes that made up the Southern Kingdom were taken captive by the Babylonians. 70 years later many of these people returned to the Southern Kingdom, known as Judah, and rebuilt the Temple. They kept the Law and sought to worship as prescribed in the Scriptures. Today, the descendants from Judea are known as the "Jews."

In 722BC the Northern Kingdom, comprised of 10 tribes from Ephraim, were scattered by the Assyrians. These Israelites mixed into the nations. Thus they lost their identity and forgot their Hebrew heritage. They continued to grow and multiply, spreading their bloodline all over the world. A recent NBC News article estimates over a tenth of today's population is directly descended from this group. Today they are known as the "lost 10 tribes of Israel."

The Jewish people began their return to the Land in 1948. As fulfillment to Biblical prophecy in Ezekiel 37 and elsewhere, the lost tribes are slowly returning to their identity as people recognize they are Israel.

The Savior said in John 4:22, "Salvation is of the Jews." This doesn't mean that a person must convert to Judaism. This means the true pathway of faith can be found within the lineage and lifestyle of the Hebrews. All of the promises in the Bible made to Israel are for today. All of the commandments in the Bible that were given to Israel are also for today. Being Israel isn't about being Jewish, but recognizing the Almighty's true plan for man.

How can you live out your Israelite identity today?

October 28

John / Yochannan 8:31-3, "Then Y'shua said to those Jews who believed Him, "If you abide in My word, you are My disciples indeed. "And you shall know the truth, and the truth shall make you free." Romans 10:17, "Faith cometh by hearing and hearing by the word of YHWH."

Y'shua used the truth of the scriptures to confront the adversary. He said, "It is written" and then quoted the Tanakh. Freedom comes the same way today. All areas of our life – thoughts and actions – need the freedom promised by Messiah.

Many people have wondered, "can a believer have a demon?" The answer is simply "no." A believer cannot have a demon for a pet like a dog on a leash. But can a "demon have a believer?" Yes! Shadim can vex, offend, and oppress believers in our actions, theologies, thoughts, and areas of life.

We need to have our mind renewed and the deception decoded about deliverance. Truth be told, we have been deceived even in the area of deliverance.

Romiyah / Romans 12:1-2, "I beg you therefore, Israelite brothers, by the rachamim of YHWH, that you present your bodies a living sacrifice, kadosh, acceptable to YHWH which is your act of reasonable worship. And be not conformed to this olam hazeh / this world: but be transformed by the ongoing renewing of your mind, that you may discern what is that tov, acceptable, and even the perfect, will of YHWH"

The Catholic church doesn't have it all together concerning this issue, nor do the Charasmatics, or the Jews. To get the best Biblical understanding of deliverance ministry we need to look to the life and the ministry of Y'shua.

October 29

Judaism and Christianity focus on the methods of exorcism and deliverance. We are told to "say this prayer" and do that action. Some preachers even say we should talk to the demons and get to know their names and their hobbies. Y'shua's deliverance ministry was much MORE about staying free than just getting free. Y'shua was more concerned about the true freedom from demons than the methodology of deliverance. No holy water or strong hold exams required!

On most occasions, Y'shua shared the emet / truth of YHWH, told the demons to be quiet and come out, instructed the delivered person to stop their lifestyle of sin and seek YHWH. That's it! No 40 day deliverance prayer book needed!

Luka / Luke 4:33-37, "And in the synagogue there was a man, who had an unclean spirit of a shad / demon, and cried out with a loud voice, Saying, Leave us alone; what have we to do with You, Y'shua of Nazareth? Have You come to destroy us? I know You who You are; the Kadosh-One of YHWH. And Y'shua rebuked him, saying, Be silent, and come out of him. And when the Satan had thrown him in their midst, he came out of him, and hurt him not. And they were all amazed, and spoke among themselves, saying, What a word is this! For with authority and power He commands the shadim / demons, and they come out."

Because of the life, death, and resurrection of Y'shua we have authority over all unclean evil spirits. This authority is found in proclaiming the Word of YHWH in boldness and authority. It is the truth that sets people free. Will you speak the truth to someone today?

October 30

A pig may wear lipstick, but it's still a dirty farm animal. The pig will return to its ways of rolling in the mud and eventually smear the Mary Kay paint. Like this proverbial pig, we can reason excuses for Bible believers to celebrate Halloween but the argument does no good. Does it matter that this holiday is evil? Should it concern us that the customs involved in Halloween were once used to worship demons? "Test everything. Hold on to the good. Avoid every kind of evil," 1 Thessalonians 5:21-22. Halloween practices, from dressing in costumes to bobbing for apples, were once part of pagan worship. These actions are repeated today by people who are unaware or simply don't care about their true meaning. Time may have passed but their origins and true purpose remains the same.

The history of Halloween as an evil day of satanic worship can't be denied. It is a historical fact. "The observances connected with Halloween are believed to have originated among the ancient Druids, who believed that on the evening, Saman, the lord of the dead, called forth hosts of evil spirits, New Encyclopedia, Vol. 12, p. 152.

The Druids, an order of priests in ancient Britain, believed that on Halloween, ghosts, spirits, fairies, witches, and elves came out to harm people. They thought the cat was sacred and believed that cats had once been human beings but were changed as a punishment for evil deeds. From these Druidic beliefs comes the present-day use of witches, ghosts, and cats in Halloween festivities. The Druids had an autumn festival called Samhain, or summer's end. It was an occasion for feasting on all the kinds of food which had been grown during the summer," The World Book Encyclopedia, volume 9, page 25.

Is Halloween really an evil celebration? "During this time interval on October 31 the normal order of the universe is suspended, the barriers between the natural and the supernatural are temporarily removed, the sidh lies open and all divine beings and the spirits of the dead move freely among men and interfere sometimes violently, in their affairs," Celtic Mythology, p. 127. Clearly, Halloween is an ancient religious holiday that over time has evolved into a secular celebration. Be careful with this holiday.

The only thing worse than blatant outright Satanic worship is secret homage to demons that is disguised behind seemingly normal practices of society. Bible believers have been called to be "in the world but not of the world." Halloween is an excellent opportunity to take a stand for righteousness and be a light to society. Today ancient customs that were once used to conjure up spirits have been adopted by the modern world of entertainment and profit. Some cultures call it the "Day of the Dead" or "All Saint's Day" but the holiday is still the same.

October 31

Dressing up children for trick-or-treating or walking through a haunted house may be fun, but such actions are inherently immoral. The Scriptures tells us to "Abstain from all appearance of evil," 1 Thessalonians 5:22.

How did Halloween become part of the current society? What does church history teach? "The celebration of All Saints' Day is attributed to Pope Boniface IV, who dedicated the Roman temple, the Pantheon, to St. Mary and the Martyrs on the thirteenth of May, 610. Boniface set the day aside as a memorial to early Christians who died for their beliefs without official recognition of their sanctity, so that 'the memory of all the saints might in future be honored in the place which had formerly been devoted to the worship, not of gods but of demons'. The clergy encouraged their flock to remember the dead with prayers instead of sacrifices. People were taught to bake 'soul cakes' - little pastries and breads - to offer in exchange for blessings rather than trying to appease the spirits with food and wine. Villagers were also encouraged to masquerade on this day, not to frighten unwelcome spirits, but to honor Catholic saints. On All Saints' Day, churches throughout Europe and the British Isles displayed relics of their patron saints. Poor churches could not afford genuine relics and instead had processions in which parishioners dressed as saints, angels and devils. This religious masquerade resembled the pagan custom of parading ghosts to the town limits. It served the new church by giving an acceptable religious basis to the custom of dressing up on Halloween. In addition, the Church tried to convince the people that the great bonfires they lit in homage to the sun would instead keep the devil away - God's mortal enemy in the new Christian religion, "from Halloween, An American Holiday, An American History, by Lesley Pratt Bannatyne. Thanks to Pope Boniface, new Christian meanings were given to ancient pagan practices. Is this acceptable to the Almighty?

In Matthew 10:5 the Savior said, "do not go in the way of the pagans." Paganism is practices and principles that are not Christian or Biblical in origin. Many Pagan practices, like Halloween and other holidays have been borrowed by contemporary religion and thus polluted much of the faith. Bible believers should sway from such practices and create a distinction in the world.

Some churches compromise with Halloween alternatives like harvest festivals or Biblical costume parties. Again, such compromise is not allowed by the Scriptures. Pagan practices cannot be transformed into holy deeds. Paganism cannot be redeemed. Paganism can only be avoided. The truth about Halloween can be found in encyclopedias, Internet searches, and even on the History Channel television network. This holiday is evil and should be avoided by those who claim to worship the Almighty of the Bible. Lipstick on a pig doesn't change the pig and nothing can change Halloween.

November

Truth For Today

November 1

"Throughout the generations to come you are to make tassels / tzittzit on the corners of your garments, with a blue cord on each tassel. You will have these tassels to look at and so you will remember all the commands of the Almighty, that you may obey them and not prostitute yourselves by going after the lusts of your own hearts and eyes. Then you will remember to obey all my commands and will be consecrated to your Mighty One," Numbers 15:38-40.

This section of Scripture is not alone when it comes to speaking of the tassels or fringes that are to be worn by all Bible believers. Though you may not remember reading them, throughout the Old and the New Testament there are many references to tassels / tzittzit. The Israelites dressed with them. Zechariah 8:23 and Ruth 3:8 speak of them. And the Messiah Himself wore tassels. Remember the woman who was suffering from chronic bleeding? Luke 8:44 teaches that she was healed when she touched the tzittzit / tassles upon the Savior's clothing. "The Messiah observed this Old Testament requirement," says the Holman Bible Dictionary, a Baptist publication. Many people say they want to WWJD; multitudes say that they want to follow the Savior. Well, the Savior wore tzittzit / tassles! Which means His followers should do the same.

This doesn't have to be intimidating. This subject is pretty simple to grasp in light of the Scriptures. "For whoever is ashamed of Me and My words, of him the son of Man will be ashamed when He comes in His glory, and in His Father's glory, " Luke 9:26.

These twisted cords are to be a constant reminder of the Almighty and His promises. They serve as an outward sign of the covenant much like a wedding band. Tzittzit speak to the believer, and the world, that YHWH's word is still valid today. When someone once asked the Messiah what was required to receive eternal life the Savior responded "keep the commandments" in Matthew 19:16-17.

Nowhere in the Bible is the command to wear fringes rescinded. In fact the Scriptures say just the opposite; they are to be worn "throughout the generations to come." Saints should follow the Messiah's example and dress with strings attached to their outer garments. The Bible doesn't specifically say how these strings are to look, except they must contain a chord of blue and be visible. "Make tassels on the four corners of the cloak you wear," says Deuteronomy 22:12. Tzittzit are often worn by Jewish people on the ends of a four-corned shawl called a "tallit." They can also be attached to belt loops, t-shirts, or any other outer garment. A common thread is for the tzittzit / tassles to be tied with white string to make the blue stand out. The point is that the tzittzit / tassles are worn, and that the commandments of the Bible are remembered.

November 2

Have you read verses like Psalm 7:17, "I will sing praise to the name of the Lord most high" and questioned to yourself who you are supposed to be praising. Sure, you know it's the Lord, but does he have a name? Does the Father have a name?

In Exodus 3 Moses is attracted to the mountain by a bush that burns, yet is not consumed. Here he comes face to face with the creator of the universe. The Almighty wants Moses to deliver His people Israel from the bondage of Egypt's Pharaoh. The only problem is Moses is a novice when it comes to leading people. It's been many years since he left Egypt and he's doubtful the people will even accept this worn out old man as a legitimate deliverer sent from above. For the people to accept him, Moses needs a miracle. What Moses needs the YHWH is.

This is Moses' first encounter with the mighty one of Abraham, Isaac, and Jacob and it is certainly a memorable one. Here on Mt. Horeb the YHWH passes before Moses and "the YHWH said moreover unto Moses, Thus shalt thou say unto the children of Israel, The YHWH God of your fathers, the God of Abraham, the God of Isaac, and the God of Jacob, hath sent me unto you: this is my name for ever, and this is my memorial unto all generations." Here in Exodus 3:15 the YHWH reveals His eternal name as "YHWH." This is His memorial name forever.

Wow! The YHWH does have a name and it's not Billy or Bob - it's YHWH. From here on throughout the Bible, YHWH is used over 6,000 times exclusively as the name of the Father. According to most scholars YHWH is the personal name of the YHWH! In the King James Version whenever you see the words "YHWH" or "GOD" in all capital letters the translators are alerting you that YHWH is the Hebrew word behind the English. Whenever you find the English word "YHWH" in capital letters the translators are letting you know that the sacred name of YHWH is being used. The KJV sometimes even uses the poetic form of "Jah" to reference the mighty name of YHWH (see Psalm 68:4). But, YHWH says emphatically in Exodus 3 that YHWH "is my name forever, and this is my memorial unto all generations." This name was not intended to be hidden by scribes and translators; rather YHWH Himself gave it to man as a sign of His existence and as a means of personal relationship.

Other titles such as Adonai and El Shaddai are just that – they are titles that describe His attributes and actions. These titles have reference to qualities and are derived from actions. But "YHWH" indicates nothing but His existence. It is peculiar to HIM alone! Moses needed a miracle to give him favor before Pharaoh and the leaders of Israel. That miracle was found in the power of a name. Here YHWH reveals Himself to Moses as the great I AM, the One who Was and who Is, and who Is to come. And from here on out His name is exalted, revered, praised, and hallowed as YHWH.

November 3

“Moses said, "Please, show me Your glory." Then YHWH said, "I will make all My goodness pass before you, and I will proclaim the name of the YHWH before you. I will be gracious to whom I will be gracious, and I will have compassion on whom I will have compassion. You cannot see My face; for no man shall see Me, and live." And YHWH passed before him and proclaimed, "YHWH, YHWH, the elohim, merciful and gracious, longsuffering, and abounding in goodness and truth, keeping mercy for thousands, forgiving iniquity and transgression and sin, by no means clearing the guilty, visiting the iniquity of the fathers upon the children and the children's children to the third and the fourth generation." So Moses made haste and bowed his head toward the earth, and worshiped,” Exodus / Shemot 33:19-21, 34:5-8.

Moshe prayed to see YHWH’s glory. YHWH revealed Himself through calling forth His Name and His character traits. YHWH’s glory is the revelation of His nature. Moshe prayed for the glory and YHWH’s response was “I will cause my goodness to pass before you.” The goodness of YHWH is the kavod of YHWH. We see this again in the Newer Testament, in John 1:14. “And the Word became flesh and dwelt among us, and we beheld His glory, the glory as of the only begotten of the Father, full of grace and truth,” John / Yochannan 1:14. When the people saw the Messiah they were looking upon the glory of YHWH wrapped within human skin.

Both Moshe and David longed to see and experience the glory because they understood its significance. Moshe the great prophet and David the man after YHWH’s own heart prayed for His kavod. How about you? When was the last time you prayed to see YHWH’s glory? How often do you cry out to know YHWH more intimately?

When was the last time the presence of YHWH quickened your pulse? When was the last time you were surprised by YHWH’s glory? If we are honest, we can agree that most believers have lost the hunger for the kavod. We haven’t prayed for His glory and THEREFORE we haven’t seen His glory! Sure, we’ve worshipped and prayed and studied but have we really experienced His kavod, His goodness? Think about it. The only time the Bible says that Moshe bowed and worshipped was when He encountered the kavod. Moshe was amazed when the bush burned. But Moshe worshipped when the kavod came. We all need a fresh glimpse of glory.

TRUTH FOR TODAY

November 4

Long before the Savior called the twelve to follow Him, the Rabbi-talmid or teacher / student pattern was well established within the Biblical faith. The Torah, or the instructions for living given to Moshe in the first five books of the Bible, was passed from teacher to student. Teachers of the Torah, also called Masters or Fathers, would pass their interpretations on to their followers, who then would teach the original words of their Rabbi. For example, Paul (Sha'ul) was taught from the teacher Gamaliel, who was the grandson of the famous Rabbi Hillel. Rabbinical writings teach that the Rabbi is actually to be held in greater esteem than your birth father, "because your birth father brought you into this world, but your teacher brings you into the next world," says the Pirkei Ahvot. It is believed that Adam discipled Noach who discipled Avraham in the truth of Torah.

Jewish history and the Talmud prove in many places that teachers would have students that would be disciplined in their leader's ways. Many sages of Judaism from Hillel to Shammai had disciples. The Pharisees and the Sadducees were made up of groups of teachers and students. "Moses received the Torah from Sinai and transmitted it to Joshua (his disciple). Joshua gave it to the elders; the elders to the prophets, the prophets to the men of the Great Assembly. The men of the Great Assembly said three things, 'Be deliberate in judgment, raise up many disciples, and make a fence for the Torah,' Ahvot 1:1, 2. Discipleship is not a New Testament idea. Instead, making disciples is a continuation of a pattern already in place within the religion of Judaism when the Messiah came. This is where discipleship comes from. The purpose of the talmid / disciple was to totally duplicate the lifestyle of their Teacher. While a student only learns for a simple grade, a talmid or disciple learns because of an innate desire to become like his teacher.

Talmidim, or disciples, would learn what their Rabbi knew, talk like their Rabbi talked, pray as their Rabbi prayed, and keep the mitzvot just like their example did. All of this could take place as the talmidim stayed at the feet of their Rabbi, learning his ways. The talmidim would follow their Rabbi everywhere and model every aspect of their Master's life. Disciples would know exactly how their Rabbi felt about the hardest to understand areas of Torah. The Tanakh speaks about the talmidim's high honor of Torah "bind up the testimony (torah) seal the instruction among My disciples," says Isaiah / Yesha'yahu / Isaiah 8:16. Talmidim were taught to teach. Their main objective was to make more followers of their Rabbi. How are you making followers for Y'shua?

November 5

Many times we feel that we can protect ourselves from this world of pain. We reason that we're too busy to stop and pray. We act as if we can face the storms of life without the Holy One. Well, this is not the case. Exodus 14: 14 makes clear what our job is and what YHWH's job is when it comes to the problems of life, "YHWH shall fight for you, and you shall hold your peace." Here's our answer to those bad hair days, plain and simple. YHWH does the combat. All we have to do is hold on to Him. He fights for us while we hold our ground.

In Hebrew the words for "hold your peace" are "charash Shalom." Charash means "to scratch, to engrave, to plough; to be deaf, imagine, speak not a word, be still." This same word is used many times in the Scriptures for a "craftsman" or "engraver." The implication here is that we are to take the Shalom of heaven and carve it deeply into our situation. "Charash Shalom" is translated in many verses "hold your peace" but could also be understood as "engrave His Shalom upon your life," or "imagine His Shalom." Like a farmer ploughs through the top soil, we too should dig His shalom deep into the dirt of life. This is where the fruit of shalom is to be farmed – in our mind, soul, and heart.

Shalom is more than just a friendly greeting. It is an expression of our hope of salvation in the Messiah. It is a fruit of the Spirit. Like the peace offering during Temple times, because of Messiah we have fellowship with YHWH. "Therefore being justified by faith, we have shalom with Elohim through our Master Y'shua Ha Moshiach," Romiyah / Romans 5:1. Shalom is the Messiah's wholeness, His presence, and His joy in our life. YHWH has healed our brokenness through His shalom.

Will we just talk about His peace or will we strive to experience it? Like the woman with the issue of blood, let us reach out to the Messiah and allow Him to heal us. Trust YHWH and hold your peace today.

November 6

In the Scriptures, Light is the Hebrew word "ore." According to Strong's Exhaustive Concordance and Dictionary "ore" literally means "to be luminous literally and metaphorically: break of day, glorious, kindle, set on fire, shine." The word "ore" appears 5 times on the first day of creation, representing the 5 books of the Torah that bring Light to the world. Light is also used as a synonym or Hebrew idiom for the Torah. So when the scriptures speak of Light they are in fact many times speaking of the Word of YHWH, the Torah. "Thy word is a lamp unto my feet and a light (Torah) unto my path," says Tehillim Psalm 119.

Light is also symbolic of the Messiah Y'shua. "When Y'shua spoke again to the people, he said, "I am the light of the world. Whoever follows me will never walk in darkness, but will have the light of life," Yochannan / John 8:12. So, light symbolizes Torah and light symbolizes Y'shua. This makes sense because Y'shua is the living Torah! Living in the Light is living in the Spirit or in deveikut.

In the Sermon on the Mount Y'shua told his followers to let their light shine. He was saying to let their Torah observance shine as a witness to everyone that the Messiah has come. Y'shua was reminding them of the principle that inside man is the darkness of the flesh yet inside man was ability to choose Light. "Let your light (Torah) so shine before men, that they may see your good works, and glorify your Father which is in heaven," Mattitiyahu / Matthew 5:16

When Light/Torah/Y'shua penetrates through the darkness, lives are changed, hurts are healed, and people understand their purpose in life. What happens in your life occurs to bring forth Light. This doesn't mean YHWH has causes the events that are occurring but He has allowed them. Stuff occurs to provide you an opportunity to grow. Hardships and suffering fan the flame of Light in the darkness of your world.

Light and darkness cannot coexist at the same time. Remember that in the beginning the Father said "let there be Light" and from the darkness came Light. Well, by simply understanding how Light shines you will discover your destiny as a person and find fulfillment in your life. How does the Light of Messiah shine? How do you experience your purpose in life? How do you deveikut? First of all, when you have a sickness, hardship, trial, problem, or area of conflict don't immediately ask YHWH to remove it. When you have a bad day, don't go into super rebuking mode and cast out everything including the demon of wrinkled clothes. Before you pray to the Father to release you from a sickness, hardship, or circumstance first ask Him what you are supposed to learn from it. Maybe you are going through something just to learn a specific lesson in the process. Y'shua knew in advance that Kefa / Peter would be tempted to deny the Messiah but Y'shua did not pray that the trials would be removed. Instead Y'shua prayed that Kefa's "faith would remain." Kefa / Peter needed the trials to prove his faith!

November 7

Do you ever wonder why a lion tamer would enter the circus ring with bar stool? Sure, the whip and the pistol make excellent tools to ward off dangerous lions, but why a bar stool? Well, lion tamers use the stool to confuse the lion. They hold the stool out by its seat and push the ferocious animal away with the legs. The lion actually tries to watch all three legs at one time and gets dizzily confused. The stool is the most important item used in the ring because it messes up the focus of the beast. The king of the jungle is nothing but a baby kitten when its focus is off. We, too, are easily off guard when our concentration is broken and we don't control our thoughts.

In life, we get that on which we focus. The person at the summit of a mountain did not fall there. Likewise, it takes effort to reach the pinnacle in our spiritual life. If we are negative, if we complain a lot, if we just can't seem to have any joy, then, we probably need to really engage our focus. There is a Biblical principle that states that we reap what we sow. When we plant positive, Torah-based thoughts, our life will then reap positive, Torah-based outcomes. This doesn't mean that things will be easy or everything will go our way. What engaging our focus does though, is preparing our soul to look to YHWH in the good times and in the bad. If we are focused, then we are determined, we are alert, and we are unwavering. The key here is found in Tehillim 16:8. "I have set YHWH always before me. Because of his right hand, I will not be shaken." We need to memorize this pasuk / verse. We can write this verse down on a note card and keep it before ourselves. "I have set YHWH always before me. Because of his right hand, I will not be shaken," Psalm 16:8.

Looking to YHWH, really seeing His hand throughout the events of our day will lead to a great transformation. The seemingly bad things that happen will turn into learning events. The good things will bring about praise to the Almighty. The humdrum stuff will provide even more opportunities to learn and rejoice. "Remember the YHWH in a distant land, and think on Yerushalyim / Jerusalem," says Yermi'yahu / Jerusalem 51:50. And even Rabbi Sha'ul wrote that, "whatever is true, whatever is noble, whatever is right, whatever is pure, whatever is lovely, whatever is admirable—if anything is excellent or praiseworthy—think about such things," Philippians 4:8. We can't let our mind wander, or wonder, when things go crazy or bad. We look to YHWH. We pray. We control our thoughts. We can ask, "How would Y'shua handle this situation?" Reading the Torah daily strengthens our renewal. What we put in is what we get out. Now is the time to start putting Torah into our mind.

November 8

Unity is key to this walk of faith. We must decide to meet and agree with one another in unity. At the congregation we should put personal differences and personal convictions aside and come together in unity. We should submit to leadership, support leadership, and work with leadership to accomplish YHWH's will. There is no such thing as the perfect congregation or the perfect rabbi or teacher. You will never find a group that has it "all together" or a teacher who is 100% doctrinally correct. Instead of seeking perfection we should seek unity and a leader with a heart that longs after YHWH. With unity comes trust. Trust is NOT supporting the leader when you agree with him. Trust is supporting the leader when you DON'T agree with him. Y'shua prayed for this type of relationship in John 17. This is the real Master's prayer – he wanted us to be unified! Do you trust your leadership? Have you submitted yourself to a local congregation? Unity is like the oil of anointing that fell from Aharon's beard.

What else came from the priest's beard? This blessing of YHWH and the name of YHWH! We see another connection in Song of Solomon 1:3, "Your Name is as anointing oil poured forth." YHWH's name is like the anointing oil. His name is power. His name is powerful. His name and His blessing is what changes us to be made in His image. We learn in Isaiah 10:27, that the "anointing breaks every yoke."

Whatever is holding you back or causing you pain is broken by the anointing / by the name of YHWH! We should take hold of this blessing and His name and begin to expect! We should start expecting good things to happen! We should see ourselves as blessed and lay hold of the promises that YHWH has set before us. Romans 4:21 states that Avinu / Father Avraham was fully persuaded that what YHWH had promised, YHWH was fully able to accomplish. We too must be determined to believe YHWH and recognize our lives as blessed beyond all measure.

One Chassidic Rebbe taught the following: "Thus shall you bless the Children of Israel — bless the Hebrew people as you find them. Do not look for the best or the most important, or for the greatest scholars or righteous men, for every Israelite deserves to be blessed."

Remember that this is the priestly blessing that was to be spoken by a kohen. In the Bible and in Judaism a person is born a priest. In the true faith we are all BORN AGAIN as priests of YHWH as seen in Exodus 19 and 1 Peter 2:9. We are to use, speak, pray, sing, and meditate upon this blessing. May we walk in His way and know that we have been blessed from the very face of YHWH!

Truth For Today

November 9

Every day on earth has 1440 minutes in it. We all have the same amount of time. How we choose to spend this time, is left up to us to decide. One of the greatest attacks of the enemy is to keep us busy and preoccupied with the lies of this physical world. We worry about work, we complain about our food, and we fret about our momentary physical happiness. All the while, our spiritual self seeks the hidden, spiritual world. If we really want to tap into the spiritual power of the Creator the only question to answer is 'how badly do I want it?' Will we take the time to dwell in His presence? Will we press on through the mask of this world? Here are three simple steps to help break away from this world of lies and cleave to Elohim. Our desire has to be coupled with actions. If we want to be different, then we have to start acting differently. If we want to tap into YHWH's power, we have to "come near to YHWH and He will come near [to us]," says the book of Ya'acov.

Consider these verses today:

- Hosea 10:12, "Sow to yourselves in righteousness, reap in mercy; break up your fallow ground: for it is time to seek YHWH, till he come and rain righteousness upon you."
- Deuteronomy 4:29, "But if from thence thou shalt seek YHWH thy Elohim, thou shalt find him, if thou seek him with all thy heart and with all thy soul."
- Matthew 6:33, "But seek ye first the kingdom of Elohim, and his righteousness; and all these things shall be added unto you."

Take a few of the 1440 minutes of your day today and seek YHWH more.

TRUTH FOR TODAY

November 10

When we read in Genesis about Adam and Eve we see that YHWH did some pretty good things for them. YHWH created the man, gave him a wife, let him name the animals, put him in the garden, and met his every need. If anyone had a reason to be thankful it was Adam. But, do you ever see Adam offering sacrifices in the creation account? Do you ever see Adam saying, "Thank you" in Genesis? Is Adam a grateful person? It doesn't seem that Adam is grateful and appreciative of all that YHWH has done for him. Instead of being thankful, Adam rebels. He sins. When we are not grateful, we are susceptible to sin, to problems, to negativity, and to pain. On the other hand is the example of Abraham. Every other page in the Torah we read of Abe offering sacrifices. He is tested but he makes it through because he is focused on praising YHWH. Gratitude makes a huge difference in our lives.

Being thankful is YHWH's will for our lives. It is interesting to note that the Jewish Rabbis have taught that after the coming of Messiah all Temple sacrifices would cease EXCEPT for the "korban todah." The "korban todah" is the "thanksgiving offering. Even though Y'shua has come and even though the Temple does not stand, we can still offer the sacrifice of praise and thanksgiving. The korban todah will never cease because we will never cease to offer thanks throughout all eternity. When we keep Messiah in mind we will forever be thankful. He is the reason we offer our lives to obedience and our mind to be renewed. In Him we live and move and have our being. In view of Y'shua sacrifice we give ourselves to heaven. We obey and we love because He first loved us. "In view of YHWH's mercy, offer your bodies a living sacrifice to YHWH. To be conformed to the pattern of this world but be transformed by the renewing of your mind," Romans 12:1-2. May we be thankful today and every day for all that YHWH has done for and in us.

TRUTH FOR TODAY

November 11

The expressions of the mouth prove who we are. The words we speak are indications of what the state of our heart is. For example, the Bible divides people into two categories; first there are the wise whose words are full of encouragement, truth, love, and inspiration. Second there are the wicked or foolish, whose words are many and whose expressions are often evil.

The wise person speaks blessings continually. "The tongue of the wise brings healing," Mishlei / Proverbs 12:18. The scriptures also say in Mishlei / Proverbs 15 that a wise or righteous person speaks the right things at the right times and these words are pure and pleasant. Can you bless those who disagree with you? Can you release others who choose to serve YHWH differently with a blessing?

The Bible often speaks of the wicked in reference to the terms of their speech. The wicked are full of violent words, which are of little value. The wicked pour forth curses like a sewer and "the advice of the wicked is deceitful," Mishlei / Proverbs 12:5. To the wicked Y'shua said, "You brood of vipers, how can you who are evil say anything good? For out of the overflow of the heart the mouth speaks," Mattityahu / Matthew 12:34. While the righteous pray that YHWH will use their tongue for good, the wicked say "our lips are our own, who is YHWH over us," Tehillim 12:4.

The story is told of Rabbi Gamaliel who once told his servant that he was going to have some friends over for dinner and the servant should prepare the absolute best meal. The servant was to go to the local market and purchase the best food for the guests of honor. Dinnertime came and Rabbi Gamaliel and his guest found their table full of tongue. Surprisingly even, tongue was the main course served to the distinguished guests. The Rabbi wasn't happy about this and inquired to the servant why tongue was purchased and served. The servant replied, "I got the best for your dinner party, Rabbi. Isn't the tongue the organ of scalability, the organ of eloquence, kindness, and worship?" The Rabbi then responded, "Well if this is the best food to offer then tomorrow we will have another meal and I want you to go to the market and get the worst food possible." The next day the servant went to market, prepared the dinner, and served beautiful dishes for the Rabbi and his guests. Again all of the food served contained tongue in some manner or another. By now the Rabbi had lost his patience and said, "Didn't I tell you to get the worst food at the market?" The servant said, "Sir I did get the worst food possible. Isn't the tongue the organ of folly, the organ of blasphemy, of defamation, lying, and cursing?"

Will you use your mouth to speak blessing today?

TRUTH FOR TODAY

November 12

The scriptures are true; man is not under the curse of the Law but under grace or "chesed" through trusting in Y'shua as the Messiah. Galatians 3:13 & 14, "Messiah redeemed us from the curse of the law by becoming a curse for us, for it is written: 'Cursed is everyone who is hung on a tree.' He redeemed us in order that the blessing given to Abraham might come to the Gentiles through Y'shua Ha Moshiach, so that by faith we might receive the promise of the Spirit." But, the "age of grace" did not necessarily begin with Messiah. Grace, or loving kindness, began in Eden when Father YHWH forgave man for breaking His Torah.

"For it is by grace you have been saved, through faith—and this not from yourselves, it is the gift of Elohim—not by works, so that no one can boast," Ephesians 2:8 & 9. This popular New Testament does not mean that the Law has been done away with. "I tell you the truth, until heaven and earth disappear, not the smallest letter, not the least stroke of a pen, will by any means disappear from the Law until everything is accomplished," Mathew 5:18. Everything has not been accomplished and the new heavens and new earth are not present, therefore the Law has not "disappeared." The Torah remains to define exactly what sin is and to be the guideline for all believers to follow.

Romans 6:15 makes this point well, "What then? Shall we sin (break the Torah) because we are not under law but under grace? By no means!"

"Sin is lawlessness" so to live an obedient life to Elohim then man must follow the Law and not break it!

It is all a matter of WWJD? Yes, the popular phrase "What Would Jesus Do" sums up how believers should live their lives. Y'shua followed the Law in perfection and commands all believers to do so also.

Understand that the Law was not some religious system that the Messiah just happened to be born into; rather it was and is Elohim's pattern and plan for man. Y'shua kept the seventh day Sabbaths, celebrated the feasts, ate kosher, and was circumcised all according to YHWH's Torah. Y'shua did not come to "do away with the Torah" (Matt.5:17-20) but present to the world a perfect life that it should strive to be a model. All of the commands of the Bible still apply and are still valid as a life-style for all Messianics, see 1 John 3:4,7,22,24;5:2-3.

TRUTH FOR TODAY

November 12

Y'shua, the living Law or living Torah, is the standard of righteousness and all Scripture remain as valid for practice if the circumstances remain available today or disobedience will lead to sin. For example, the Temple laws cannot be performed without a Temple in place. And many commands cannot simply be performed unless a person is living in the Promised Land under the rule of a Torah keeping government. Also, several of the laws given in the Torah were only for the Levites and can only be carried out by the Levitical priesthood.

Rav Sha'ul uses Galatians chapters 1 and 2 to defend the good news. Chapters 3 and 4 are written to define the good news and in chapters 5 and 6 Sha'ul shows followers how to display the Gospel. Paul begins the letter detailing his own conversion through the power and message of the Moshiach / Messiah.

Apparently, some false teachers brought a different message than Rav Sha'ul so he wanted to write and expose their impure motives (6:12 & 13). These false teachers espoused the doctrine that one must be circumcised and follow the Torah to be born again. But, Sha'ul told the Messianic Community "do not frustrate the grace of Elohim: for if righteousness comes by the law, then Messiah is dead in vain." The Law/Torah is not to be followed for salvation through performance. Follow the Torah for sanctification yes, but for salvation no. Think about that last statement during your day today. We are to follow the Torah for sanctification but not salvation. Praise YHWH for His gift of salvation in grace through faith in Y'shua.

November 13

Though salvation is not earned by our earnest following of YHWH's commandments the Torah is still to be obeyed. Y'shua said in Matthew 5:17 &18 "Think not that I am come to destroy the law, or the prophets: I am not come to destroy, but to fulfill. For verily I say unto you, till heaven and earth pass, one jot or one tittle shall in no way pass from the law." The book of Romans says the Torah is "holy, righteous, and good." And Isaiah 40:8 says, "The grass withereth, the flower fadeth: but the Torah of our Elohim shall stand forever."

The Torah was given by YHWH as a way of life. Even in Galatians we are called to follow it in this manner. Galatians 5:13 & 14, "For, brethren, ye have been called unto liberty; only use not liberty for an occasion to the flesh, but by love to serve one another. For all the law is fulfilled in one word, even in this; Thou shalt love thy neighbor as thyself." Here love is esteemed as the way to follow the Torah. Galatians 6:2 goes even farther to prove this point, "Bear ye one another's burdens, and so fulfill the law of Messiah." By walking in love, through bearing the burdens of our neighbor we are walking out Torah. For it is in the Torah, in Leviticus 18:18, that the commandment "thou shalt love thy neighbor as thyself" is first found.

The freedom spoken of throughout the book of Galatians is in reference to the freedom mankind has been given to walk out the Torah without the bondage of man's traditions and the fear of evading ones eternity. "Christ hath redeemed us from the curse of the law, being made a curse for us: for it is written, Cursed is every one that hangeth on a tree," Galatians 3:13. This verse shows that Y'shua freed us from the curse quoted in Galatians 3:10, "For as many as are of the works of the law are under the curse: for it is written, Cursed is every one that continueth not in all things which are written in the book of the law to do them." The curse that Y'shua took upon Himself enables believers to walk out the commands of the whole Bible without the fear of being cursed for not fulfilling the instructions completely. Through His life and sacrifice He did not bring the Torah to an end, rather He modeled how we as followers should live the Torah.

Who can you share this message with today?

November 14

The Savior said, "Shabbat was made for man." It is a gift to us so that we can experience Heaven's rest. It's a day to emulate YHWH. Ephesians 5:1 says to "Imitate YHWH like dear children." YHWH rested on the Shabbat day and we are to do the same. He didn't stay in bed until two o'clock because he was tired and weary. "Have you not known? Have you not heard, that the Everlasting Elohim, YHWH, the Creator of the ends of the earth, faints not, neither is tired," Isaiah / Yesha'yahu 40:28. He rested to enjoy His creation. We are to do the same. Stop working, stop creating, stop whatever and simply seek Him. When was the last time you took a long walk and just prayed aloud? Or sat outside and just watched the blowing of the leaves? Or played with the children? Or read the Bible out loud to just hear His word? When was the last time you simply joined with others in unity and spent a day seeking YHWH with your whole heart? Shabbat is a day to seek YHWH and hear from His Spirit.

One rabbi described Shabbat as compared to a king in the field. The king's usual place is in the capital city, in the royal palace. Anyone wishing to approach the king must go through the appropriate channels in the palace bureaucracy and gain the approval of a succession of royal secretaries and ministers. He must journey to the capital and pass through the many gates, corridors and antechambers that lead to the throne room. His presentation must be meticulously prepared, and he must adhere to an exacting code of dress, speech and mannerism upon entering into the royal presence.

However, there are times when the king comes out to the fields outside the city. At such times, anyone can approach him; the king receives them all with a smiling face and a radiant countenance. The peasant behind his plow has access to the king in a manner unavailable to the highest ranking minister in the royal court when the king is in the palace. The Shabbat is a time when the king is in the field of the earth. Will you be ready to meet him on this next Shabbat?

Hebrews 4 says "there remains a Sabbath rest for us." Shabbat is a day to rest in Him – to totally fall into his arms and trust Him that everything will be ok. That's what trust is. When you trust someone, you are simply believing that everything is going to be alright. Do you trust YHWH enough to keep Shabbat with joy and shalom?

Also in Hebrews 4, the Bible makes it clear that we fail to enter into the rest of Shabbat because of unbelief. We fail to trust YHWH and therefore we fail to experience His rest. "There remains therefore a Shabbat-keeping duty to the people of YHWH. For the one that is entered into His rest, he also has ceased from his own works, as YHWH did from His. Let us labor therefore to enter into that future Shabbat, lest any man fall into unbelief.

November 15

Praying three times a day is a lofty idea and tradition that has long held the Hebrew people. This tradition was already present during the times of Dani'el and David. "Evening, morning and noon I cry out in distress, and he hears my voice," says Tehillim (Psalms 55:17). Also Dani'el 6:11-14 shows it was the keeping of this tradition that landed Dani'el in the trouble he was in.

First, by keeping this custom, your day can start with the shacarit" or "morning or dawn" time of devotion. Many people spend "quiet time" each day with the Almighty; yet have nothing structured to do each day. Praying in the morning has its origin with Avraham. "Early the next morning Abraham got up and returned to the place where he had stood before YHWH," Beresheet / Genesis 19:27. The Gospels teach that Y'shua the Messiah also kept this tradition. He prayed in the morning. "Very early in the morning, while it was still dark, Y'shua got up, left the house and went off to a solitary place, where he prayed," Mark 1:35. So from these examples it is easy to see that praying in the morning is a Biblical idea.

Prayer in the afternoon is modeled after the "mincha" or "afternoon offering." In traditional Judaism this prayer time has its origin in Beresheet / Genesis 24:63. Eliyahu / Elijah also battled the false prophets of ba'al in the afternoon. The afternoon was also the time that Y'shua offered Himself upon the tree in Mattitiyahu / Matthew 27:45.

During times of spiritual refreshing many people say they want to return to the faith as it was in the book of Acts. If this is true for you, then you should consider afternoon mincha prayers. Possibly one reason why the believers in the book of Acts had power is because they prayed three times daily. "One day Kefa / Peter and Yochannan / John were going up to the temple at the time of prayer—at three in the afternoon," Acts 3:1. Cornelius also had his vision during afternoon prayer in Acts 10:1-3. Afternoon prayer time is an occasion for miracles from heaven!

"Maariv" or "avrit" are the Hebrew terms for "evening prayers." This time of prayer has its beginning with Ya'acov who experienced the Almighty in the evening in Beresheet / Genesis 28:11. Evening time is also when the Israelites were led out of Egypt. It was during this time of nightly prayer that Dani'el had an exciting encounter. "While I was still in prayer, Gavri'el, the man I had seen in the earlier vision, came to me in swift flight about the time of the evening sacrifice," Dani'el 9:21. "May my prayer be set before you like incense; may the lifting up of my hands be like the evening sacrifice," says Tehillim 141:2. Y'shua also did many powerful works during the nighttime setting. Rabbi Sha'ul (Paul) received a vision of YHWH at night in Acts 18:9. From these examples it is pretty easy to see that praying three times a day is a Biblical custom that has many advantages. Would it hurt you to take time to pray and seek YHWH three times a day?

November 16

When Y'shua celebrated Passover he lifted the cup and said "this is the blood of the brit / covenant, unless you drink my blood and taste my flesh you cannot enter the kingdom of YHWH." Again, He was proclaiming that life is in the blood. His blood was the fulfillment of the prophetic blood of the Nile and the lamb's blood on the doorposts. We read in the book of Mattitiyahu / Matthew that the disciple that betrayed Y'shua dipped his hand in the dish before the cup was offered. Even in the face of death, Y'shua offered eternal life to those at his table, including the one who would trade his life for silver. The blood covers all sin and all reproach, no matter what you have done, said, or thought. "And the dahm / blood of Y'shua ha Moshiach His Son cleanses us from all sin," Yochannan Aleph / 1 John 1:7. Forgiveness is found in the blood.

The story is told of a man who has built up a huge debt and can't pay it. The man's wealthy boss comes along and pays the bill without telling his employee -- then calls him in to give him the good news. The man sits down, is handed the dossier of debts, and flips through the pages to see the list of bills he has accumulated. He thinks, "I'll never be able to pay all this. They're going to throw me in jail!" When the CEO sees the man's fearful countenance, he is perplexed. He says, "Excuse me -- did you look at page one?" The man flips back to the first page, which reads: "Paid in full." Our sins have been covered the debt of sin has been paid in full!

When Y'shua returns the world will once again see a sign of blood and be given another chance to repent. On that day millions will look upon the one whom was pierced and call upon Y'shua for salvation. As we await His return let us continually keep the dahm / blood of Y'shua in our minds. It is through His blood that we have been redeemed, forgiven, and given the victorious life. "And they overcame him by the dahm / blood of the Lamb, and by the word of their testimony; and they loved not their lives even to the end," Revelation 12:11.

We have the right to draw a faith blood line that the enemy cannot cross. By remembering the blood of Y'shua and applying it to the door posts of our lives, no evil can triumph over us.

"Knowing that you were not redeemed with corruptible things, like silver, or gold, from your futile spiritual conduct received by tradition from your ahvot / fathers. But with the precious dahm / blood of Moshiach, as of a Lamb without blemish and without spot," 1 Peter / Kefa Aleph 1:18-25. Think on this today.

TRUTH FOR TODAY

November 17

The Holy Spirit or Holy Ghost as we know Him in English is actually "Ruach HaKodesh" in Hebrew. This Hebrew term brings to mind more than just some mystical manifestation of the Almighty. "Ruach HaKodesh" is literally the "set apart breath." This power is the direct presence of YHWH. The Set Apart Spirit is eternal and can be found throughout the Bible.

Again, the importance of using the Hebrew name brings to mind the correct Biblical understanding of just who the Holy Spirit is. The term "Ruach HaKodesh" relates to us that the Holy Spirit is actually the "breath of the Holy One." The Ruach HaKodesh is the divine presence manifest. It not just some ghost that flutters and flies about doing anything it desires. The Ruach HaKodesh is a power, not a person. Nor is it the third person in the "trinity."

John 4:24 teaches that YHWH is a Spirit, which means He is a person. But YHWH's Spirit is power, "And the Spirit of Elohim moved upon the face of the waters," Gen 1:2. "He breathed on them and said receive the Holy Spirit," John 20:22. The Holy Spirit is part of YHWH from YHWH but is not necessarily YHWH. In Hebrew and Greek breath is "Pneuma." Pneuma means breath. In each reference of the "Holy Spirit" or just "Spirit" in the Scriptures it is clear that it is a power and not a person. Take for example Acts 1:8, "But ye shall receive power, after the Holy Ghost is come upon you." Romans 15:13 also speaks to this, "Now may the Elohim of all hope fill you with all joy and peace in believing, that ye may abound in hope, through the power of the Ruach HaKodesh."

Many times in the Scriptures the Holy Spirit is referred to as the "Spirit of truth" but just because the Ruach HaKodesh has so many titles does not make the Ruach a person. The Ruach is also seen as fire, wind, rain, oil, and a dove (see Acts 2:2,3, John 7:37-39; Zechariah 10:1; Hebrew 1:9; Ephesians 1:13; Matthew 3:16).

Unfortunately it seems that many religious groups have lately encouraged people to "worship" the Spirit. This was never meant to be. The Spirit or Ruach has come to bring power not receive praise. The Ruach points to Y'shua who in turn points to and gives all glory to Father YHWH. The Spirit is the power of YHWH present on this earth reflecting the personality of YHWH Y'shua.

How can you "walk in the Spirit" today?

Truth For Today

November 18

Worshippers during temple times would bring special offerings to YHWH. These gifts were sacrifices that often included the slaughter of animals for a meal that would be consumed by the priest and the giver. Other offerings, of blood or wine, were poured out upon the altar and used as a libation. One of the most interesting sacrifice in the Scriptures is the "thanksgiving offering" or in Hebrew, the "korban todah."

Before any of the sacrifices can be understood we should have our mind renewed to the truth of this subject. Today we shudder at the idea of killing an animal for an offering but people during ancient times used the sacrificial system as a way of drawing near to YHWH. In fact, the Hebrew word "korban" means "offering" or "gift." As a gift, the offering was like an engagement ring that brought the worshipper and YHWH closer together. Intimacy is the purpose of the engagement ring and any sacrifice to YHWH. The "korban todah" or the "thanksgiving offering" was to bring the giver closer to YHWH through a special meal of praise.

The Hebrew word "todah" is derived from the Hebrew word "yadah" which means "to praise" or "to know." This word "yada" is used in the story of Adam and Eve to explain how they "knew" each other and begot children. When we praise YHWH we become pregnant in the Spiritual sense and can bring about great things for the kingdom. Together the phrase "korban todah" means "a gift of thanks that brings intimacy." During temple times, the korban todah was a totally voluntary offering. It wasn't commanded or even expected from people. It was simply a willing sacrifice that would signify the greatness of YHWH and the deliverance of His power. Psalm 54:6 says, "Willingly I will sacrifice to you; I will give thanks to your name, O YHWH, for it is good."

The korban todah was a huge offering that was intended for much more than just one person. The Thanksgiving Offering consists of 4 different types of bread (10 loaves of each type), as well as an animal offering (cow, sheep or goat) that had to be consumed in one day. (And you thought your Thanksgiving turkey meal was a big deal!)

From this willing sacrifice we can learn many things about our worship and the offerings of praise we offer today. Of course we can see the similarities between the korban todah and the meal of Thanksgiving we share each year. On the fourth Thursday of each November, families join together for turkey and sides to celebrate the goodness of life. While Christmas is all about receiving the holiday of Thanksgiving is all about gratitude and appreciation of what we already have. And though Thanksgiving comes only once a year, the thanksgiving offering could be offered at any time by anyone. We can and should give thanks at all times. This is YHWH's will for our lives.

November 19

YHWH gives His righteousness to man as a reward/gift for faith and trust exhibited through Torah obedience. "And it shall be our righteousness, if we observe to do all these commandments before the YHWH our Elohim, as he hath commanded us," Deuteronomy 6:25. Romans 2:13 makes this point very clearly, "it is those who obey the law who will be declared righteous."

The Holman Bible Dictionary, a Baptist publication, says "rather than being a ladder that Israel climbed to get to YHWH, the Torah was understood to be a divine program of the maintenance of a healthy relationship between Israel and Elohim (Leviticus 16.) YHWH expected Israel to keep the Torah not to earn merit but to maintain the status Elohim had already given the nation. As Israel kept the covenant, the nation was righteous. Thus human righteousness in relation to Elohim was understood as faithful adherence to the Torah (Leviticus 19.)"

Right standing and fairness with YHWH is granted as a GIFT when a person walks in accordance with the mitzvah of the Bible, "a righteous man does what is lawful and right," Ezekiel 18:5. Man cannot and has never merited himself spiritual righteousness. "For there is not a righteous man upon earth, that doeth good, and sinneth not," Ecclesiastes 7:20. According to the Bible tzedekah / righteousness simply cannot be earned. Tzedekah must be given by YHWH to repentful and faithful man, "If we confess our sins, he is faithful and just and will forgive us our sins and purify us from all unrighteousness," 1 John 1:9. Because of sin man does not deserve tzedekah / righteousness but YHWH gives it when man turns from the path of wickedness and returns to Yah. Romans 5:19, "For as by one man's disobedience many were made sinners, so by the obedience of one shall many be made righteous." Breaking or not obeying the Torah is sin which leads to unrighteousness. "All unrighteousness is sin," 1 Yochannan / John 5:17.

It was because of Abraham's faithful obedience he was considered a righteous person or a tzadik in YHWH's eyes. "Avraham / Abraham believed Elohim, and it was accounted to him for righteousness," says the Scriptures. Avraham's belief and faithful trusting led him to follow the instructions of the Almighty, thus making Avraham a tzadik.

Abraham is called the father of our faith. As his children we must believe YHWH and act upon that belief by acting righteous. How do you behave righteously? That's simple. Just do what is right and your righteousness will shine to others. Choose to do right today.

November 20

When it comes to the faith of the Bible, there is a bad taste in the mouth of millions of people. All over the world, the hungry have been fed a faith that is anything but fulfilling. At best the church system meets the physical needs of the helpless while at worst the system is full of money hungry preachers and perverted priests. Yet in some groups, the pattern of discipleship is being restored. The truth of being a talmidim or "disciple" is washing away the yuck of self, religion, and pain. True discipleship can usher in unity of the faith that is so badly needed. Being a talmid / disciple feeds the spiritual hunger found in so many people.

While Evangelical Christianity teaches evangelism and numbers Y'shua's call in the great commission was to make talmidim. This was his pattern for ministry and his call for us today.

Most people aren't going to share the gospel with 500 people a month and hear 500 prayers of repentance. This type of ministry is NOT practical or productive.

But, could YOU disciple just ONE person every six months? Could you teach the love, mercy, and commandments of Torah to just one person in a six month period? That may not seem like much BUT, after twelve years, if each continued to reproduce themselves every six months, there would be no one left on earth to evangelize. Y'shua's method of raising talmidim to reach the lost, would have produced nearly 6 BILLION disciples in less than thirteen years!

Discipleship is the pattern Y'shua used and is the pattern that should be used today. Make a decision today to be a student of Y'shua, the living word. Turn from a life of sinful torahlessness and be immersed in the Name of Y'shua. Sit at the Savior's feet, and learn from the Tanakh and the Brit Chadasha / Newer Testament. Memorize your Rebbe's words. Learn what traditions are Biblical and keep them. Be diligent in what you decide. Put fences around your life to help you stay pure. Raise up and mentor other talmidim / disciples like yourself. As you do these things you will return to the way the faith was meant to be lived and your spiritual life will finally bring fulfillment.

November 21

Y'shua came to offer a clear path to eternal life. "Ani ha derech, ani ha emet, ani ha chayim - I am the way, the truth, and the life," John 14:6. He gave His life and shed His blood to pay the penalty for sin. In John, He spoke to a leader of the Jews and said emphatically "you must be born again." Even Jews must each personally accept Y'shua to enter the Kingdom of Heaven.

Part of Y'shua's mission was to restore the relationship with YHWH that had been lost by Adam. Y'shua was to right the wrongs of Adam and to accomplish what the first Adam could not. Indeed, the Bible actually calls Y'shua the "second Adam." Therefore to truly grasp and understand the second Adam we need to have a true biblical understanding of the first Adam. By knowing more about the first Adam, we can have better knowledge of the second.

In the beginning, Adam was created perfect. He was given dominion and power over the entire earth. YHWH instructed him to guard the garden. Adam was commanded not to eat from the tree of the knowledge of good and evil. These instructions or "torah" from YHWH were to protect Adam and help him accomplish all that YHWH had for him. If Adam would have obeyed then He would have been blessed abundantly. He was given simple instructions, yet He disobeyed. He broke the "torah" that was given to Him by Abba YHWH. We all know that he fell from perfection. This disobedience to Torah is what the Bible calls "sin." Sin is violation of the will of YHWH. Sin is selfishness. A person sins when they enact their desire to receive for self alone. Different religious groups differ on their definition of sin but 1 John 3:4 clarifies the subject. "Whoever commits sin commits lawlessness; sin is lawlessness," 1 John 3:4.

Adam's sin caused humanity and even the ground of the earth to fall under certain curses. Indeed, the serpent, the woman, and the man each faced punishment because of the disobedience of Adahm. Adahm and Eve (Chava in Hebrew) were kicked out of the Garden of Eden and separated from the presence of YHWH. Death entered the world because of the first sin. "The wages of sin is death," says Romans 3:23.

Though Adam tried to cover his sin with fig leaves, he failed to truly deal with the sin issue. This shows us that man alone cannot correct the sinful nature. Nothing you do will counteract the effects of sin. Good deeds, tithing, prayer, church attendance, or even obedience to the commandments will not conquer the power of sin. Sin leads to death. The only answer to sin is blood atonement. Genesis / Beresheet 3:21 shows YHWH making the first couple coats of skin to wear in place of their frail fig leaves. This is the first example of animal sacrifice to cover the penalty of sin. Hebrews 9:22 says, "Without the shedding of blood there is no remission of sin." Man sinned and the wages of sin is death. Blood was shed as a covering of all sin.

TRUTH FOR TODAY

November 22

In as much as tzedekah or "righteousness" is a gift it is also a deed carried out by faithful man. In today's Jewish society if you mention the word tzedekah, most Jews will recognize that this is a term used for giving aid, charity, or assistance to the poor. Again, this understanding sheds more light on the true meaning of the word. Tzedekah, or fairness and justice, is a gift from YHWH that is to be passed on towards fellow mankind. This teaching is based on Proverbs 29:7, "The righteous considereth the cause of the poor: but the wicked regardeth not to know it." Tzedekah is like a two sided coin.

Remember that in the book of Devarim / Deuteronomy Moshe told Israel to pursue righteousness from Avinu / our father YHWH. It is not just something that is handed over lightly. Y'shua commented on this when he said, "Blessed are those who hunger and thirst for righteousness, for they will be filled," Mattityahu / Matthew 5:6. Before the filling of righteousness comes there must be a hunger and a thirst; before you scratch your back it has to itch; and before man considers another man to be righteous there must be justice and fairness.

Moshe and Y'shua were calling the people to chase after and seek tzedekah / righteousness as a gift from YHWH AND as a behavior towards man. Notice Y'shua said to "hunger and thirst for righteousness" and not just "have a spiritual understanding and confess." Tzedekah in YHWH's sight is given by trusting obedience to Torah commands while tzedekah in man's sight is given by how a believer treats other individuals. Torah obedience always leads to life. "The labor of the righteous tendeth to life," Proverbs 10:16. Biblical righteousness shows others a life of Torah submission. "But the path of the tzedek is as the shining light, that shineth more and more unto the perfect day," Proverbs 4:18. Or to paraphrase "The works, actions, and words of a tzedek is a shining light to the world, pointing to the day of the full restoration of tzedekah / righteousness."

Now take a moment and reflect on the duality of tzedekah / righteousness and the ten words. The ten words, or the Ten Commandments as they are better known as, were given to Israel from YHWH as some basic guidelines for living. These mitzvah are divided into rules for man's two most important relationships – that with individuals and that with the Almighty. Just like the ten words, righteousness has everything to do with how other people are treated. "The righteous man leads a blameless life; blessed are his children after him, Proverbs 20:7. Again, tzedekah is received from YHWH and is performed towards man. Avi Ben Mordechai once wrote that "righteousness always begins with trusting faith in the Name. However, trusting faith is not the end of the story. Trusting faith produces actions of righteousness and therefore, the righteous are ultimately defined as those who walk in the covenant of YHWH of the Torah as found in Devarim / Deuteronomy 6:25." How can you live out tzedekah today?

November 23

Thanksgiving is more than just a time to gather with family to enjoy a good meal. It is a religious holiday that calls Americans to reflect upon their life, examine their ways, and give thanks for their blessings. History records many lessons that can be learned from Thanksgiving. In 1621 a group of religious Puritans left England to seek a land that would allow them religious freedom. Persecution pushed them to make a "pilgrimage" to America. It is from this journey that they became known as the "pilgrims."

These Christian Puritans were conservative Bible believers who kept much of the Law of Moses. They were similar to the "Quakers" in that they promoted separation from pagan influences that still remain in Protestant Christianity. The Puritan's desire was to achieve and preserve simplicity or 'purity' of faith that they felt had been lost amid Christianity. They came to America in order to continue the reformation away from Catholicism and the Church of England. The Pilgrims very likely kept a kosher diet and celebrated the feast days of Leviticus 23 like Passover or Sukkot. "The pilgrims based their customs on the Bible," says Gloria Kaufer Greene, a food and holiday expert. "They knew that Sukkot was an autumn harvest festival, and there is evidence that they fashioned the first Thanksgiving after the Jewish custom of celebrating the success of the year's crops."

When the Pilgrims settled in America they were greeted by the Wampanoag Indians. History records about 90 Indians and 50 Puritans shared a meal of thanksgiving together sometime between September 21 and November 9. Based on the numbers, it was probably the Indians who brought most of the food. And let us not be mistaken, it was the Pilgrims who were the visitors and not the hosts to this meal.

For that first and historic Thanksgiving there was no football and there was most likely no turkey. The only written eye witness account of the first meal was by colonist Edward Winslow to his friend in England. In this letter he states that they ate "wild fowl and venison." He doesn't specify if there was deep fried turkey or not.

This year, millions will bow to their television and pay homage to sports. Most will gorge with the gods of appetite and gluttony. Some will recognize the spiritual significance of this day, reflect upon their blessings and give thanks. May we all desire to be like the Pilgrims and return to a purity of faith that has been lost over the years.

TRUTH FOR TODAY

November 24

Read, think on, or study these verses today. Ask YHWH to help you have a thankful attitude!

- Chronicles 16:8, "Oh give thanks to YHWH, call upon His name; Make known His deeds among the peoples."
- Psalm 107:29-32, "He caused the storm to be still, So that the waves of the sea were hushed. Then they were glad because they were quiet; So He guided them to their desired haven. Let them give thanks to YHWH for His lovingkindness, And for His wonders to the sons of men! Let them extol Him also in the congregation of the people, And praise Him at the seat of the elders."
- 1 Chronicles 16:34, "O give thanks to YHWH, for He is good; For His lovingkindness is everlasting."
- Psalm 34:1, "I will bless YHWH at all times; His praise shall continually be in my mouth."
- Psalm 100:4, "Enter His gates with thanksgiving, And His courts with praise. Give thanks to Him; bless His name."
- Jonah 2:9, "But I will sacrifice to You With the voice of thanksgiving. That which I have vowed I will pay Salvation is from YHWH."
- Ephesians 5:3-4, "But immorality or any impurity or greed must not even be named among you, as is proper among saints; and there must be no filthiness and silly talk, or coarse jesting, which are not fitting, but rather giving of thanks."
- Colossians 3:15, "And let the peace of Messiah rule in your hearts, to which indeed you were called in one body; and be thankful."
- 1 Timothy 4:4-5, "For everything created by Elohim is good, and nothing is to be rejected, if it is received with gratitude; for it is sanctified by means of the word of YHWH and prayer."
- 1 Thessalonians 5:18, "in everything give thanks; for this is YHWH's will for you in Messiah Y'shua."

November 25

Does Matthew 9:13 confuse you? It is here that Y'shua said, "I desire mercy and not sacrifice, now go and learn what that means." How many of us have done what Y'shua commands here? He tells us to go and learn what this statement means. Is Y'shua ending the sacrificial system with these words? Or is there a better understanding to His statement?

First, Y'shua is NOT saying that the sacrifices should end. Those that heard His words were already making their offerings at the Temple. He simply said that they didn't need to kill any more animals. Nor did they need to kill any fewer animals either. The problem was that their formula was wrong. They gave YHWH the burnt offerings but their actions were mostly through religious or selfish intentions. Rachamim (mercy) and devotion are the MAIN part and idea of the sacrificial system. Though some sacrifices were for praise, thanksgiving, covenant making, or food for the priests, we know that there was much blood shed for the remission of sins.

Many times, the animals were sacrificed to stop judgment upon a person. When Y'shua spoke these words He was actually quoting a text from the Tanakh. The people to whom He spoke knew exactly what He was talking about. He wasn't saying "just show mercy and don't bother with the Torah." Instead, He was reminding the multitudes of the importance to show mercy through the Torah. Y'shua was quoting the book of Hosea and revealing a mystery about His coming and the restoration of the nation of Israel. All sacrifices before Y'shua pointed to His coming. All sacrifices after His coming pointed back to Him. Y'shua is the ultimate sacrifice. Everything in the Torah, including the sacrifices is about Him!

TRUTH FOR TODAY

November 26

Chanukah is an eight-day festival, commemorating the historic victory of the Maccabee family over the Syrian tyrant, Antiochus, in the 2nd century B.C. The story of this holiday is amazing.

We are told that after conquering Jerusalem, to show his utter contempt for the Holy One of Israel, Antiochus sacrificed a pig on the altar and put to death any Jewish people who dared to observe the commands of Torah. Basically, Antiochus declared that everyone had to become Greek and no one could study Torah or continue in true worship. Judah Maccabee, son of Mattathias, an Hasmonean priest, lead a revolt against this man and his Hellenistic oppression. Noted for courage and military genius, Judah led an outnumbered, unskilled guerilla army to a decided victory over superior Syrian forces. Upon entering Jerusalem, they cleansed and rededicated the Temple. In honor of this victory, an eight-day festival was begun. Since that time, Judah Maccabee has become a popular folk hero, a symbol of religious freedom and national liberation. The hero of Hanukkah plays, poems, and songs, he is considered a type of the Jewish warrior in modern Israel, he symbolizes many military victories over great odds. Tradition interprets the name "Maccabee" to mean "hammer," a symbol of Judah's might and the power of the Israeli people.

Chanukah not only commemorates this military victory but also a tradition about the miracle of oil. According to legend, after the Maccabee family gained control of the desecrated temple they found only one undefiled cruse of oil. Tradition tells us that one day supply lasted a full eight days thus keeping the temple menorah lit while allowing time to consecrate more oil. That is why this is an eight day festival and the Chanukah menorah has nine branches

Some groups light the candles from right to left, while others light the menorah from left to right. You can even start your own tradition and light all the candles each night. Or maybe place a menorah in the window so others can be blessed by seeing it. Some people believe that everyone in the home should light their own menorah while other families just have one menorah. That's the beauty of this holiday – you can do what is best for your family. Its eight days to rejoice in being YHWH's special people and the victory we have over paganism and anti-torah living. It is about the spiritual survival over many who have liked to destroy Israel through cultural assimilation. More recently the custom of gift giving has become a major part in this festival but doing such should not be expected. Chanukah isn't a replacement for Christmas. Instead it is a set apart time to rejoice in YHWH's Messiah and share the truth of the Scriptures with others. Let your light shine before men that they may glorify your Father in heaven!

TRUTH FOR TODAY

November 27

Have you considered what the Bible and the Apocrypha say about Chanukah? Read below for more details on this holiday:

- John 10:22-23, "And it was at Jerusalem the feast of the dedication, and it was winter. And Y'shua walked in the temple in Solomon's porch."
- Dani'el 12:11-13, "And from the time that the daily sacrifice shall be taken away, and the abomination that maketh desolate set up, there shall be a thousand two hundred and ninety days. Blessed is he that waiteth, and cometh to the thousand three hundred and five and thirty days. But go thou thy way till the end be: for thou shalt rest, and stand in thy lot at the end of the days."
- I Maccabees 1:21-24, "Insolently breaking into the Sanctuary, he removed the golden altar and the lampstand for the light with all its fittings, together with the table for the loaves of permanent offering, the libation vessels, the cups, the golden censers, the veil, the crowns, and the golden decoration on the front of the Temple, which he stripped of everything. He made off with the silver and gold and precious vessels; he discovered the secret treasures and seized them and, removing all these, he went back to his own country, having shed much blood and utter words of extreme arrogance."
- I Maccabees 4:2-7,52-59 "They found the sanctuary deserted, the altar desecrated, the gates burn down, and vegetation growing in the courts as it might in a wood or on some mountain, while the storerooms were in ruins. They tore their garments and mourned bitterly, putting dust on their heads. They prostrated themselves on the ground, and when the trumpets gave the signal, they cried aloud to Heaven....On the 25th of the ninth month, Kislev, in the year 164 BCE, they rose at dawn and offered a lawful sacrifice on the new altar of burn offering which they had made. The altar was dedicated at the same time of year and on the same day on which the gentiles had originally profaned it. The whole people fell prostrate in adoration and then praised Heaven who had granted them success. For eight days they celebrated the dedication of the altar, joyfully offering burn offerings, communion and thanksgiving sacrifices. They ornamented the front of the Temple with crowns and bosses of gold, renovated the gates and storerooms, providing the latter with doors. There was no end to the rejoicing among the people, since the disgrace inflicted by the gentiles had been effaced. Judas, with his brothers and the whole assembly of Israel, made it a law that the days of the dedication of the altar should be celebrated yearly at the proper season, for eight days beginning on the 25th of the month Kislev, with rejoicing and gladness."

November 28

Ya'acov / Jacob saw the vision of the ladder when he rested his head upon a stone. The Hebrew word in this passage for stone is "eben" which is spelled with the ancient letters aleph – bet – nun sofeet. This term for stone contains the Hebrew word for son – ben. This word is spelled bet - nun sofeet. From the word play, we can see that when Ya'acov rested in the Son's stone, he was able to experience the presence of Y'shua in a profound way. It was an awesome manifestation!

Ya'acov's ladder was more than just a dream. It is an actual portal to heaven. It is the place where angels ascend and descend to earth. Jacob's ladder – the person of Y'shua of Nazareth – is the gate to Father YHWH (Genesis 28:13). A ladder is like a bridge that grants access to something higher. This is the perfect representation of Y'shua. We are told in Philippians 2:5 to put on the mind of Christ / Messiah. We are also told in Isaiah 55 that "His thoughts are not your thoughts, neither are your ways His ways. For as the heavens are higher than the earth, so are His ways higher than your ways, and His thoughts than your thoughts." As we climb Jacob's ladder our life, our mind, our heart, and our will changes. Our thinking is elevated and each rung takes us closer to being like Him.

A ladder involves effort. Y'shua is not an escalator that briskly pushes us higher. We must make the effort to move forward with Him. This effort is to first be made in "tefillah" or prayer. The sages of Judaism have recognized Yaakov's ladder as the power of prayer. The Hebrew word for ladder is "sulam." The numerical value of its letters is 136. The word "kol" has the same numerical value. "Kol" is Hebrew for voice, as in the voice of prayer. When we pray and seek YHWH's face we can come into His presence and transcend the cares of this world. Our worries and concerns change when we begin to see things from His perspective. From the height of a tall ladder everything below seems so much smaller. Through Tehillim we become one with YHWH's thoughts we see the bigger picture. Our huge problems are actually very small from the height of YHWH's glory.

How much time do you spend in prayer climbing Jacob's ladder?

November 29

Tis the season to be jolly? In remembering Christmas we cannot forget that tree decorating, gift giving and even the date of December 25th were part of winter celebrations long before Christ came. Christmas before Christ? Though the celebration of Christmas seems "harmless" and modern, it has actually evolved from ancient times. The Encyclopedia Britannica reports that "The traditional customs connected with Christmas have developed from several sources as a result of the celebration of the birth of Christ mixed with the pagan agricultural and solar observations at midwinter. In the Roman world Saturnalia was a time of merrymaking and exchange of gifts. December 25 was also regarded as the birth date of the Iranian mystery god Mithras, the Sun of Righteousness."

On their website, www.christmas-tree.com, The Christmas Tree Farm Network reveals, "The Romans celebrated the winter solstice with a feast called Saturnalia in honor of Saturnus, the god of agriculture. They decorated their houses with greens and lights and exchanged gifts. They gave coins for prosperity, pastries for happiness, and lamps to light one's journey through life. Centuries ago in Great Britain, woods priests called Druids used evergreens during mysterious winter solstice rituals. The Druids used holly and mistletoe as symbols of eternal life, and place evergreen branches over doors to keep away evil spirits. Late in the Middle Ages, Germans and Scandinavians placed evergreen trees inside their homes or just outside their doors to show their hope in the forthcoming spring. Our modern Christmas tree evolved from these early traditions. Legend has it that Martin Luther began the tradition of decorating trees to celebrate Christmas. One crisp Christmas Eve, about the year 1500, he was walking through snow-covered woods and was struck by the beauty of a group of small evergreens. Their branches, dusted with snow, shimmered in the moonlight. When he got home, he set up a little fir tree indoors so he could share this story with his children. He decorated it with candles, which he lit in honor of Christ's birth." The idea sounds ridiculous, but the truth of Christmas is a part of history. The Pilgrims who first settled in America understood this. History records that the Pilgrims actually outlawed any celebration of Christmas, from 1620 to 1681. And England's parliament outlawed Christmas in 1643.

Today, most people are more concerned about checking off their wish list than learning about the history of Christmas. The majority of parents are guilt-free while they mislead their children with stories of Santa and flying reindeer. Surely the excitement of gifts and the family traditions outweigh the truth of any ancient customs? Proverbs 19:2 says differently, "It is not good to have zeal without knowledge, nor be hasty and miss the way." The excitement and good feelings of Christmas does not outweigh its pagan roots. The knowledge of Christmas past taints the celebration of Christmas present and future. The end does not justify the means.

Truth For Today

November 30

"YHWH is merciful and gracious, slow to anger and abounding in steadfast love," says Psalm 103:8. In this verse as well as many others, the terms "merciful and gracious" are used together. In Hebrew this reads "rachum v'chanun."

This is YHWH! He has compassion and patience towards us at all times. To be merciful is to show empathy to a person. Empathy is the ability to recognize, relate, and directly feel the emotion of another person. To have empathy is to have rachamim. YHWH emphasizes with us.

It has been said that mercy is "not getting what you deserve." Well, that definition is just a small portion of the truth. Rachamim is so much more.

YHWH's mercy is the force that sustains creation and allows the world to spin on its axis.

Many describe the "God of the Old Testament" as an angry judge of the world that sent His son to save mankind from the religion of Judaism. This is not so. Such an idea of a bearded man with lightning bolts and a huge throne relate more to Greek Mythology than the Bible. The Scriptures state that "YHWH did not send His son into the world to condemn the world but that the world through Him might be saved," John 3:17.

Part of Y'shua's ministry on Earth was to restore the mercy and grace of the Torah. He did not come to start a new religion or write a second portion of the Bible called the "New Testament." John 1:17 states, "The Torah was given by Moses and its unmerited favor and truth were revealed by Y'shua." Pray today for a revelation of Y'shua's mercy and truth.

December

December 1

The world celebrates Christmas. The Messiah celebrated Chanukah in John 10:22-23, "And it was at Jerusalem during the Feast of Dedication, and it was winter. And the Messiah walked in the temple in Solomon's porch." Chanukah isn't just a Jewish holiday. It is a set apart time of rejoicing and reflection for all followers of the Bible. Believers are to follow the Savior's every example. Remember that the Savior was a Hebrew-speaking Jew. What Jew would be at the Temple during Chanukah and not join the celebration? John 10 clearly indicates that He rejoiced at Chanukah and thus put his seal of approval upon this day.

The Hebrew word "Chanukah" literally means “dedication." Chanukah is an eight day celebration that commemorates the dedication of the Temple, after it was desecrated by the Greek army. Christmas has a pagan past but the account of Chanukah is historical fact. Chanukah is based upon an actual military battle won by a small group of Hebrews. The Maccabee family led victory over the Syrian tyrant, Antiochus Epiphanies, in the 2nd century B.C. Chanukah is NOT the "Jewish Christmas," but an altogether separate celebration of victory over paganism. There are games, songs, and traditions that recall the miracle of Chanukah without pagan roots.

December 2

To fear YHWH is a direct command of the Scriptures, it is one of the 613 mitzvot / commandments of the Torah, yet it is forgotten. "You shall fear YHWH your Elohim, and serve Him, and shall swear by His Name. You shall not go after other Elohim," Devarim / Deuteronomy 6: 13, 14. We know a lot about many of the commandments in the Torah, now it is time to learn about fearing YHWH!

Unfortunately our faith has taught us to become an awful lot like a gas oven, without the pilot light burning. What purpose can a non-working stove accomplish? See, we have some knowledge about the fear of YHWH, yet this information is rarely used and seldom considered. We have the oven, but the heating force is missing. The power that gives purpose to an oven and to our lives is unlit. Let's turn up the heat, by searching the scriptures and applying what we learn. "Therefore receiving a malchut / kingdom that cannot be moved, let us have favor, by which we may serve YHWH acceptably with reverence and fear: For our Elohim is a consuming fire," Ivrim / Hebrews 12: 28, 29.

Perhaps one reason this matter is not a motivating force within our daily walk is because of how it has been presented to us in the past. Mainstream Christianity teaches the fear of the Lord to be exclusively, a deep reverence and respect for the Almighty. The evangelist says that we are to be in awe of the Creator, not scared of Him. Religion preaches that the fear of the YHWH is NOT to be understood as being related to judgment, punishment and sin. We are told to just confess our sins to a priest or that 'love is all that matters'. "Christians tend to de-emphasize the fear of God in the New Testament by placing the love of God above the fear of Him. There is indeed a greater emphasis on the love of Elohim in the New Testament. However, the element of fear was part of the proclamation of the early believers," says the Holman Bible Dictionary, a Baptist publication. This begs the questions, 'Are we really to reverence the power and majesty of YHWH and not expect His judgment and punishment in our lives?'

To reference the fear of YHWH only as awe though, is to present only part of the case. It is to portray a lion without its teeth; or a King without His scepter. We pacify the Almighty, to the point that we'll accept anything. This idea presents a type of "god" on Prozac, one who doesn't care about motives, ethics, or actions. We reason that there's no need to fear the Creator because His Son died for us. Thinking like this betrays only being sorry when we are caught doing something wrong. How does such an understanding of the fear of YHWH help or hurt your faith?

December 3

The scriptures are clear that a person's spiritual walk should be based upon the first five books of the Bible. These are the teachings of Moses and the foundation that the whole of the Bible is built upon. These teachings were given as the basis for all believers to make clear what is expected of people who walk by faith. They were not replaced with the Gospels and the Messiah did not do away with these teachings. 2 Timothy 2:19a, "A solid foundation stands firm."

The problem is, when most people are born again the first thing they do is turn directly to the middle of the Bible for instruction and inspiration. New believers begin reading the Gospels without any prior knowledge of what is required of man or how the Most High relates to humanity. A person's spiritual walk should not begin with Matthew! That's because without reading and understanding Genesis, Exodus, Leviticus, Numbers and Deuteronomy it is impossible to correctly understand the books of Matthew, Mark, Luke and John.

Suppose you walk into an Algebra class with no prior knowledge of math. The teacher starts the first day of the class by instructing everyone to turn to the middle of the book so she can begin teaching. You would be lost wouldn't you? Well, that is exactly what happens when people lay a foundation of the New Testament without knowledge and understanding of the Old Testament teachings and way of life.

If we are going to walk as the Savior walked then we must believe as the Savior believed. It is clear that the Messiah used, read, and lived the Torah.

The key to comprehending the scriptures is by viewing everything in the Bible through the lens of the "Torah." Every other scripture passage in the Bible, every doctrine of the Church, and every teaching a person listens to should be filtered through the "Torah."

"Torah" is the Hebrew word for teaching and instruction usually translated as "law" in English Bibles. Overtime, "Torah" has become the title for the first five books of the Bible, which were given to Moses by the Almighty. The Torah is the revelation of the Creator's will for mankind. It is also the Bible Y'shua read and used. Will you allow the Torah to be your foundation for life?

December 4

One Chanukah tradition that delights people of all ages is the dreidel. The dreidel is a spinning top with Hebrew letters on its four sides. The toy is spun and gelt can be exchanged in various games. The song "I have a little dreidel" is one of those tunes that can get caught in a person's head very easily. It's a tune known by people throughout the world and is often times synonymous for Chanukah. As "Rudolph the Red Nosed Reindeer" is to Christmas so "I have a little dreidel" is to Chanukah.

Don't be fooled though, the dreidel is no ordinary toy. For this little top has many deep spiritual insights for us if we will simply watch it spin. The rabbis have said that "The prophets are like children and the children are like prophets." This shows us that if we can simply view the world as little children then there are many spiritual principles that we can learn.

The dreidel doesn't look special. Most are made from wood (not clay). And most are basically a square block with Hebrew letters and a pointed bottom. The four letters found on the dreidel are the nun – gimel – hey – shin.

The dreidel was first used many years ago when the Hebrew people faced harsh persecution from King Antiochus. The evil ruler forbid the study of Torah. Believers would meet secretly to discuss the Torah portions in defiance to the ban. Syrian officers would raid the meetings or watch the gathering. The Jewish people would study hidden Torah scrolls when the enemy wasn't look. When the enemy did watch or raid the gatherings, the Hebrews would simply pull out their dreidel and take it for a spin. They weren't gambling. Instead they would play as if they were playing. The dreidel didn't start as a children's game. Instead this spinning top was used to aid the study and discussion of Torah.

Adults would spin the dreidel and then view the letter that fell on top. They would then use that letter to determine the subject of their Torah discussion. If the sevivon / dreidel landed on "nun" then perhaps their midrash would be on the "ner tamid" or "everlasting light." If the top fell on "shin" then maybe they spoke of the "shekinah" glory or "shalom" or even the prophesied Messiah that would come from "Shiloh."

The people back then didn't have modern entertainment to consume their time. Instead they engrossed their lives in their faith. They knew Torah and Tanakh so well that by simply viewing one letter they could recall passages of scripture and recite the glory of YHWH. May we return to such a love and knowledge of YHWH's word. May this simple toy become a symbol of our devotion to raise our awareness of the Torah. Spin that dreidel this year and have fun!

December 5

At His birth the angels appeared in glory and proclaimed the kavod / glory. "And behold, an angel of the YHWH stood before them, and the kavod of YHWH shone around them, and they were greatly afraid. And suddenly there was with the angel a multitude of the heavenly host praising YHWH and saying: "Glory to YHWH in the highest, And on earth peace, goodwill toward men," Luke 2:9. Y'shua came to earth amidst the glory in order to bring glory to YHWH by establishing peace between YHWH and men. He came as "A light to bring revelation to the Gentiles, and the glory of Your people Israel," Luke 2:32. Y'shua came to reveal the full kavod / glory of YHWH. He traded His crown of glory for a crown of thorns in order to restore the kavod to mankind. "For YHWH, who commanded the light to shine out of darkness, hath shined in our hearts, to give the light of the knowledge of the glory of YHWH in the face of Y'shua Ha Moshiach," 2 Corinthians 4:6.

Y'shua came to restore the glory of YHWH lost by Adam's sin. Believers can experience His glory through a relationship with Y'shua. We can see how we are to be changed by YHWH's glory in the story of Moshe, the Prince of Egypt. Moshe was different after he came face to face with the glory of YHWH. Exodus 34 speaks of how Moshe had to wear a veil over his face because it was so bright from the glory of YHWH. This is a picture of how YHWH wants to change His people today. We are to behold His face and be changed by His kavod. "But we all, with open face are changed into the same image from glory to glory, even as by the Spirit of the YHWH," 2 Corinthians 3:18. We are changed by His glory when we acknowledge His presence and power.

Psalm 82:9 says, "the whole earth is filled with His glory." This means that His presence is as close as our realization. The kavod is all around us. YHWH's glory can be revealed through a religious prayer, beautiful scene of nature, a love song, a good doctor, a strong businessman, or a loving mother. CS Lewis once wrote, "If there lurks in most modern minds the notion that to desire our own good and earnestly hope for the enjoyment of it is a bad thing, I submit that this notion has crept in from Kant and the Stoics and is no part of the Christian faith. Indeed, if we consider the unblushing promises of reward and the staggering nature of the rewards promised in the Gospels, it would seem that our YHWH finds our desires, not too strong, but too weak. We are half-hearted creatures, fooling around with drink and sex and ambition when infinite joy is offered us, like an ignorant child who wants to go on making mud pies in a slum because he cannot imagine what is meant by the offer of a holiday at the sea. We are far too easily pleased." This concept is truly a Hebrew idea, as the Talmud teaches that each person will be judged in Heaven according to the pleasures they allowed themselves to experience. The Talmud says that we will be held accountable if there is a fruit in this world we didn't at least taste once to see if we enjoyed it. What an awesome idea of how each of us should experience YHWH's kavod in the little things in life. How can you experience YHWH's kavod today?

TRUTH FOR TODAY

December 6

"Chesed" is the Hebrew term often translated as "grace" or "mercy" in English Bibles. Chesed or grace is usually understood to mean unmerited favor, yet its real definition is much greater. This is because chesed is one of the sefirot / attributes of YHWH. YHWH is gracious and imparts grace because chesed is part of who YHWH Is. To receive chesed is to receive YHWH. To better understand chesed is to better know YHWH. But, how can you comprehend the incomprehensible? How can you understand the unfathomable? How can the "amazing grace" of YHWH be realized? This is done through YHWH's word, His Torah.

YHWH's grace or "chesed" is so great that translators have to use various words to describe it. It is hidden in this verse…"In your unfailing love / chesed you lead the people you have redeemed," Shemot / Exodus 15:13. According to this verse through chesed, redemption or salvation comes. Sound familiar? "You are redeemed/saved by chesed through trusting belief—and this not from yourselves, it is the gift of YHWH," Ephesians 2:18. Chesed is sometimes translated as grace and at other places mercy. Though the words may change the definition remains the same. Chesed is YHWH doing for man what man cannot do for himself. To help you better understand the vast scope of chesed here are a few other potentials:

Loving-kindness, favor, faithfulness, unconditional giving, deep love, bliss, tenderness, abundance, achievement, preservation, respect, enthusiasm, leadership, optimism, caring, safety, protection, trust, success, rewards, generosity, gratitude, love, union, insight, knowledge, understanding, and learning, loyalty, kindness, benevolence, and commitment.

Chesed is all of the above and more. Friend, much can be learned about chesed from numerous verses in the Tanakh. For example Tehillim (Psalms) 89:3 teaches that, "the world is built through chesed." The act of creation and every act of the Almighty that has followed has happened through grace/chesed. YHWH created because of and through His chesed. He did not have to create, yet through His love he chose to. Through His own sefirot or attributes YHWH brought forth creation, redemption, and restoration. This is because through grace flows the merciful qualities of the Divine. Man deserves absolutely nothing yet because of chesed man receives everything.

Chesed is not only given from YHWH to humankind, but also from man to fellow man as this Parasha reading shows. We receive chesed from El Shaddai and we should reflect that chesed to those around us. "Each one should use whatever gift he has received to serve others, faithfully administering YHWH's chesed in its various forms," 1 Kefa / 1Peter 4:10.

December 7

Historical writings prove that the early followers of Y'shua were so Jewish that most people could not tell them apart from the majority of the Jews. "The Nazarenes do not differ in any essential thing from [the Orthodox Jews], since they practice the customs and doctrines prescribed by Jewish Law; except that they believe in Messiah. "They believe in the resurrection of the dead, and that the universe was created by the Almighty. They preach that YHWH is One, and that Y'shua is his Son... They are very learned in the Hebrew language. They read the Law," wrote the early Church Father Epiphanius in his doctrinal book: "Adversus Haereses (Against Heresies)" Panarion 29 – sacred names added. And remember that the Savior did say, "what we do know is salvation is from the Jews," in John 4:22.

To know and live in a Hebraic mindset, the traditions and customs of Judaism are a great asset. It is difficult and maybe, even impossible, to have a world-view based upon Torah without looking to Judaism for answers as to how the Jewish people live. The Jews have kept the Torah for thousands of years. They have an understanding of what it means to obey the majority of the commandments. The Rabbis and Sages of Judaism have studied, discussed, fussed, and made decisions on the various mitzvah or commands. A single action of obeying a Torah command has over time developed into a tradition, through repetition. The action has, also progressed into the culture as an accepted practice, thus becoming part of the Jewish identity.

When we look to Judaism for answers on the Hebrew mindset, we must deal with the issue of tradition. The Hebrew word for tradition is "masoret." The Encyclopedia Judaica says, "Masoret is the general name for tradition. It is found in Ezekiel 20:37 and means originally 'bond' or 'fetter'." Tradition is the discipline that establishes the correct practice and interpretation of the Torah and was therefore regarded as a hedge or fetter about the Law (Avot 3:14). Since this knowledge was handed down by successive generations, it was also associated with the Hebrew word masor, denoting "to give over." In the Talmudic literature, the term masoret is used to include all forms of tradition, both those which relate to the Bible and those which concern custom, law, historical events, folkways, and other subjects." Masoret remain virtually unchanged over long periods of time to provide examples, uniformity, and help with belief. What traditions in your life need to be changed? What traditions in your life can be found in the Scriptures?

December 8

"May YHWH bless you, and keep you; May YHWH make His face shine on you, and be gracious to you; May YHWH lift up His countenance on you, and give you peace," Numbers 6:24-26.

For Christianity and Judaism this is the final benediction of many worship services. It is a prayer of mercy, protection, substance, and peace. This blessing calls for the Creator's favor and holy name to be upon all who follow the Scriptures. It is not some magical practice on the part of the priests, as they have no power over the divine. The text makes it very clear that while the priests may pronounce the words, it is the Almighty who does the actual blessing. This prayer is often used as Jewish leaders raise their hand in the fashion of the Star Trek vulcan hand symbol and speak the benediction.

The Jewish people have a rich faith that is full of symbolism and Spiritual power. Such traditions have great meaning that can be lost if one is totally closed to the Hebrew roots of Christianity. "What advantage then has the Jew? Much in every way; chiefly as they were entrusted with the very oracles of YHWH," Romans 3:1-2. Judaism isn't all bad. Judaism isn't all good either. One must earnestly search for the true path of faith that hangs between the balance of our ancestor's practices and the Almighty's divine will.

The Almighty chose the Jewish people to preserve the Scriptures from error. Many of the traditions that surround their devotion, like the Vulcan hand symbol, bring added significance to life. Such traditions can be adopted by Bible believers if they are void of pagan origin, not prohibited in the Scripture, and if the action does not grieve the Holy Spirit. The Bible never bans tradition but it does speak against actions that make void the word of YHWH. There are many customs of Judaism and Christianity that are beneficial for the Believer. For example, during the synagogue service the worshippers are not to look at the person who gives the blessing of Numbers 6. This is because the focus should be placed on the words of the prayer and not the personality of the one speaking. Christianity often uses this blessing at the end of funerals and other events.

The words of Numbers 6 were never meant just to be shared at worship gatherings or graveside ceremonies. Instead, these words describe our relationship with Y'shua and all that it brings. Ephesians 1 states we have been blessed with "every spiritual blessing in heavenly places." As a born again follower of Messiah YHWH has blessed us and has promised to keep up. Nothing can separate us from His love. YHWH has also shined his face upon us and been gracious to us through Y'shua's life, death, and resurrection. Finally, YHWH has lifted his blessing upon us and given us peace through Y'shua the prince of peace.

December 9

Shabbat is a day and time of physical rest and spiritual reflection. It is a time and dimension that is infused with the energy and power of YHWH. Shabbat is a day to lay aside the cares of the world. The Bible states that this world is not our home. We are simply traveling through the valley of the shadow of death. "Our citizenship is in heaven," says Philippians 3:20. This means that we are illegal aliens in this world. We've simply been granted a work permit to be in the world. Our home is with YHWH. The problem with illegal immigration in the natural world is just a reflection of the spiritual problems we face today. We are to say "no" to amnesty and remember that this is not our home!

To help us while on the journey, YHWH has given us a travel size experience of heaven / shamayim called the Shabbat. In Hebrew the word for Sabbath is "Shabbat." "Shabbat comes from the Hebrew verb 'shavat,' which literally means "to cease." Although Shabbat is almost universally translated as "rest" or a "period of rest," a more literal translation would be "ceasing", with the implication of "ceasing from work." Thus, Shabbat is the day of ceasing from work; while resting is implied, it is not a necessary denotation of the word itself. For example, the Hebrew word for "strike (as in a work stoppage) is shevita, which comes from the same Hebrew root as Shabbat. This word has the same implication, namely that striking workers actively abstain from work, rather than passively," wikipedia.com.

When we keep Shabbat we are to go on strike against work and the rest of the world. Sabbath keeping is not about just abstaining from the time-clock but abstaining from this entire existence. Shabbat is a supernatural time in which the heavens are closer to earth in the spiritual realm.

The Shabbat was given to man as a gift; a taste test of eternity. To further prove this point, let's consider the numerical value of Shabbat. In Hebrew, each letter is assigned a numerical value. The letter-numbers can be added together and compared to find similarities and hidden messages. The value of Shabbat is 702. The Hebrew word for "emerald" has the same value (bet-resh-kof-tav). The fourth chapter in the book of Revelation makes the connection for us as it describes an emerald throne in Heaven. Shabbat isn't a time of labor or worry; rather it's a day to spend with the King of Heaven! Shabbat is when we can praise the King and approach His throne of grace to help us during our time of need. When is our time of need? The remaining 6 days of the week.

December 10

"And if ye go to war in your land against the enemy that oppresseth you, then ye shall blow an alarm with the trumpets; and ye shall be remembered before YHWH, and ye shall be saved from your enemies. Also in the day of your gladness, and in your solemn days, and in the beginnings of your months, ye shall blow with the trumpets over your burnt offerings, and over the sacrifices of your peace offerings; that they may be to you for a memorial before YHWH," Numbers 10:9-10.

Numbers 10: says that when we "teruah" or "cry and shout aloud" that YHWH remembers us! And when YHWH remembers his people, great things happen. When the storms were at their climax and humanity had perished, YHWH remembered Noach and the floodwaters receded. Genesis / Beresheet 19:29 says that YHWH remembered Abraham and gave him many military victories. And finally, the Bible says that "YHWH remembered Rachel, and YHWH heard her, and opened her womb," in Genesis 30:22.

Did you get that? YHWH will remember you as you shout and cry out to Him in urgency. Shout to Him if you need the flood of the world to stop. Cry out to Him if you want victory over your enemies. Lift your prayer in fervency if you need new life. Come near to Him and He will come near to you!

The Messiah Y'shua spoke about the importance of urgency when praying. "Hear what the unrighteous judge said; now, will not YHWH bring about justice for His elect who cry to Him day and night, and will He delay long over them? I tell you that He will bring about justice for them quickly. However, when the Son of Man comes, will He find faith on the earth?'" Luke 18:7-8. YHWH certainly hears the sincere prayer. However, when a fervent shout is lifted then positive results abound. Much of our prayer lacks the kind of fervency that YHWH seeks for active results. Remember, it's not the volume of the voice but the cry of the heart that YHWH hears. YHWH longs to hear us cry out to Him.

December 11

Just open up any encyclopedia or browse the Internet, to see the proof that Christmas is an ancient pagan day of worship. But, does its origin really matter? When a person celebrates Christmas, surely they are not worshipping trees, nature, and the sun?

Today, most people are more concerned about checking off their wish list than learning about the history of Christmas. The majority of parents are guilt-free while they mislead their children with stories of Santa and flying reindeer. Surely the excitement of gifts and the family traditions outweigh the truth of any ancient customs? Proverbs 19:2 says differently, "It is not good to have zeal without knowledge, nor be hasty and miss the way." The excitement and good feelings of Christmas does not outweigh its pagan roots. The knowledge of Christmas past taints the celebration of Christmas present and future. The end does not justify the means. For fundamental believers, the holiday of Halloween is often forsaken because of its witchcraft and pagan roots. Why then is the origin of Christmas glossed over by visions of sugarplums dancing in our heads?

Every single tradition of this holiday can easily be traced to ancient rituals. The same exact practices that were once used in cultic worship to conjure up evil spirits are now being repeated in schools, churches, and homes as part of Christmas celebrations. Many Pastors and Priests defend Christmas traditions by stating that these actions now point to Christ. "Put Christ back into Christmas," they say. Can believers conquer the pagan influences of ancient times, by giving these customs Christian religious meanings? The Scriptures emphatically answer 'No.' Consider this passage from the Prophet Jeremiah (10:2) speaking six centuries before the Savior came: "Do not learn the practices of the heathen." What did the heathen do that was so despicable? What practices are believers to stay clear from? What custom was so horrible that it should never be repeated? "Do not learn the practices of the heathen... For the customs of the people are vain: for one cutteth a tree out of the forest, the work of the hands of the workman with the axe. They deck it with silver and gold; they fasten it with nails and with hammers, that it move not," Jeremiah 10:2-4.

Will you follow the crowds to keep Christmas or will you take a stand against this day?

December 12

Self-control, or the mastery of self is expressed in justice, bravery, and judgment. The Hebrew term for this is "gevurah." Gevurah repels and restrains while ahava / love accepts and encourages. The two must act in harmony within man. The attribute of gevurah allows one to make wise and correct choices. The fruit of self-control separates the wheat from the tares. "What is the difference between the righteous and the wicked? The wicked are under control of their heart while the righteous have their heart under their control," says the Talmud.

In a world full of road rage, abuse, obesity, drunkenness, envy, and drug dependency, the idea of self-control seems foreign. Yet self-control demands the believer to control tempers, emotions, and actions. "Let every man be swift to hear, slow to speak, and slow to anger," James / Ya'acov 1:19. To have self-control is to prevail over the flesh and conquer the sinful desires. Gevurah is strength manifest as control. "Who is strong? One who is able to overcome his evil inclination," Pirkei Avot, 4:1. Self-control means to restrain power. It is to willingly give up a "right" in order to do what is "right." It's the idea of everything being permissible but not everything being beneficial. This fruit abruptly stops the modern culture of desire from overtaking a believer. It is not easy. Having gevurah is not popular. Saying "no" never is. Yet, the more a saint says "no," the more the fruit of self control matures. Gevurah grows each time it is expressed. Each time we restrain from sinning in a specific way, gevurah's fruit matures. What tempts today should be easier to deny tomorrow because of the increase in gevurah.

To overcome the flesh takes a choice to follow the Messiah in a lifestyle of Torah observance and total dependence upon YHWH. "My children I have created the evil impulse, and I have created the Torah as an antidote to it. If you occupy yourselves with the Torah you will not be delivered to the power of the flesh," says the Talmud. Winning the war over self is not done in a day; it is a daily battle to walk in the Spirit. The fruit of the spirit must be pursued over time. What can you do today to pursue YHWH?

December 13

Love. The English term has many meanings. People say that they "love spaghetti" and they "love the Atlanta Braves." Girls fall in and out of love all through high school. All of this makes defining love very difficult. In modern thought love is an emotion that can be turned on and off like a light switch. Love or "ahava" in the Hebrew mind is very different in today's culture. In the Hebrew, love is connected directly with action and obedience. Strong's Exhaustive Dictionary defines ahava as "to have affection, sexually or otherwise, love, like, to befriend, to be intimate." It brings to mind the idea of longing for or breathing for another. Biblically, ahava is a verb and a noun, it is an act of doing. Ahava is not just a feeling. To get a clear understanding of ahava, let's examine the Hebrew word itself and learn how to love Biblically.

First, most Hebrew words can be broken down to a three-consonant root word that contains the essence of the word's meaning. The root word of ahava is "ahav." The term ahav in Hebrew means, "to give." True ahava, true love, is more concerned about giving than receiving. Being the center of someone's attention isn't love. And love isn't about getting some feeling or fix. Ahava is about giving devotion and time. For giving is the vehicle of love. YHWH so loved the world that He GAVE His only Son. Meaningful relationships have mutual giving. Love may focus on receiving, but ahava / love is all about giving. There is a difference.

Y'shua said the greatest commandment is to love YHWH first and then love our neighbor as you. "The first of all commandments is, Shema O Yisra'el; the Master YHWH is our Elohim, the Master YHWH is Echad: and you shall love the Master YHWH with all your lev / heart, and with all your being, and with all your mind, and with all your strength: this is the first commandment. And the second is like it, namely this; You shall love your neighbor as yourself. There are no other commandments greater than these," said the Messiah Y'shua in Mark 12:29-31. Ahava starts with Aleph, the first letter of the Hebrew alphabet. Real ahava / love starts with loving YHWH first. Then, as a person has a relationship with YHWH, one can love his neighbor.

The Hebrew root word for love is "ahav," spelled "aleph, hei, bet." The aleph reminds us that we are to love YHWH first. Hei shows us to express that love by conforming our thoughts, words, and deeds to the five books of the Torah. When love is directed first to YHWH, then a beit, a house, is built to sustain His presence. Wow! Ahava is the greatest! How can you show love today?

TRUTH FOR TODAY

December 14

Daily we are to seek YHWH's glory in everything that we do. By acting and doing until your power is spent is the most effective way of increasing the kavod Shamayim / glory of the Heavens. This desire to live life for the sake of Heaven is part of the restoration of all things as promised in the book of Acts.

The restoration will NOT be to the glory of Moses but like that of Adam. Remember, that after Moshe returned from the mountain of YHWH, his face had such a bright glow that he had to wear a veil. Over time the glory around Moshe faded. For a time, Moshe wore the crown of glory that Adam lost. But that crown faded. Today, YHWH is fully restoring the crown of kavod. It is YHWH's will that man be crowned with a kavod that does not fade but permeates everything we do. YHWH wants His kavod to be proclaimed and experienced in suffering and in work; in play and in worship; in sickness and in health. The Saints will soon fully experience the kavod when Y'shua returns and establishes His malchut / kingdom. "And when the Roei-Hagadol / Chief Shepherd shall appear, you shall receive a keter / crown of glory that fades not away," 1 Peter 5:4.

As we await His return we should seek His glory daily and pray like Moshe – "show me your glory." In Exodus 34 Moshe prayed to see YHWH's glory. YHWH responded to Moshe's plea by revealing His goodness, attributes, and name – all manifestations of His kavod! "And YHWH passed by before him, and proclaimed, YHWH, YHWH. An El, full of rachamim and favor, longsuffering, and abundant in, chesed, and emet / truth, Keeping chesed for thousands, forgiving iniquity and transgression and sin, and will by no means clear the guilty; visiting the iniquity of the ahvot / fathers upon the children, and upon the children's children, to the third and to the fourth generation. And Moshe hurried, and bowed his head toward the earth, and worshipped," Exodus / Shemot 34:6-8.

The kavod of YHWH is the significance of His personality as displayed through His attributes. To have the kavod and walk in the anointing is to know YHWH and walk in His ways. Pray like Moses to see YHWH's glory. Begin to acquaint yourself with YHWH like never before. Study the scriptures concerning His attributes. Understand that Messiah in you is the hope of glory. Having the anointing in your life is like wearing the crown of kavod that adorned Adam. "Arise, shine; for your Light has come, and the tifereth of YHWH has risen upon you. For, see, the darkness shall cover the earth, and gross darkness the nations: but YHWH shall arise upon you, and His tifereth shall be seen upon you. And the nations shall come to Your Light, and melechim to the brightness of Your rising," Isaiah / Yesha'yahu 60:1.

December 15

The fruit that we are to bear is the fruit of the Spirit. "The fruit of the Holy Spirit (Ruach Hakodesh) is ahava / love, simcha / joy, shalom / peace, patience, chesed / kindness , rachamim / goodness, trust worthiness, gentleness, self-control. Against such there is no true Torah (law)" Galatians / Galutyah 5:22, 23. Man is a tree, planted in this world to produce fruit. People aren't drawn to YHWH by laws and rules but by love, joy, peace, patience and goodness. This fruit is the result of walking in accordance to YHWH's word as revealed in the Torah.

"Torah" is the Hebrew word for teaching and instruction usually poorly translated as "law" in English Bibles. It gives us YHWH's will. Torah includes guidelines on every part of life, including how and when to worship, what to eat or wear, and how to get along with others. The Holy Spirit / Ruach HaKodesh is the manifested power of YHWH. The Ruach HaKodesh leads, teaches, and guides the believer. The Spirit will always lead one towards obedience to the Scriptures, including the Torah / Law of Moses. The Torah and the Spirit are NOT at odds but are identical – "against such there is no true torah." The Ruach HaKodesh aides the believer to keep the Torah and manifest the kingdom of Heaven. The fruit we produce spreads the seed of the Gospel. This fruit is the most dynamic witnessing tool. A life devoted to yielding the fruit of the Spirit will reach many.

As a person walks is submission to the Torah, the fruit of the Spirit is able to develop. "I am the Emet Vine, and My Abba is the Gardener. Every branch in Me that bears not fruit He takes away and every branch that bears fruit, He purges it, that it may bring forth more fruit. Now you are clean through the word that I have spoken to you. Remain in Me, and I in you. As the branch cannot bear fruit by itself, except it stays in the Vine; neither can you, except you remain in Me. I am the Vine, you are the netsarim / branches: He that stays in Me, and I in him, the same brings forth much fruit: for without Me you can do nothing," John / Yochannan 15:1-5. Here, Y'shua identifies Himself as the Vine. In John Chapter 1 the Messiah is called the "Torah made flesh." So, if Y'shua is the Torah made flesh and Y'shua is the Vine, then... the Vine is the Torah!

The Torah is "a tree of life / eytz chayim to them that take hold of her: and happy is everyone that takes hold of her," Mishlei / Proverbs 3:18. To walk in the Spirit is to eat from the Tree of life and produce much fruit. Torah explains how we abide in Y'shua and produce the fruit of the Spirit. How can you abide in the vine of Y'shua today?

TRUTH FOR TODAY

December 16

There are many ways that we become unclean and this subject is very challenging for believers today. However, t'vilah mikvah mayim / immersion in a collection of moving waters was, and is, a central part in dealing with uncleanliness. For example, the leper would go through washing rituals found in Vayikra / Leviticus 14, not for physical cleansing but spiritual cleansing. Like Naaman who immersed seven times and was healed, mikvah / immersion completed the healing process for leprosy. The priests also went through immersions in preparation for temple service in Vayikra / Leviticus 16. Throughout the Torah, mikvah / immersion is established as a vital and necessary part of Temple worship. Thus, ritual baths were built at the Temple site to be used by those seeking to immerse themselves for ritual/spiritual cleanliness. People who became unclean were not allowed to approach YHWH without first immersing themselves. Those who are clean were allowed access to the temple site while many who were unclean were put outside the camp. Immersion and sometimes a wait, was and is simply a part of the remedy for becoming unclean. "You must keep the Israelites separate from things that make them unclean, so they will not die in their uncleanness for defiling my dwelling place, which is among them," Vayikra / Leviticus 15:31.

All believers have been called to the priestly worship of YHWH through our covenant with Him. We are to walk in cleanliness, to be free of defilement and daily, to demonstrate YHWH's high moral standards. We become unclean when we cross the lines that YHWH has set for living with His Torah.

There are three various degrees of being unclean: temporary, punishment, and a person can become unclean through natural bodily functions. Believers today must still deal with the issue of being spiritually and ritually clean. One may become impure for many different reasons: eating unclean foods, turning to a medium or spiritualist, and even, sinning defiantly. Y'shua did not abolish uncleanliness from the world. "Think not that I am come to destroy the law, or the prophets: I am not come to destroy, but to fulfill," Mattitiyahu / Matthew chapter 5. What Y'shua did though was reach out to us in our unclean state.

In Mark 1 we read of Y'shua and an unclean leper. In this chapter we actually see that Y'shua made Himself unclean by touching the leper! The Messiah could have spoken a word of healing or waived his hand to heal the person but he chose to touch the leper and minister healing. This is a powerful example of how the spirit of the law and the letter law must meet. The letter of the law says not to touch an unclean person and thus make you unclean but the spirit of the law allows us to minister love and compassion.

How can you reach out to those who are unclean today?

TRUTH FOR TODAY

December 17

Part of Y'shua's ministry on earth was to confront the false teachings of many religious leaders and replace their perception of the Torah with His Divine way to walk. Take for example the Savior's words in Matthew 5:21 & 22, "You have heard that it was said to the people long ago, 'Do not murder, and anyone who murders will be subject to judgment.' But I tell you that anyone who is angry with his brother will be subject to judgment..." Y'shua was not removing the physical prohibition of murder. Murder is still wrong! What He was doing was showing the original intention of the Torah commandment: that man should respect life and examine the heart intention behind the physical actions of anger.

Y'shua used the Torah to teach his disciples. He even quoted the Torah to defeat the Adversary in Matthew 4:4. Deuteronomy 8:3, "Man does not live on bread alone but on every word that comes from the mouth of the YHWH."

You see, the Torah is not a boring manuscript full of laws and commands. Rather, these teachings, which have survived thousands of years present how the Heavenly Father relates to man and how we should properly relate to Him. In the books of Moses, the character of the Ruler of the Universe is proven through His involvement with mankind. Proverbs 3:18 teaches that the Torah is a "tree of life to them that lay hold of it." While Romans 7:12 says, "Wherefore the law is holy, and the commandment holy, and just, and good."

Think about this, when you first meet someone you inquire about their likes and dislikes, their family, and their occupation. But when you really want to know someone you ask them about their past. As your new friend reveals their life's story you really get to know them. And as their history unfolds you begin to see and appreciate their character because you understand that the events a person experienced in the past will shape how they face the future. How much more with our Heavenly Father! Surely He will continue as He has acted in the past, because He never changes! Malachi 3:6, "I am YHWH; I change not."

Truth For Today

December 18

"Therefore come out from among them and be set-apart, says the Master YHWH, and touch not the unclean things; and I will receive you, and will be an Abba to you and you shall be My sons and daughters, says the Master YHWH the Almighty," 2 Corinthians 6:17-18. What does this verse mean to you? Really, what does this verse speak to you today? Have you ever compromised your faith?

In Hebrew the word for compromise is "p'shara." This term means to "expose or make liable to danger, suspicion, or disrepute." It also means to, "resolve differences by mutual concessions esp. to prevent or end a lawsuit." How? P'shara is a choice to give in and even give away. Compromise, as the definition states, is a mutual agreement. It is an action that must be taken and accepted – compromise is not forced. Some Hebrew chose to p'shara and others did not. Interestingly, there is not a word for "compromise" in the ancient Arabic language that the Muslims speak. One reason why there is no compromise in the Middle East is because the Islamic belief system does not believe in giving in. They don't even have a word for compromise in their dictionary. The war against p'shara is one of the greatest fights Torah followers face today. The world is calling us to conform. Our children are bombarded with musicians, actors, and the media who set the trends and fan the fads. We must resist.

How can you take this truth and apply it to your life today?

TRUTH FOR TODAY

December 19

In a sense we as Israelites have to defy gravity. We must resist the pull of the world. We have to reject mixture. It is hard to swim upstream and resist the influences of those around us. The Talmud says, "All beginnings are difficult." Yet it will get easier each time we choose not to "p'shara"or compromise. There is a principle of spiritual momentum that states every time you perform a mitzvot or refuse to go along with the ways of the world your spirit is strengthened. Barriers are broken down as you reject the urge to compromise. Take for example the feasts of YHWH. At first they are new and perhaps even difficult to celebrate. But as time goes by, the new actions become habit; they become part of you and don't seem so strange. As the actions are repeated, it gets easier each time to just perform the mitzvot. And each time you refuse to allow your life to mix with the world, you stand as a witness and example of how a follower of YHWH should live. Resist the urge when you are confronted with the option to follow YHWH or not. Do not allow the adversary a foothold. "Do not give satan a chance or opening," Ephesians 4:27.

Be faithful in the small matters. Most people won't compromise their faith by disobeying a 'big' commandment like murdering or stealing. Yet will your faith stand strong when faced with small choices about Sabbath observance, kosher eating, or words that are spoken? It is hard to resist p'shara in the small areas of life. The next time you are tempted to cross the line remember how the priests would not even compromise the oil they used in the temple.

As you are faithful to YHWH, you can expect miracles to happen. In fact, you can make miracles happen through your devotion. Expect the unexpected and experience the unthinkable as your heart is molded in the Father's hands. Just as the Israelite rededicated the Temple, recommit yourself to YHWH and His service. Clean out the areas of compromise and evil influences. Turn off that racy TV show. Put away those clothes that reveal too much. Look at how much money you spend on things that are just not necessary. Say 'no' when friends and co-workers tease or tempt you to disobey Torah.

December 20

YHWH spoke the world into existence. The universe and everything it contains was made for the glory of YHWH. "All things were created by him, and for Him," Colossians 1:13. Everything that is came from Him; therefore the entire universe contains His divine spark. From the Glorious One came a world filled with glory. "And blessed be his glorious name for ever: the whole earth is filled with his glory," Psalm 72:19. The crown of creation was mankind, made in the image of the Holy One. Like YHWH, man was originally crowned with glory. Psalm 8:5, "For thou hast made him a little lower than the angels, and hast crowned him with glory and honor."

Adam lived in perfection and had an unhindered relationship with YHWH. He walked with YHWH with a fullness of love and acceptance. But because of the fall, man was separated from YHWH. When Adam sinned, mankind lost the glory. Sin removed the crown of glory. "All have sinned and fallen short of the glory of YHWH," Romans 3:23. Sin drove Adam out of the garden and pushed the glory away.

The glory / the significance of our relationship was broken because of disobedience. This is a pattern throughout the Scriptures. "So they sinned against me, therefore I will turn their kavod / glory into shame," Hosea / Hoshea 4:7. We see this again in the book of 1 Samuel 4:22, "The glory is departed from Israel: for the ark of YHWH is taken."

Sin separates man from the kavod / glory. Adam tried to replace his crown of glory and cover his shame by sewing fig leaves together. Like Adam, we too have tried to replace YHWH's glory with our own works – our own garments. But these efforts are futile. Man cannot earn the crown of glory lost in Eden. This crown can only be replaced by King of Glory, YHWH Himself. It is to this purpose YHWH sent His only begotten Son. Y'shua came not to start a new religion or inspire a franchise chain of bookstores, but to bring back the glory! Y'shua wrapped Himself in human flesh to redeem the fall of Adam and restore mankind's position as the crown of creation. This was His purpose. Is our desire to bring Him glory?

December 21

Can you imagine America without Christmas? The idea seems preposterous as the jolly holiday has become engrained in the American culture. A recent poll shows that 92% of Americans, including atheists and Muslims, celebrate Christmas. This holiday brings people together with the hope of love and peace on earth. Right? Well, history records a different perspective.

The first settlers understood the dangers of Christmas. The yuletide was actually outlawed in America during the 1600s. In Boston from 1659 to 1661 those who exhibited the Christmas spirit were fined five shillings. In England Sir Oliver Cromwell led the ban as a means to rid the society of mistletoe, nativity scenes, and eggnog. Why ban Christmas? Besides the obvious lies about Santa Clause, is there something wrong with the holiday?

"The traditional customs connected with Christmas have developed from several sources as a result of the celebration of the birth of Christ mixed with the pagan agricultural and solar observations at midwinter. In the Roman world Saturnalia was a time of merrymaking and exchange of gifts. December 25 was also regarded as the birth date of the Iranian mystery god Mithras, the Sun of Righteousness," Encyclopedia Britannica. Mithras worship started before Messiah was born and continues unchanged to this day. "Do not learn the practices of the heathen... For the customs of the people are vain: for one cutteth a tree out of the forest, the work of the hands of the workman with the axe. They deck it with silver and gold; they fasten it with nails and with hammers, that it move not," Jeremiah 10:2-4.

Followers of the Savior have been called to be "in the world but not of the world." 1 Thessalonians 5:21-22, "Prove all things; hold fast that which is good. Abstain from all appearance of evil." The principle is that one should abstain from all practices of evil origin. This would include Christmas.

Will you celebrate Christmas this year or will you take a strong stand for YHWH?

December 22

Many people go through the motions of an empty existence. They continue as normal until they suddenly stop and consider what is most important. Sometimes it takes a national tragedy or a doctor speaking the word "cancer." Others live for pleasure and thrills. Yet, even if your purpose is to live a moral life or raise children to have a good future, it is easy to stay in the grind of the normal life. Without tapping into the Almighty's purpose and high calling, living is simply aimless, boring, and based on momentary happiness. What about the "abundant life" the Savior promised? Wouldn't you like to have the Messiah's power in life?

For some real answers on living a life of meaning and fulfillment let's look into the Torah and discover YHWH's plan for man. Back to the beginning we shall turn as the creation account reveals much about YHWH's original intention for mankind. "We were made like YHWH, created in His image. We were given a free will to follow Him or follow our own path. We were formed with an evil inclination, or fleshly desire called the 'yetzer hara.' We were also formed with an eternal light called our "spirit." When "YHWH formed man from the dust of the ground He breathed into his nostrils the breath of life, and the man became a living being," Beresheet / Genesis 2:7. This breath of life is the part of YHWH that was breathed into mankind. "There is one Elohim and Father of all, who is over all and through all and in all" says Ephesians 4:5.

The Scriptures declare that everything, including man, was made specifically for YHWH's tov pleasure and fulfillment. "Thou art worthy, O Master, to receive glory and honor and power: for thou hast created all things, and for thy pleasure they are and were created," Revelation 4:11. The book of Colossians also speaks of this "For by him were all things created, that are in heaven, and that are in earth, visible and invisible, whether they be thrones, or dominions, or principalities, or powers: all things were created by him, and FOR him." YHWH made us for His tov pleasure. The sages asked, "What motivated Elohim to create the world in the first place?" A Midrash answers, "Elohim desired a dwelling in the physical world." We were also made in YHWH's image. This means that within each of us is a desire to experience pleasure.

YHWH created us like Himself to actually fulfill His desires. So, we too have desires that long to be filled. Paschal once said that there exists a "god shaped vacuum inside all humanity." This vacuum within the soul longs and craves for fulfillment, for pleasure. When this desire turns inward the result is a dangerous lifestyle concerned only about self. This is how the fall came about. Adam and Chava wanted to be more like YHWH; they wanted to know tov from evil, to experience more of the pleasures of the Creator. And so they made a decision to disconnect from YHWH's will and do their own desire. The consequence was the law of sin and death and their banishment from the Almighty. How can you allow this truth to change you?

TRUTH FOR TODAY

December 23

Christianity claims that legend of Santa Claus dates back to a fourth century Turkish monk. Stories abound about this man of kindness who reportedly gave away his wealth and even walked on water to save the life of a drowning sailor. He also supposedly rescued three sisters from a life of prostitution by sliding bags of gold down their chimney. Because of his piety he became known as the patron saint of schoolchildren and sailors. The Christmas Almanac states, "By the height of the Middle Ages, St. Nicholas was probably invoked in prayer more than any other figure except the Virgin Mary and Christ Himself" (The Christmas Almanac. New York: Random House, 2004, p. 131)

For almost 1,000 of years, the “Feast of Saint Nicholas” was held on December 6th with merry-making and gift giving. The Feast of St Nicholas is still celebrated in several countries, including Holland and the Netherlands. (Here St. Nicholas or Sinter Klass travels from Spain instead of the North Pole to bring gifts to children.) The popular idea of a chubby St. Nick with red priestly robes and white beard was created by author Washington Irving around 1809. Just a few years later reindeer were introduced by Clement Moore in the poem ‘Twas the Night Before Christmas. This poem also promoted the idea of St. Nicholas delivering presents on the night before Christmas and not on December 6. Together Moore and Irving morphed the legendary Catholic bishop into an elf that would travel the world spreading holiday cheer. The Coca-Cola Company solidified the idea of a standard image of Santa through years of advertising.

Today, the religious undertones involving Santa Claus are obvious. He is known as a carpenter/toy-maker with God-like powers. He records naughty or nice behavior in his giant book and is all knowing. Children pray to him through wish lists of toys and then wait in line to ascend his throne to sit on his lap. Like a thief in the night he distributes rewards and punishment. His crown of holly thorns, white beard, red robes, and feet that do not burn by the furnace all mimic the appearance of the Savior in Revelation 1:14-15, Isaiah 63:2, and Mark 15:17. Isn’t this interesting?

The fantasy of Santa Claus is real to children who are often led astray by parents who see no problem in St. Nick taking the place of the Almighty. For centuries, the legend of Santa has changed to match the whims of the world. It is quit puzzling how anyone who claims to know the Elohim of the Bible can also encourage gullible children to believe in Catholic Monk-Elf figure named Saint Nicholas. Perhaps this Christmas more parents will not mislead their children and abruptly stop the worship of Santa Claus. What will you do? Who can you gently share this truth with today?

TRUTH FOR TODAY

December 24

When a person performs a commandment, like keeping the Shabbat, this action of obedience affects the physical realm and the spiritual realm. A simple act of faith is much more than just a simple act of faith.

At what time you fulfill the smallest mitzvah (commandment) you are bridging the gap that exists between heaven and earth. When you obey you are actually bringing heaven to earth. It is the power of obedience that does this. In the Hebrew language this is called "tikkun olam." Tikkun olam is Hebrew for literally "fixing/repairing/restoring the world."

There is much more to the mitzvah than you think. When you do something, as simple as resting from work on the Shabbat, you are not just resting on the Shabbat. You are doing tikkun olam, you are restoring the world to the way it was created to be, and you are establishing the kingdom. While religion teaches people to sit on the pew and await the rapture bus, the scriptures teach that man should live out his faith through obedience and faith, thus being the kingdom of heaven while on earth. "YHWH's ultimate plan is to bring heaven to people on earth. It is not to bring His people on earth to heaven," wrote Angus Wooten in the book Restoring the Kingdom of Israel. (This is not Kingdom Now or Dominion theology, which is a gross twisting of scripture and totally anti-truth)

A person once came to Y'shua and asked Him specifically what He must do to have eternal life. His response was that man must do tikkun olam. "Now a man came up to Y'shua and asked, "Teacher, what good thing must I do to get eternal life?" Y'shua replied, "Why do you ask me about what is good? There is only One who is good. If you want to enter life, obey the commandments," Mattitiyahu / Matthew 19:16-17.

The Messiah also said, "Not everyone who says to me, 'YHWH, YHWH,' will enter the kingdom of heaven, but only he who does the will of my Father who is in heaven. Many will say to me on that day, 'YHWH, YHWH, did we not prophesy in your name, and in your name drive out demons and perform many miracles?' Then I will tell them plainly, 'I never knew you. Away from me, you evildoers!" Mattitiyahu / Matthew 7:21-23.

Tikkun olam brings the spiritual to the natural and restores life to the way it was supposed to be. Obedience to YHWH restores man to the Gan Eden and proclaims, "the Malchut Shamayim / kingdom of heaven is among you!" You see, Adam's original job after the fall was to "work the ground" to do tikkun olam but because he failed the second Adam did it for man. You can right Adam's wrongs today by walking in step with the Spirit of YHWH.

December 25

The term "in Christ" is found 76 times in the Authorized King James Version. These occurrences are often associated with powerful promises that we will examine. But first, Strong's Exhaustive Concordance writes the Greek the word used in this phrase is "Christos." Literally, Christos literally is defined "anointed, the Messiah." Christos is a poor Greek substitute for the Hebrew "Moshiach" which according to Strong's means exactly the same thing. To be "in Christ" is to be "in Moshiach." And believe it, or not, to be "in Moshiach" is to be "in Torah." John 1:14, "And the Word was made flesh, and dwelt among us" teaches that Y'shua is the Torah embodied in human form. Y'shua lived, breathed, walked, talked, studied, taught, and prayed Torah. Torah is in Y'shua Ha Moshiach. Therefore to be "in Moshiach" or to be "in Christ" is to literally be "in Torah."

"Torah" is the Hebrew word meaning "teaching." When Torah is mentioned it is most often associated with the teachings of Moses. The first five books of the Bible are the words which YHWH gave to Israel in the wilderness. These teachings of Moses are the building blocks YHWH uses to base the entire Bible; therefore, Torah signifies His instruction throughout the Hebrew Scriptures, including the Prophets and the Psalms.

Since all of His Word is His Teaching, all of it is His Torah. Torah is all the written teaching of YHWH, from Genesis to Revelation. And according to scripture Torah is holy, right and good; and useful for everyone who belongs to YHWH. To be "in Moshiach" or "in Christ" is to be in the teachings of the word. It is important to note that most believers do not have a strong understanding of the teachings of Moses and therefore misunderstand other scripture passages. Though the word "Torah" does not appear in various Bible translations, it is there, hidden beneath English words like "law," "word," "commandment."

Torah itself was stolen from the early believers by religious leaders whose desire was to create a separate religion from Judaism that was not based on anything Jewish. Therefore, Torah with its festivals, diet, and way of living was dismissed as a heavy burden not posed to Christians. This false teaching contradicts the fact that Torah was given as YHWH's gift to man. This gift provides the way sinful man may approach a holy Elohim. The teachings of Moses (the first five books of the Bible) are the foundation upon which the whole Bible is based. Nothing has passed away, nothing has been dismissed, and nothing has been abolished. Without properly understanding the words of the Creator to man, as spoken of in the Torah of Moses, a person cannot understand how YHWH dealt with His people through the ages and how YHWH deals with man today. For more on the importance and power of Torah read Psalm 119. Now, the question is "Are you in Torah?"

December 26

Many years ago, Avinu Avraham / our father Avraham was told by YHWH to travel with his son to the Mountain of Moriah. Yitzchak was to be bound as a sacrifice. The promised son, Avraham's own flesh and blood, was to be killed. Somehow, Avraham obeys in total faith. He rises early the next morning and starts on the three-day journey. Avraham and Yitzchak (Isaac) reach the mountain. The wood for the altar is placed on the back of Yitzchak, while Avraham carries the knife and the fire. The two ascend to worship. When they arrive, Avraham makes the preparations to offer his only true son to the Almighty. As the father raises his hand to slaughter his son, an angel from Shamayim / heaven stops the act. A ram is substituted for the son. The animal is sacrificed and the son is saved. The Jewish people call this account "the Akeidah."

"Akeidah" is the Hebrew word for "binding." It is only used one time in the entire Bible. This is in Beresheet / Genesis 22:9, when Avraham tied up his son to the altar to kill him. The specific usage of this Hebrew word is found nowhere else in the Scriptures. It appears here to stress the fact that Avraham was willing to sacrifice everything for YHWH. The Encyclopedia Judaica says that the "Akeidah has become in Jewish thought the supreme example of self-sacrifice in obedience to the Almighty's will." Avraham's obedience is so great, that he was willing to submit his own son to death.

During the Akeidah, Avraham set an example for his seed to follow. We are to give up that which is most precious, in order to receive life anew. One ancient Jewish writing teaches that it was during the Akeidah that "water was crowned with fire." This phrase reveals that YHWH's attributes of mercy and judgment are totally equal. Water is crowned with fire. Through true sacrifice, a person can walk in the balance of the two extremes of judgment and mercy. When a person sacrifices, mercy is extended and judgment is given, at the same time. How? The sacrifice itself is judged, while the one offering the sacrifice is pardoned. Mercy kisses judgment.

What does the Akeidah mean to you?

TRUTH FOR TODAY

December 27

The mitzvot / commandments are more than just commands for obedience and blessing. The mitzvot are the way we fix our will in order to receive pleasure from YHWH. Like an extension cord that connects power from a major source to an adapter is the mitzvot of Torah. They are to be followed not for salvation or to become good but to connect to the Good one. "Taste and see that YHWH is good," Tehillim / Psalms 34:8. The way to taste of Yah's goodness is through the mitzvot. These commands lead to our closeness to Him. Rabbi Schneerson teaches that "the primary reason we study Torah and perform the commandments is to reveal godliness in the world. It follows that every mitzvah produces its own, specific illumination of divinity. Every mitzvah we do creates its own Paradise, reserved to benefit the person who fulfilled it. The Talmud tells us, 'A mitzvah's reward is not given in this world.' The inference is that we enjoy its benefit only in the Olam Haba. The Mishnah Avot confirms, 'A mitzvah's reward is the mitzvah itself.' By observing the mitzvot we reveal the Gan Eden of this physical world."

For example, the mitzvot of keeping Shabbat gives us an eternal perspective as it reminds us to be opposite of the world. It's a day to break patterns from the entire week. What is your week like? Shabbat should be different. Shabbat is a day to break and not continue the normal routines of life.

How can you make Shabbat extra special this week? How do the commands of Torah connect you to YHWH?

December 28

Our days are normally crammed with anything but focused thoughts on the shamayim / heavens. Yet the Bible says in Colossians 3:2 that we are to "set your mind on things above; not on things of the earth." In the book of Isaiah, the Bible explains how a Shabbat should be observed and how we are blessed for keeping Shabbat.

"If you turn away your own foot from the Shabbat, from doing your own pleasure on My kadosh day; and call the Shabbat a delight, the kadosh day of YHWH, honorable; and shall honor Him, not doing your own halachot, nor finding your own pleasure, nor speaking your own words: Then shall you delight yourself in YHWH; and I will cause you to ride upon the high places of the earth, and feed you with the heritage of Ya'acov your abba / father: for the mouth of YHWH has spoken it," Yesha'yahu / Isaiah 58:13-14. Shabbat was meant to be a taste of heaven. Here in Isaiah, YHWH says that when we keep the Sabbath that he will feed us with the heritage of our ancestor Jacob. A heritage is a physical attribute or item that is passed down from one generation to the next. What is the heritage of Ya'acov? What did he do that was so great that it has been passed down for thousands of generations? Besides being the Father of Israel, Ya'acov kept Shabbat! He tasted heaven and now we can be fed with his very own meal. In Genesis 28 Ya'acov took a stone and used it for a pillow. He rested upon the rock. While asleep he saw a ladder with angels / melechim ascending and descending. He then poured oil on the stone and called it "Beth-el," or the "house of El."

"And Ya'acov awoke out of his sleep, and he said, Surely YHWH is in this place; and I knew it not. And he was afraid, and said, How awesome is this place! This is no other place but Beit Elohim, and this is sha-ar ha shamayim. And Ya'acov rose up early in the morning, and took the stone that he had put for his pillow, and set it up for a pillar, and poured oil upon the top of it. And he called the name of that place Beth-El," Genesis 28:16-19. While asleep, Ya'acov dreamed a prophecy concerning the Messiah. This is the heritage of Ya'acov! Judaism teaches that sleep is one sixtieth of death and dreaming is one sixtieth of prophecy. Here on the rock, Ya'acov tasted Heaven and dreamed of Moshiach! When we keep Shabbat we are fed with his heritage and experience heaven on earth.

What will you do differently on the next Shabbat? How can you set apart this day of worship better?

December 29

Do a Bible search for the word "rapture." Go ahead, flip through some Bible pages and look for the word. No luck? This term just can't be found in the Scriptures. It isn't in the Bible. Anywhere. The idea of Christians being suddenly taken to heaven comes from preachers who misinterpret 1 Thessalonians - "For the YHWH himself shall descend from heaven with a shout, with the voice of the archangel, and with the trump of Elohim: and the dead in Messiah shall rise first: Then we which are alive and remain shall be caught up together with them in the clouds, to meet the YHWH in the air: and so shall we ever be with the YHWH. Wherefore comfort one another with these words," I Thessalonians 4:16, 17.

Many churches now teach that believers will suddenly disappear at the beginning of a seven-year period of Tribulation. Then they say that the time of the anti-Christ will then begin, until the visible Second Coming of the Savior. Yet, this doctrine is fairly new when compared to the major tenets of the Christian faith.

The false teaching of the pre-tribulation rapture first surfaced around the 1830's. This is when a thirteen-year old little girl had a vision that those baptized in the Spirit would be raptured before the antichrist came to power. She also saw that a second group of believers would then be raptured at the end of the tribulation. About the same time, a book was released about the Savior coming first to rapture His church and then, again to defeat the anti-Christ. Bible publisher C.I. Scofield promoted these ideas in his popular study bible, and the religious hasn't looked back since. From movies to TV preachers to best-selling books, the church is taken with the pre-tribulation rapture theology.

The New Testament does speak of a certain event taking place, "In a moment, in the twinkling of an eye, at the last trump: for the trumpet shall sound, and the dead shall be raised incorruptible, and we shall be changed," 1 Corinthians, chapter 15:52.

Again, many suppose this is the sudden disappearance of Christians. Is this really what Paul meant? No. The Bible does not teach a pre-tribulation catching away where unbelievers are "left behind." Man teaches this. Don't get caught up, in this false hope.

Watch and pray that you may be counted worthy to escape all these things that come to pass and stand before the Son of Man.

December 30

When we keep the mitzvot (the reminders of YHWH), our obedience in the physical has profound impact upon the spiritual. Our submission to YHWH's word sends ripple effects within our souls and puts into motion the divine will of Elohim. The Talmud teaches that these living emblems are the insignia of a believer. "Whosoever has the tefillin on his head, the tefillin on his arm, the tzittzit on his garment, and the mezuzah on his doorpost is secure against the commission of sin. Beloved is Israel, for the Holy One, blessed be he, surrounded it with mitzvot," Menachot 43b. What we do in the natural realm is a direct reflection of our spiritual walk and beliefs.

As we have the reminders of YHWH present around our daily activities, we live in constant awareness of the Almighty and our mind will rest in Him. "You will keep in perfect peace him whose mind is steadfast, because he trusts in you. Trust in YHWH forever, for YHWH, the Master, is the Rock eternal," Yesha'yahu / Isaiah 26:3, 4.

Which commandments are you hesitant to keep? Why? What can you do today to follow YHWH's word better?

Obedience to the Torah must flow from a heart of love. Our actions should reflect our gratitude and appreciation for all that YHWH has done for us in this life and in the world to come. We obey in view of YHWH's mercy. Romans 12:1-2 say that "in view of YHWH's mercies" we are to "offer our lives a living sacrifice" and be "transformed by the renewing of our minds." We don't obey to get his mercy. We follow His Word in consideration of all that He has done for us.

Your obedience today can change the future of generations to come. Will you make a stand for righteousness?

December 31

One fundamental aspect of the Biblical faith is the issue of "halakhah." The true faith is not just a set of beliefs but a way of life, filled with various guidelines. This set of rules is known as "halakhah." Halakhah is a Hebrew word that literally means the "way to walk." YHWH has a set way of halakhah for His people. To the observant Jew, halakhah is "Jewish laws." To the Christian, halakhah is often mistaken for "doctrine." Biblical halakhah is neither. True halakhah is the path a believer follows through life. This is more than just rules or doctrine. Instead – true halakhah is THE way to live. James 1:27,"Religion that YHWH our Father accepts as pure and faultless is this: to look after orphans and widows in their distress and to keep oneself from being polluted by the world."

The word "halakhah" is derived from the Hebrew root "halek," which means to walk. The true faith should be walked out before the world. We have been called to be a light to the nations through our actions. Halakhah is different than doctrine as doctrine is mostly concerned with a belief system in agreement with various tenets. Halakhah is the outward expression of faith. Proverbs 4:2, "For I give you good doctrine: Do not forsake my Torah." The Newer Testament also says, "Study to show thyself approved unto Elohim, a workman that needeth not to be ashamed, rightly dividing the word of truth," 1 Timothy 2:15.

Many local assemblies establish their own "halakhah" or "way to do the Torah." The Torah is eternal and binding upon all believers. However, how the Torah is kept may vary from group to group. This is the difference of halakhah. Torah is the doctrine while halakhah is the way to walk. There is much freedom in halakhah.

Theology leads to walls of separation that shout, "If you don't believe exactly as I do, then, you are not welcome or you are not going to heaven." Halakhah provides freedom and room for growth. Halakhah says, "We do it this way, yet you may do it another way. The important thing is that we are doing YHWH's Will of the Torah." The Scriptures allow congregations, Rabbis, and families to fulfill the mitzvot in different yet meaningful ways. Theology on the other hand, leaves no room for differences. Such thinking is often sadly exalted by people who push their personal convictions upon others.

James 1:25, "But the one who looks at the perfect law of freedom and remains committed to it-thereby demonstrating that he is not a forgetful hearer but a doer of what that law requires-will be blessed in what he does."

How can you share your "halakah" with someone today? What can you do different this coming year to be more faithful to YHWH?

About the Author

Daniel Rendelman and his wife April are the founders of Emet Ministries, a teaching outreach located in Newberry, South Carolina with the five children: Nickolas, Judah, Joshua, Isaiah, and Rebkah.

Together, the family has spent over eleven years studying the original faith of the Apostles, church history, and the Hebrew roots of Christianity. Through the years, Daniel has taught children, youth, and adults the restoration of Israel and the importance of the Torah. His first book was titled "Finding the Truth" and offers a beginning look at religious practices and the Bible. Daniel's second book is an extensive Bible commentary and study guide called "The Open Bible." In 2011, Daniel released a 19 lesson plan book for children's classes called "Shabbat School Is Cool."

These titles have sold internationally and helped people experience the abundant life promised in the Scriptures.

"Emet" is the Hebrew word for truth. The vision of Emet Ministries is to teach, live, and share the truth of the Scriptures. Emet Ministries has grown into an international ministry, reaching people with teachings, audio messages, free resources, school of ministry, prayer support, and various outreach programs. The mission of Emet Ministries is to strengthen families worldwide, expose pagan practices, experience true worship, and share the Hebrew roots of the Scriptures.

Please visit www.emetministries.com
for audio teachings, articles,
videos, music, or to order additional
copies of this book.

Help Children Learn

Guide your children or class to the basics of the faith. Find 19 reproducible lessons with crafts, music, snacks, drama skits, and more. This material is perfect for children ages 7 – 12 and can be easily adapted to younger or older groups. Learn more at www.emetministries.com.

Study the Torah

Walk through the weekly Torah portion with this extensive study guide. This book gives an in depth look into the Torah portion from a viewpoint that keeps the Messiah in mind. Each week you will read a quick overview, find ways to apply the Torah to your life, learn about the Messiah in the Torah, and use many discussion questions to peak your interest. Open your Bible and use this guide to learn all about the truth of the faith. Learn more at www.emetministries.com.

Discover More

"Finding the Truth" has insights on over 95 subjects. Get this work with short essays on various subjects like tattoos, sin, the rapture, end times, satan, grace, heaven, the cross, and more. This book is impossibly honest as it gives a fascinating glimpse behind many customs and practices that have become the "normal." As you read, you will be challenged to confront the origins of your practices and place them in proper context. Visit www.emetministries.com to learn more.

Truth For Today

Made in the USA
Charleston, SC
02 February 2012